Fabien Grolleau & Jérémie Royer

AUDUBON

On the Wings of the World

NOBROW

LONDON - NEW YORK

FOREWORD

Jean Rabin. Fougère. Laforêt. Jean-Jacques Audubon. John James Audubon.
A man of many names and many lives – an adventurous and complex spirit.
Though his journey was rich in real life stories and incidents, these weren't
always enough for the man who lived through them: there is no doubt
he invented, embellished or modified certain episodes – sometimes in good
faith or forgetfulness, perhaps finally believing in his own confabulations.

His writings in particular have inspired our own retelling, which should
be read as a more 'romanticised' version of Audubon's life. We hope this will give
a fuller sense of the man than the mere facts ever could. The views expressed
in Audubon's writings and in the speech of the characters is reflective of the
oppressive attitudes and terminology of the time towards African Americans
and indigenous peoples, and does not acknowledge the destruction caused
by colonial expansion.

Despite his foibles, history will remember Audubon as an unparalleled
ornithological painter, one of fledgling America's pioneer landscape
adventurers, as well as a writer and one of the fathers of modern
American ecology.

Enjoy.

Fabien Grolleau

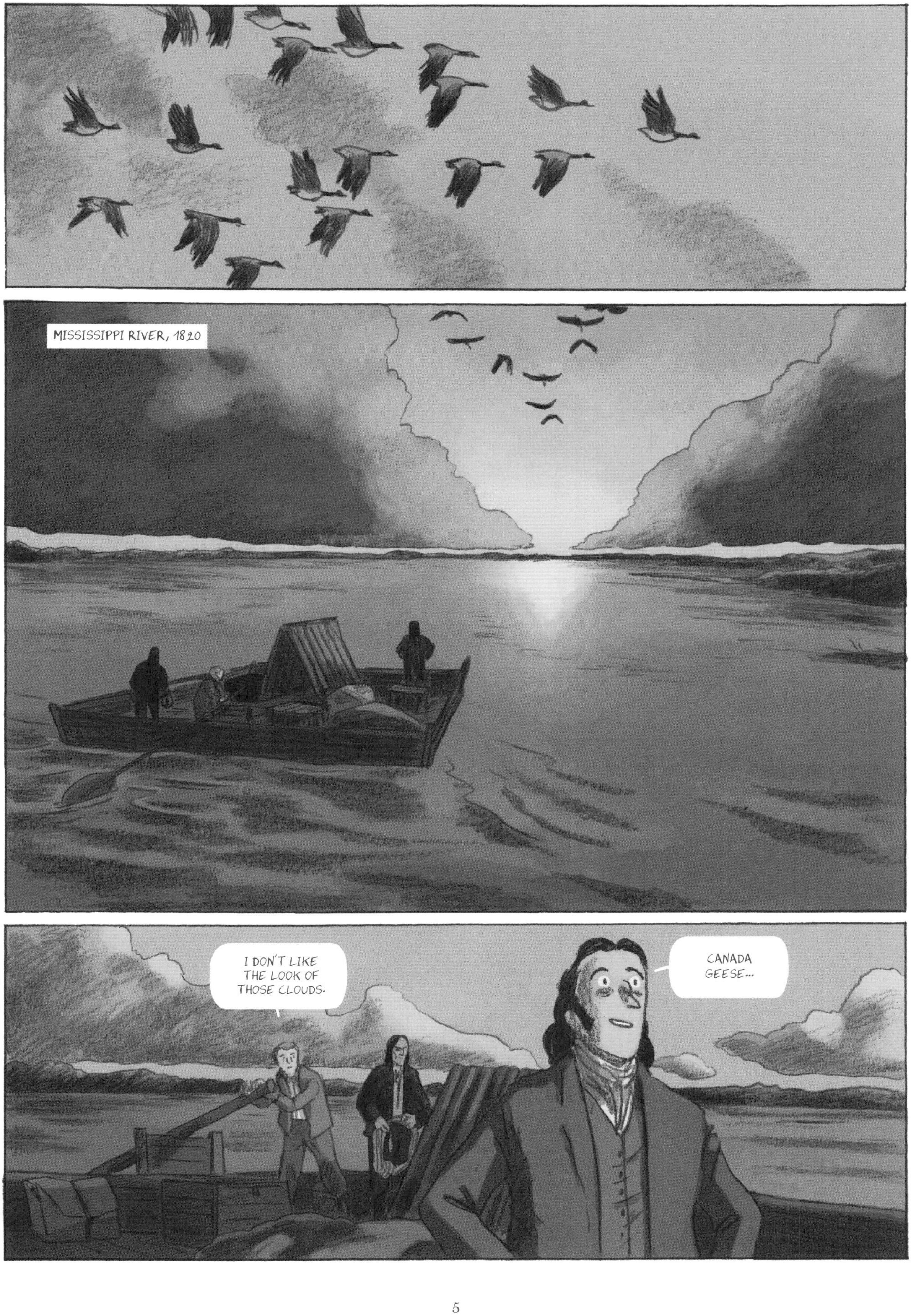
MISSISSIPPI RIVER, 1820
I DON'T LIKE THE LOOK OF THOSE CLOUDS.
CANADA GEESE...

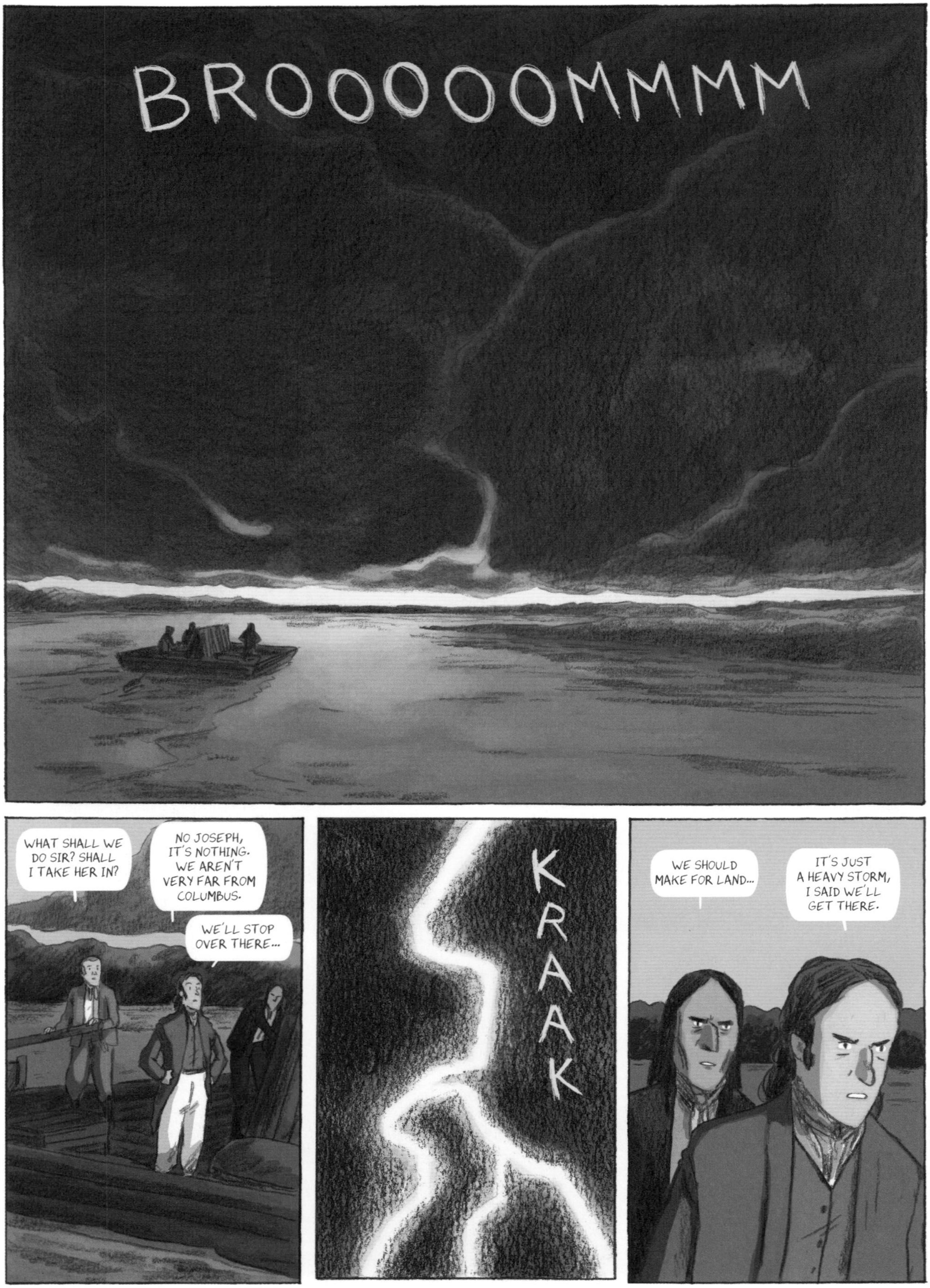
BROOOOOMMMM
WHAT SHALL WE DO SIR? SHALL I TAKE HER IN?
NO JOSEPH, IT'S NOTHING. WE AREN'T VERY FAR FROM COLUMBUS.
WE'LL STOP OVER THERE...
KRAAK
WE SHOULD MAKE FOR LAND...
IT'S JUST A HEAVY STORM, I SAID WE'LL GET THERE.

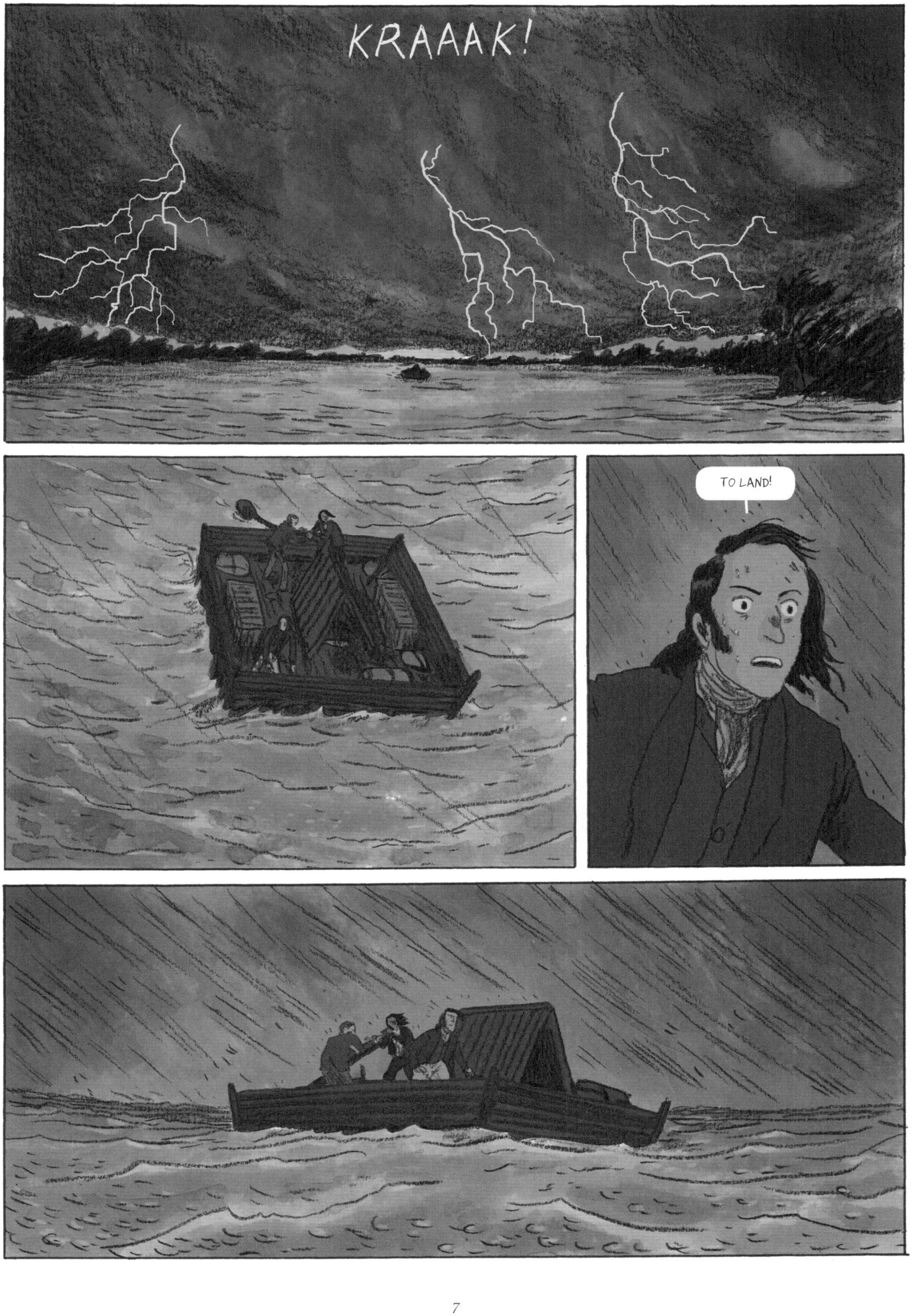
KRAAAK!
TO LAND!

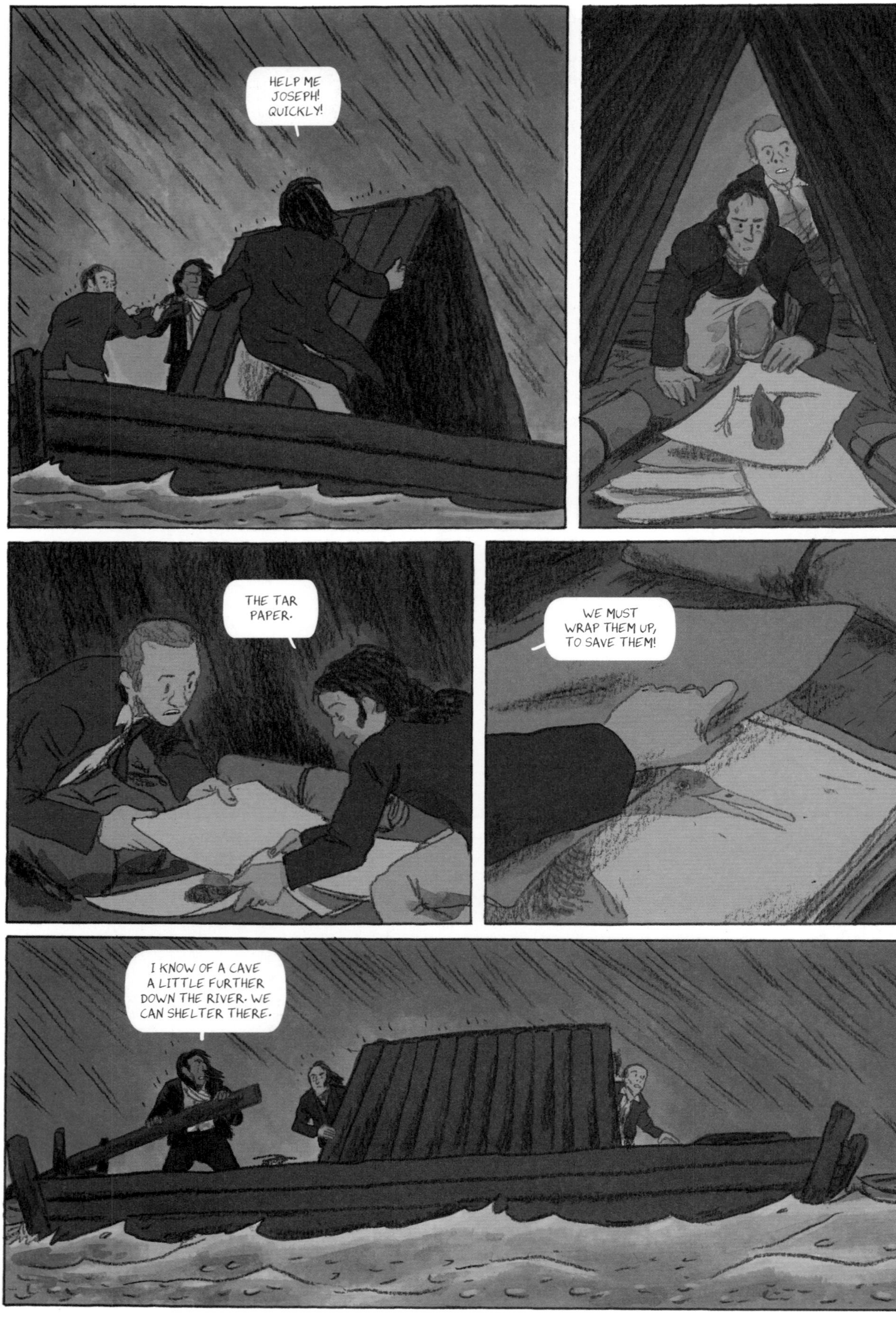
HELP ME JOSEPH! QUICKLY!
THE TAR PAPER.
WE MUST WRAP THEM UP, TO SAVE THEM!
I KNOW OF A CAVE A LITTLE FURTHER DOWN THE RIVER. WE CAN SHELTER THERE.

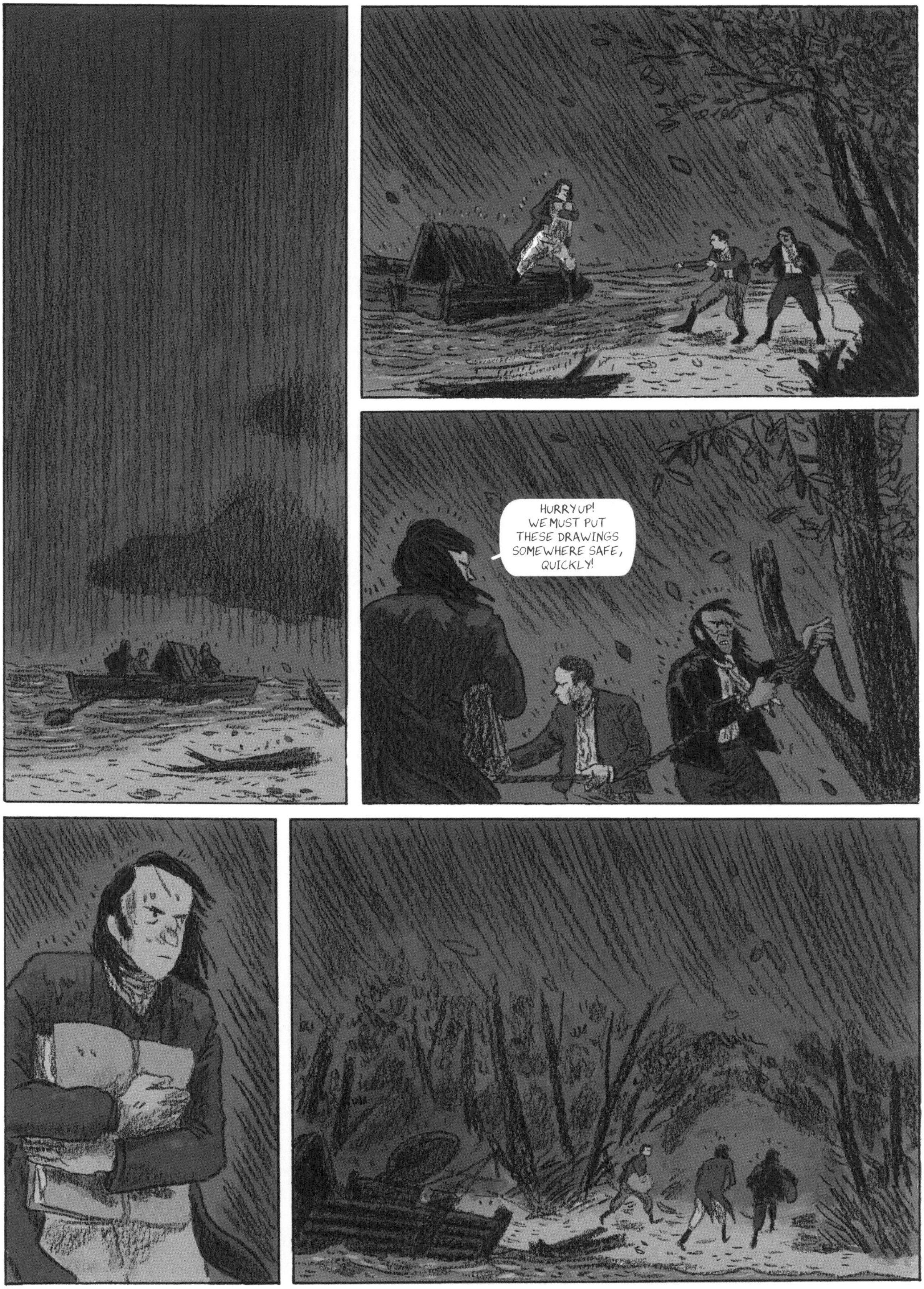
HURRYUP! WE MUST PUT THESE DRAWINGS SOMEWHERE SAFE, QUICKLY!

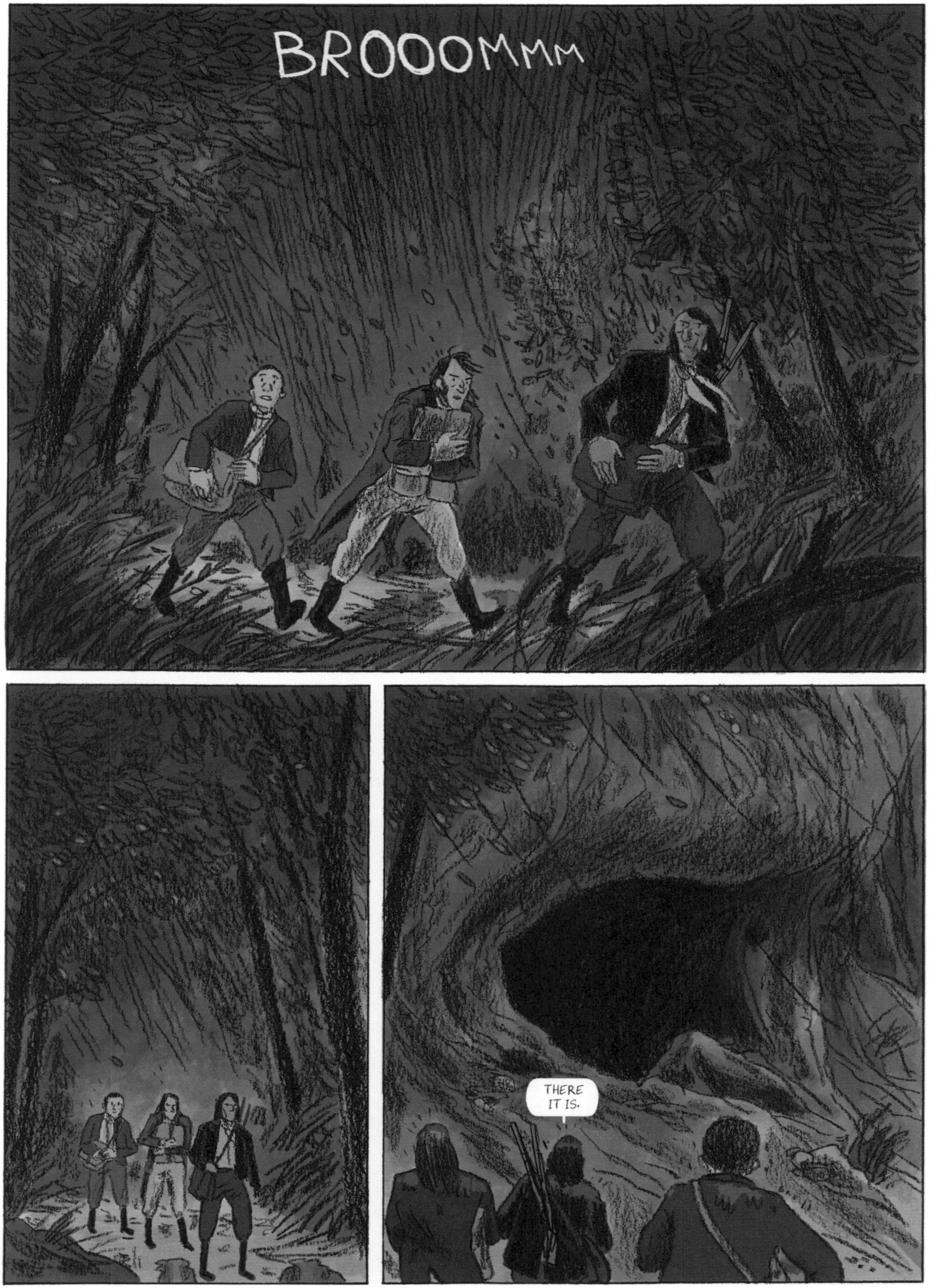
BROOOMMM
THERE IT IS.

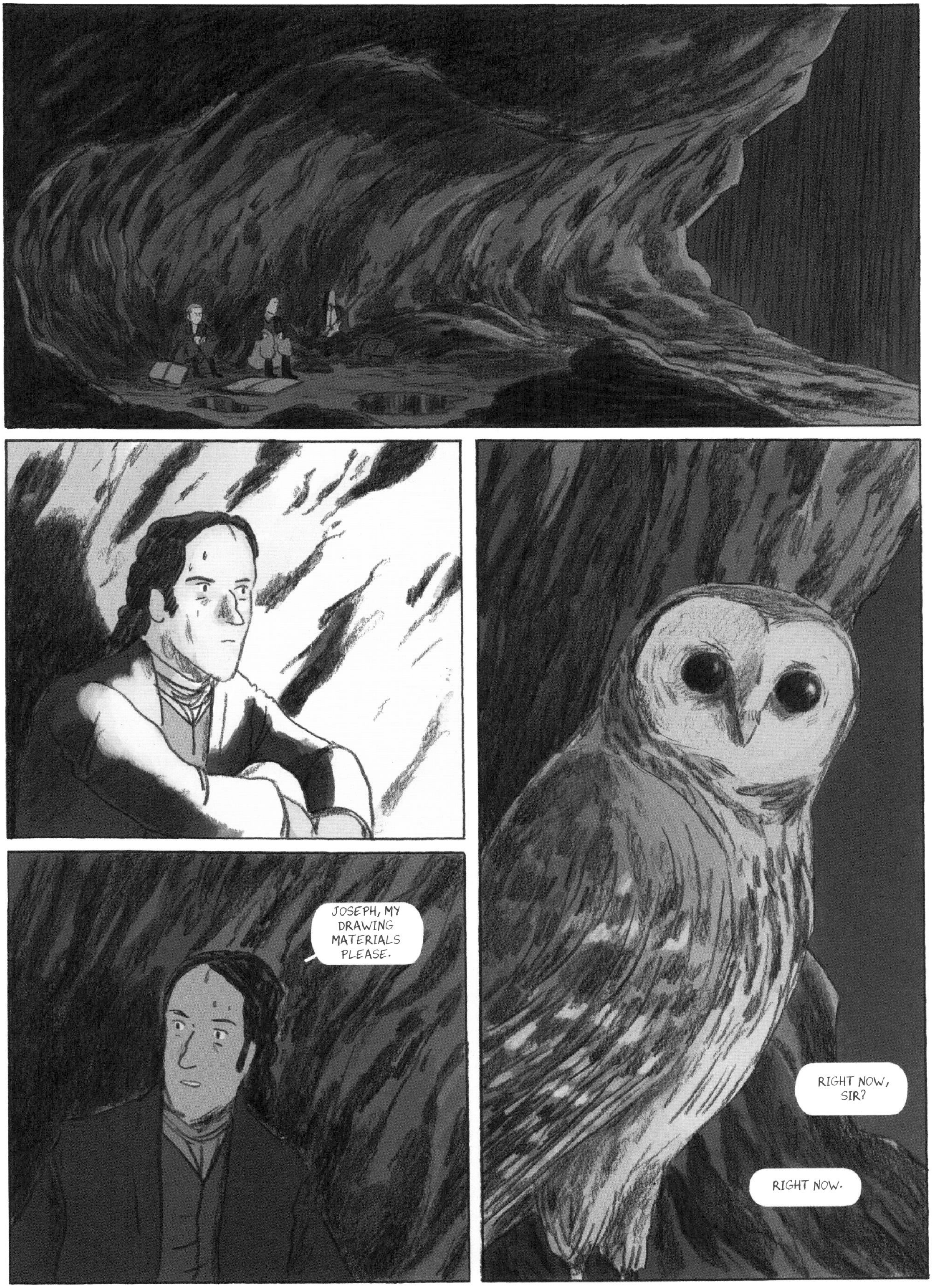
JOSEPH, MY DRAWING MATERIALS PLEASE.
RIGHT NOW, SIR?
RIGHT NOW.

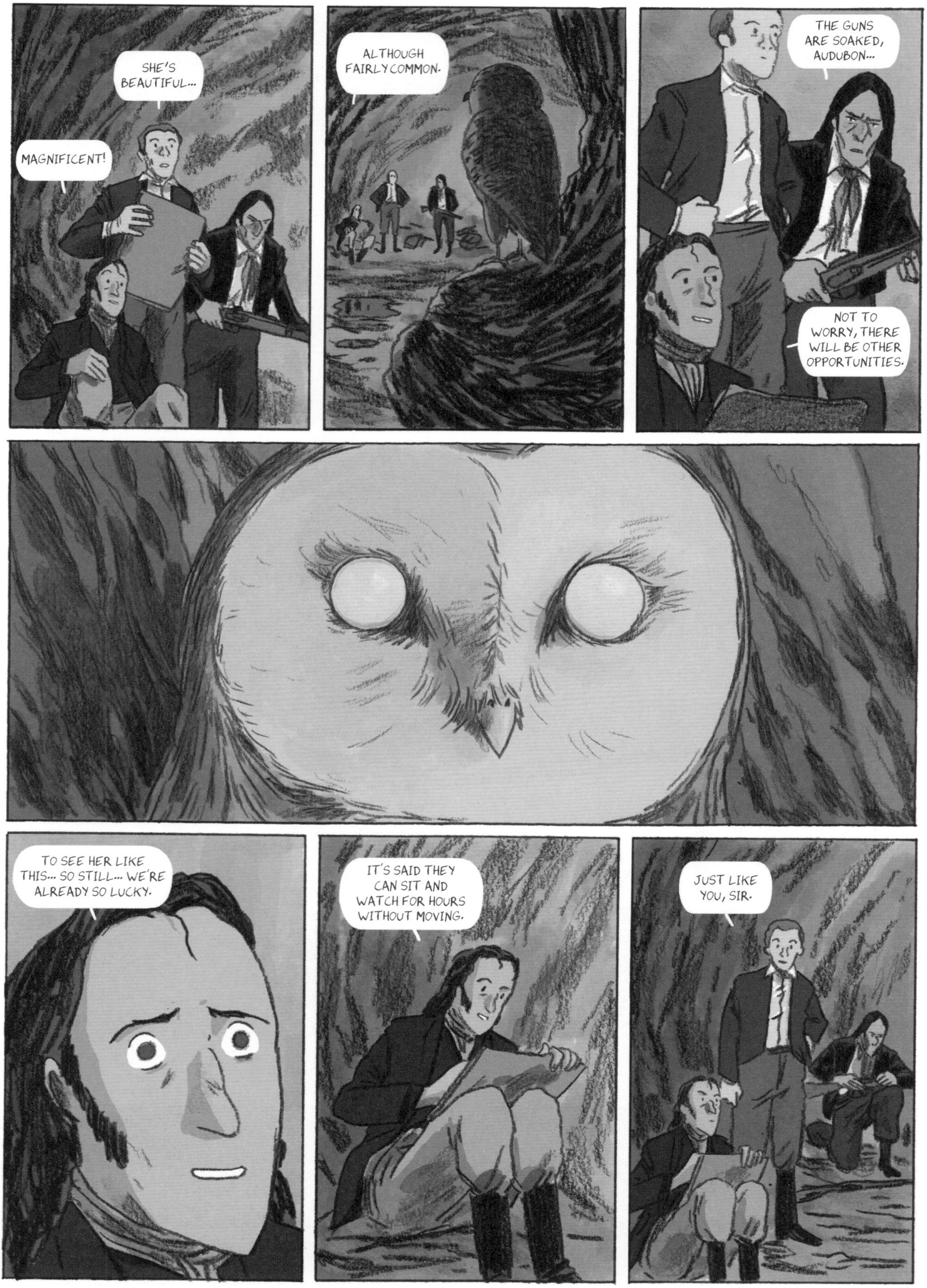
SHE'S BEAUTIFUL...
MAGNIFICENT!
ALTHOUGH FAIRLY COMMON.
THE GUNS ARE SOAKED, AUDUBON...
NOT TO WORRY, THERE WILL BE OTHER OPPORTUNITIES.
TO SEE HER LIKE THIS... SO STILL... WE'RE ALREADY SO LUCKY.
IT'S SAID THEY CAN SIT AND WATCH FOR HOURS WITHOUT MOVING.
JUST LIKE YOU, SIR.

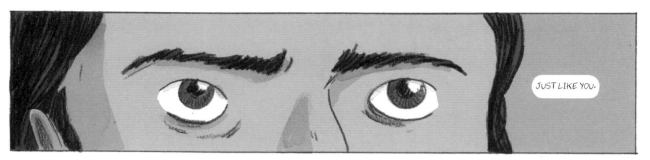

JUST LIKE YOU.

13

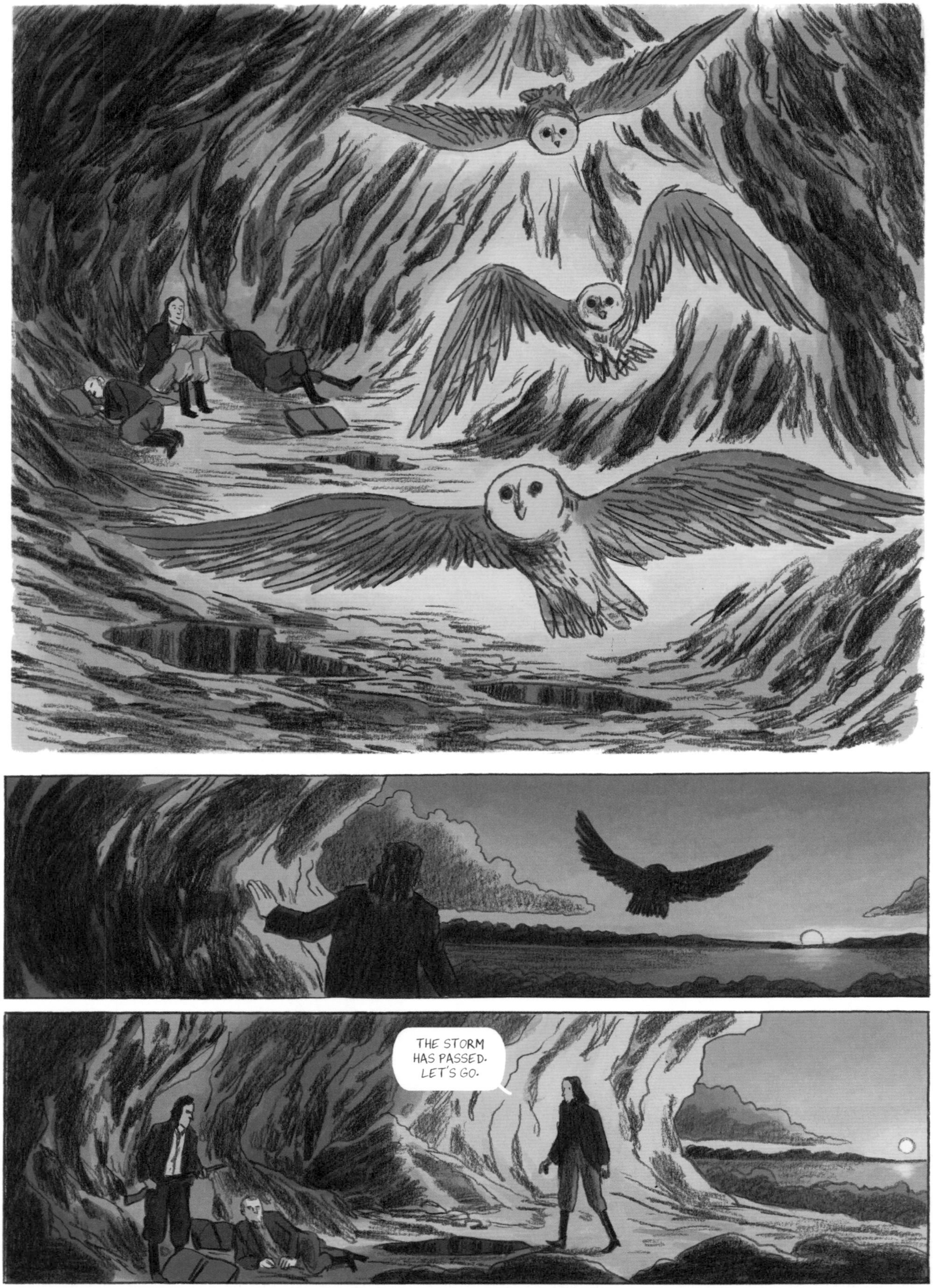
THE STORM HAS PASSED. LET'S GO.

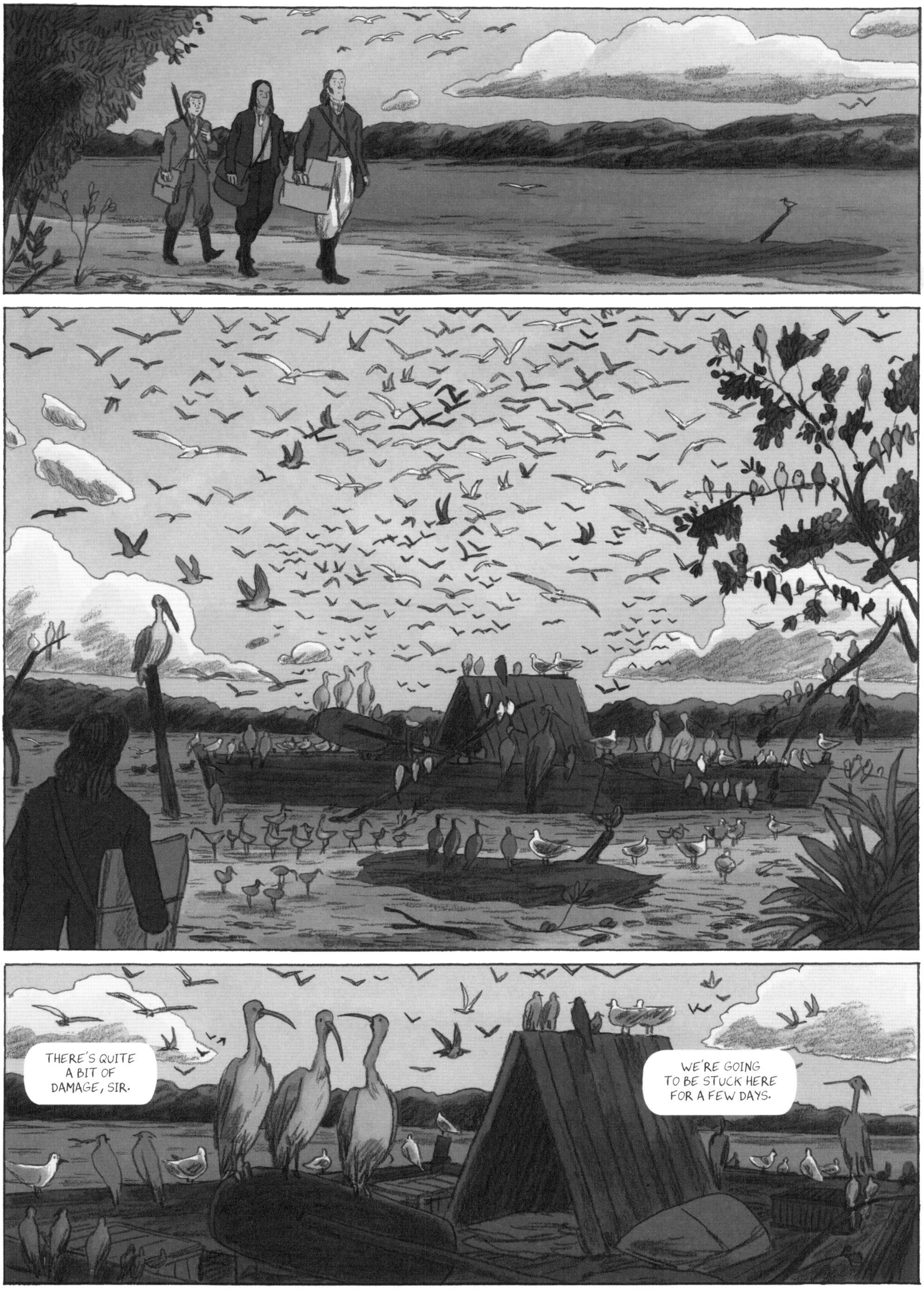
THERE'S QUITE A BIT OF DAMAGE, SIR.
WE'RE GOING TO BE STUCK HERE FOR A FEW DAYS.

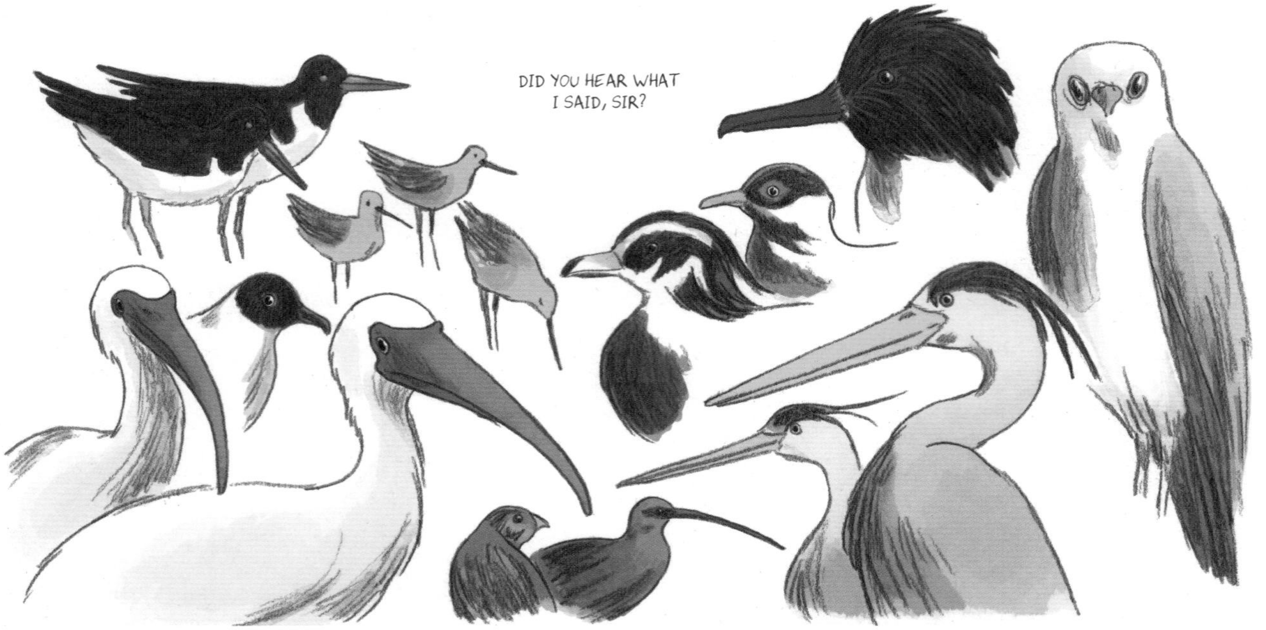
DID YOU HEAR WHAT I SAID, SIR?

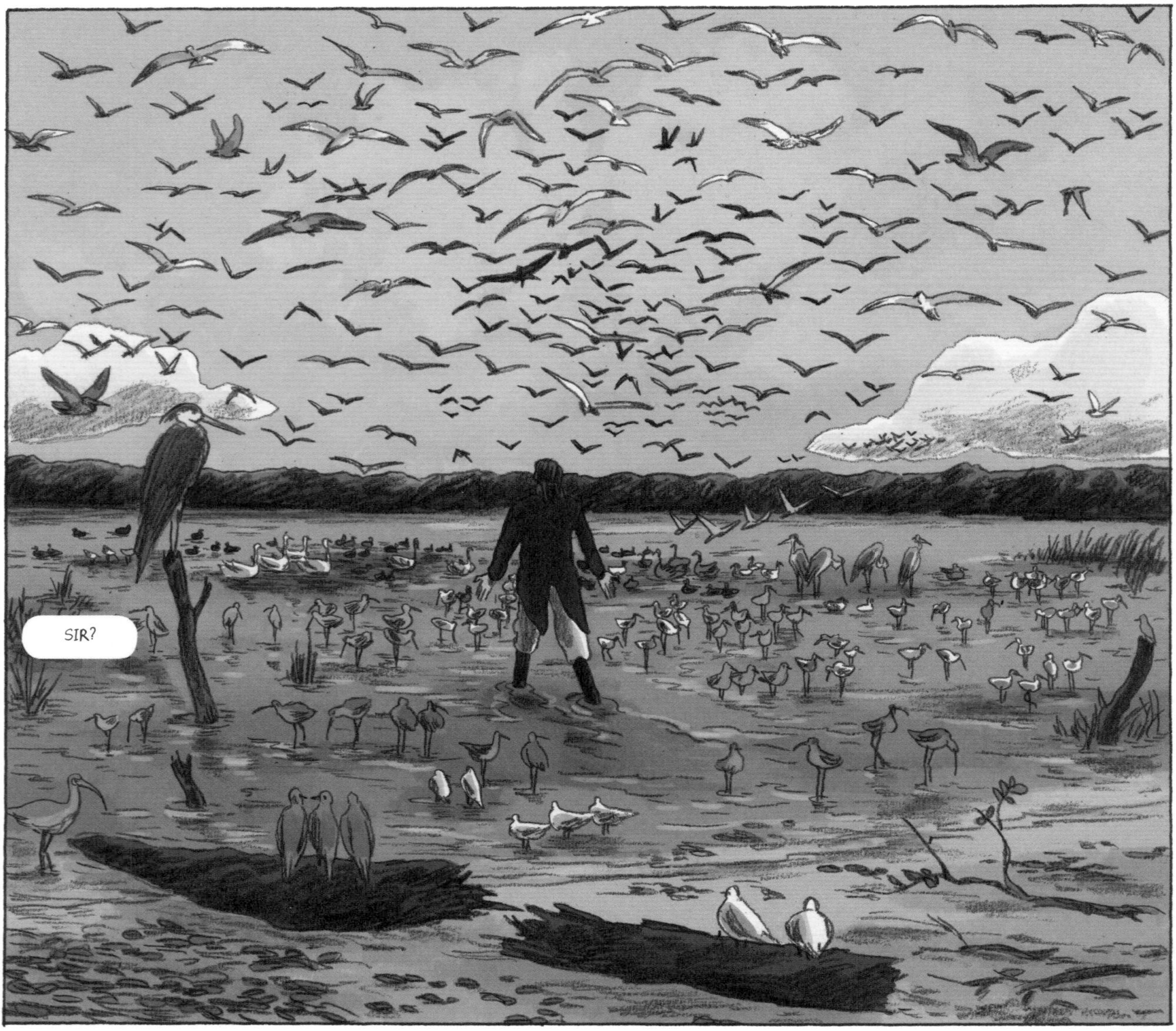
SIR?

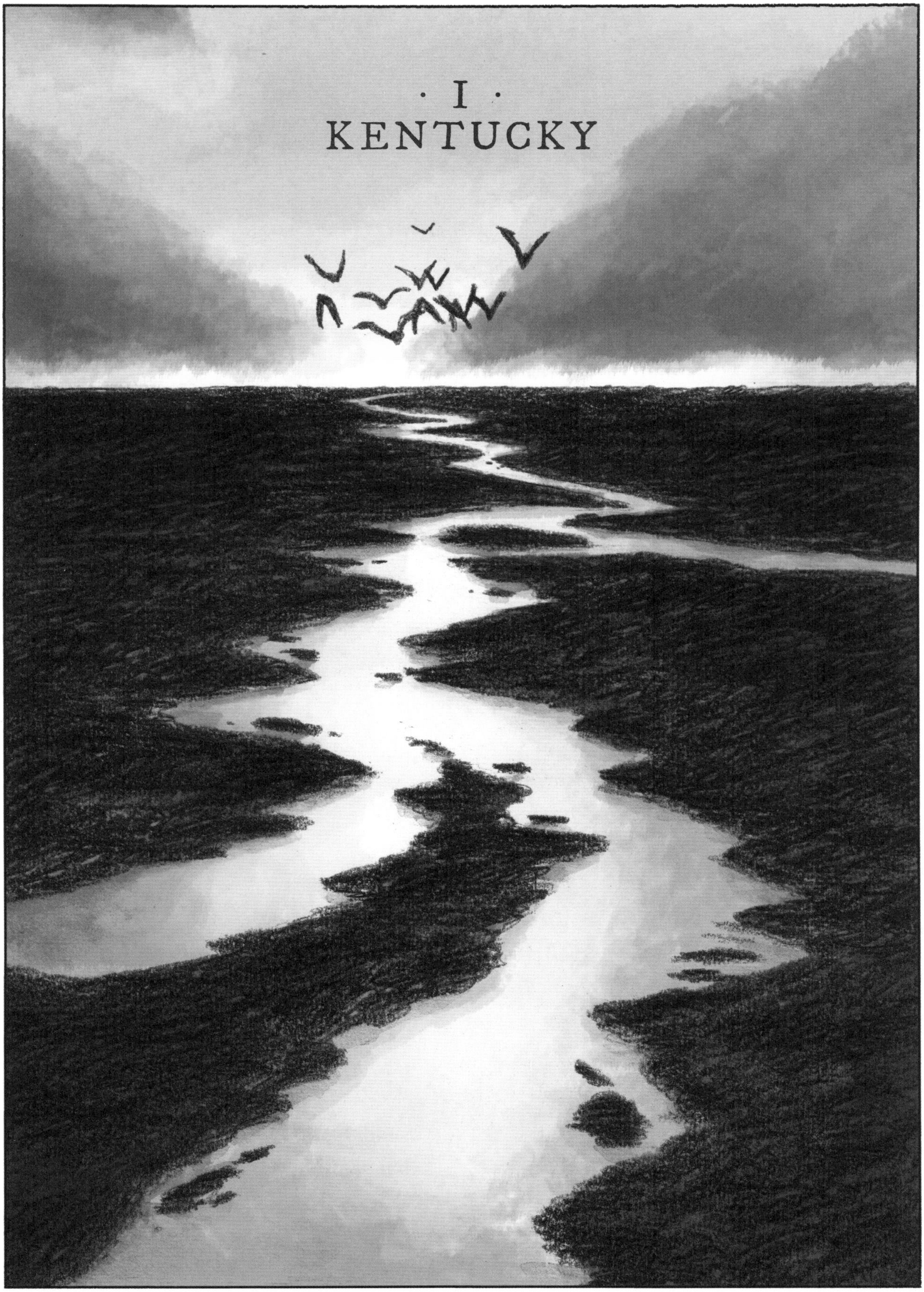
· I ·
KENTUCKY

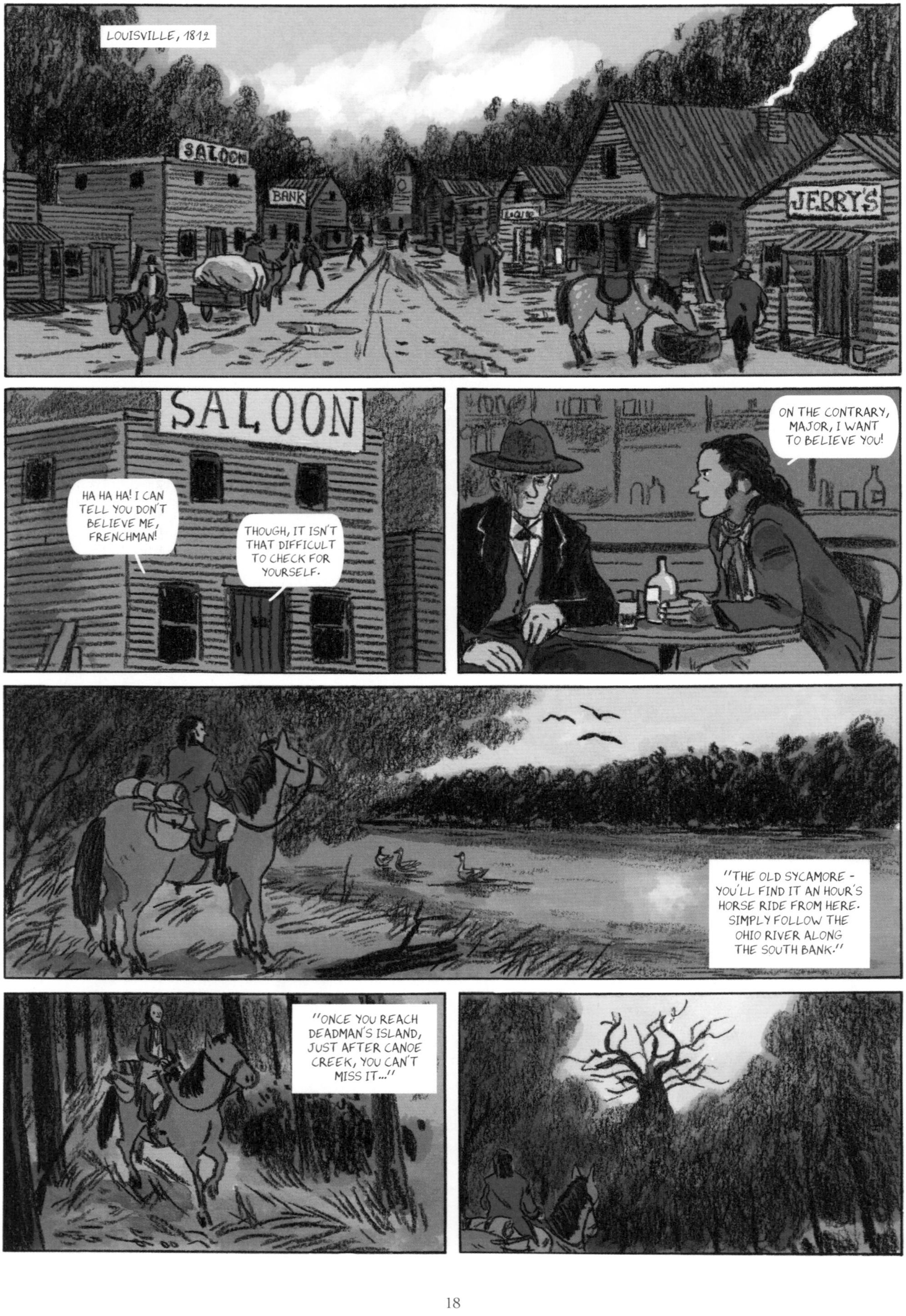
LOUISVILLE, 1812
SALOON
BANK
JERRY'S
SALOON
HA HA HA! I CAN TELL YOU DON'T BELIEVE ME, FRENCHMAN!
THOUGH, IT ISN'T THAT DIFFICULT TO CHECK FOR YOURSELF.
ON THE CONTRARY, MAJOR, I WANT TO BELIEVE YOU!
"THE OLD SYCAMORE - YOU'LL FIND IT AN HOUR'S HORSE RIDE FROM HERE. SIMPLY FOLLOW THE OHIO RIVER ALONG THE SOUTH BANK."
"ONCE YOU REACH DEADMAN'S ISLAND, JUST AFTER CANOE CREEK, YOU CAN'T MISS IT..."

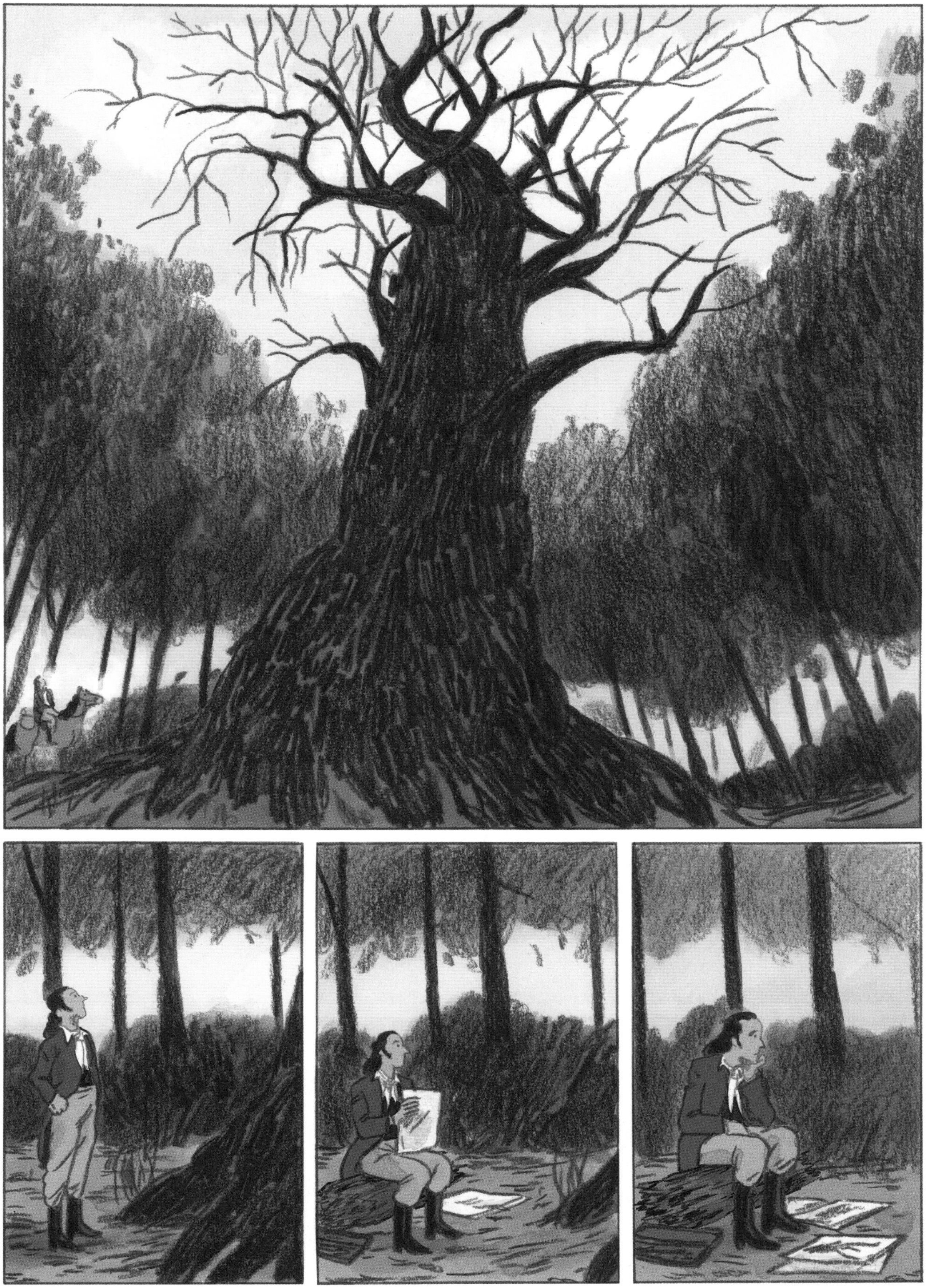

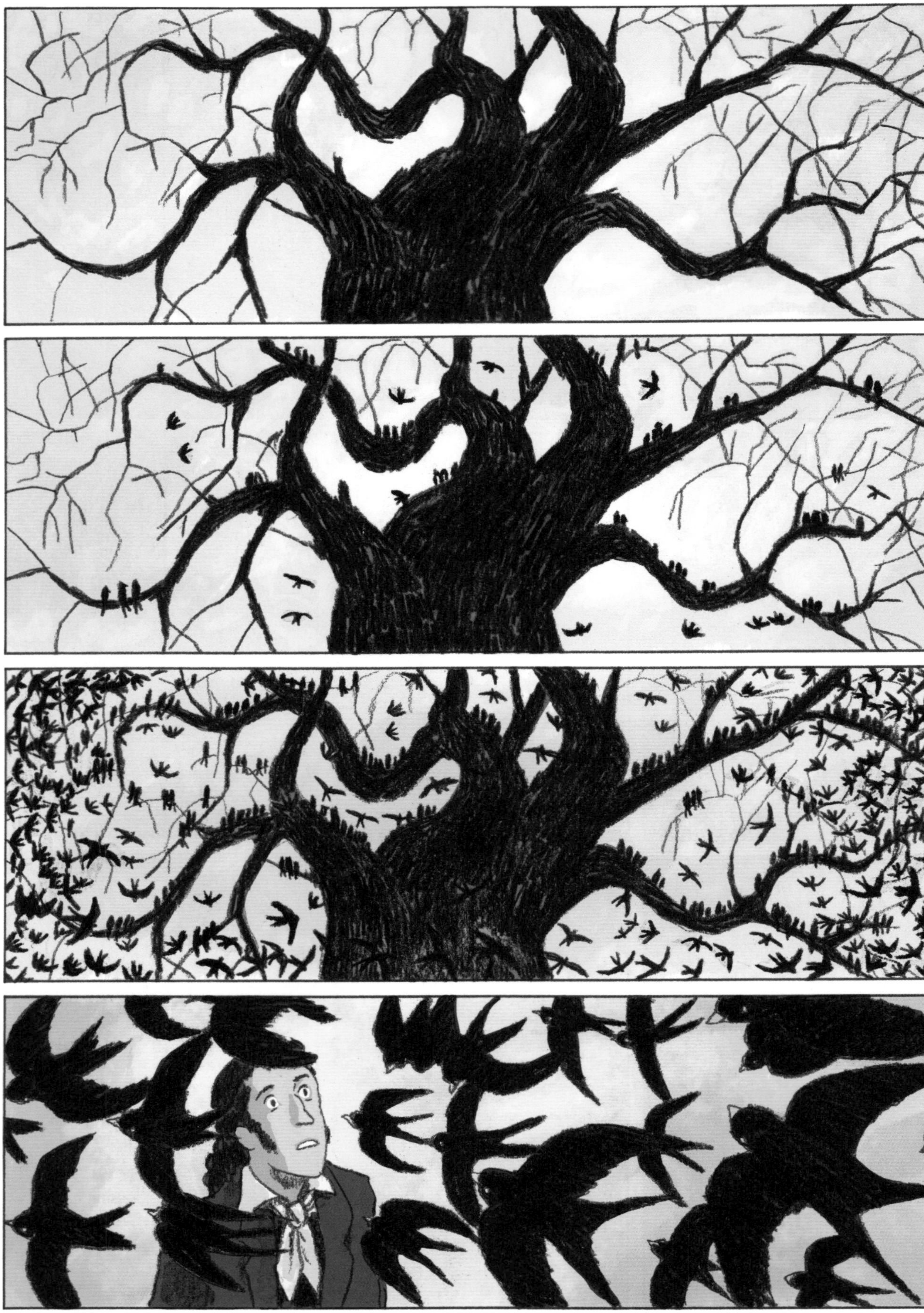

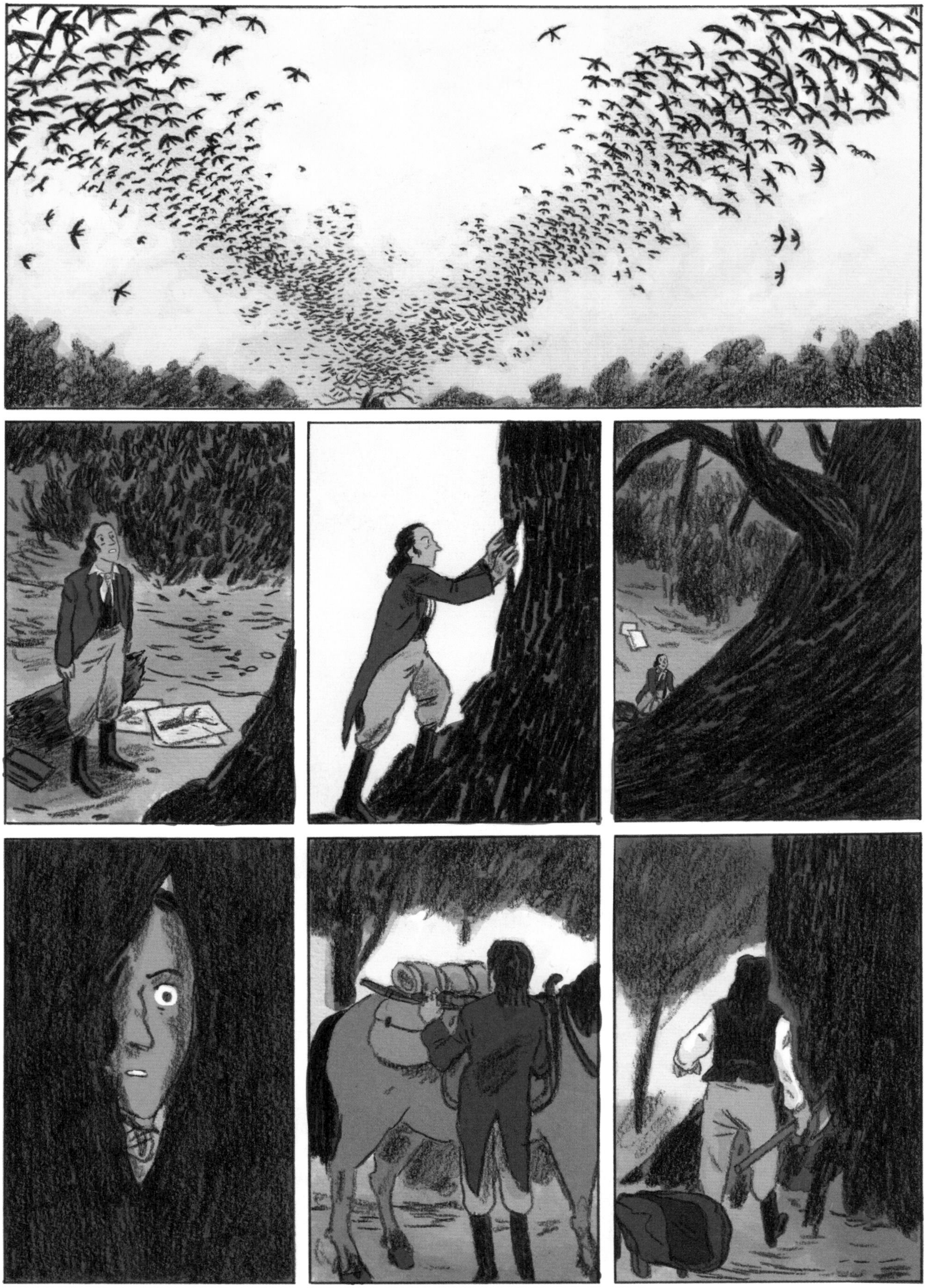

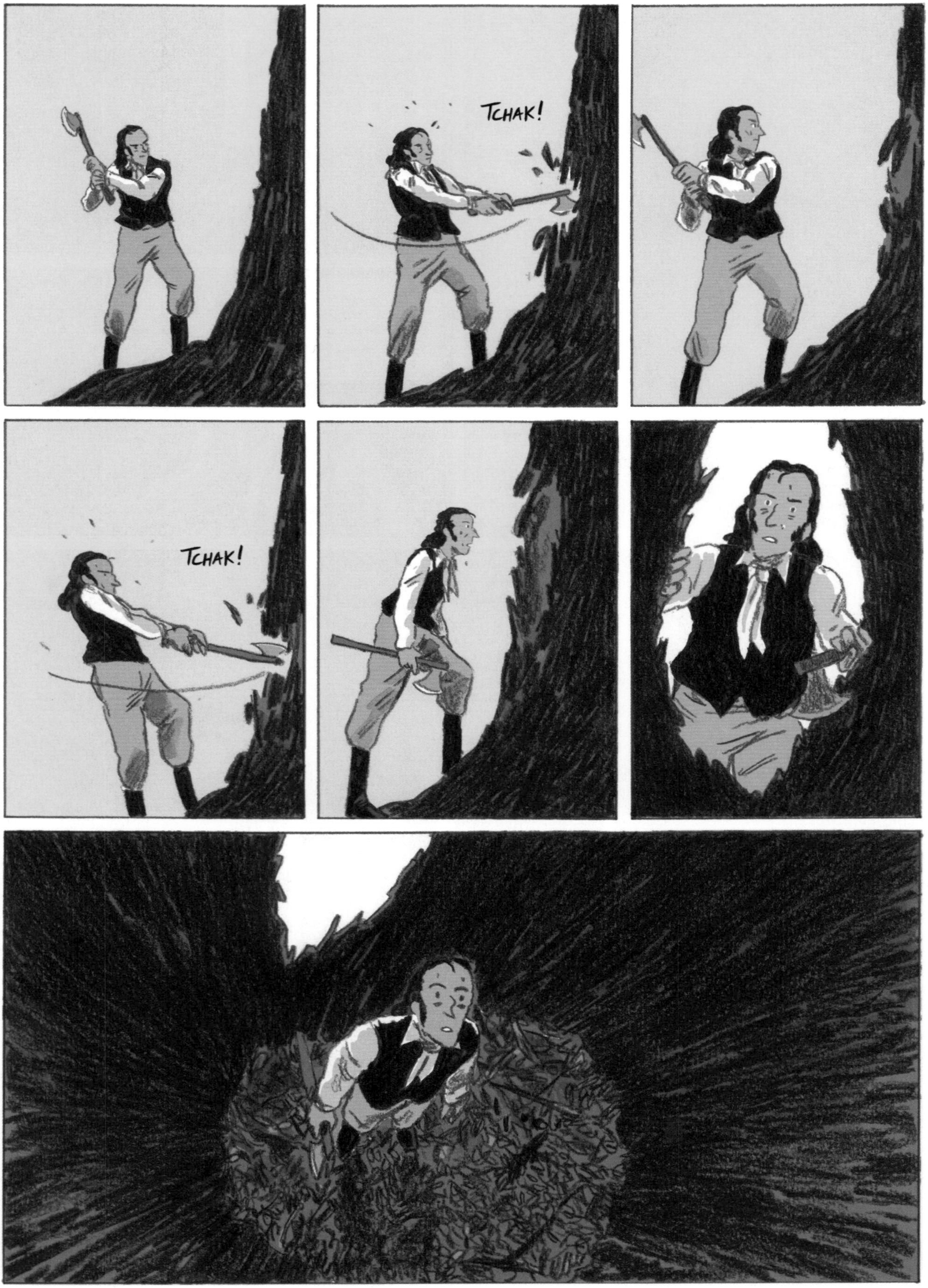
TCHAK!
TCHAK!

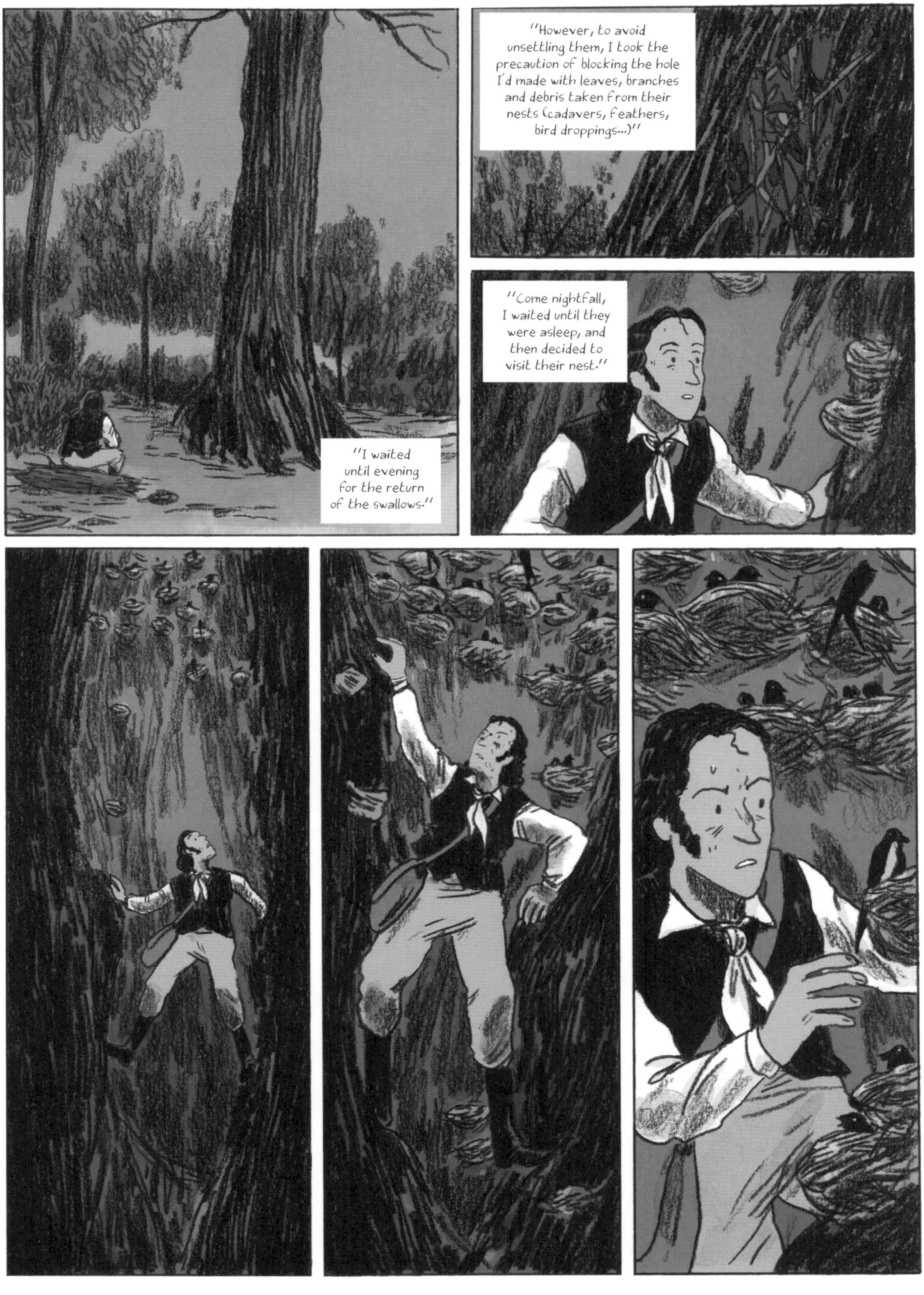
"I waited until evening for the return of the swallows."
"However, to avoid unsettling them, I took the precaution of blocking the hole I'd made with leaves, branches and debris taken from their nests (cadavers, feathers, bird droppings...)"
"Come nightfall, I waited until they were asleep, and then decided to visit their nest."

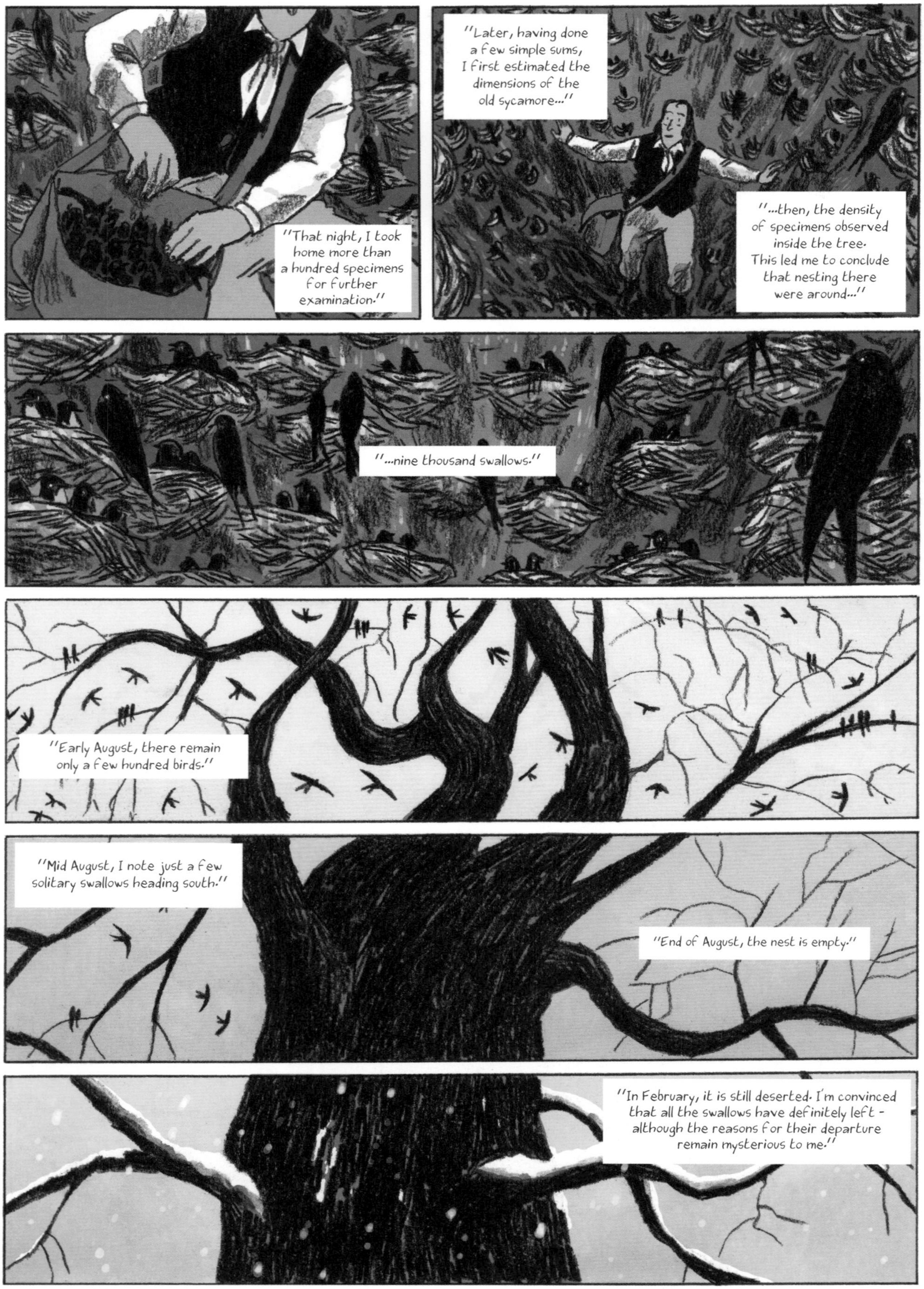
"That night, I took home more than a hundred specimens for further examination."
"Later, having done a few simple sums, I first estimated the dimensions of the old sycamore..."
"...then, the density of specimens observed inside the tree. This led me to conclude that nesting there were around..."
"...nine thousand swallows."
"Early August, there remain only a few hundred birds."
"Mid August, I note just a few solitary swallows heading south."
"End of August, the nest is empty."
"In February, it is still deserted. I'm convinced that all the swallows have definitely left - although the reasons for their departure remain mysterious to me."

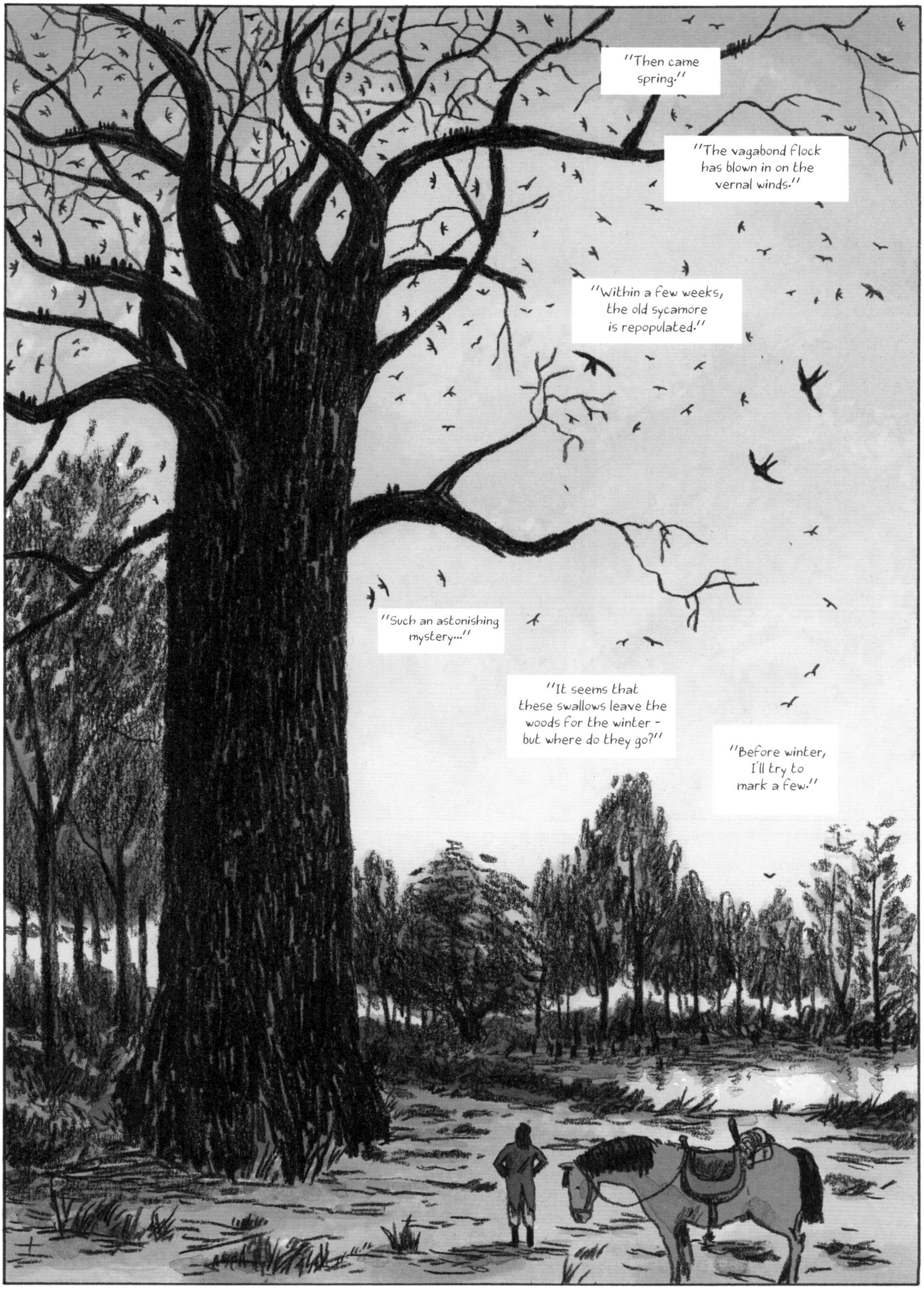
"Then came spring."
"The vagabond flock has blown in on the vernal winds."
"Within a few weeks, the old sycamore is repopulated."
"Such an astonishing mystery..."
"It seems that these swallows leave the woods for the winter - but where do they go?"
"Before winter, I'll try to mark a few."

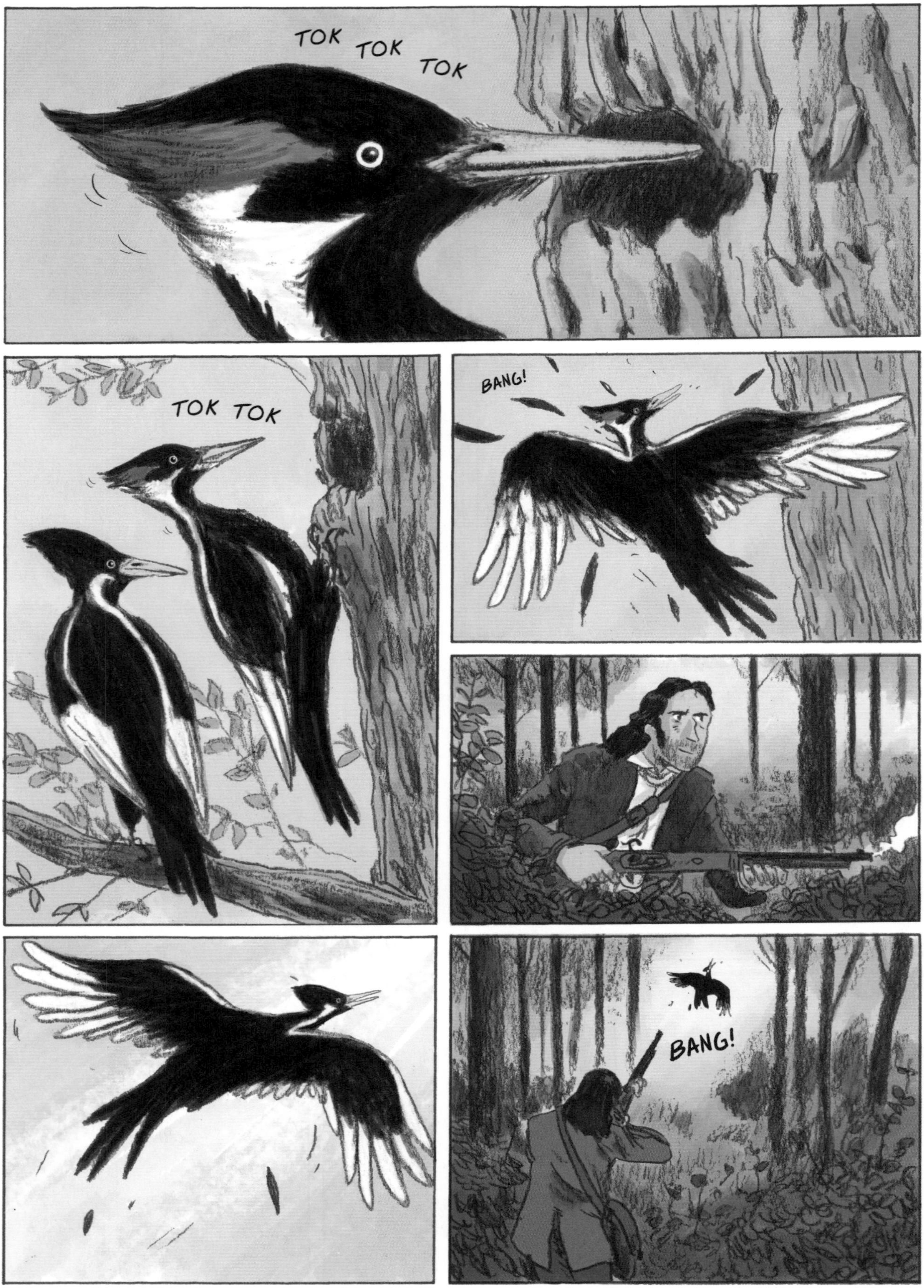
TOK TOK TOK
TOK TOK
BANG!
BANG!

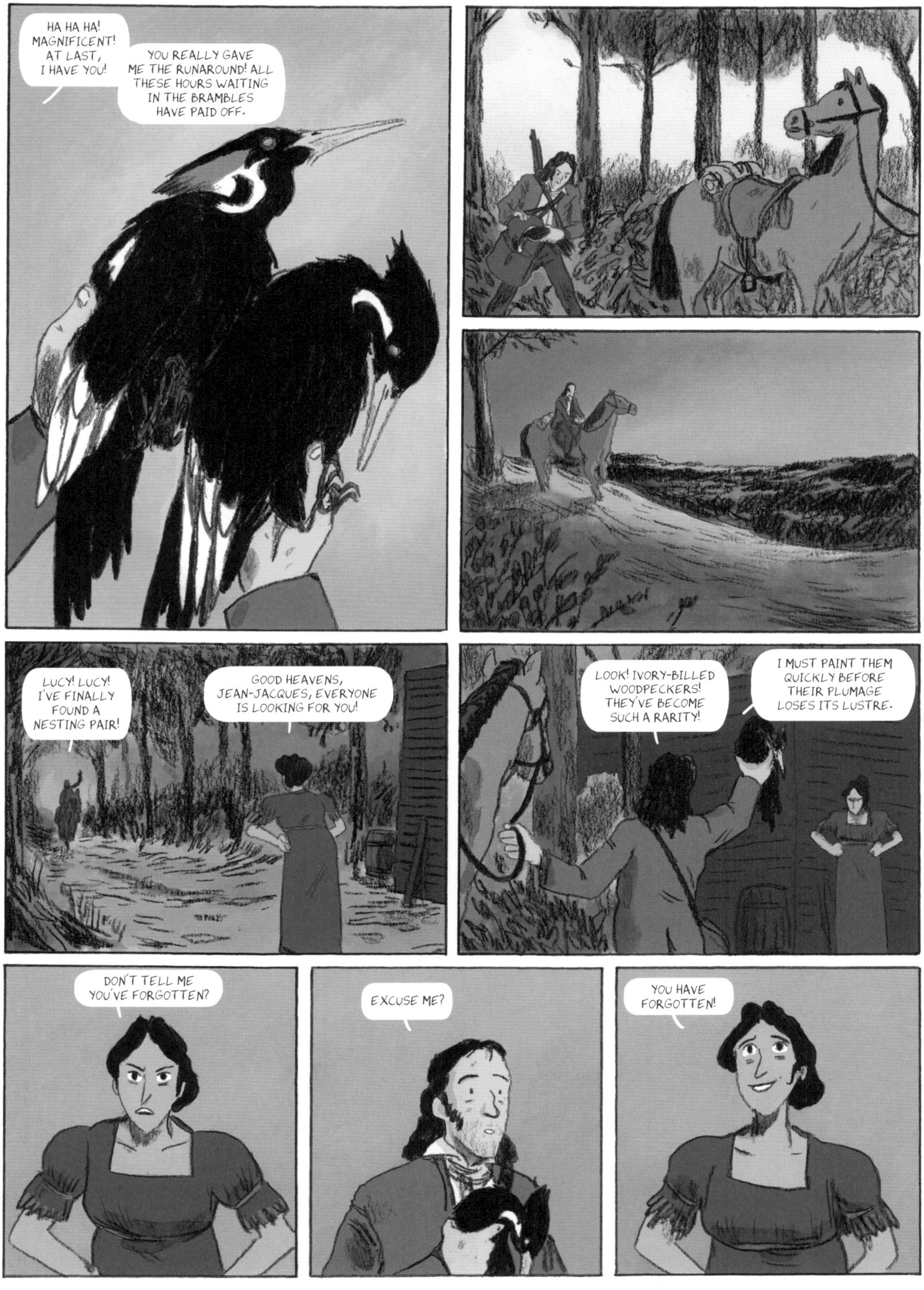
HA HA HA! MAGNIFICENT! AT LAST, I HAVE YOU!
YOU REALLY GAVE ME THE RUNAROUND! ALL THESE HOURS WAITING IN THE BRAMBLES HAVE PAID OFF.
LUCY! LUCY! I'VE FINALLY FOUND A NESTING PAIR!
GOOD HEAVENS, JEAN-JACQUES, EVERYONE IS LOOKING FOR YOU!
LOOK! IVORY-BILLED WOODPECKERS! THEY'VE BECOME SUCH A RARITY!
I MUST PAINT THEM QUICKLY BEFORE THEIR PLUMAGE LOSES ITS LUSTRE.
DON'T TELL ME YOU'VE FORGOTTEN?
EXCUSE ME?
YOU HAVE FORGOTTEN!

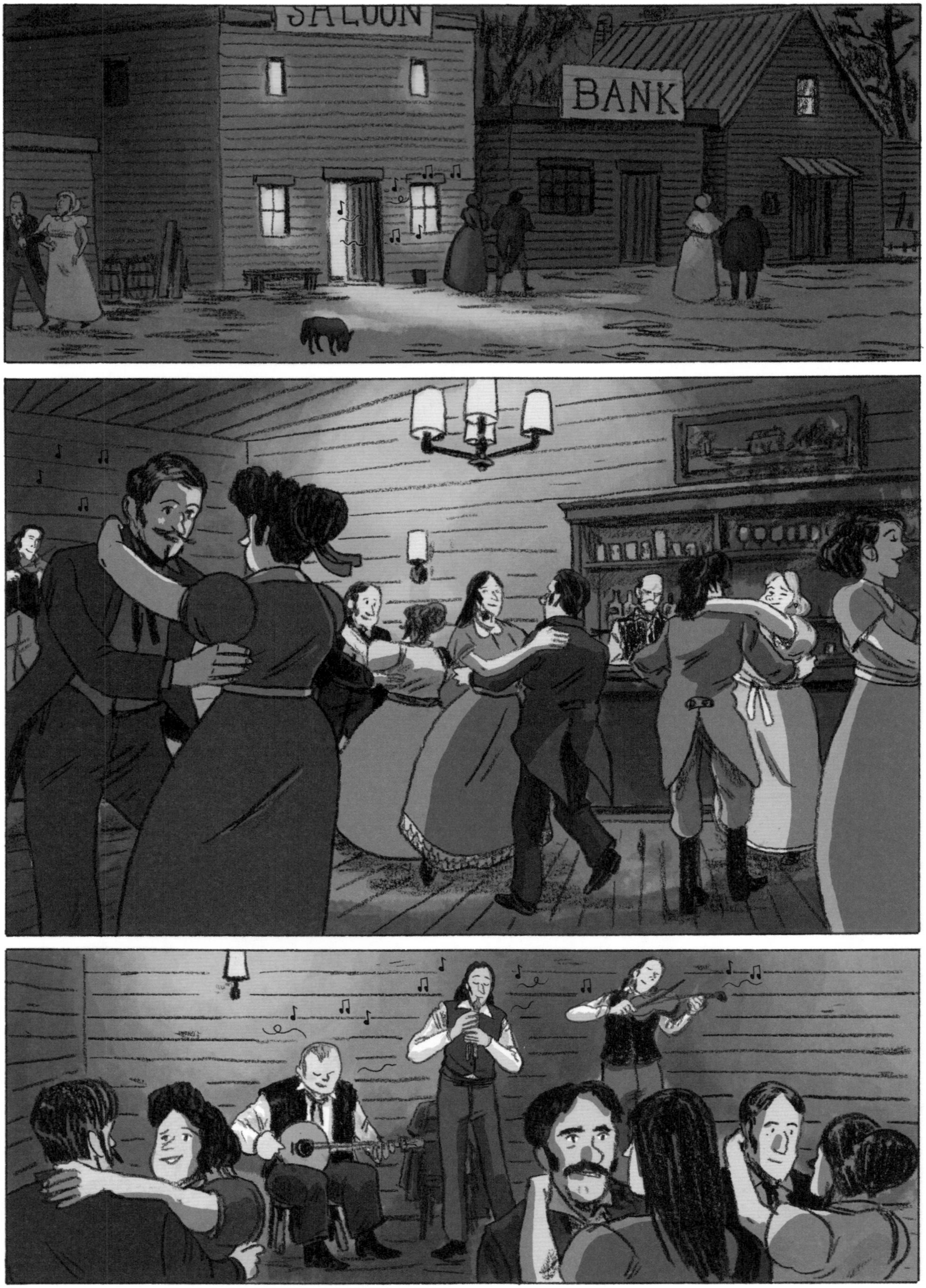
SALOON
BANK

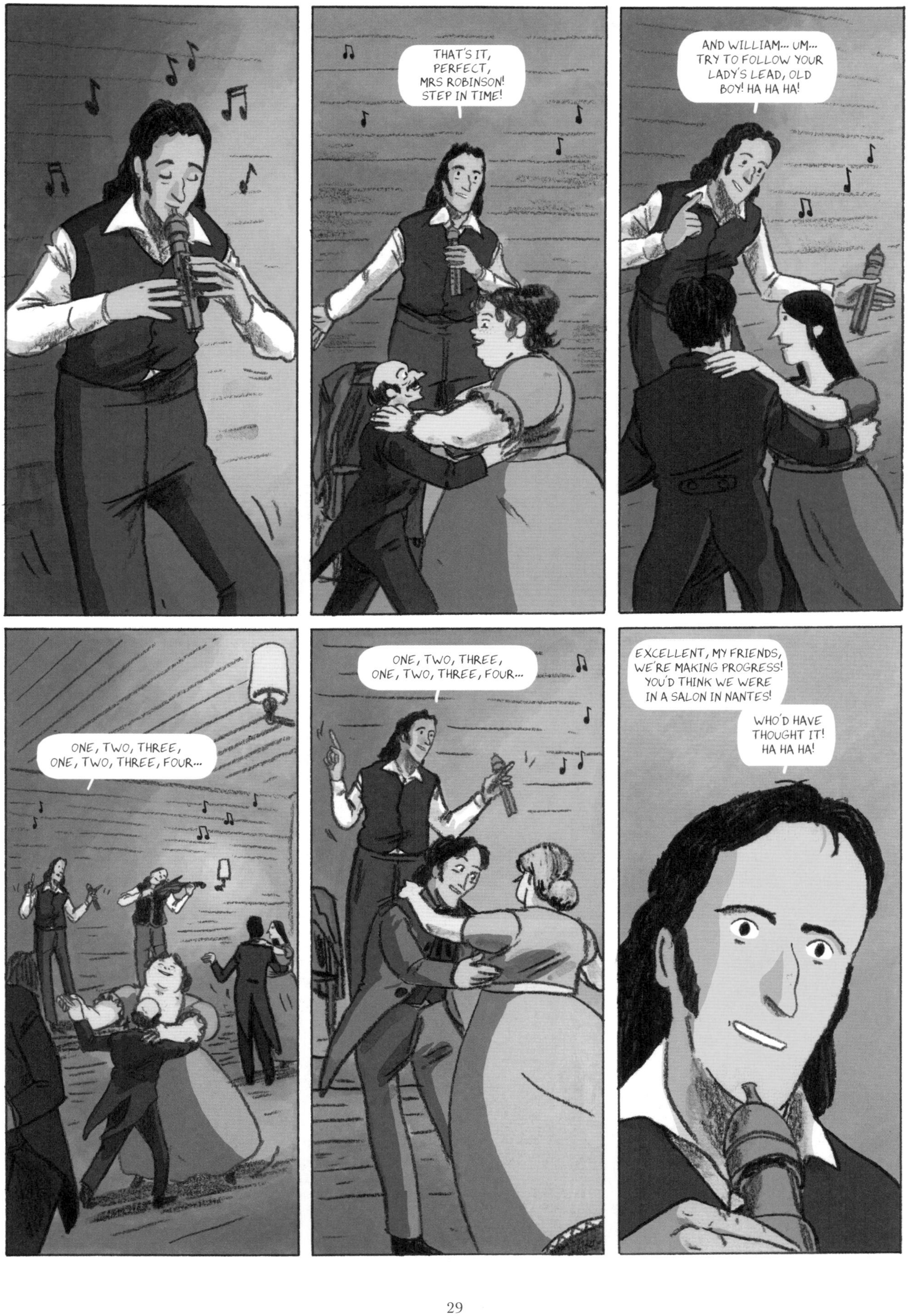
THAT'S IT, PERFECT, MRS ROBINSON! STEP IN TIME!
AND WILLIAM... UM... TRY TO FOLLOW YOUR LADY'S LEAD, OLD BOY! HA HA HA!
ONE, TWO, THREE, ONE, TWO, THREE, FOUR...
ONE, TWO, THREE, ONE, TWO, THREE, FOUR...
EXCELLENT, MY FRIENDS, WE'RE MAKING PROGRESS! YOU'D THINK WE WERE IN A SALON IN NANTES!
WHO'D HAVE THOUGHT IT! HA HA HA!

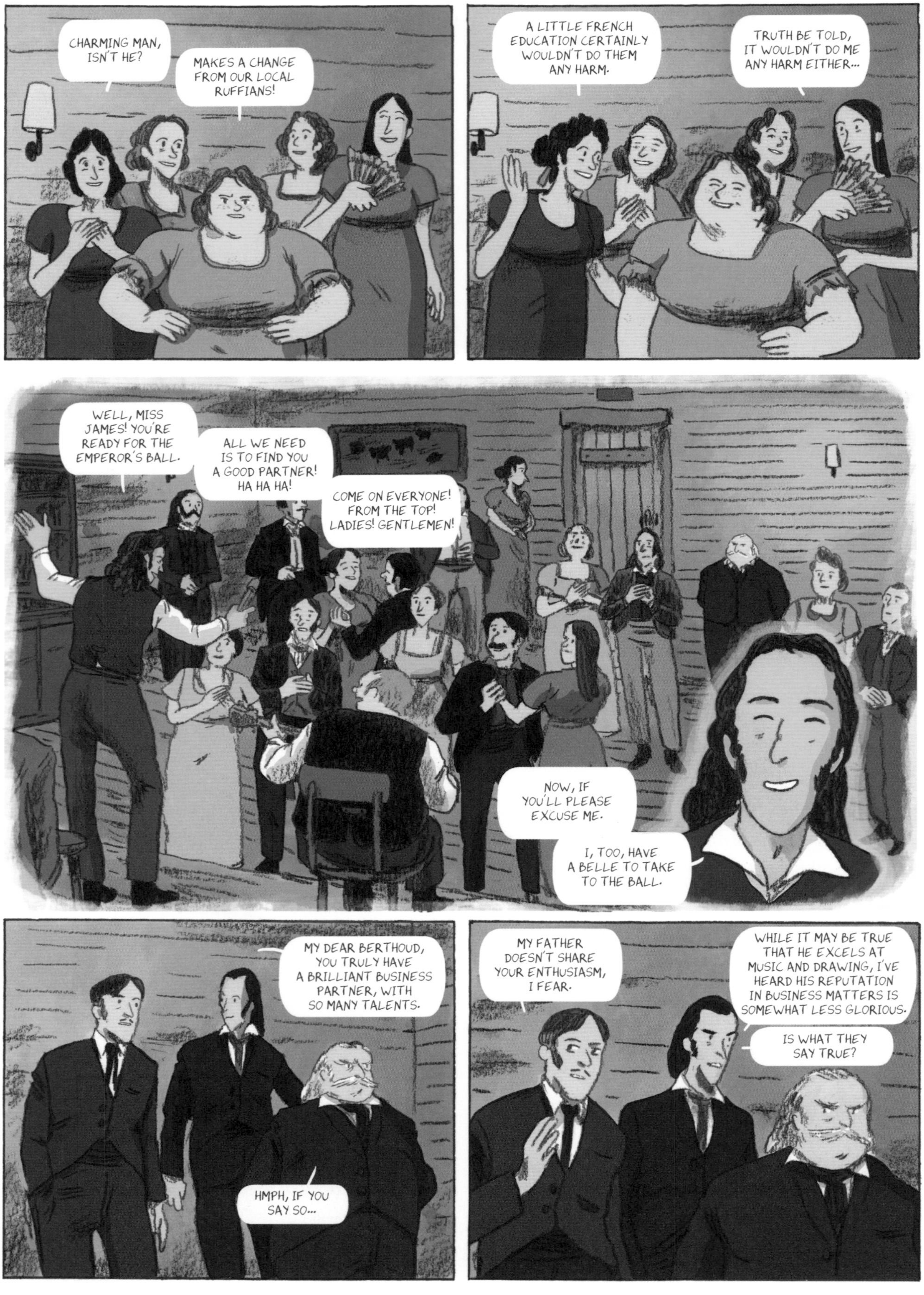
CHARMING MAN, ISN'T HE?
MAKES A CHANGE FROM OUR LOCAL RUFFIANS!
A LITTLE FRENCH EDUCATION CERTAINLY WOULDN'T DO THEM ANY HARM.
TRUTH BE TOLD, IT WOULDN'T DO ME ANY HARM EITHER...
WELL, MISS JAMES! YOU'RE READY FOR THE EMPEROR'S BALL.
ALL WE NEED IS TO FIND YOU A GOOD PARTNER! HA HA HA!
COME ON EVERYONE! FROM THE TOP! LADIES! GENTLEMEN!
NOW, IF YOU'LL PLEASE EXCUSE ME.
I, TOO, HAVE A BELLE TO TAKE TO THE BALL.
MY DEAR BERTHOUD, YOU TRULY HAVE A BRILLIANT BUSINESS PARTNER, WITH SO MANY TALENTS.
HMPH, IF YOU SAY SO...
MY FATHER DOESN'T SHARE YOUR ENTHUSIASM, I FEAR.
WHILE IT MAY BE TRUE THAT HE EXCELS AT MUSIC AND DRAWING, I'VE HEARD HIS REPUTATION IN BUSINESS MATTERS IS SOMEWHAT LESS GLORIOUS.
IS WHAT THEY SAY TRUE?

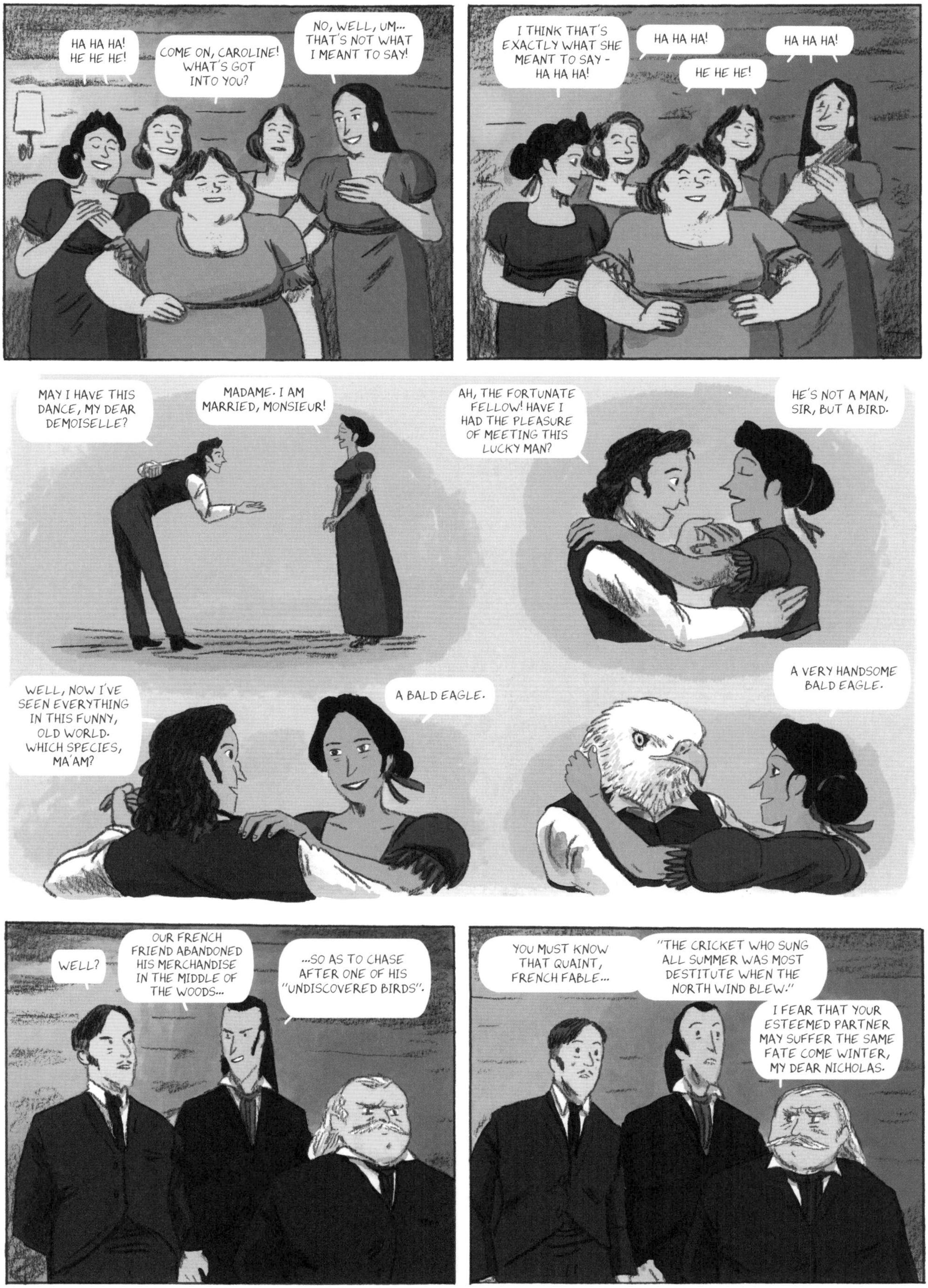
HA HA HA! HE HE HE!
COME ON, CAROLINE! WHAT'S GOT INTO YOU?
NO, WELL, UM... THAT'S NOT WHAT I MEANT TO SAY!
I THINK THAT'S EXACTLY WHAT SHE MEANT TO SAY - HA HA HA!
HA HA HA!
HE HE HE!
HA HA HA!
MAY I HAVE THIS DANCE, MY DEAR DEMOISELLE?
MADAME. I AM MARRIED, MONSIEUR!
AH, THE FORTUNATE FELLOW! HAVE I HAD THE PLEASURE OF MEETING THIS LUCKY MAN?
HE'S NOT A MAN, SIR, BUT A BIRD.
WELL, NOW I'VE SEEN EVERYTHING IN THIS FUNNY, OLD WORLD. WHICH SPECIES, MA'AM?
A BALD EAGLE.
A VERY HANDSOME BALD EAGLE.
WELL?
OUR FRENCH FRIEND ABANDONED HIS MERCHANDISE IN THE MIDDLE OF THE WOODS...
...SO AS TO CHASE AFTER ONE OF HIS "UNDISCOVERED BIRDS".
YOU MUST KNOW THAT QUAINT, FRENCH FABLE...
"THE CRICKET WHO SUNG ALL SUMMER WAS MOST DESTITUTE WHEN THE NORTH WIND BLEW."
I FEAR THAT YOUR ESTEEMED PARTNER MAY SUFFER THE SAME FATE COME WINTER, MY DEAR NICHOLAS.

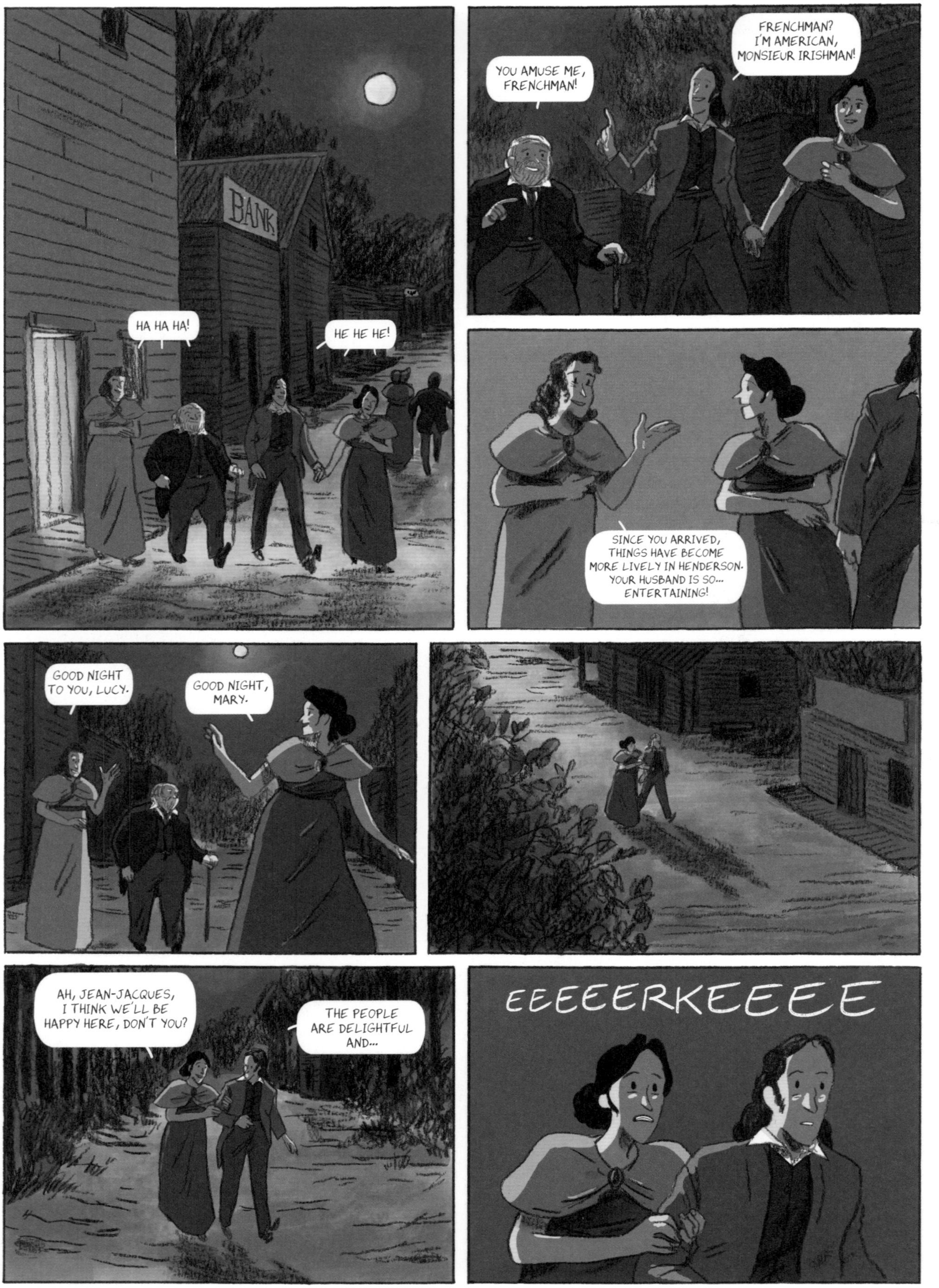
HA HA HA!
HE HE HE!
YOU AMUSE ME, FRENCHMAN!
FRENCHMAN? I'M AMERICAN, MONSIEUR IRISHMAN!
SINCE YOU ARRIVED, THINGS HAVE BECOME MORE LIVELY IN HENDERSON. YOUR HUSBAND IS SO... ENTERTAINING!
GOOD NIGHT TO YOU, LUCY.
GOOD NIGHT, MARY.
AH, JEAN-JACQUES, I THINK WE'LL BE HAPPY HERE, DON'T YOU?
THE PEOPLE ARE DELIGHTFUL AND...
EEEEERKEEEE

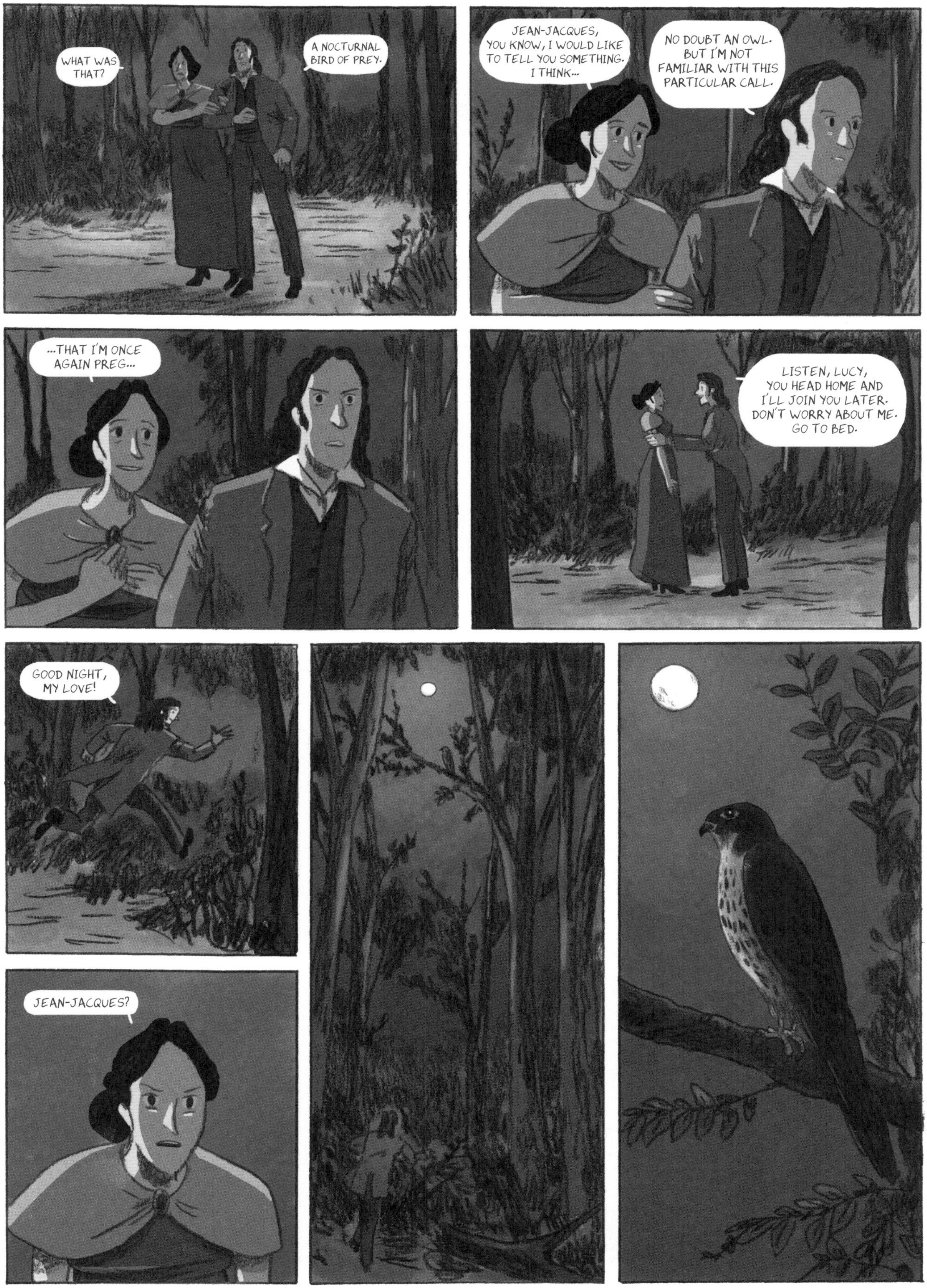
WHAT WAS THAT?
A NOCTURNAL BIRD OF PREY.
JEAN-JACQUES, YOU KNOW, I WOULD LIKE TO TELL YOU SOMETHING. I THINK...
NO DOUBT AN OWL. BUT I'M NOT FAMILIAR WITH THIS PARTICULAR CALL.
...THAT I'M ONCE AGAIN PREG...
LISTEN, LUCY, YOU HEAD HOME AND I'LL JOIN YOU LATER. DON'T WORRY ABOUT ME. GO TO BED.
GOOD NIGHT, MY LOVE!
JEAN-JACQUES?

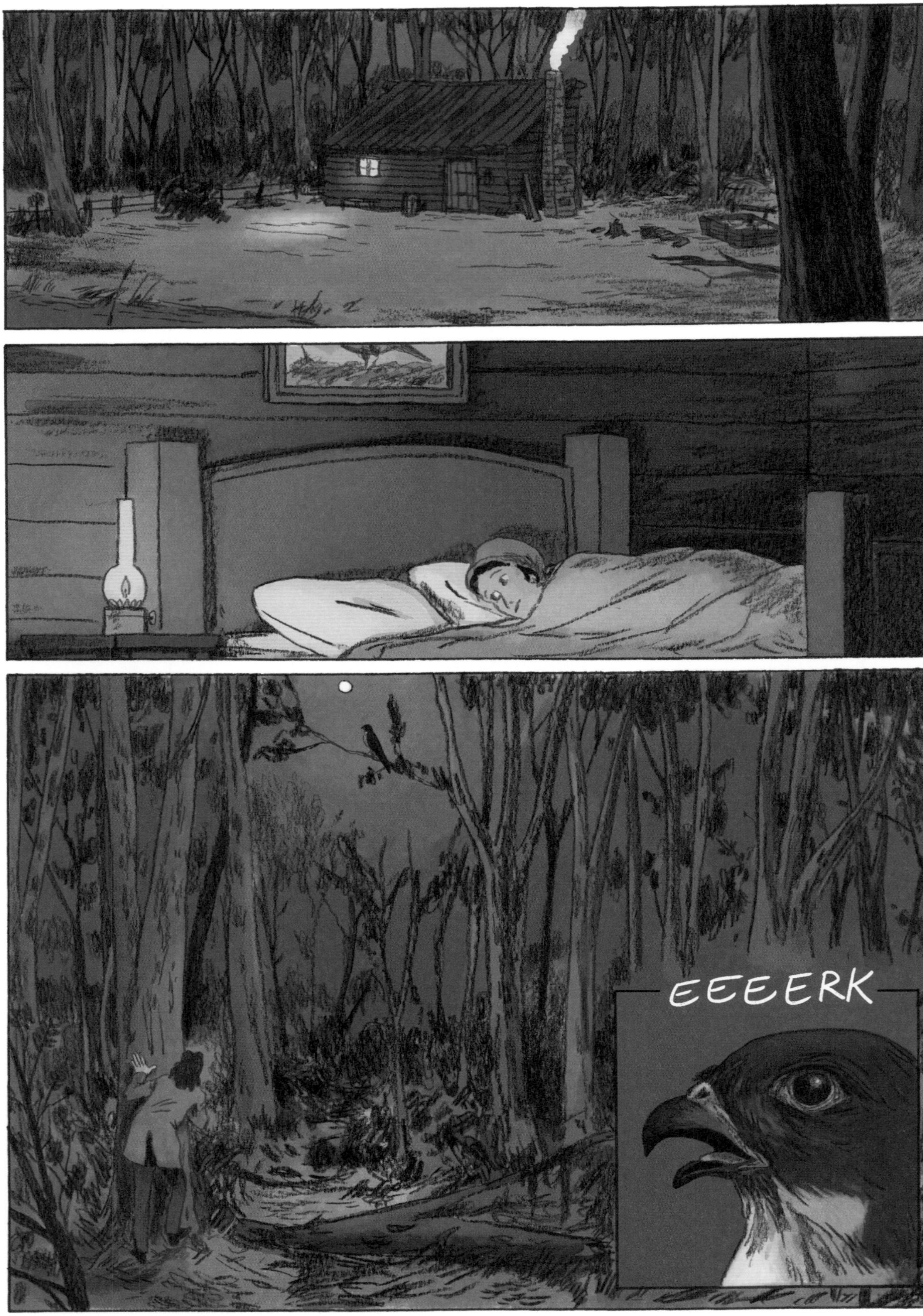
EEEERK

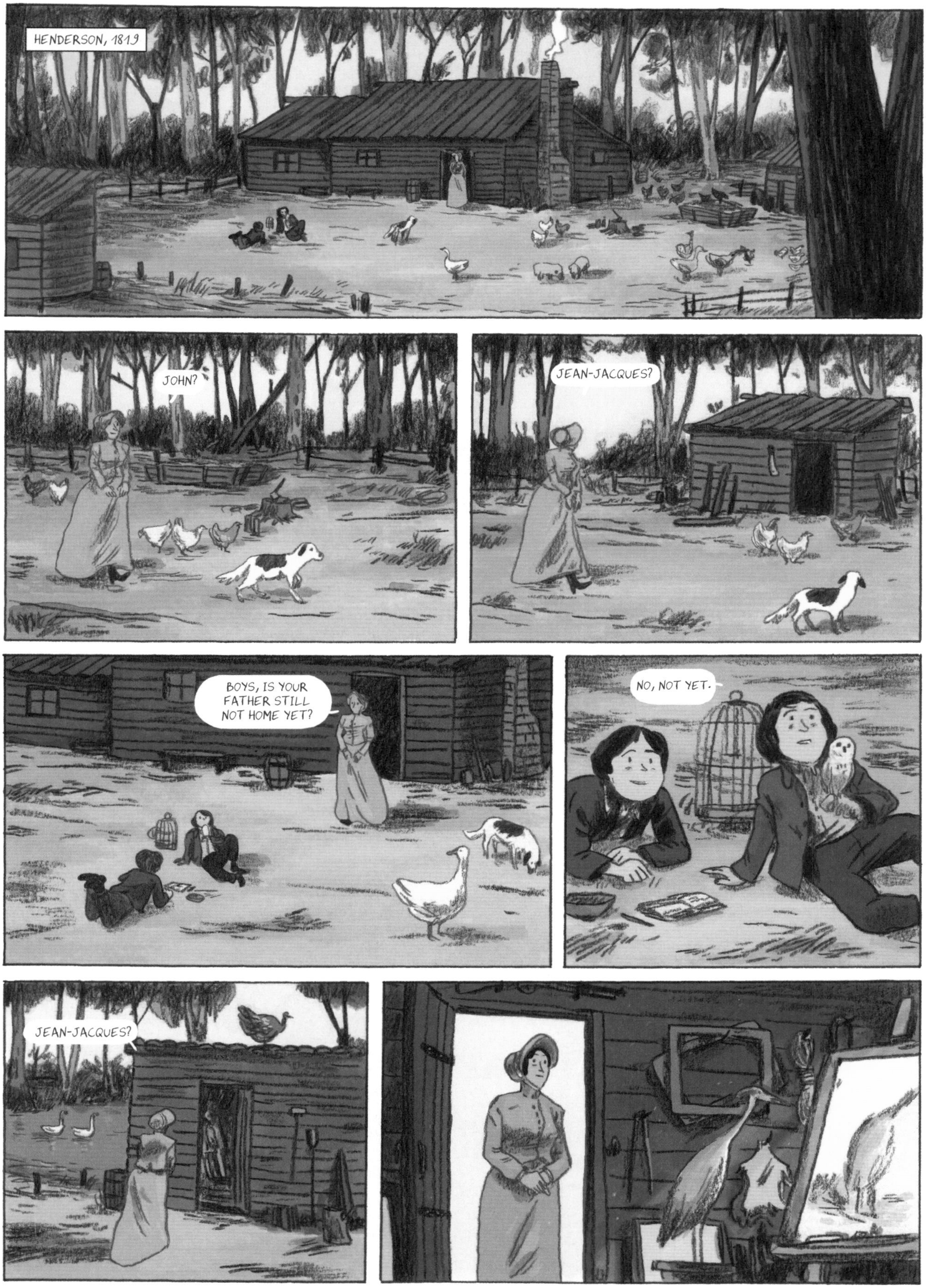
HENDERSON, 1819
JOHN?
JEAN-JACQUES?
BOYS, IS YOUR FATHER STILL NOT HOME YET?
NO, NOT YET.
JEAN-JACQUES?

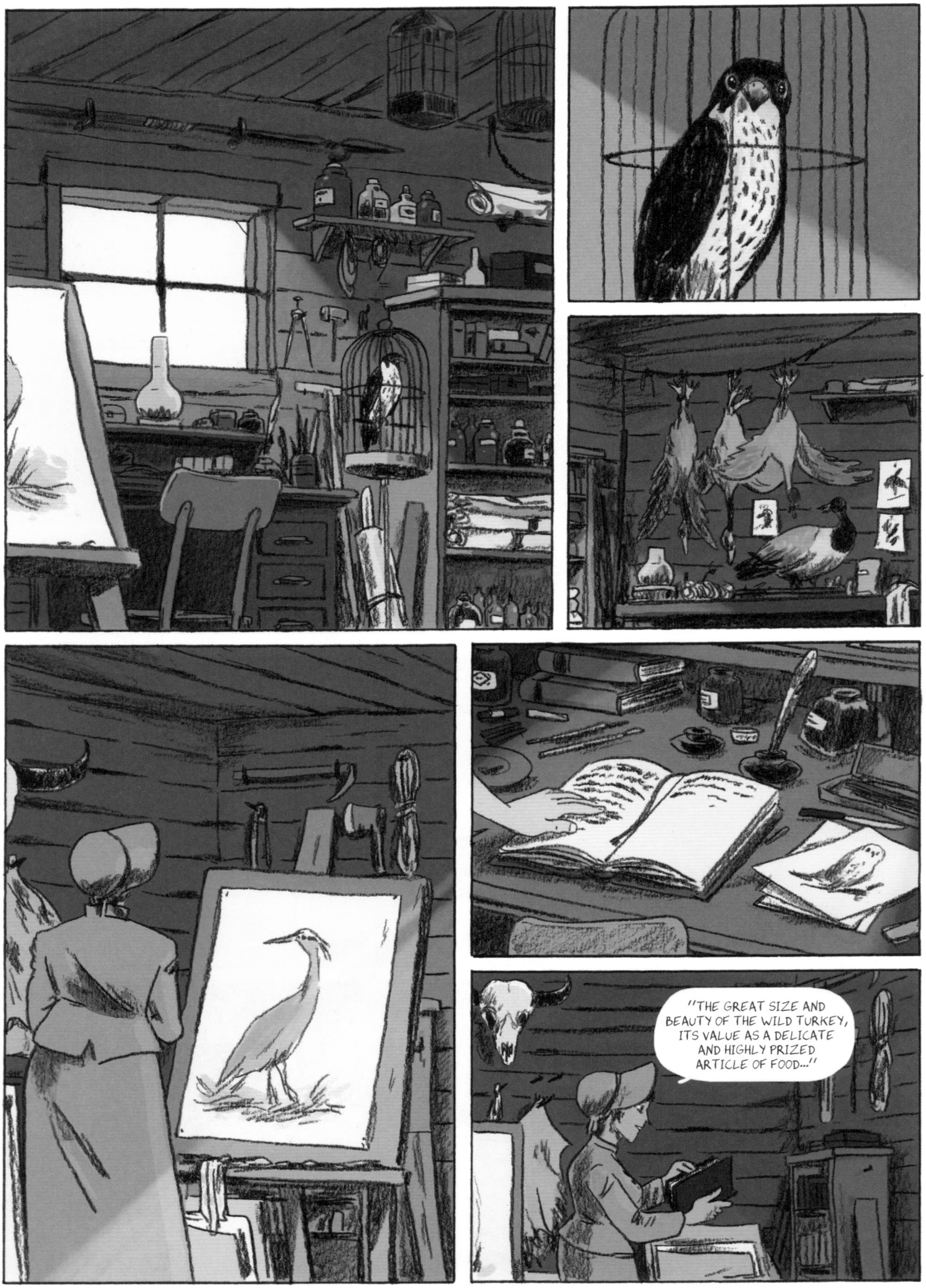
"THE GREAT SIZE AND BEAUTY OF THE WILD TURKEY, ITS VALUE AS A DELICATE AND HIGHLY PRIZED ARTICLE OF FOOD..."

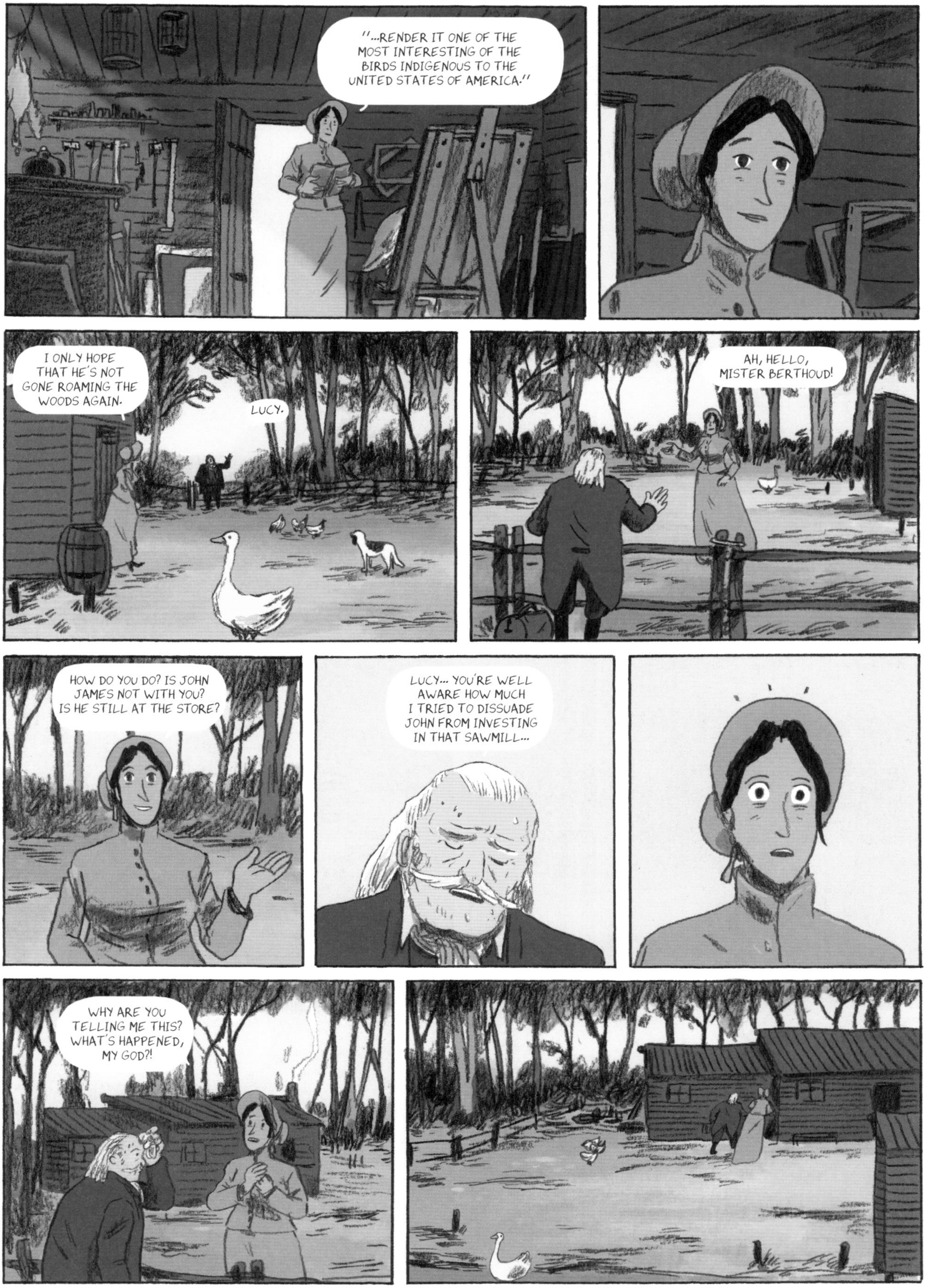
"...RENDER IT ONE OF THE MOST INTERESTING OF THE BIRDS INDIGENOUS TO THE UNITED STATES OF AMERICA."
I ONLY HOPE THAT HE'S NOT GONE ROAMING THE WOODS AGAIN.
LUCY.
AH, HELLO, MISTER BERTHOUD!
HOW DO YOU DO? IS JOHN JAMES NOT WITH YOU? IS HE STILL AT THE STORE?
LUCY... YOU'RE WELL AWARE HOW MUCH I TRIED TO DISSUADE JOHN FROM INVESTING IN THAT SAWMILL...
WHY ARE YOU TELLING ME THIS? WHAT'S HAPPENED, MY GOD?!

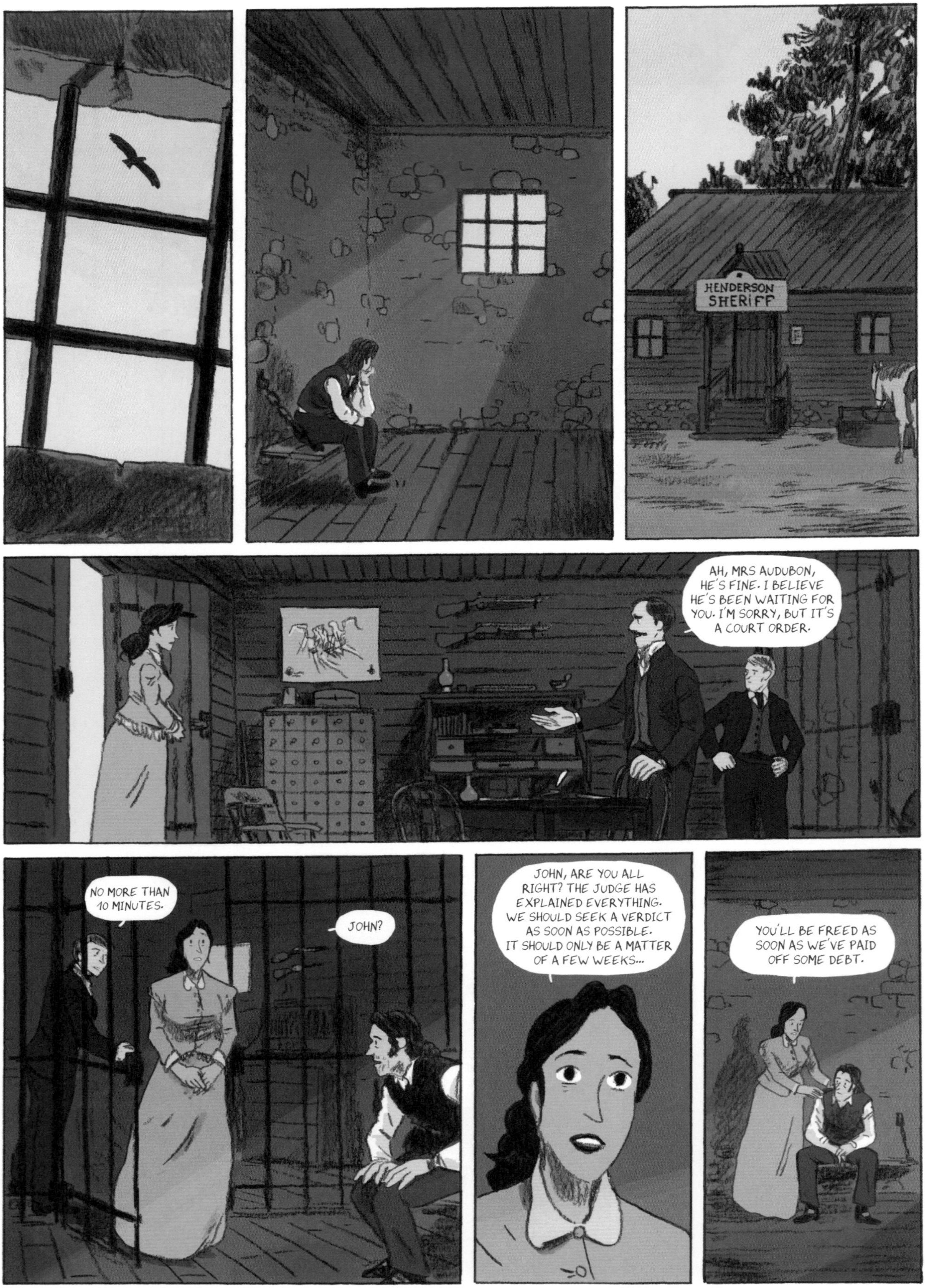
HENDERSON SHERIFF
AH, MRS AUDUBON, HE'S FINE. I BELIEVE HE'S BEEN WAITING FOR YOU. I'M SORRY, BUT IT'S A COURT ORDER.
NO MORE THAN 10 MINUTES.
JOHN?
JOHN, ARE YOU ALL RIGHT? THE JUDGE HAS EXPLAINED EVERYTHING. WE SHOULD SEEK A VERDICT AS SOON AS POSSIBLE. IT SHOULD ONLY BE A MATTER OF A FEW WEEKS...
YOU'LL BE FREED AS SOON AS WE'VE PAID OFF SOME DEBT.

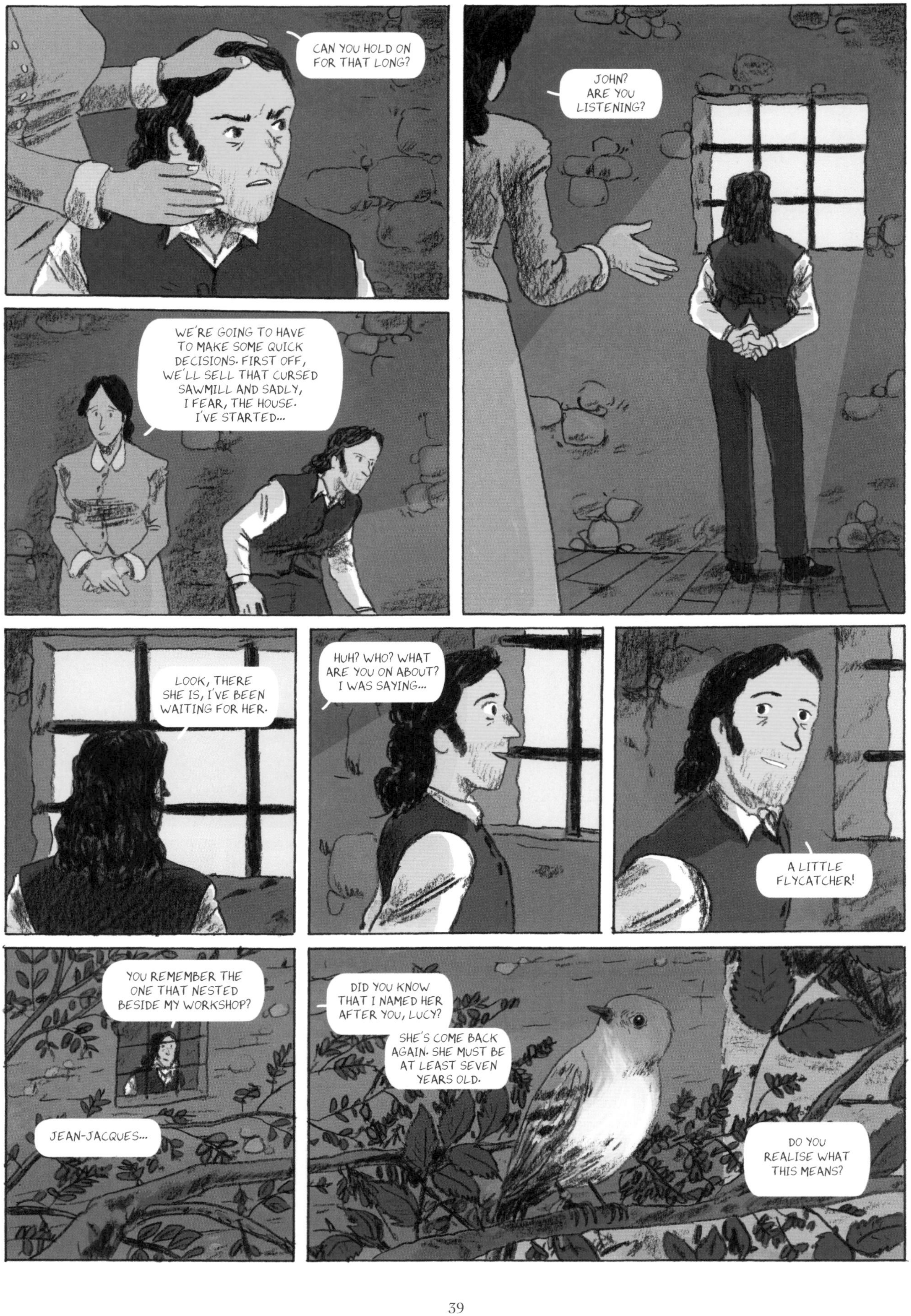
CAN YOU HOLD ON FOR THAT LONG?
JOHN? ARE YOU LISTENING?
WE'RE GOING TO HAVE TO MAKE SOME QUICK DECISIONS. FIRST OFF, WE'LL SELL THAT CURSED SAWMILL AND SADLY, I FEAR, THE HOUSE. I'VE STARTED...
LOOK, THERE SHE IS, I'VE BEEN WAITING FOR HER.
HUH? WHO? WHAT ARE YOU ON ABOUT? I WAS SAYING...
A LITTLE FLYCATCHER!
YOU REMEMBER THE ONE THAT NESTED BESIDE MY WORKSHOP?
JEAN-JACQUES...
DID YOU KNOW THAT I NAMED HER AFTER YOU, LUCY?
SHE'S COME BACK AGAIN. SHE MUST BE AT LEAST SEVEN YEARS OLD.
DO YOU REALISE WHAT THIS MEANS?

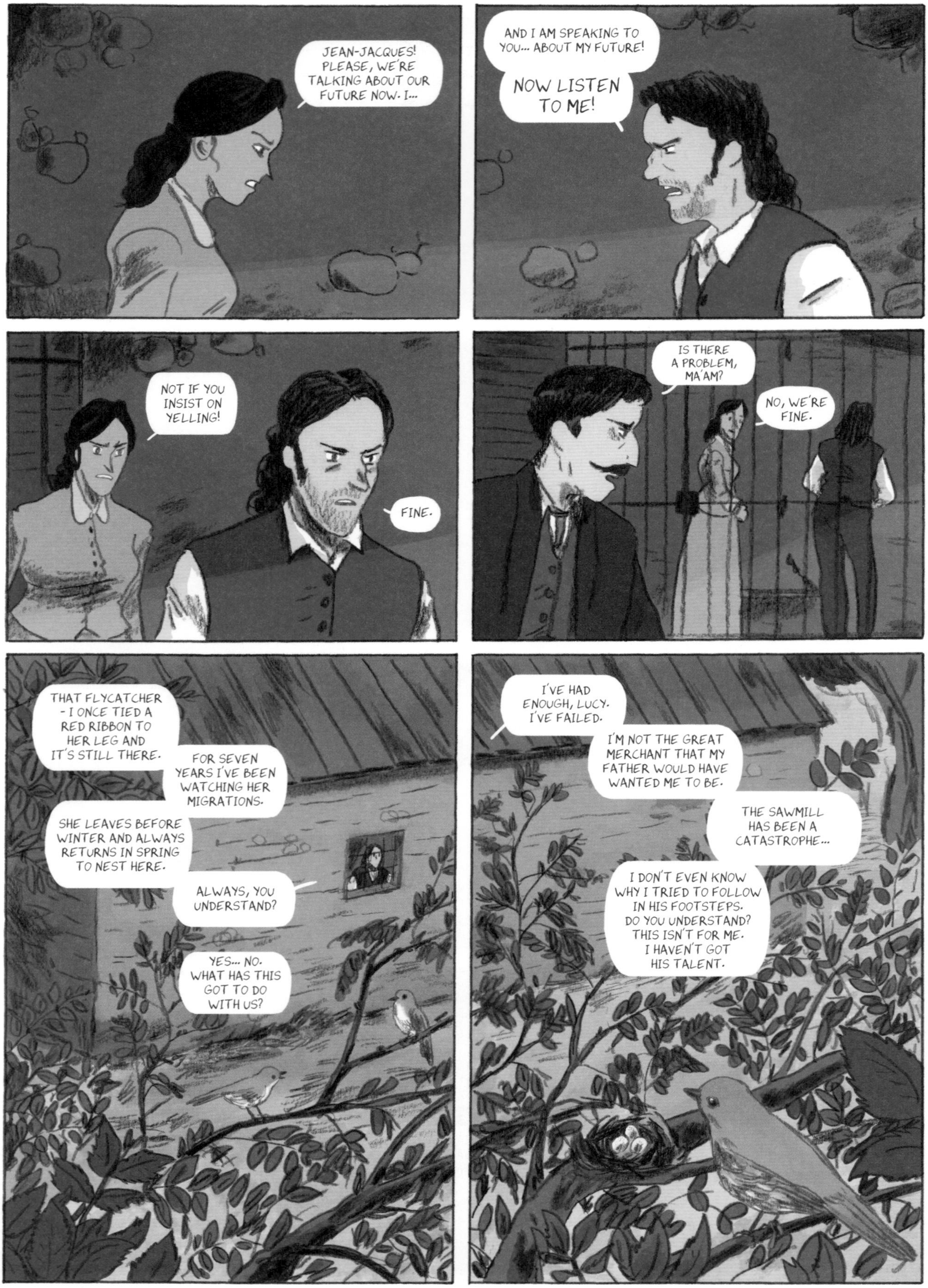

JEAN-JACQUES! PLEASE, WE'RE TALKING ABOUT OUR FUTURE NOW. I...
AND I AM SPEAKING TO YOU... ABOUT MY FUTURE!
NOW LISTEN TO ME!
NOT IF YOU INSIST ON YELLING!
FINE.
IS THERE A PROBLEM, MA'AM?
NO, WE'RE FINE.
THAT FLYCATCHER - I ONCE TIED A RED RIBBON TO HER LEG AND IT'S STILL THERE.
FOR SEVEN YEARS I'VE BEEN WATCHING HER MIGRATIONS.
SHE LEAVES BEFORE WINTER AND ALWAYS RETURNS IN SPRING TO NEST HERE.
ALWAYS, YOU UNDERSTAND?
YES... NO. WHAT HAS THIS GOT TO DO WITH US?
I'VE HAD ENOUGH, LUCY. I'VE FAILED.
I'M NOT THE GREAT MERCHANT THAT MY FATHER WOULD HAVE WANTED ME TO BE.
THE SAWMILL HAS BEEN A CATASTROPHE...
I DON'T EVEN KNOW WHY I TRIED TO FOLLOW IN HIS FOOTSTEPS. DO YOU UNDERSTAND? THIS ISN'T FOR ME. I HAVEN'T GOT HIS TALENT.

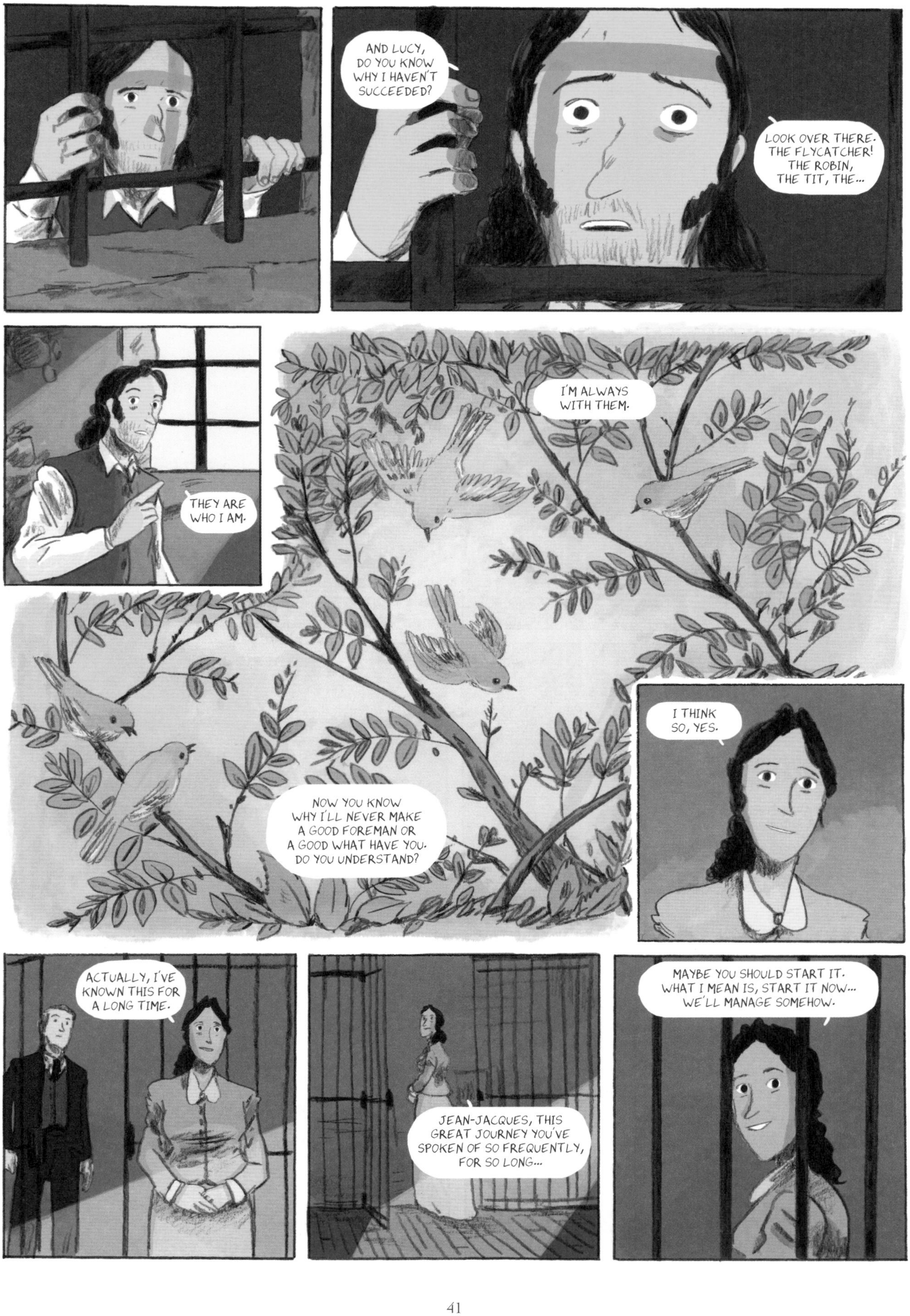
AND LUCY, DO YOU KNOW WHY I HAVEN'T SUCCEEDED?
LOOK OVER THERE. THE FLYCATCHER! THE ROBIN, THE TIT, THE...
THEY ARE WHO I AM.
I'M ALWAYS WITH THEM.
NOW YOU KNOW WHY I'LL NEVER MAKE A GOOD FOREMAN OR A GOOD WHAT HAVE YOU. DO YOU UNDERSTAND?
I THINK SO, YES.
ACTUALLY, I'VE KNOWN THIS FOR A LONG TIME.
JEAN-JACQUES, THIS GREAT JOURNEY YOU'VE SPOKEN OF SO FREQUENTLY, FOR SO LONG...
MAYBE YOU SHOULD START IT. WHAT I MEAN IS, START IT NOW... WE'LL MANAGE SOMEHOW.

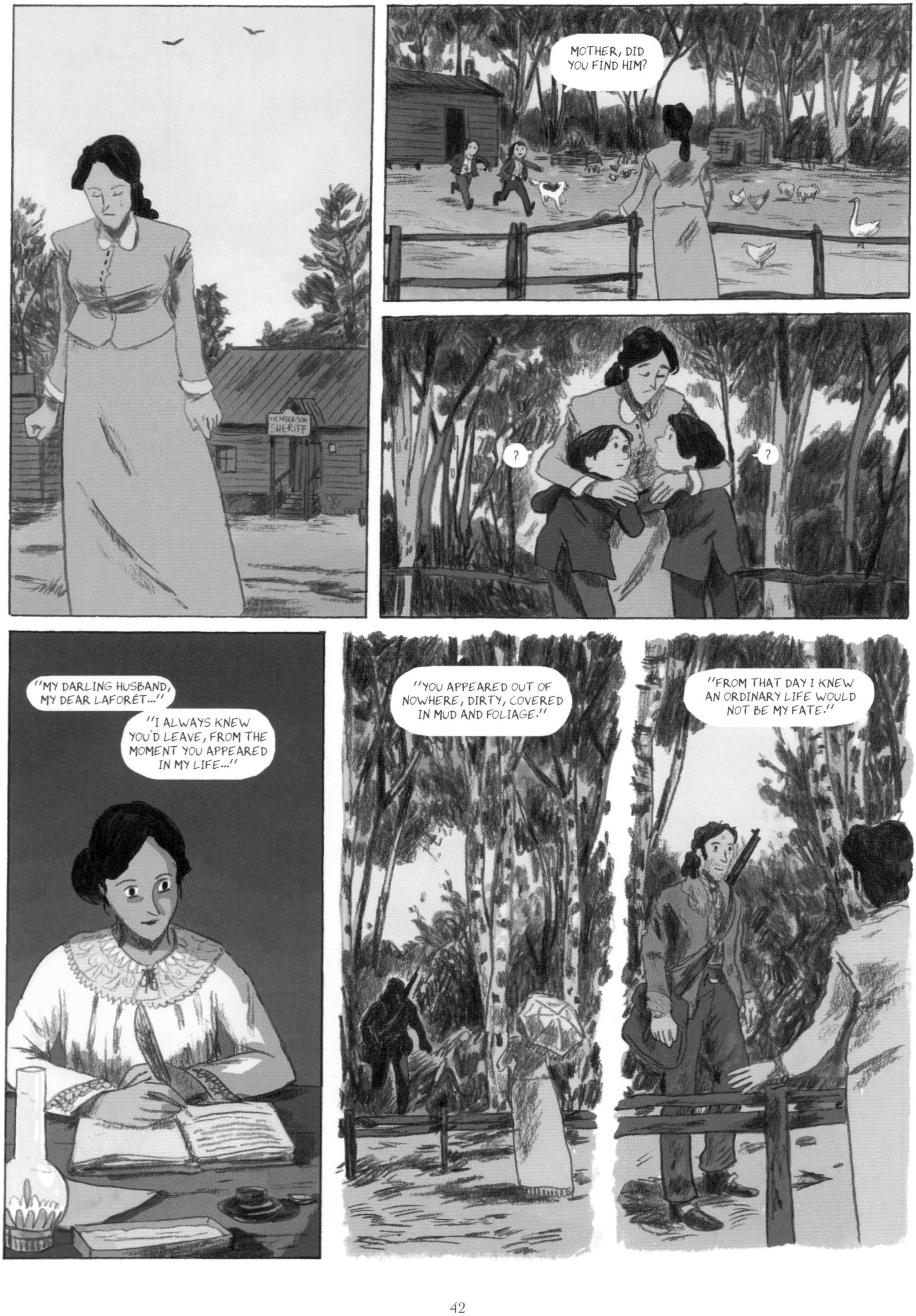
HENDERSON SHERIFF
MOTHER, DID YOU FIND HIM?
?
?
"MY DARLING HUSBAND, MY DEAR LAFORÊT..."
"I ALWAYS KNEW YOU'D LEAVE, FROM THE MOMENT YOU APPEARED IN MY LIFE..."
"YOU APPEARED OUT OF NOWHERE, DIRTY, COVERED IN MUD AND FOLIAGE."
"FROM THAT DAY I KNEW AN ORDINARY LIFE WOULD NOT BE MY FATE."

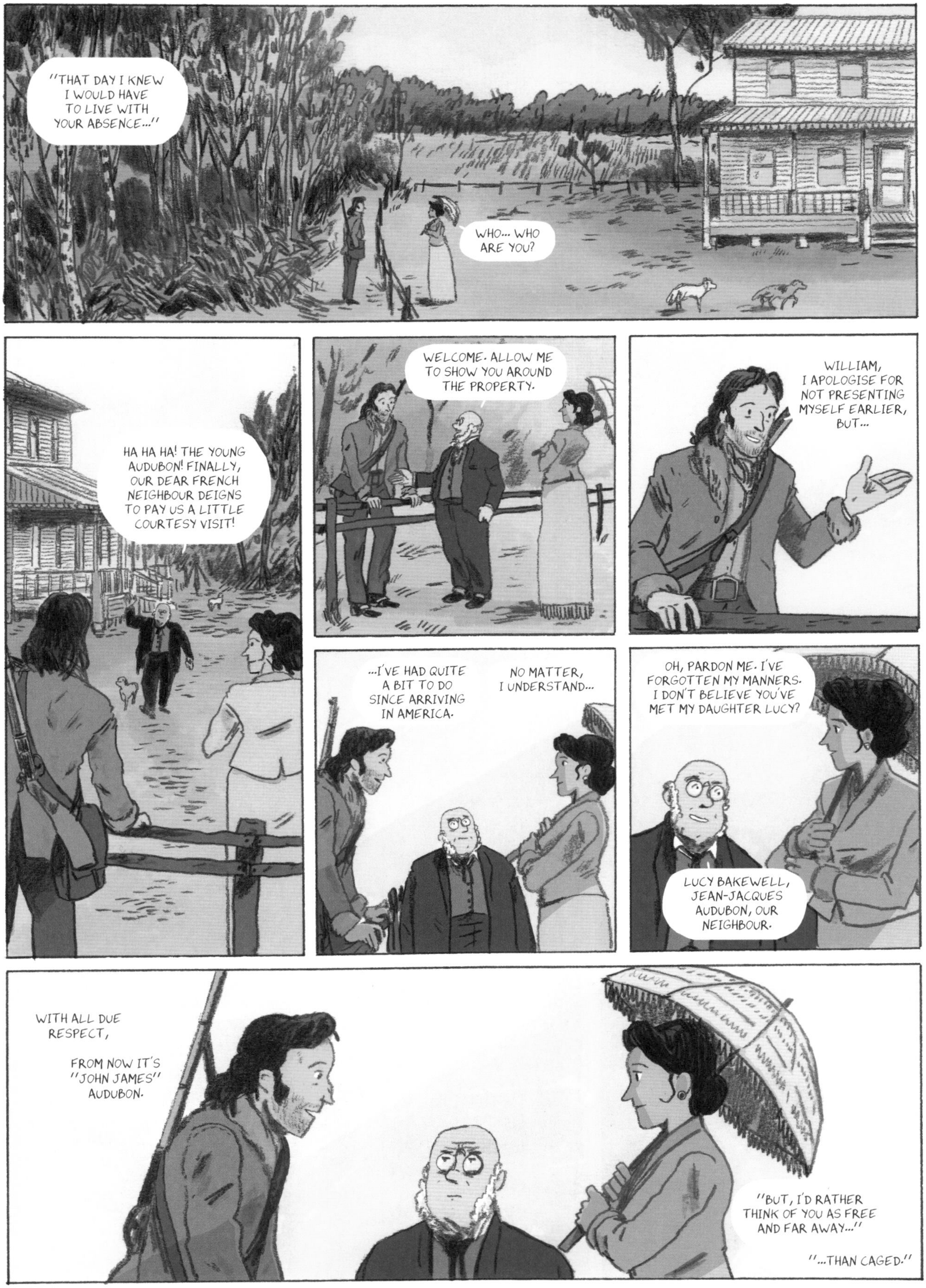
"THAT DAY I KNEW I WOULD HAVE TO LIVE WITH YOUR ABSENCE..."
WHO... WHO ARE YOU?
HA HA HA! THE YOUNG AUDUBON! FINALLY, OUR DEAR FRENCH NEIGHBOUR DEIGNS TO PAY US A LITTLE COURTESY VISIT!
WELCOME. ALLOW ME TO SHOW YOU AROUND THE PROPERTY.
WILLIAM, I APOLOGISE FOR NOT PRESENTING MYSELF EARLIER, BUT...
...I'VE HAD QUITE A BIT TO DO SINCE ARRIVING IN AMERICA.
NO MATTER, I UNDERSTAND...
OH, PARDON ME. I'VE FORGOTTEN MY MANNERS. I DON'T BELIEVE YOU'VE MET MY DAUGHTER LUCY?
LUCY BAKEWELL, JEAN-JACQUES AUDUBON, OUR NEIGHBOUR.
WITH ALL DUE RESPECT,
FROM NOW IT'S "JOHN JAMES" AUDUBON.
"BUT, I'D RATHER THINK OF YOU AS FREE AND FAR AWAY..."
"...THAN CAGED."

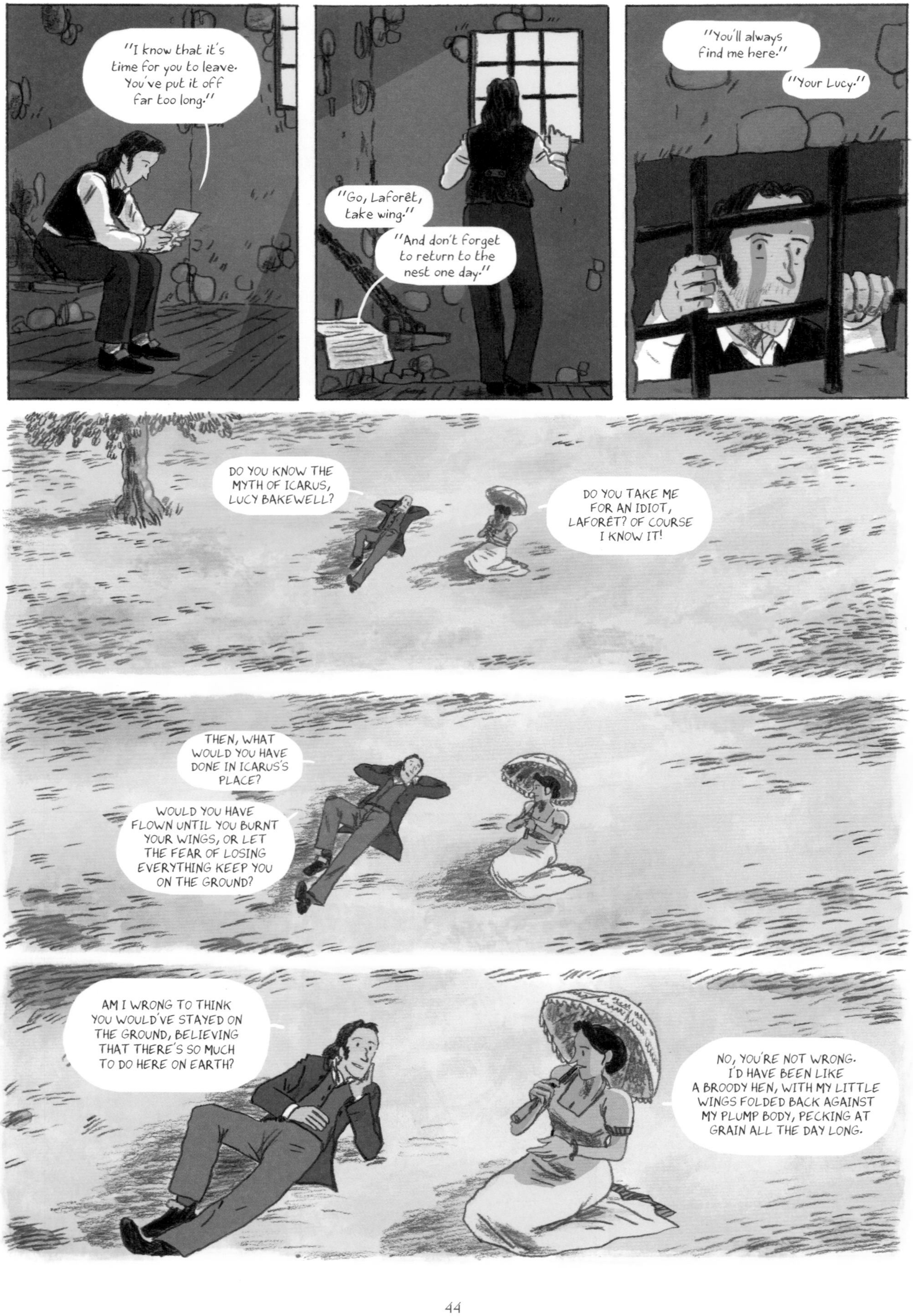
"I know that it's time for you to leave. You've put it off far too long."
"Go, Laforêt, take wing."
"And don't forget to return to the nest one day."
"You'll always find me here."
"Your Lucy."
DO YOU KNOW THE MYTH OF ICARUS, LUCY BAKEWELL?
DO YOU TAKE ME FOR AN IDIOT, LAFORÊT? OF COURSE I KNOW IT!
THEN, WHAT WOULD YOU HAVE DONE IN ICARUS'S PLACE?
WOULD YOU HAVE FLOWN UNTIL YOU BURNT YOUR WINGS, OR LET THE FEAR OF LOSING EVERYTHING KEEP YOU ON THE GROUND?
AM I WRONG TO THINK YOU WOULD'VE STAYED ON THE GROUND, BELIEVING THAT THERE'S SO MUCH TO DO HERE ON EARTH?
NO, YOU'RE NOT WRONG. I'D HAVE BEEN LIKE A BROODY HEN, WITH MY LITTLE WINGS FOLDED BACK AGAINST MY PLUMP BODY, PECKING AT GRAIN ALL THE DAY LONG.

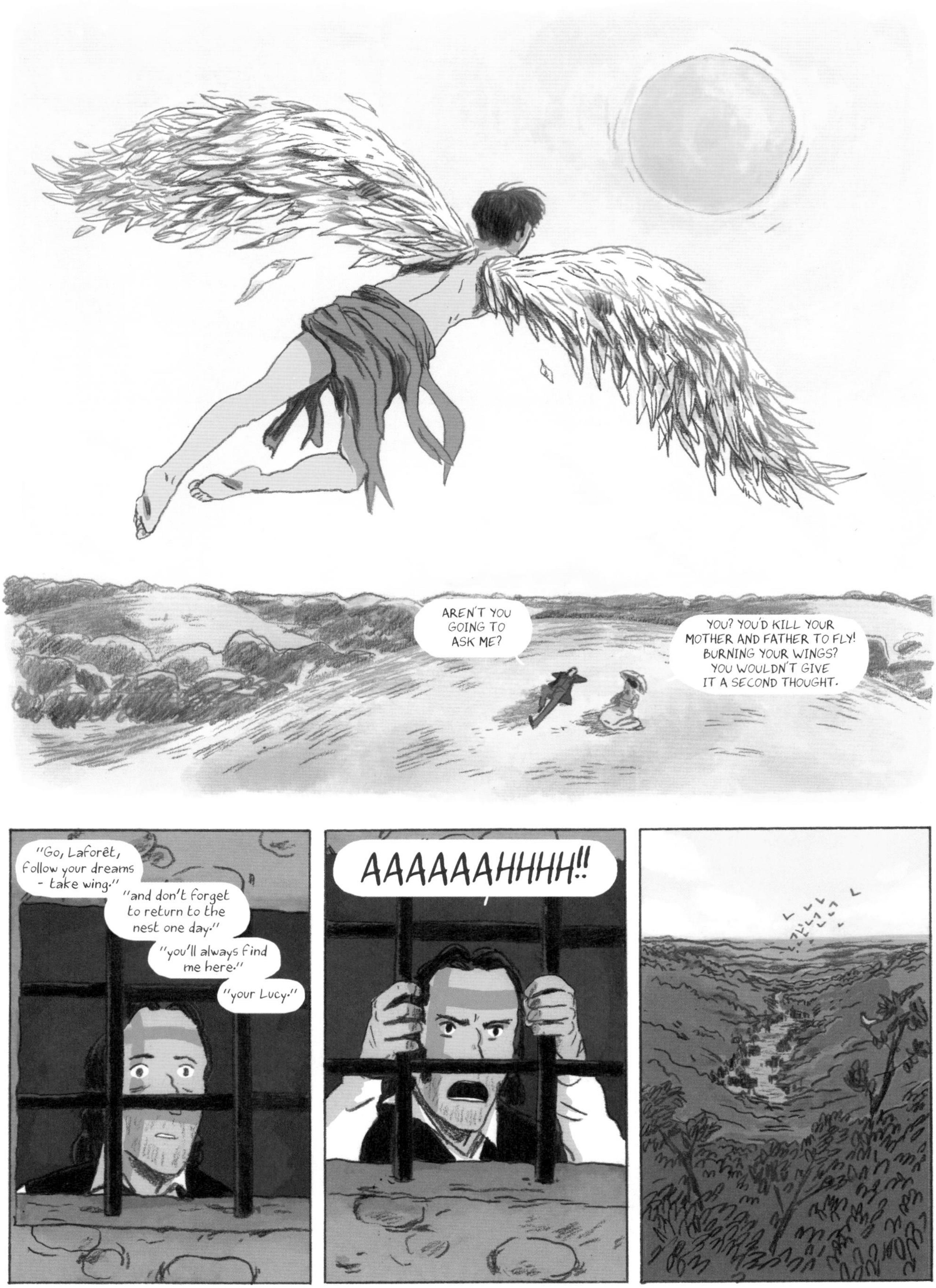
AREN'T YOU GOING TO ASK ME?
YOU? YOU'D KILL YOUR MOTHER AND FATHER TO FLY! BURNING YOUR WINGS? YOU WOULDN'T GIVE IT A SECOND THOUGHT.
"Go, Laforêt, follow your dreams - take wing."
"and don't forget to return to the nest one day."
"you'll always find me here."
"your Lucy."
AAAAAAHHHH!!

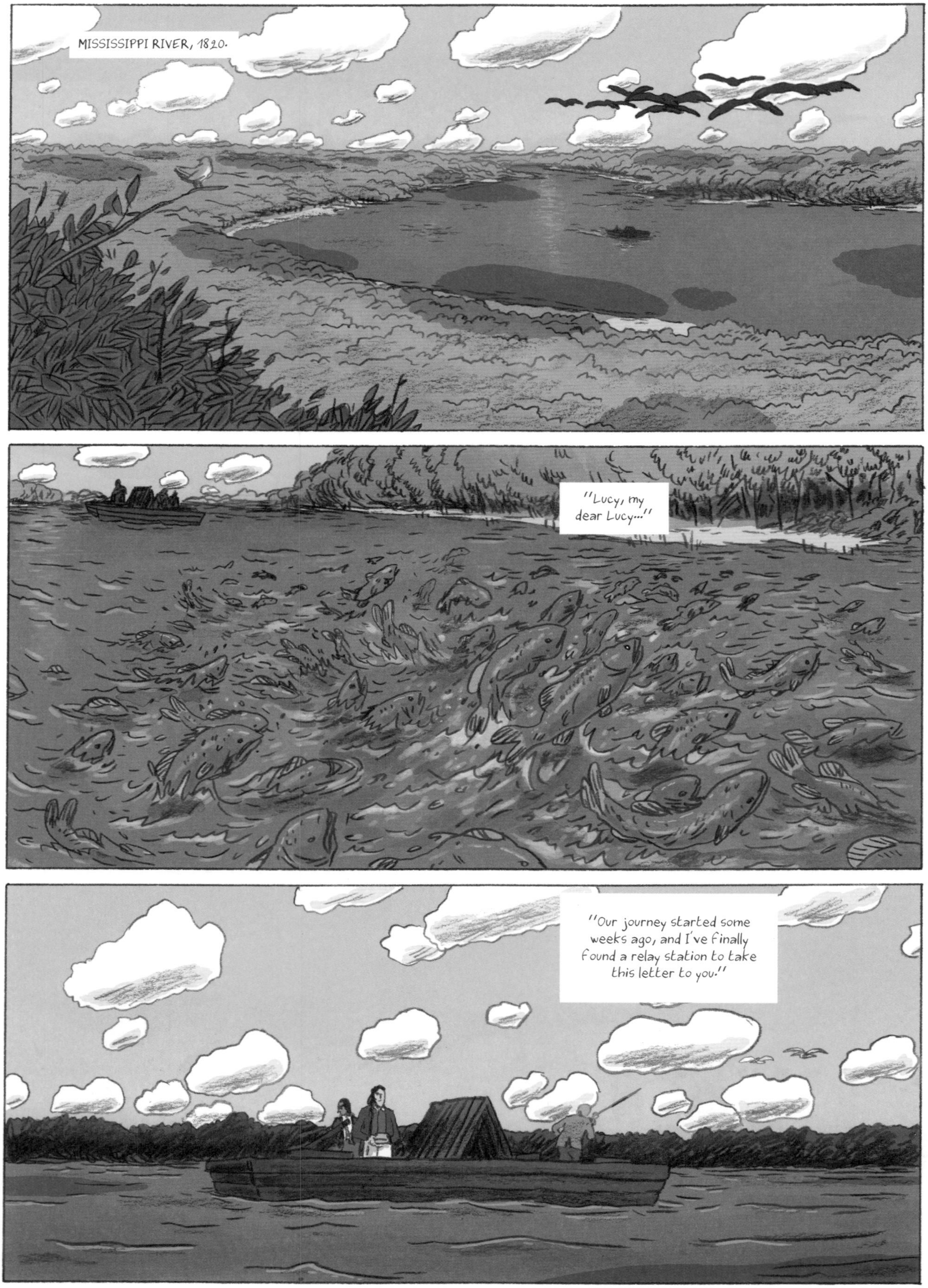
MISSISSIPPI RIVER, 1820.
"Lucy, my dear Lucy..."
"Our journey started some weeks ago, and I've finally found a relay station to take this letter to you."

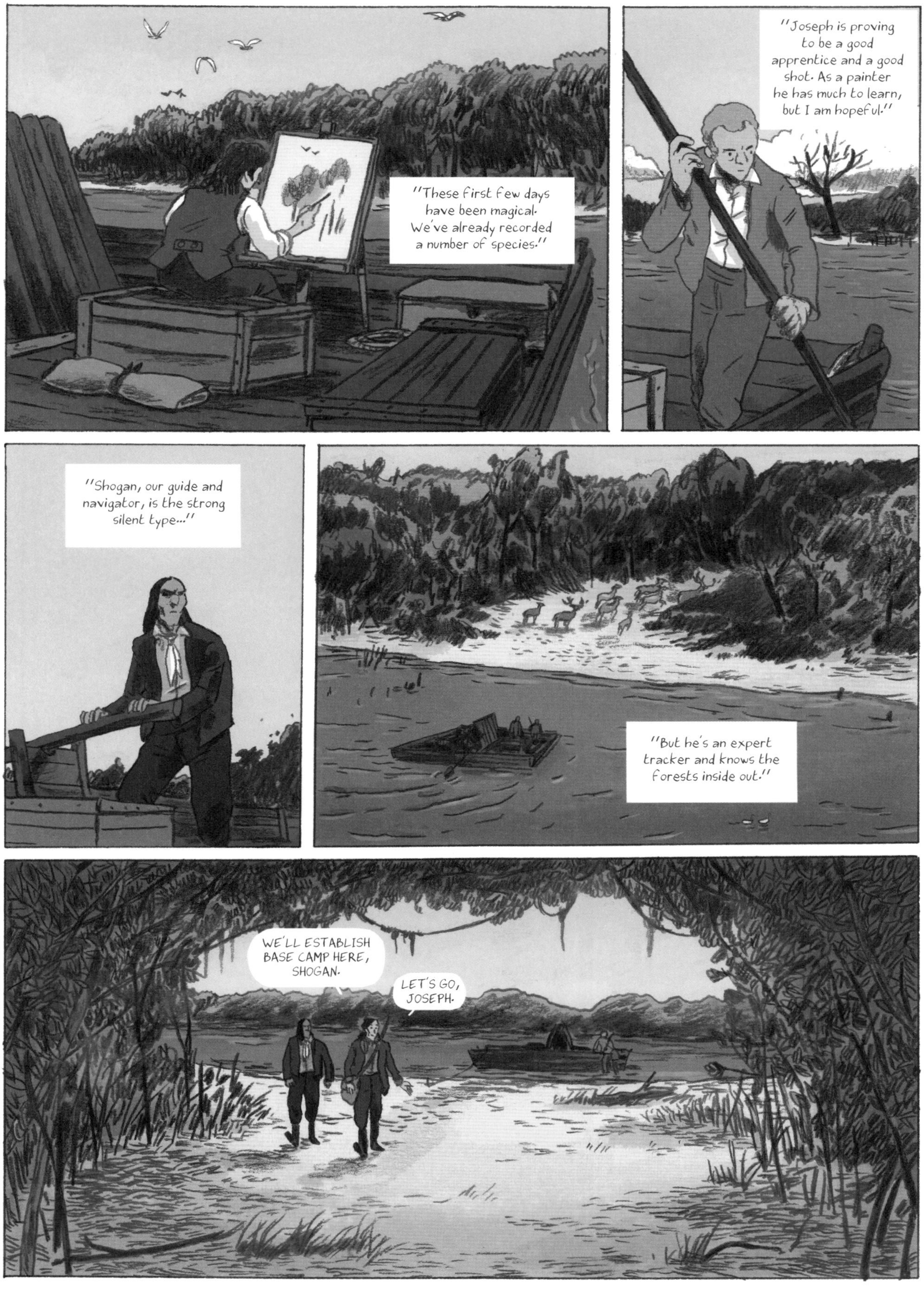
"These first few days have been magical. We've already recorded a number of species."
"Joseph is proving to be a good apprentice and a good shot. As a painter he has much to learn, but I am hopeful."
"Shogan, our guide and navigator, is the strong silent type..."
"But he's an expert tracker and knows the forests inside out."
WE'LL ESTABLISH BASE CAMP HERE, SHOGAN.
LET'S GO, JOSEPH.

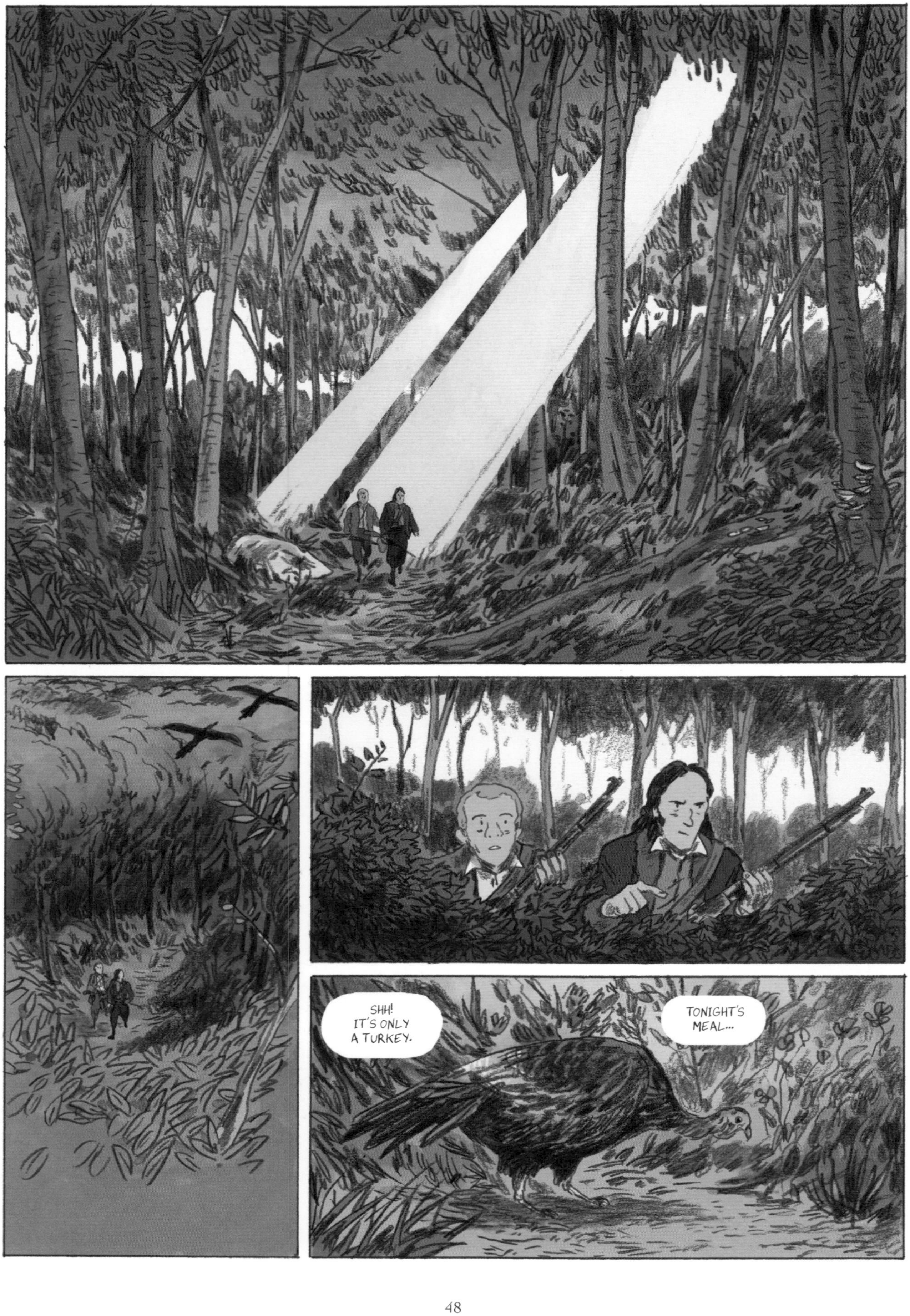
SHH!
IT'S ONLY
A TURKEY.
TONIGHT'S
MEAL...

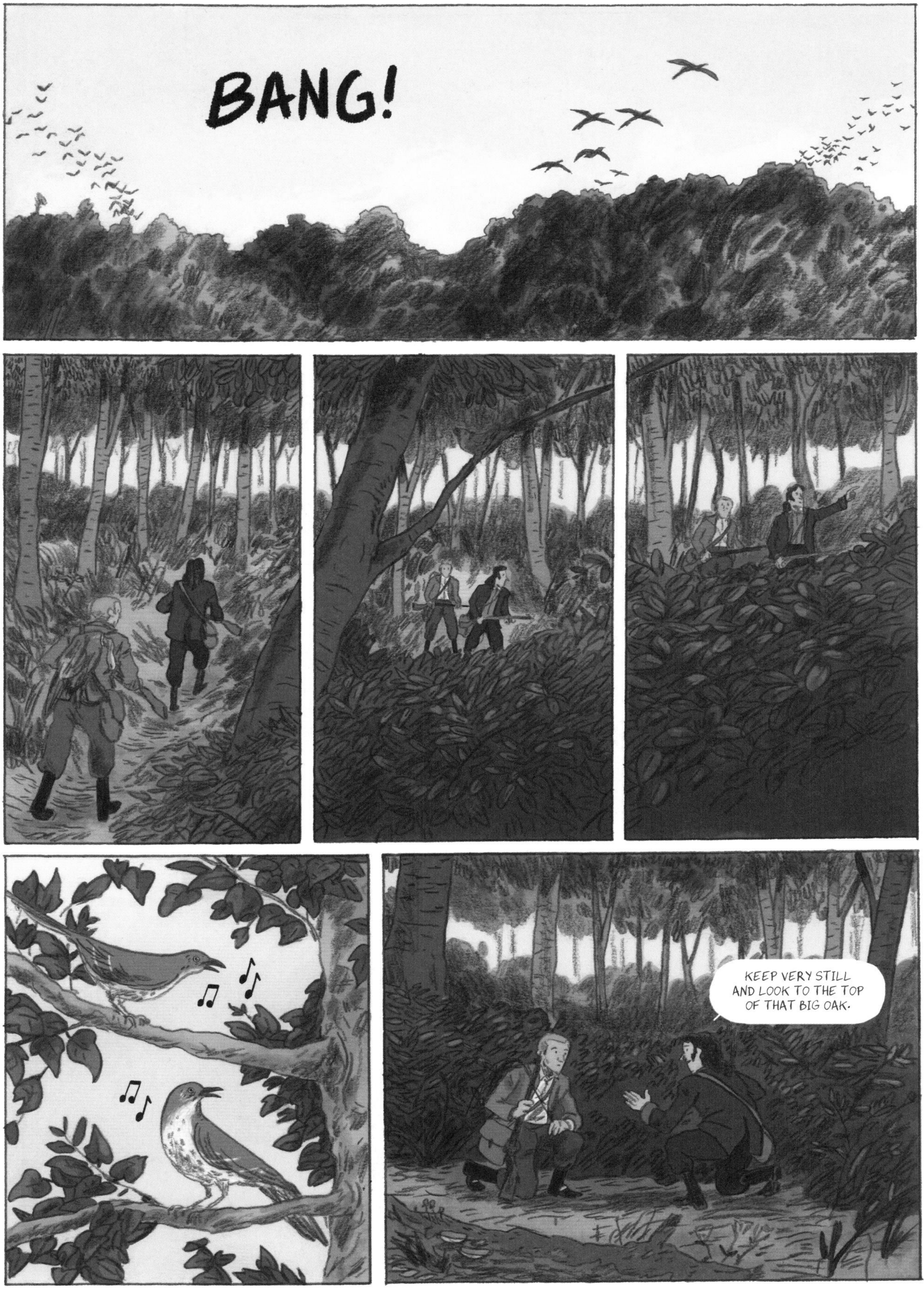
BANG!
KEEP VERY STILL AND LOOK TO THE TOP OF THAT BIG OAK.

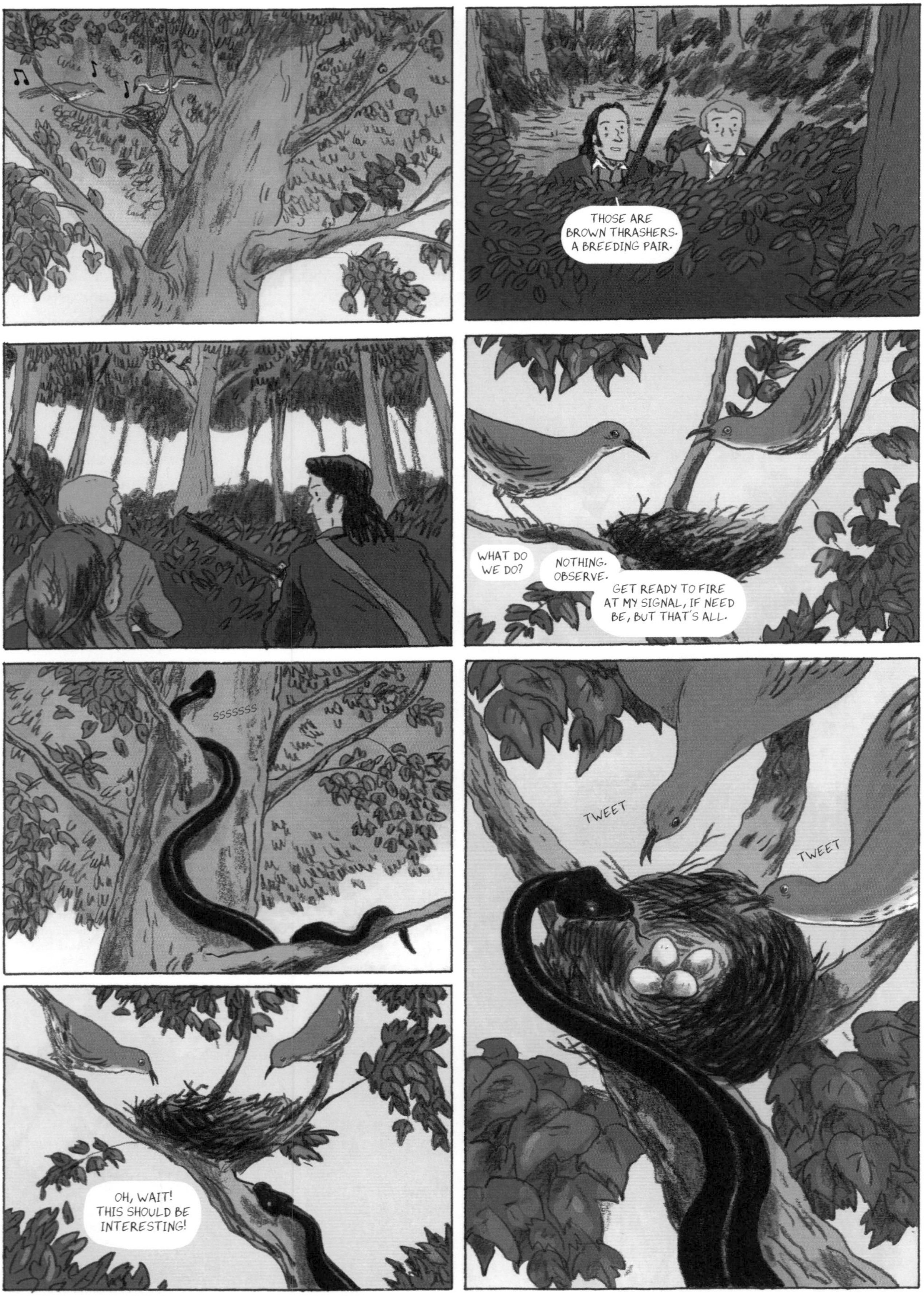
THOSE ARE BROWN THRASHERS. A BREEDING PAIR.
WHAT DO WE DO?
NOTHING. OBSERVE.
GET READY TO FIRE AT MY SIGNAL, IF NEED BE, BUT THAT'S ALL.
SSSSSSS
TWEET
TWEET
OH, WAIT! THIS SHOULD BE INTERESTING!

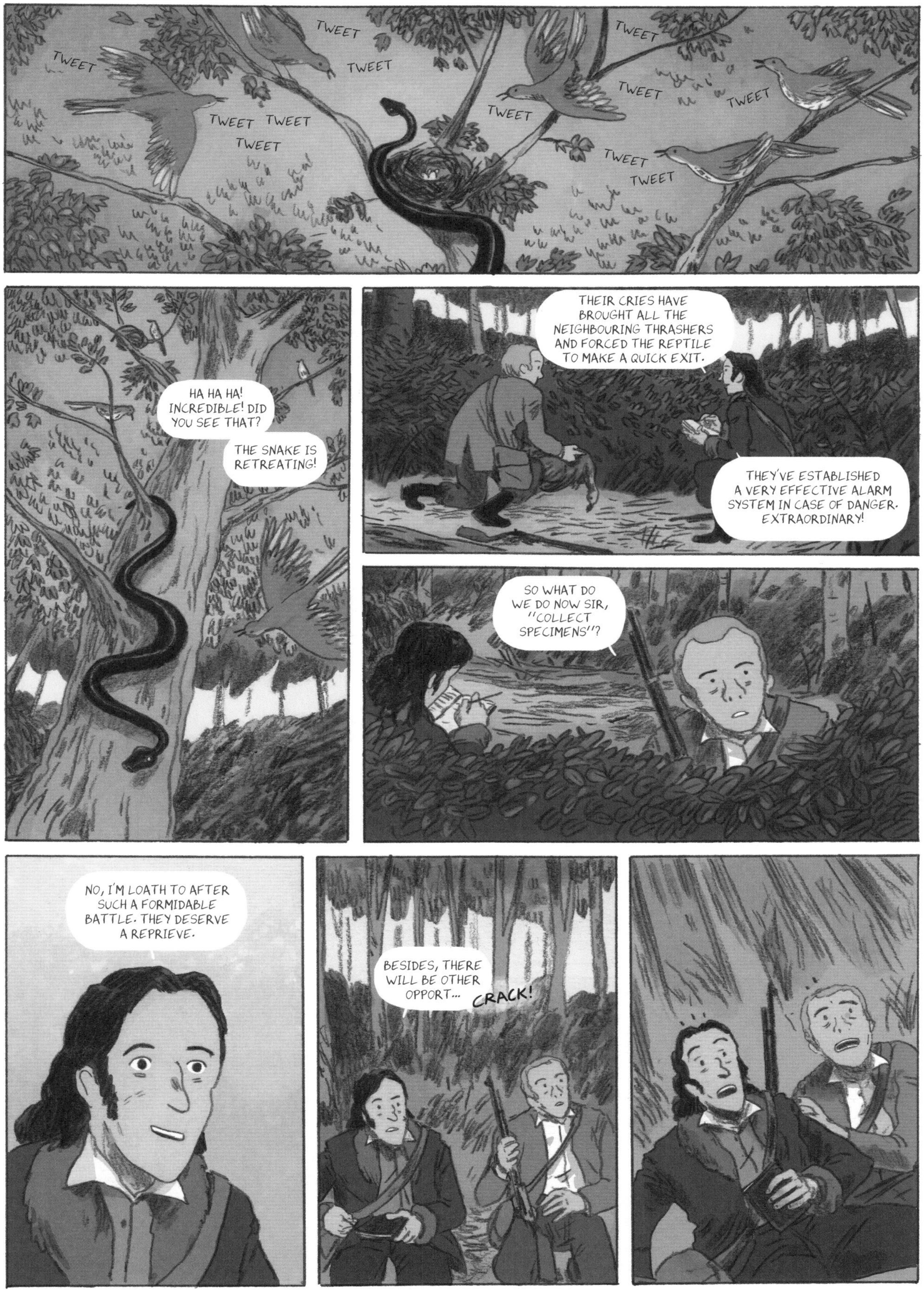
TWEET
TWEET
TWEET
TWEET TWEET
TWEET
TWEET
TWEET
TWEET
TWEET
TWEET
TWEET
HA HA HA! INCREDIBLE! DID YOU SEE THAT?
THE SNAKE IS RETREATING!
THEIR CRIES HAVE BROUGHT ALL THE NEIGHBOURING THRASHERS AND FORCED THE REPTILE TO MAKE A QUICK EXIT.
THEY'VE ESTABLISHED A VERY EFFECTIVE ALARM SYSTEM IN CASE OF DANGER. EXTRAORDINARY!
SO WHAT DO WE DO NOW SIR, "COLLECT SPECIMENS"?
NO, I'M LOATH TO AFTER SUCH A FORMIDABLE BATTLE. THEY DESERVE A REPRIEVE.
BESIDES, THERE WILL BE OTHER OPPORT...
CRACK!

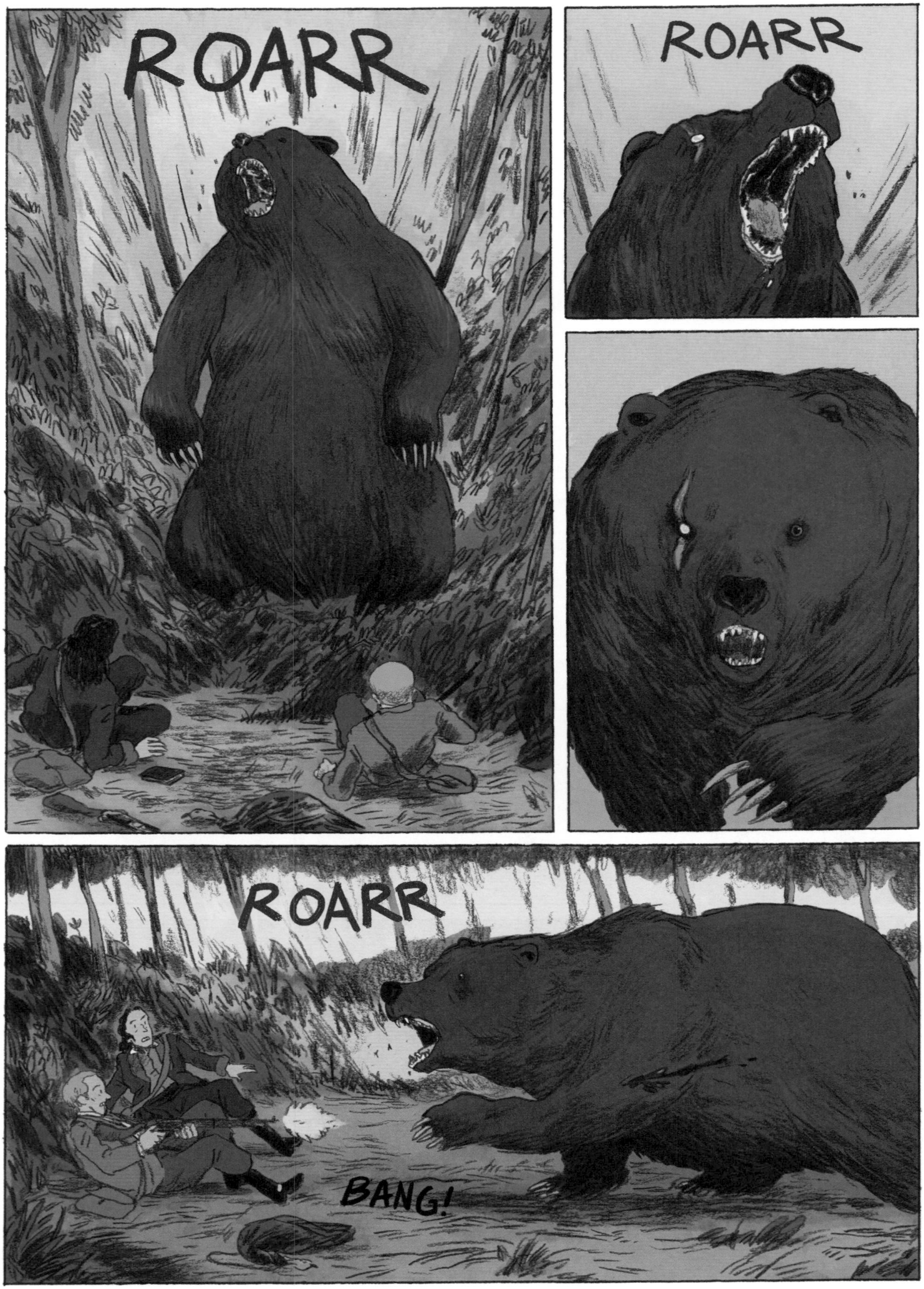
ROARR
ROARR
ROARR
BANG!

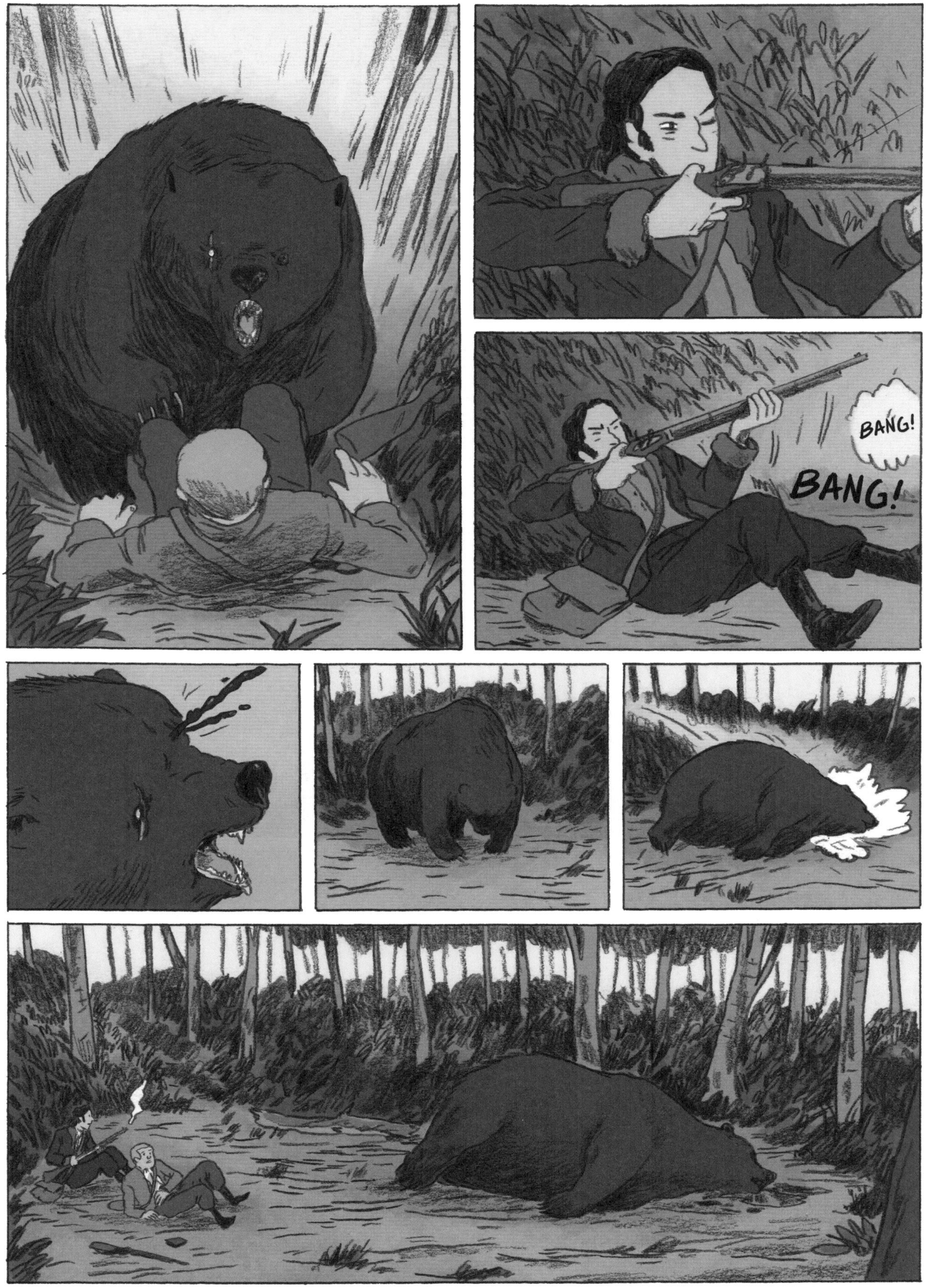
BANG!
BANG!

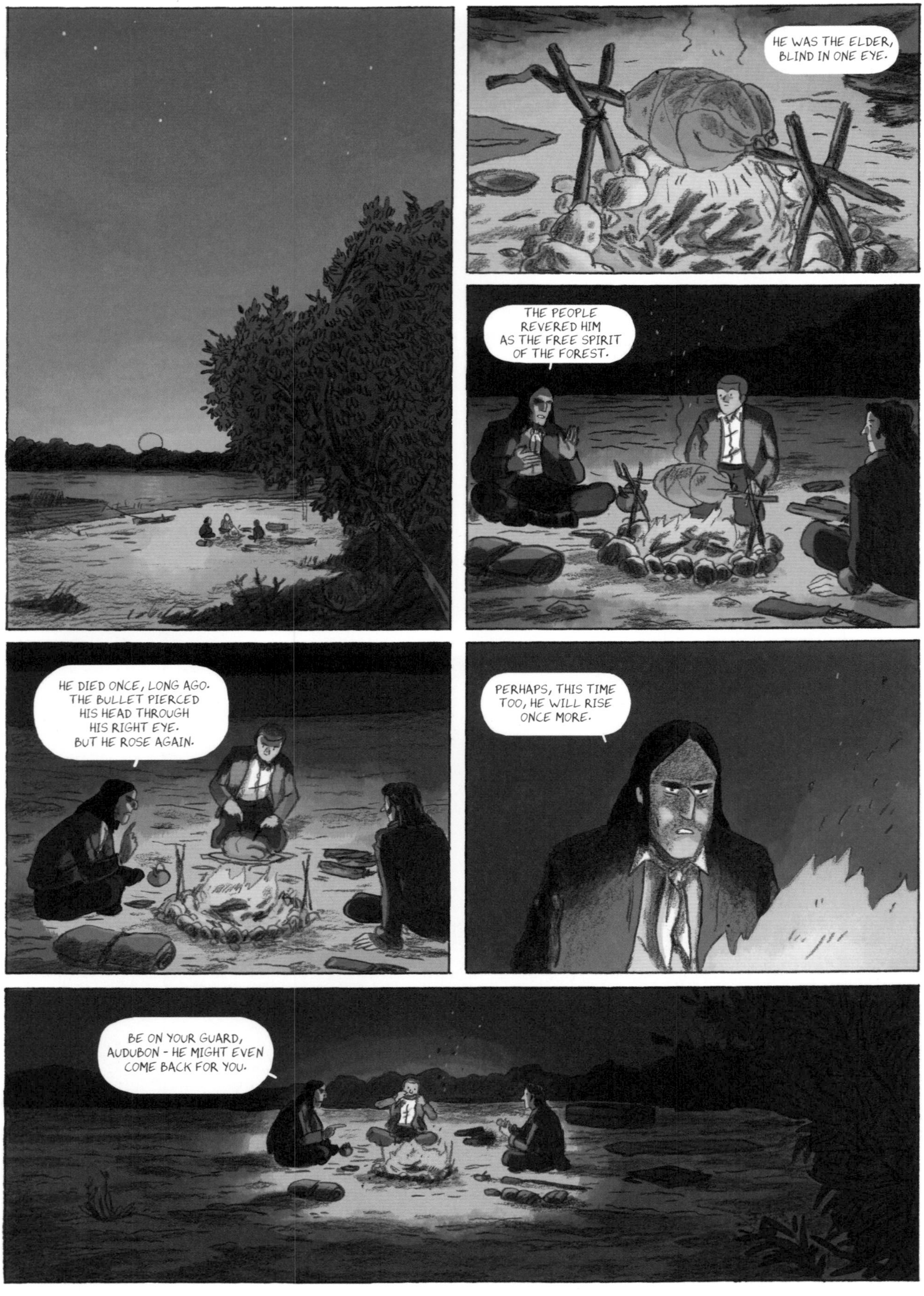
HE WAS THE ELDER, BLIND IN ONE EYE.
THE PEOPLE REVERED HIM AS THE FREE SPIRIT OF THE FOREST.
HE DIED ONCE, LONG AGO. THE BULLET PIERCED HIS HEAD THROUGH HIS RIGHT EYE. BUT HE ROSE AGAIN.
PERHAPS, THIS TIME TOO, HE WILL RISE ONCE MORE.
BE ON YOUR GUARD, AUDUBON - HE MIGHT EVEN COME BACK FOR YOU.

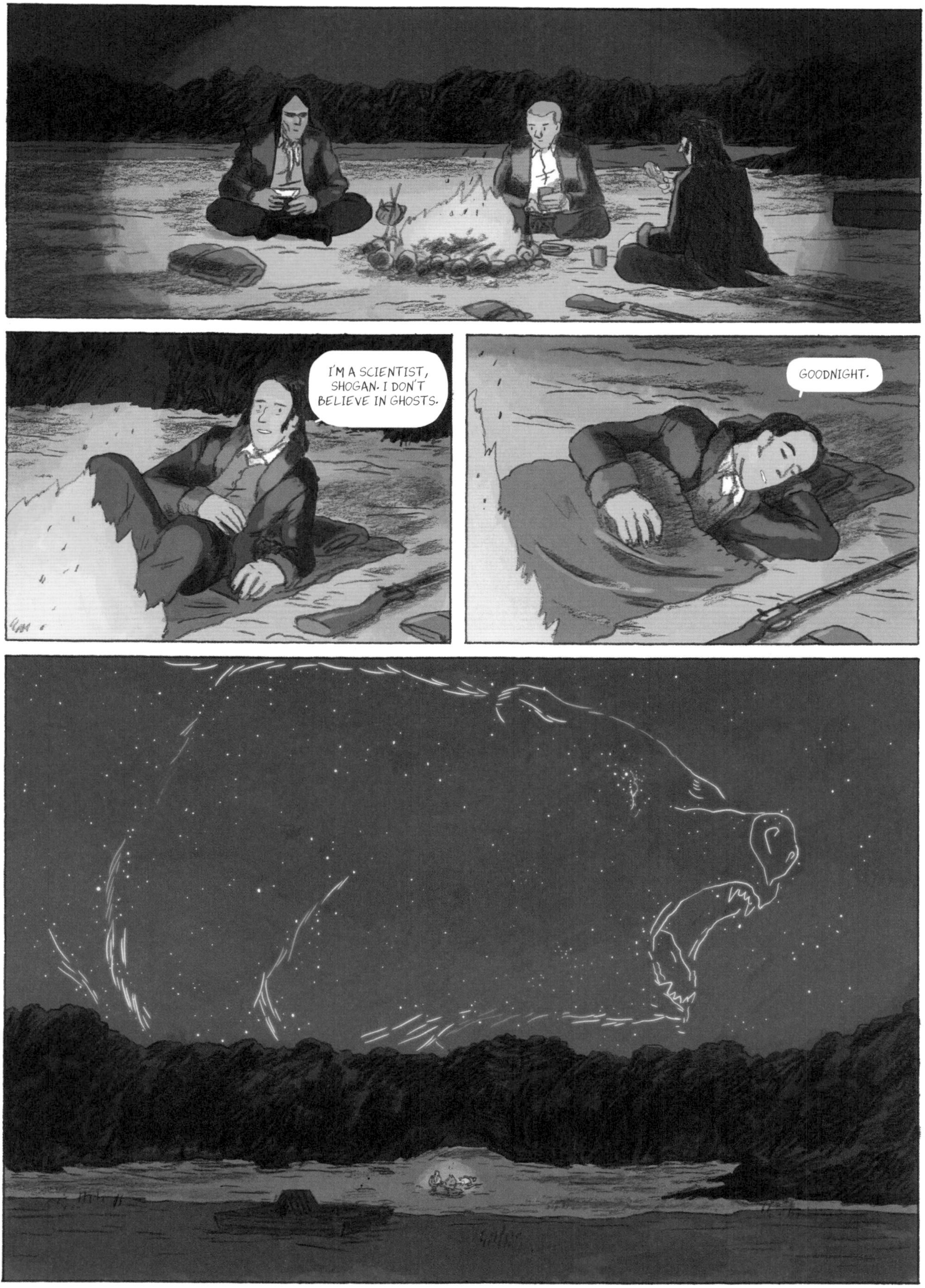
I'M A SCIENTIST, SHOGAN. I DON'T BELIEVE IN GHOSTS.
GOODNIGHT.

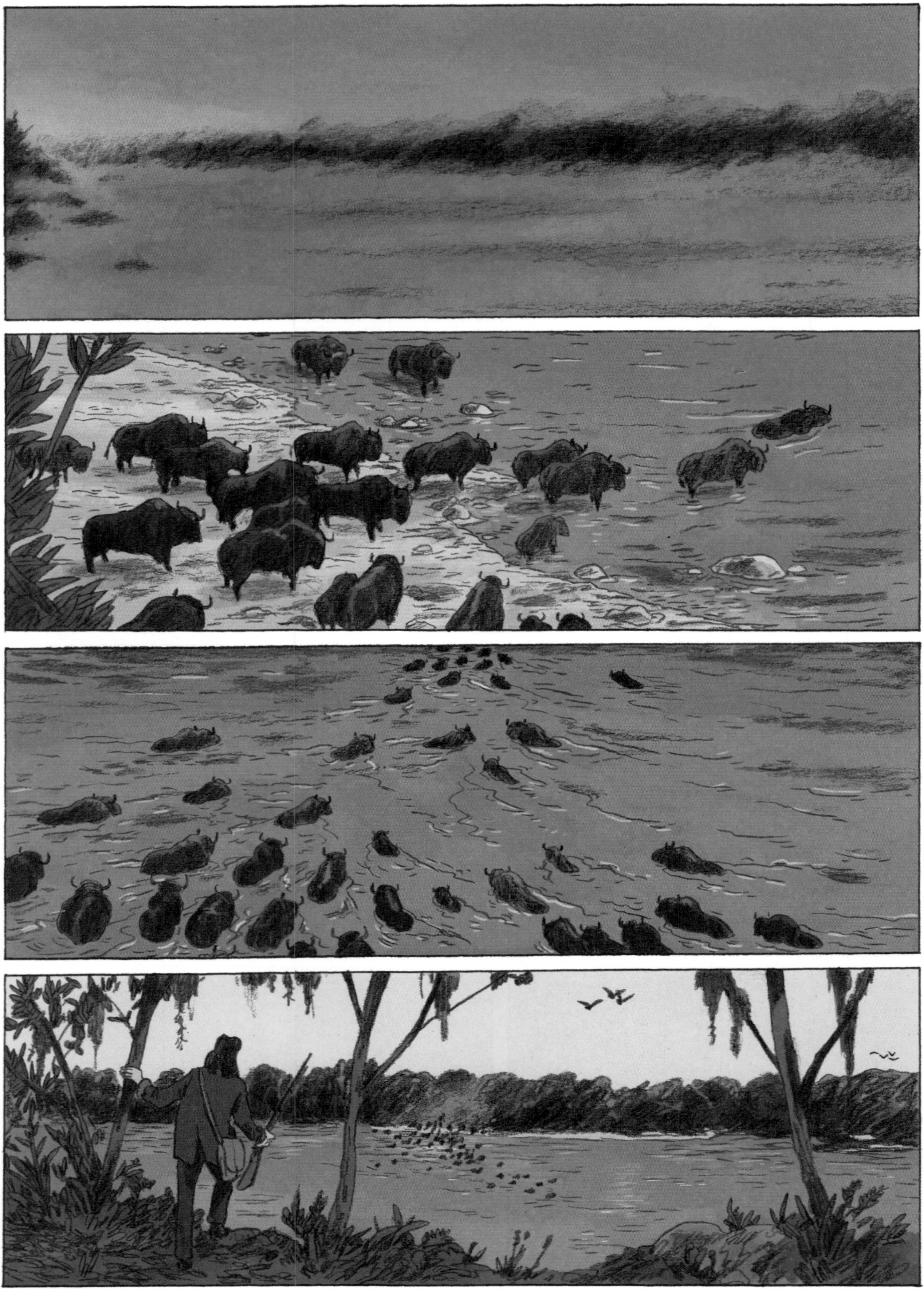

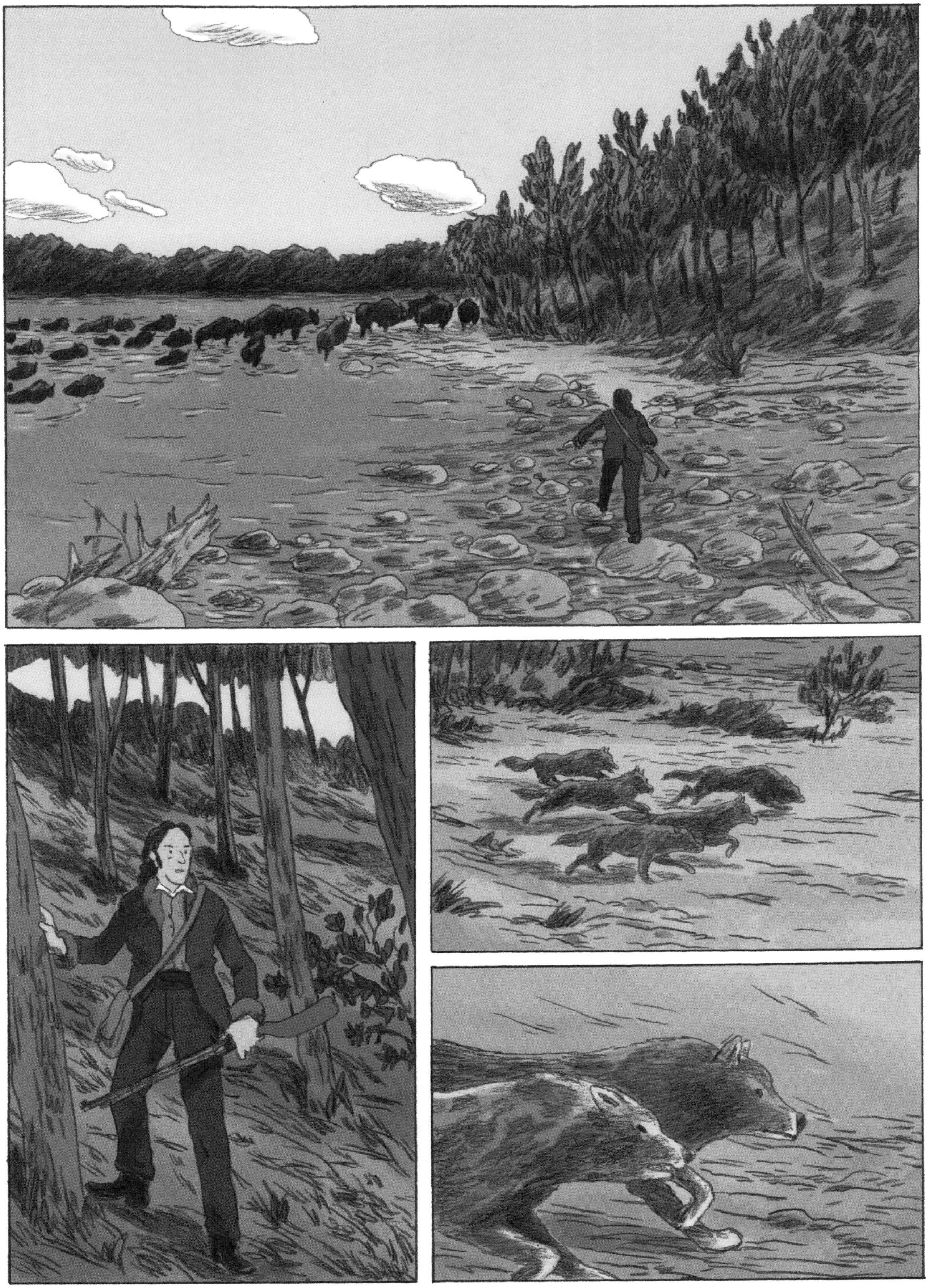

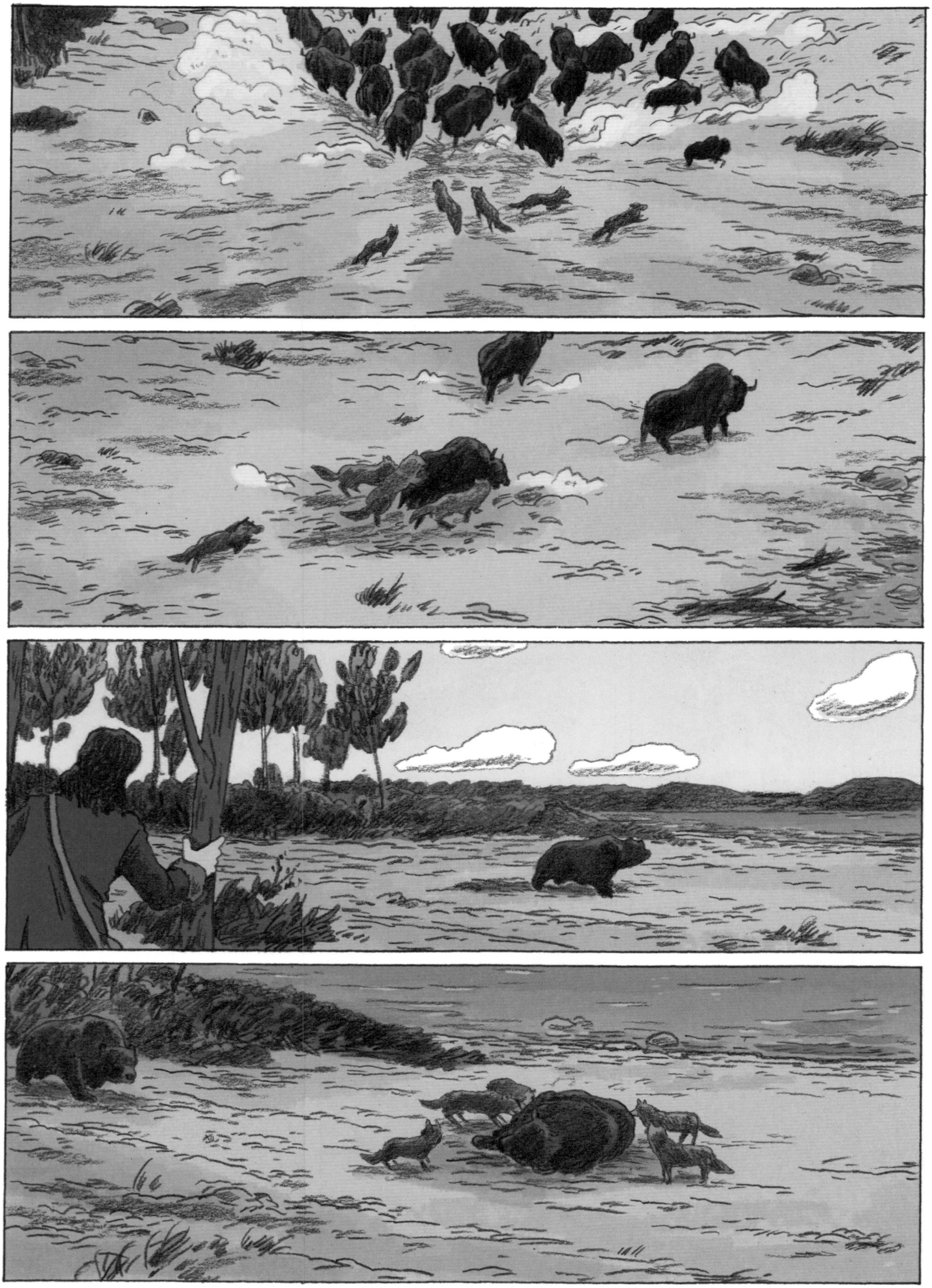

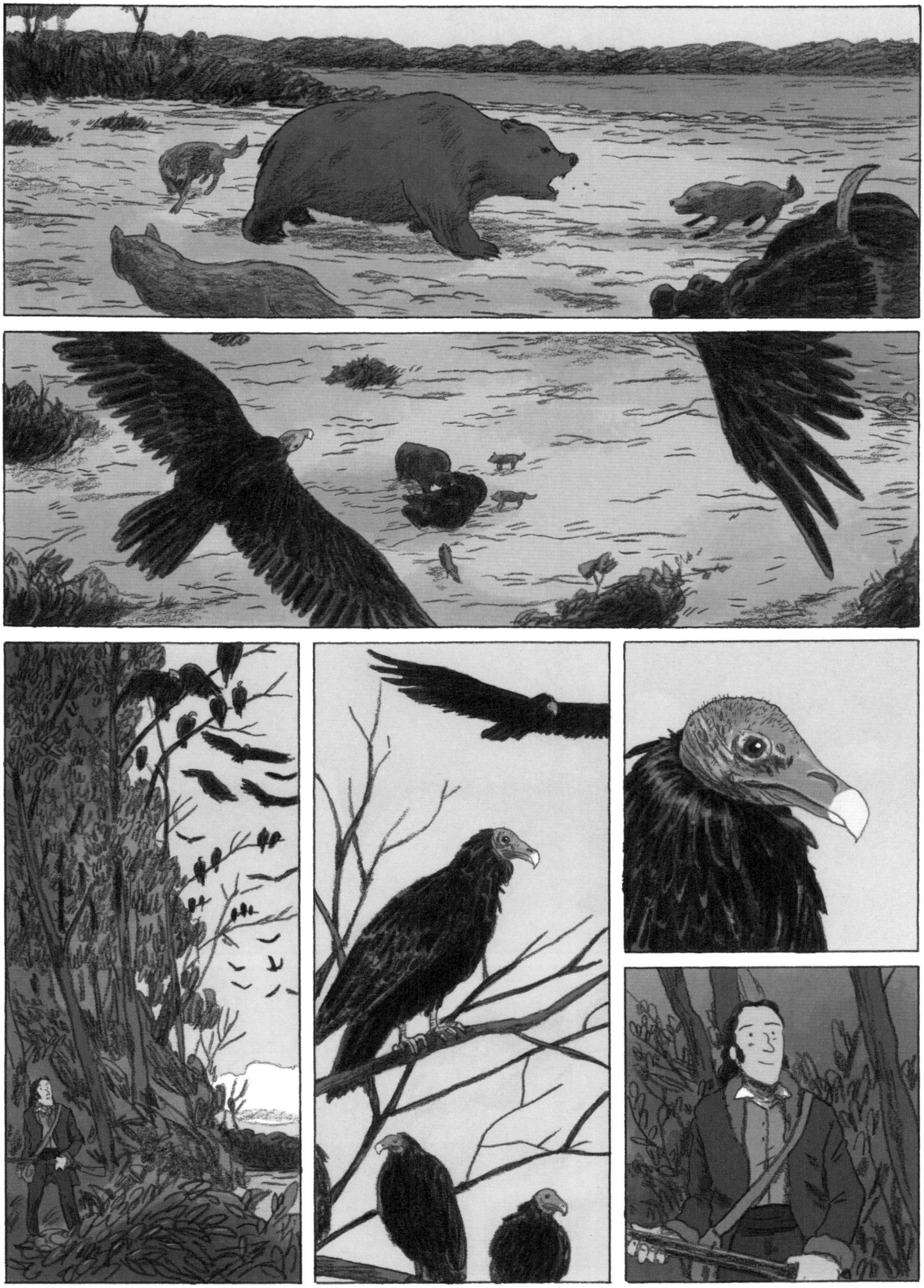

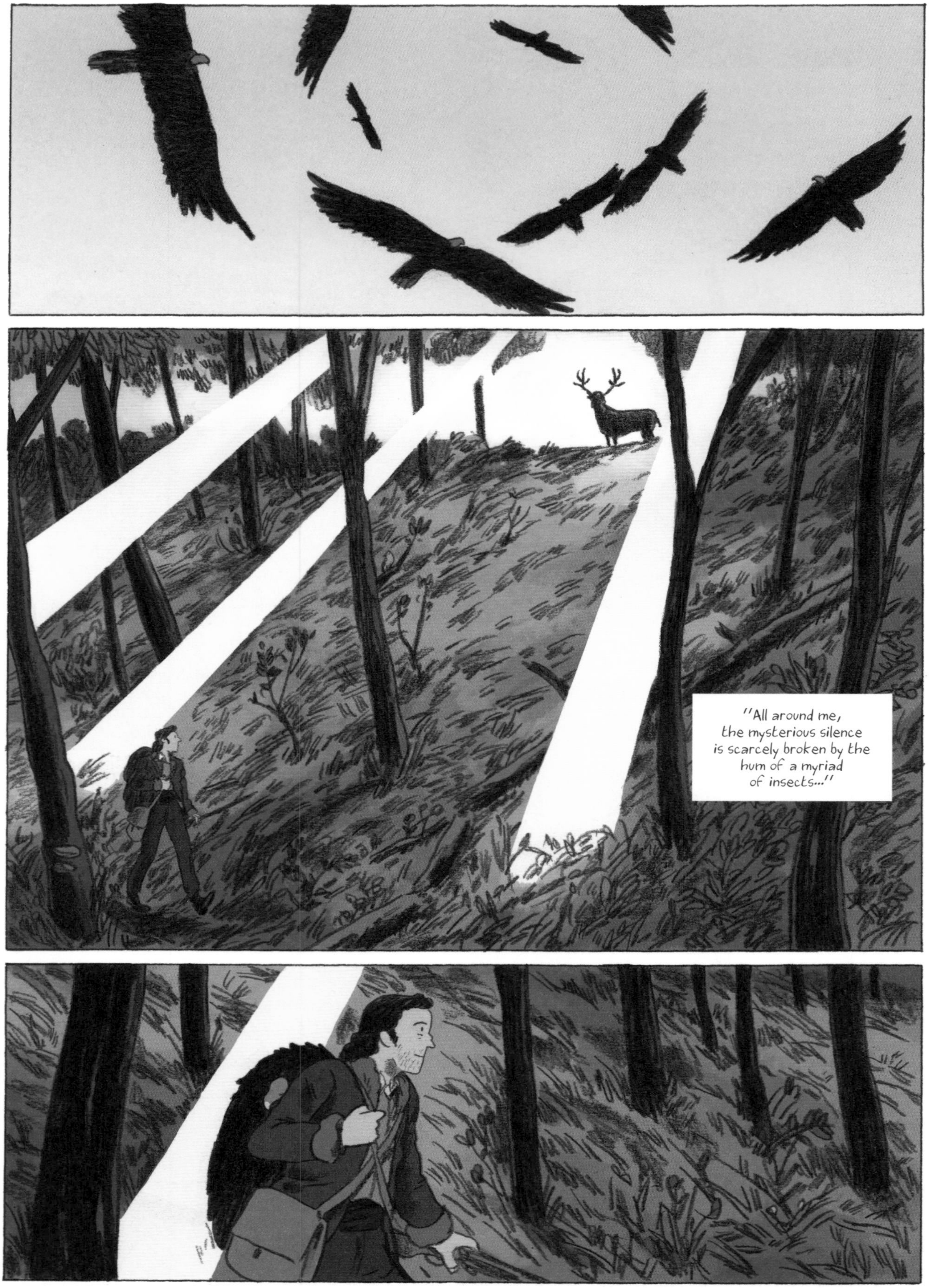
"All around me, the mysterious silence is scarcely broken by the hum of a myriad of insects..."

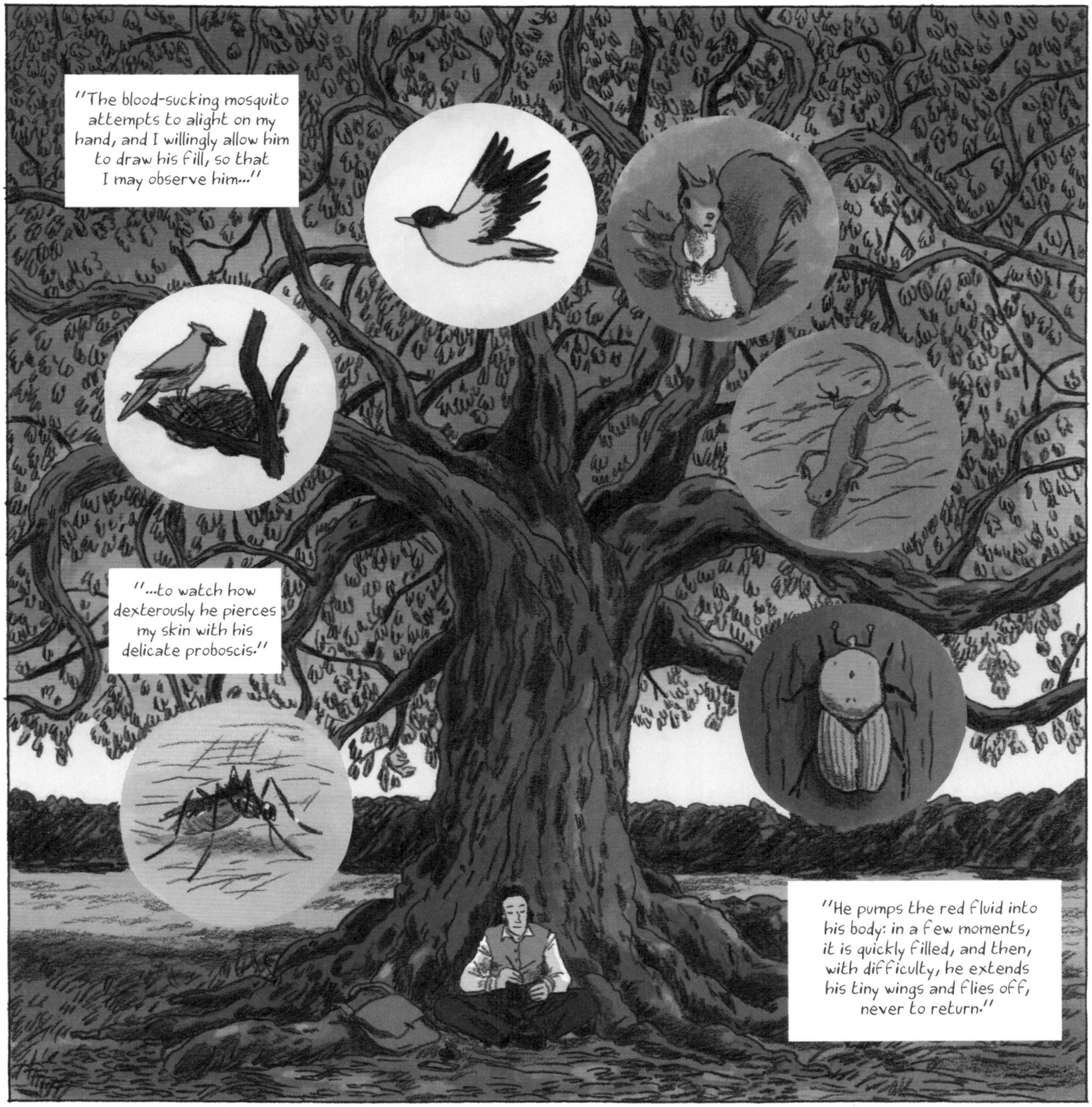
"The blood-sucking mosquito attempts to alight on my hand, and I willingly allow him to draw his fill, so that I may observe him..."
"...to watch how dexterously he pierces my skin with his delicate proboscis."
"He pumps the red fluid into his body: in a few moments, it is quickly filled, and then, with difficulty, he extends his tiny wings and flies off, never to return."

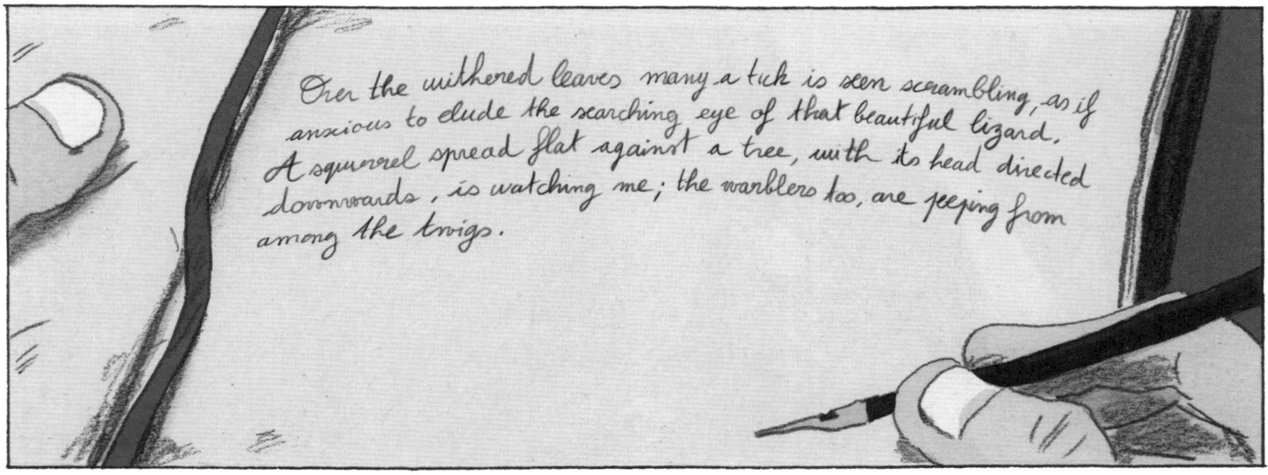
Over the withered leaves many a tick is seen scrambling, as if anxious to elude the searching eye of that beautiful lizard. A squirrel spread flat against a tree, with its head directed downwards, is watching me; the warblers too, are peeping from among the twigs.

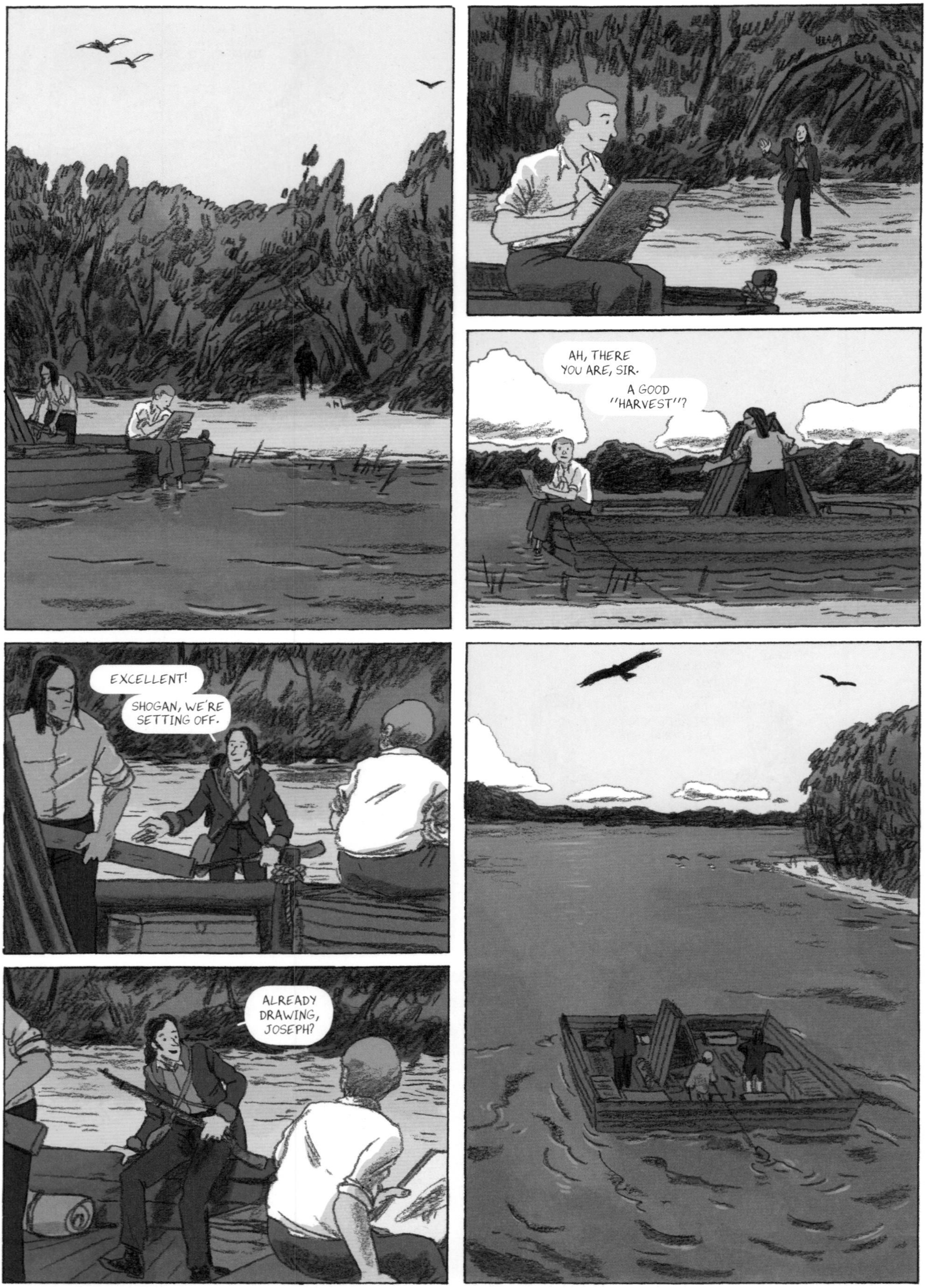
AH, THERE YOU ARE, SIR.
A GOOD "HARVEST"?
EXCELLENT!
SHOGAN, WE'RE SETTING OFF.
ALREADY DRAWING, JOSEPH?

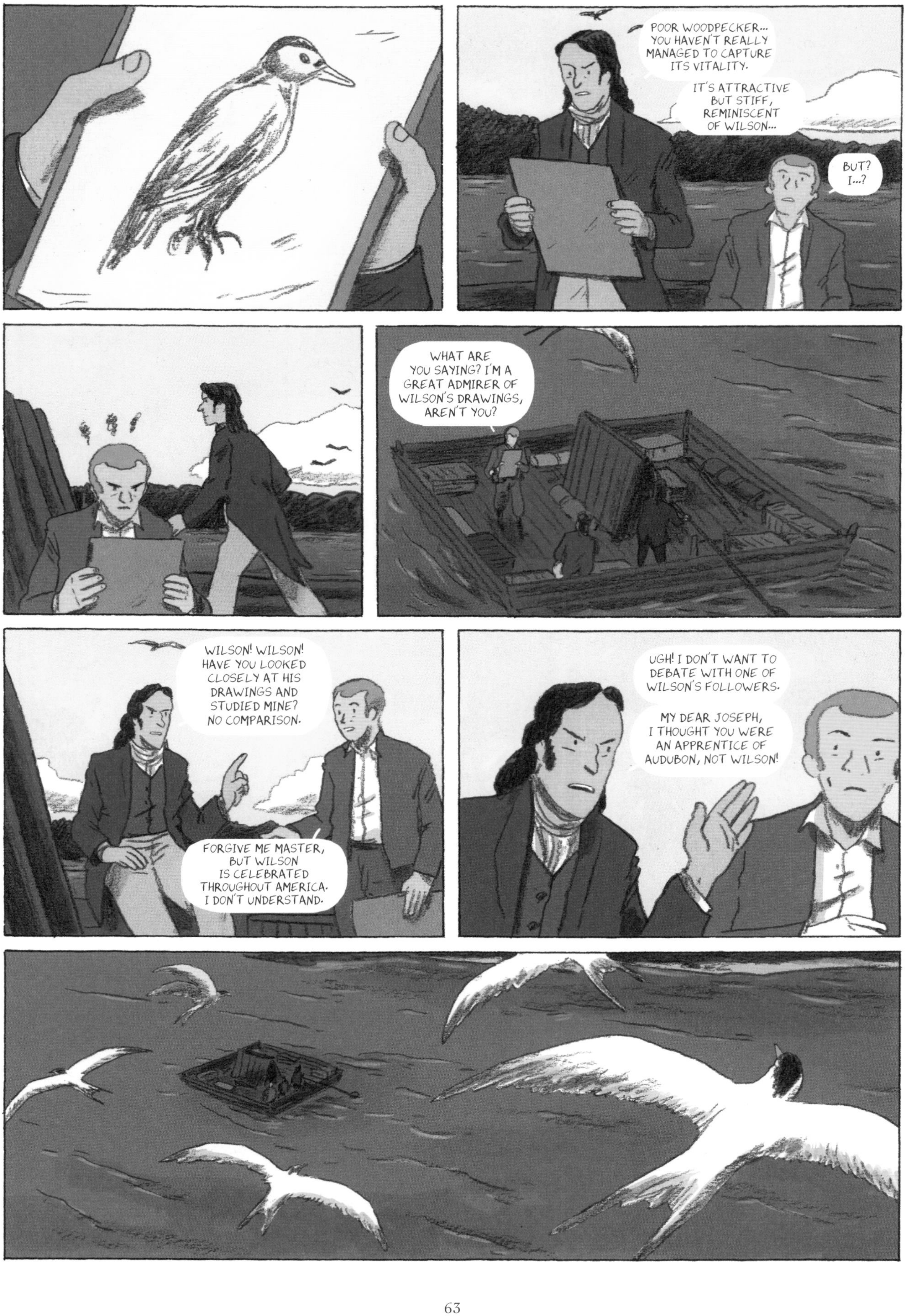
POOR WOODPECKER... YOU HAVEN'T REALLY MANAGED TO CAPTURE ITS VITALITY.
IT'S ATTRACTIVE BUT STIFF, REMINISCENT OF WILSON...
BUT? I...?
WHAT ARE YOU SAYING? I'M A GREAT ADMIRER OF WILSON'S DRAWINGS, AREN'T YOU?
WILSON! WILSON! HAVE YOU LOOKED CLOSELY AT HIS DRAWINGS AND STUDIED MINE? NO COMPARISON.
FORGIVE ME MASTER, BUT WILSON IS CELEBRATED THROUGHOUT AMERICA. I DON'T UNDERSTAND.
UGH! I DON'T WANT TO DEBATE WITH ONE OF WILSON'S FOLLOWERS.
MY DEAR JOSEPH, I THOUGHT YOU WERE AN APPRENTICE OF AUDUBON, NOT WILSON!

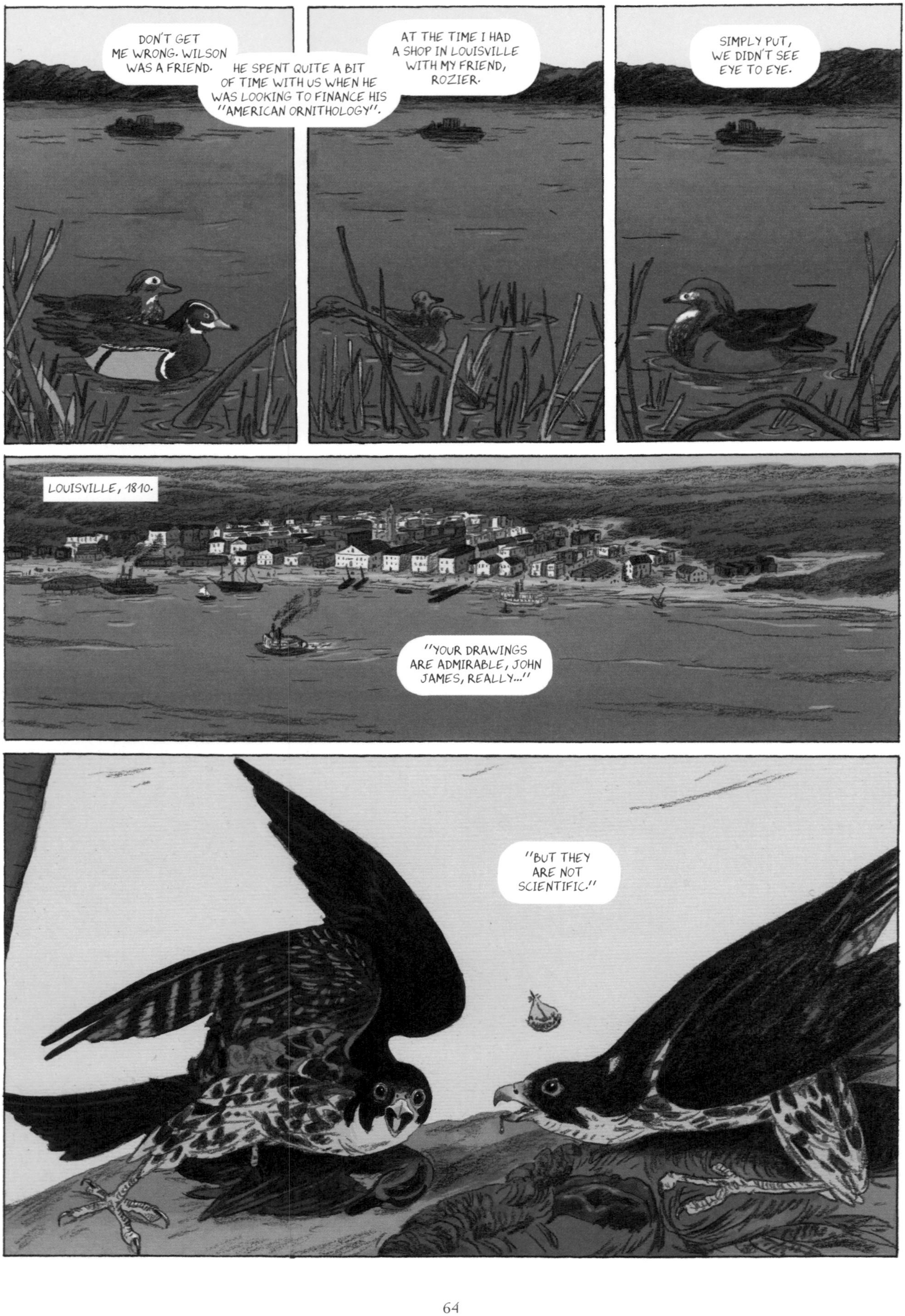
DON'T GET ME WRONG. WILSON WAS A FRIEND.
HE SPENT QUITE A BIT OF TIME WITH US WHEN HE WAS LOOKING TO FINANCE HIS "AMERICAN ORNITHOLOGY".
AT THE TIME I HAD A SHOP IN LOUISVILLE WITH MY FRIEND, ROZIER.
SIMPLY PUT, WE DIDN'T SEE EYE TO EYE.
LOUISVILLE, 1810.
"YOUR DRAWINGS ARE ADMIRABLE, JOHN JAMES, REALLY..."
"BUT THEY ARE NOT SCIENTIFIC."

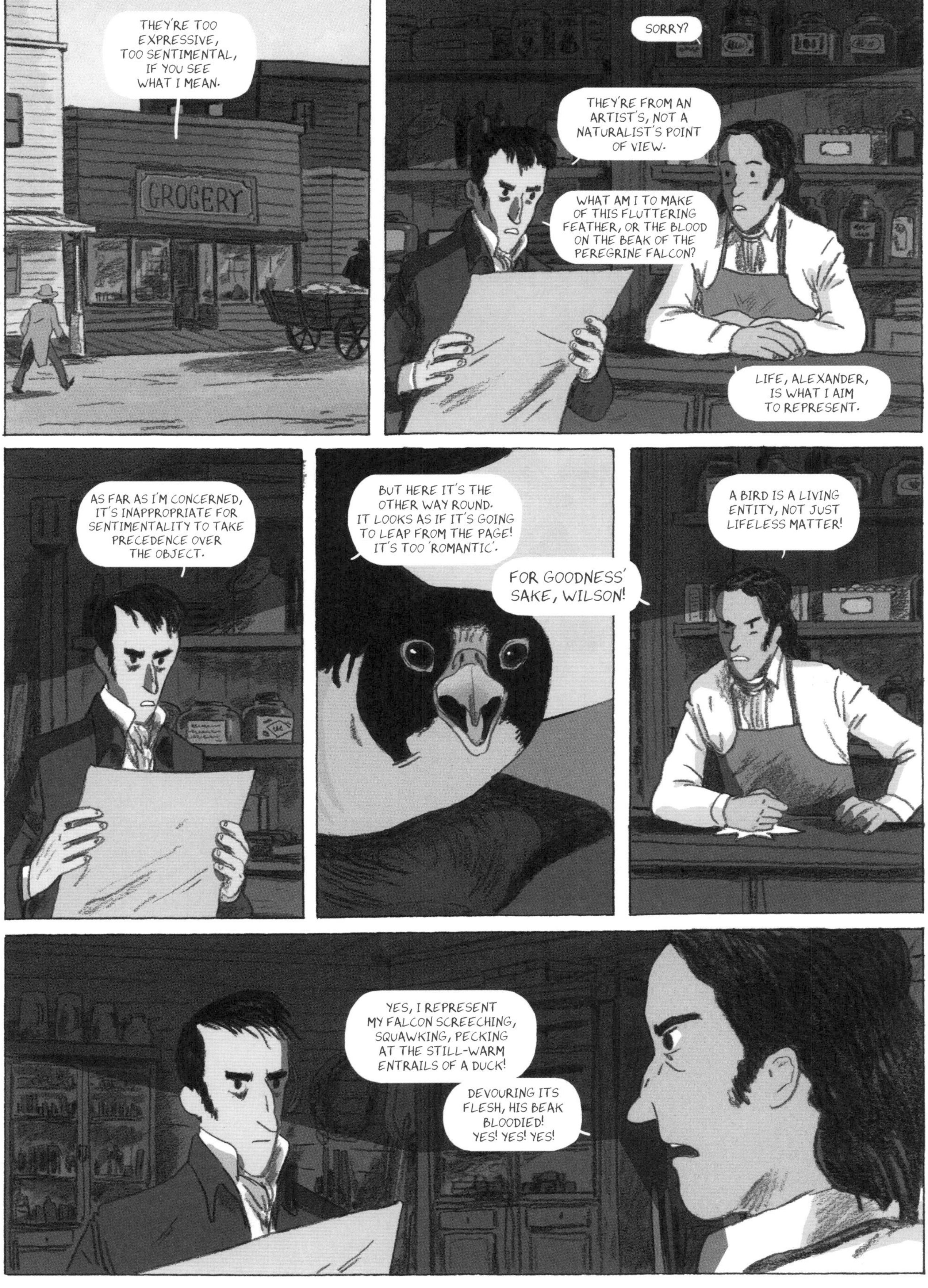
THEY'RE TOO EXPRESSIVE, TOO SENTIMENTAL, IF YOU SEE WHAT I MEAN.
GROCERY
SORRY?
THEY'RE FROM AN ARTIST'S, NOT A NATURALIST'S POINT OF VIEW.
WHAT AM I TO MAKE OF THIS FLUTTERING FEATHER, OR THE BLOOD ON THE BEAK OF THE PEREGRINE FALCON?
LIFE, ALEXANDER, IS WHAT I AIM TO REPRESENT.
AS FAR AS I'M CONCERNED, IT'S INAPPROPRIATE FOR SENTIMENTALITY TO TAKE PRECEDENCE OVER THE OBJECT.
BUT HERE IT'S THE OTHER WAY ROUND. IT LOOKS AS IF IT'S GOING TO LEAP FROM THE PAGE! IT'S TOO 'ROMANTIC'.
FOR GOODNESS' SAKE, WILSON!
A BIRD IS A LIVING ENTITY, NOT JUST LIFELESS MATTER!
YES, I REPRESENT MY FALCON SCREECHING, SQUAWKING, PECKING AT THE STILL-WARM ENTRAILS OF A DUCK!
DEVOURING ITS FLESH, HIS BEAK BLOODIED! YES! YES! YES!

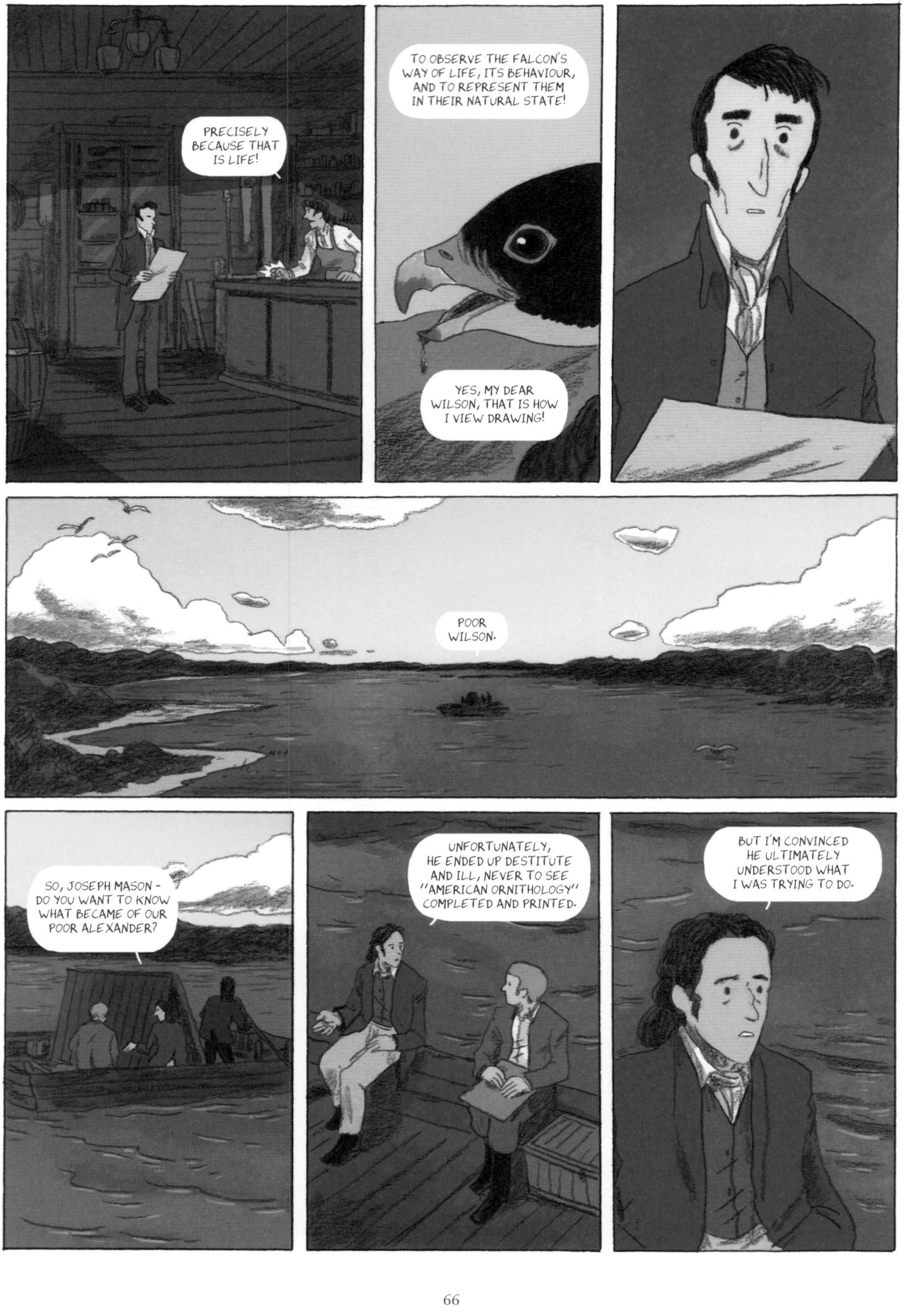
PRECISELY BECAUSE THAT IS LIFE!
TO OBSERVE THE FALCON'S WAY OF LIFE, ITS BEHAVIOUR, AND TO REPRESENT THEM IN THEIR NATURAL STATE!
YES, MY DEAR WILSON, THAT IS HOW I VIEW DRAWING!
POOR WILSON.
SO, JOSEPH MASON - DO YOU WANT TO KNOW WHAT BECAME OF OUR POOR ALEXANDER?
UNFORTUNATELY, HE ENDED UP DESTITUTE AND ILL, NEVER TO SEE "AMERICAN ORNITHOLOGY" COMPLETED AND PRINTED.
BUT I'M CONVINCED HE ULTIMATELY UNDERSTOOD WHAT I WAS TRYING TO DO.

HERE, COME AND SEE.

ADMIRE THE MAGNIFICENT BLUE OF THIS PLUMAGE!

WHAT A BEAUTY!

I SHOT THEM ONLY A FEW HOURS AGO.

I OBSERVED THESE JAYS FOR SOME TIME THIS MORNING.

ALREADY THE LIFE HAS DRAINED FROM THEIR BODIES, AND THE DULLNESS OF DEATH IS SETTING IN.

FIRSTLY, LET'S MEASURE THEM. NOTE THE LENGTH OF THE FEET... HMM, LETS SEE...

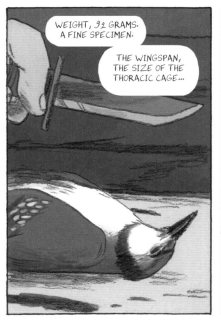

WEIGHT, 92 GRAMS. A FINE SPECIMEN.

THE WINGSPAN, THE SIZE OF THE THORACIC CAGE...

NEXT, WE WILL EVISCERATE IT AND NOTE THE STOMACH'S CONTENTS. IT'S OFTEN VERY INTERESTING.

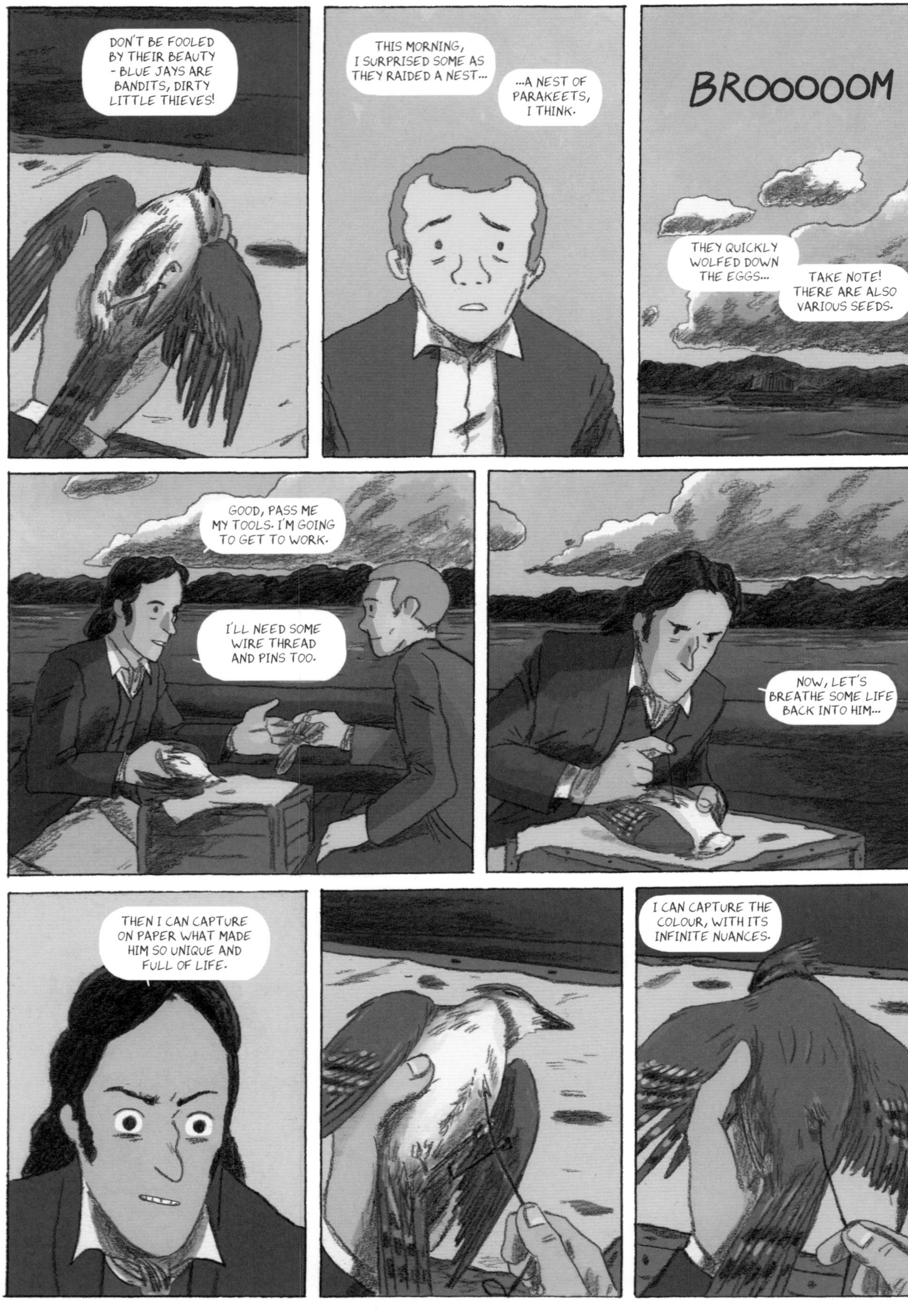
DON'T BE FOOLED BY THEIR BEAUTY - BLUE JAYS ARE BANDITS, DIRTY LITTLE THIEVES!
THIS MORNING, I SURPRISED SOME AS THEY RAIDED A NEST...
...A NEST OF PARAKEETS, I THINK.
BROOOOOM
THEY QUICKLY WOLFED DOWN THE EGGS...
TAKE NOTE! THERE ARE ALSO VARIOUS SEEDS.
GOOD, PASS ME MY TOOLS. I'M GOING TO GET TO WORK.
I'LL NEED SOME WIRE THREAD AND PINS TOO.
NOW, LET'S BREATHE SOME LIFE BACK INTO HIM...
THEN I CAN CAPTURE ON PAPER WHAT MADE HIM SO UNIQUE AND FULL OF LIFE.
I CAN CAPTURE THE COLOUR, WITH ITS INFINITE NUANCES.

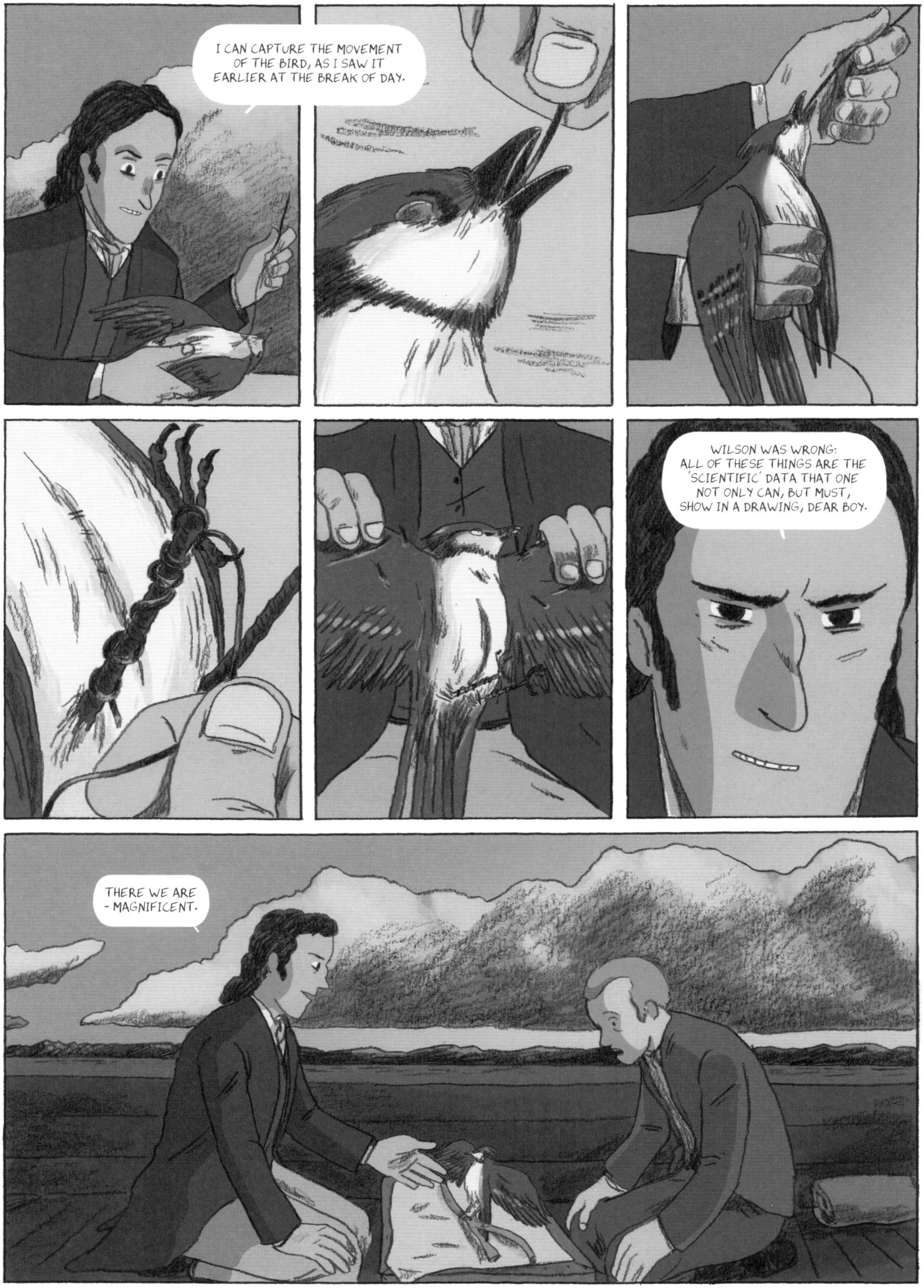
I CAN CAPTURE THE MOVEMENT OF THE BIRD, AS I SAW IT EARLIER AT THE BREAK OF DAY.
WILSON WAS WRONG: ALL OF THESE THINGS ARE THE 'SCIENTIFIC' DATA THAT ONE NOT ONLY CAN, BUT MUST, SHOW IN A DRAWING, DEAR BOY.
THERE WE ARE - MAGNIFICENT.

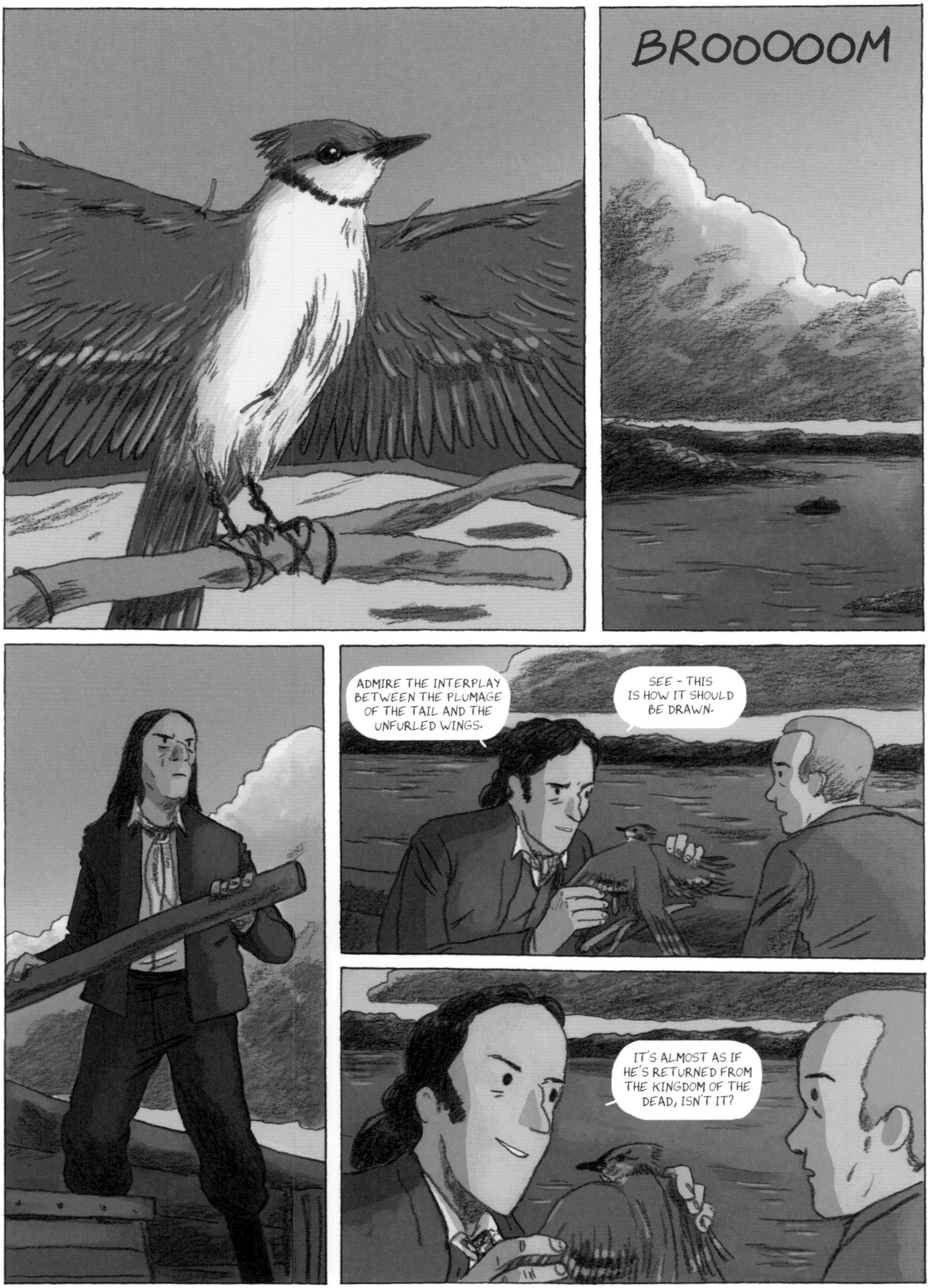
BROOOOOM
ADMIRE THE INTERPLAY BETWEEN THE PLUMAGE OF THE TAIL AND THE UNFURLED WINGS.
SEE - THIS IS HOW IT SHOULD BE DRAWN.
IT'S ALMOST AS IF HE'S RETURNED FROM THE KINGDOM OF THE DEAD, ISN'T IT?

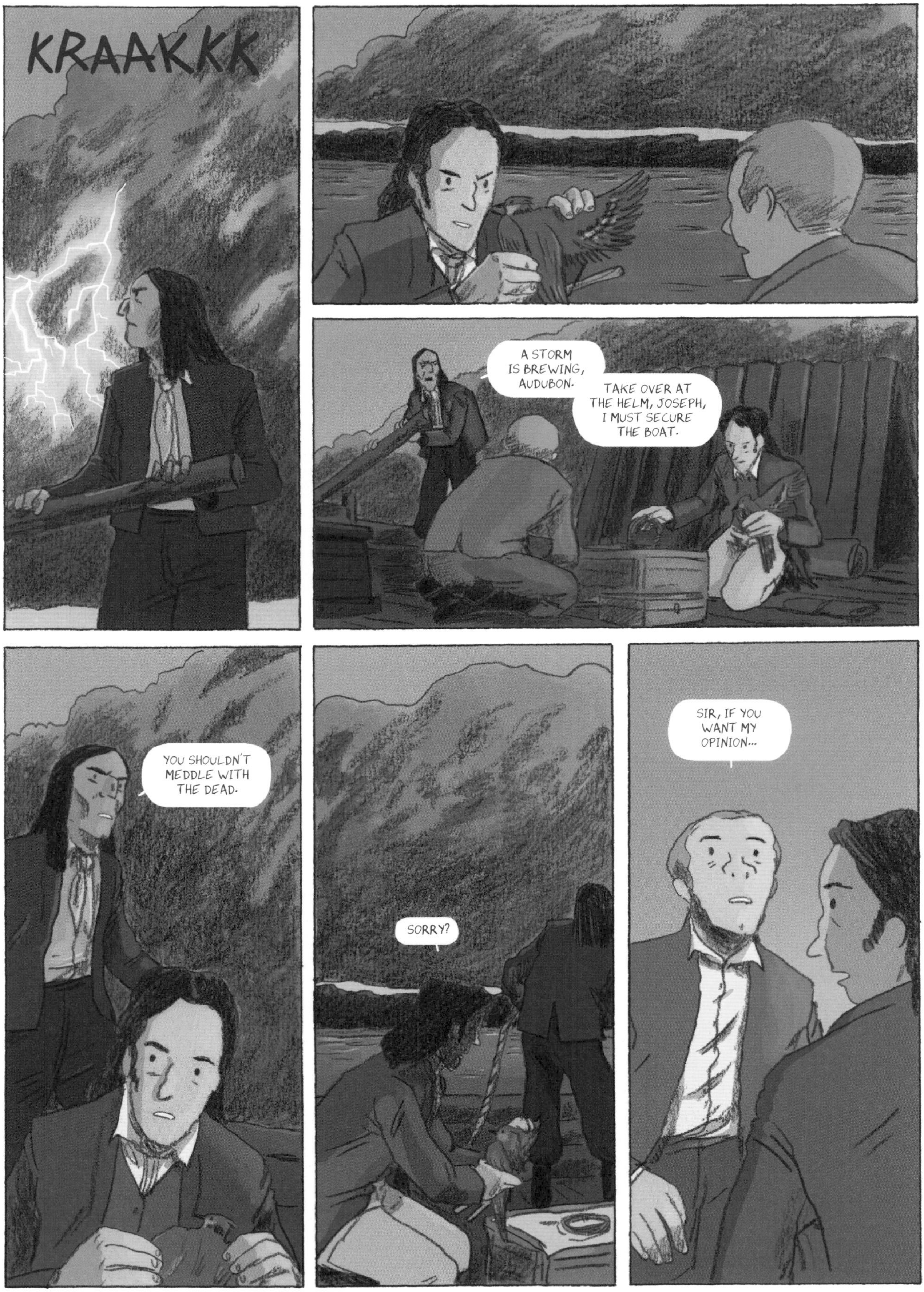
KRAAKKK
A STORM IS BREWING, AUDUBON.
TAKE OVER AT THE HELM, JOSEPH, I MUST SECURE THE BOAT.
YOU SHOULDN'T MEDDLE WITH THE DEAD.
SORRY?
SIR, IF YOU WANT MY OPINION...

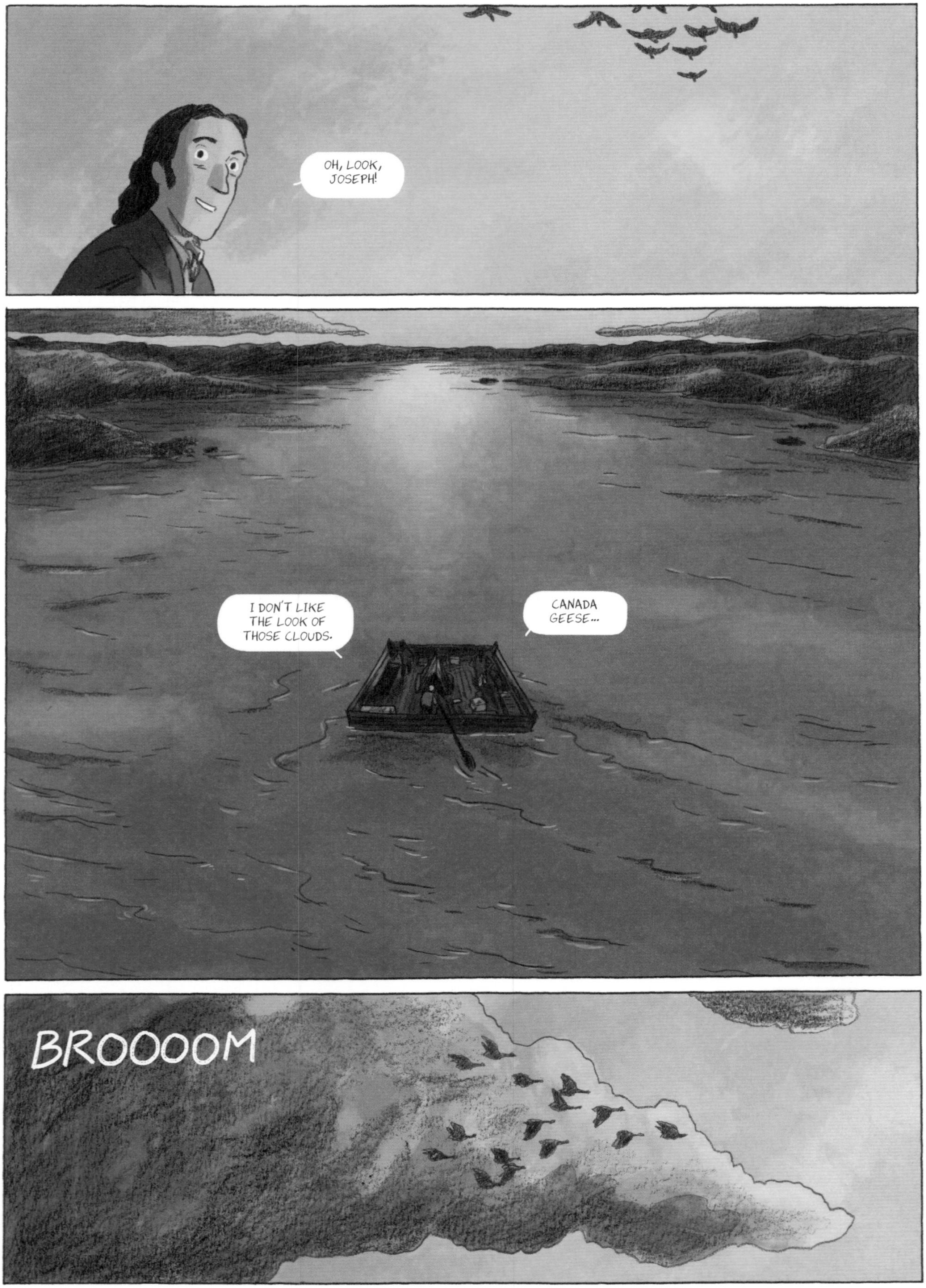
OH, LOOK, JOSEPH!
I DON'T LIKE THE LOOK OF THOSE CLOUDS.
CANADA GEESE...
BROOOOM

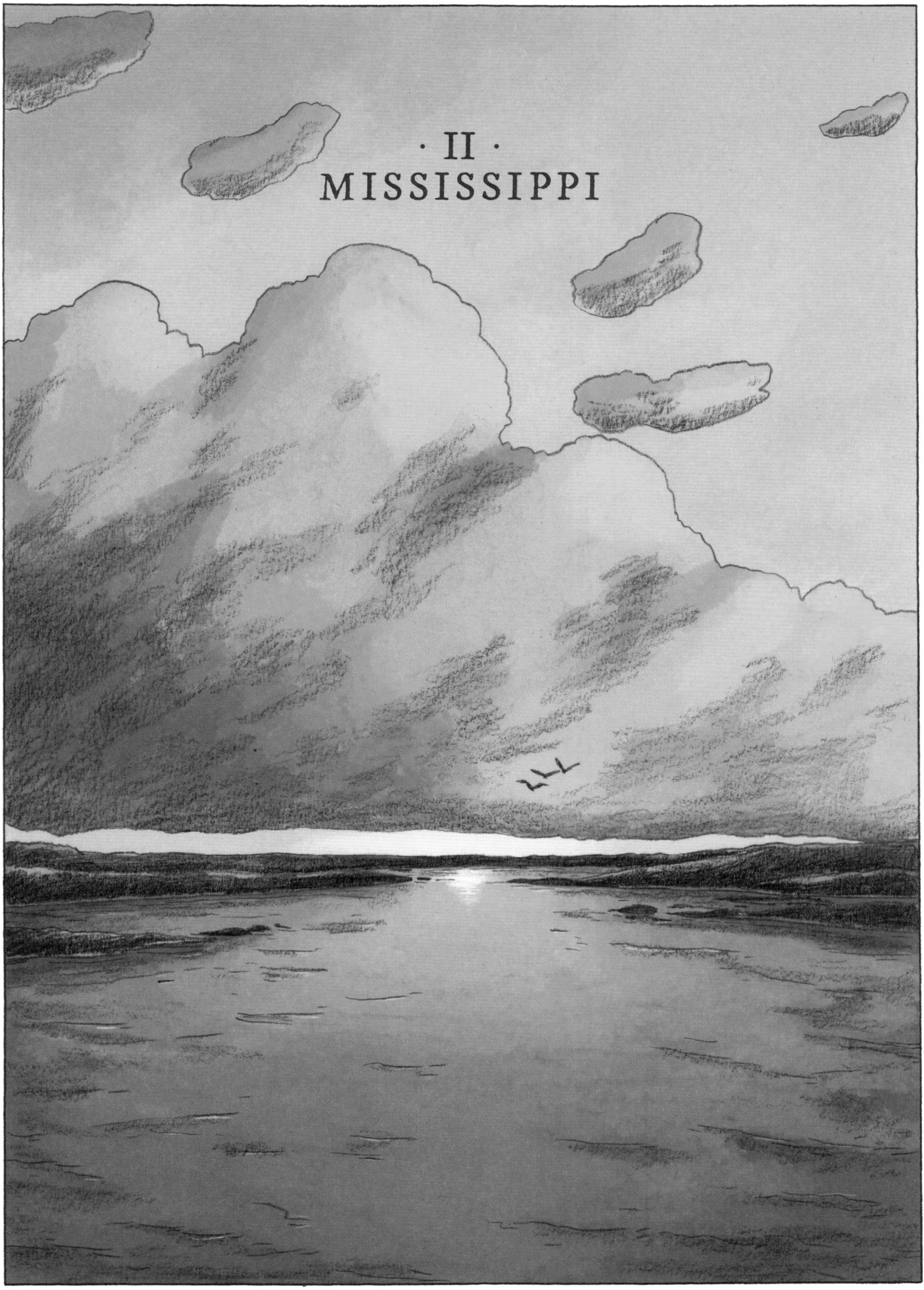
· II ·
MISSISSIPPI

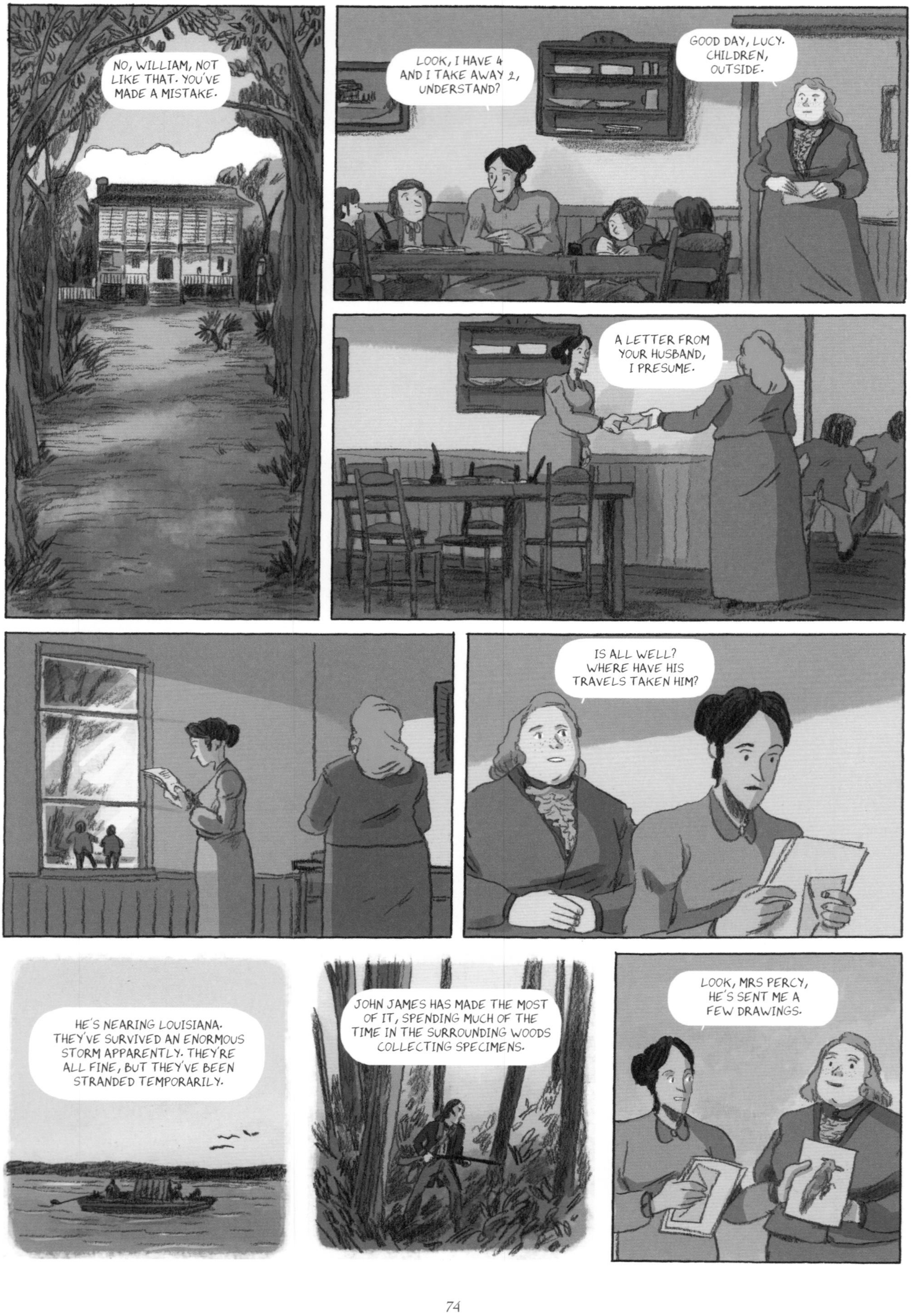
NO, WILLIAM, NOT LIKE THAT. YOU'VE MADE A MISTAKE.
LOOK, I HAVE 4 AND I TAKE AWAY 2, UNDERSTAND?
GOOD DAY, LUCY. CHILDREN, OUTSIDE.
A LETTER FROM YOUR HUSBAND, I PRESUME.
IS ALL WELL? WHERE HAVE HIS TRAVELS TAKEN HIM?
HE'S NEARING LOUISIANA. THEY'VE SURVIVED AN ENORMOUS STORM APPARENTLY. THEY'RE ALL FINE, BUT THEY'VE BEEN STRANDED TEMPORARILY.
JOHN JAMES HAS MADE THE MOST OF IT, SPENDING MUCH OF THE TIME IN THE SURROUNDING WOODS COLLECTING SPECIMENS.
LOOK, MRS PERCY, HE'S SENT ME A FEW DRAWINGS.

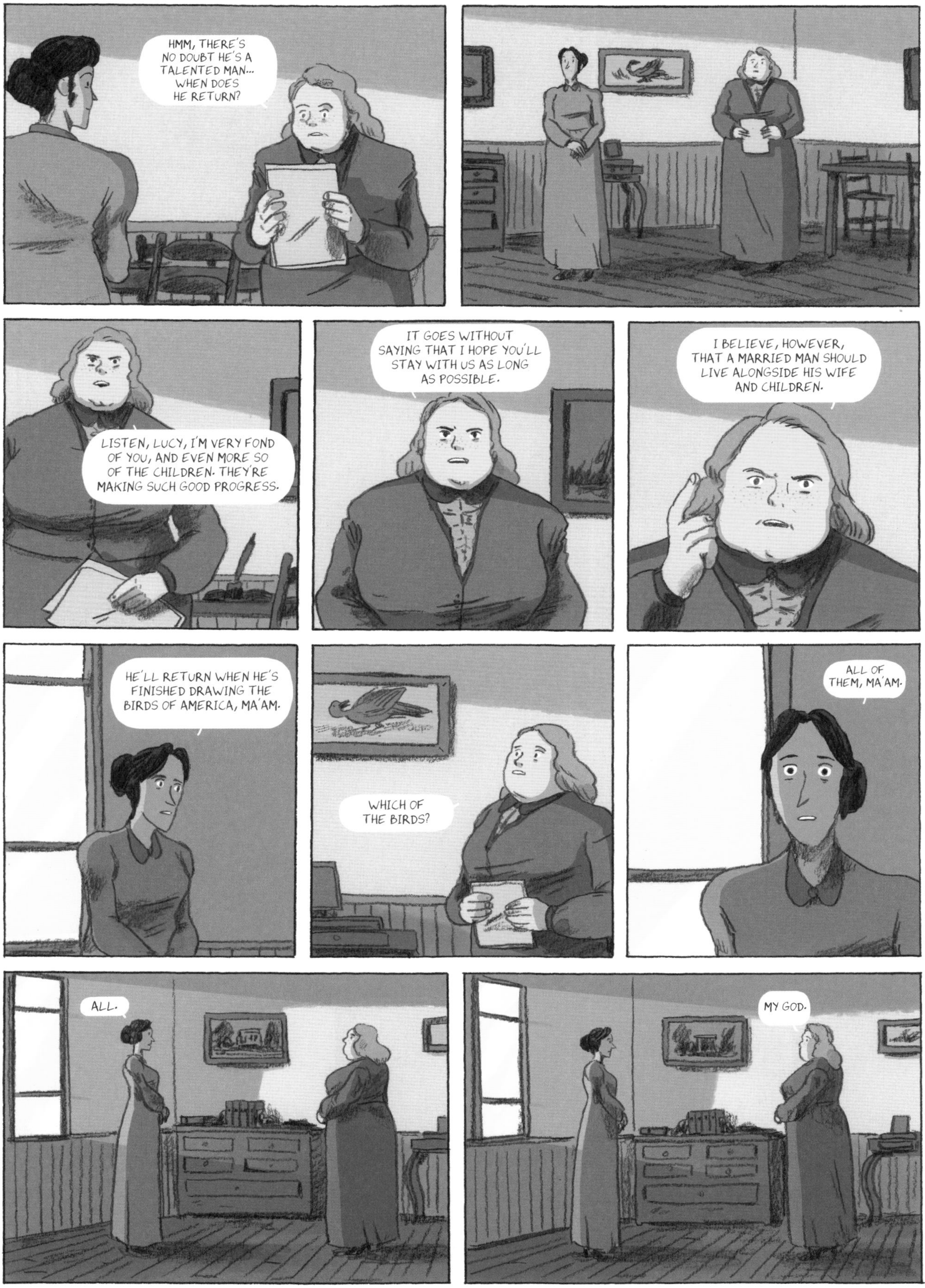
HMM, THERE'S NO DOUBT HE'S A TALENTED MAN... WHEN DOES HE RETURN?
LISTEN, LUCY, I'M VERY FOND OF YOU, AND EVEN MORE SO OF THE CHILDREN. THEY'RE MAKING SUCH GOOD PROGRESS.
IT GOES WITHOUT SAYING THAT I HOPE YOU'LL STAY WITH US AS LONG AS POSSIBLE.
I BELIEVE, HOWEVER, THAT A MARRIED MAN SHOULD LIVE ALONGSIDE HIS WIFE AND CHILDREN.
HE'LL RETURN WHEN HE'S FINISHED DRAWING THE BIRDS OF AMERICA, MA'AM.
WHICH OF THE BIRDS?
ALL OF THEM, MA'AM.
ALL.
MY GOD.

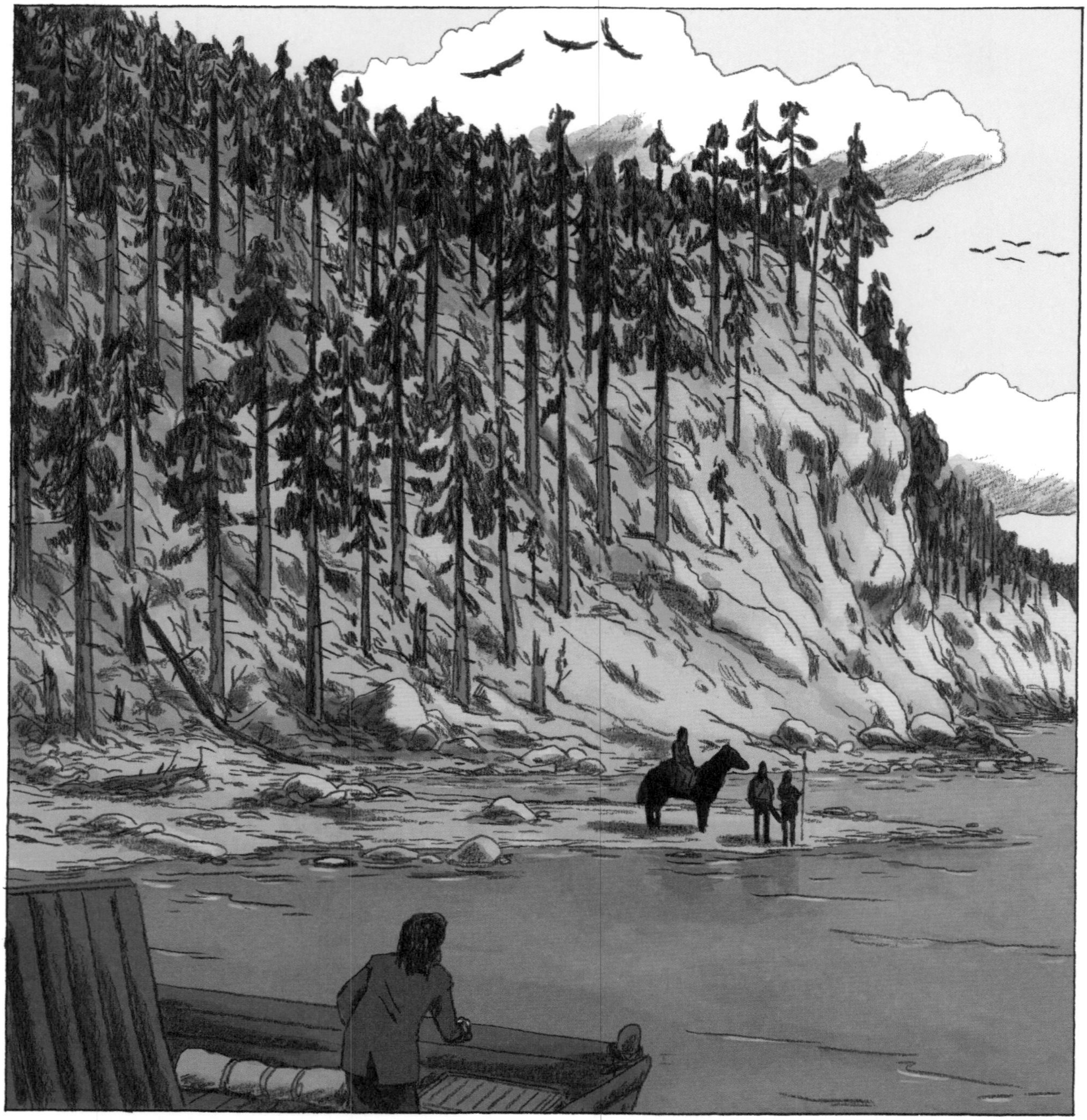

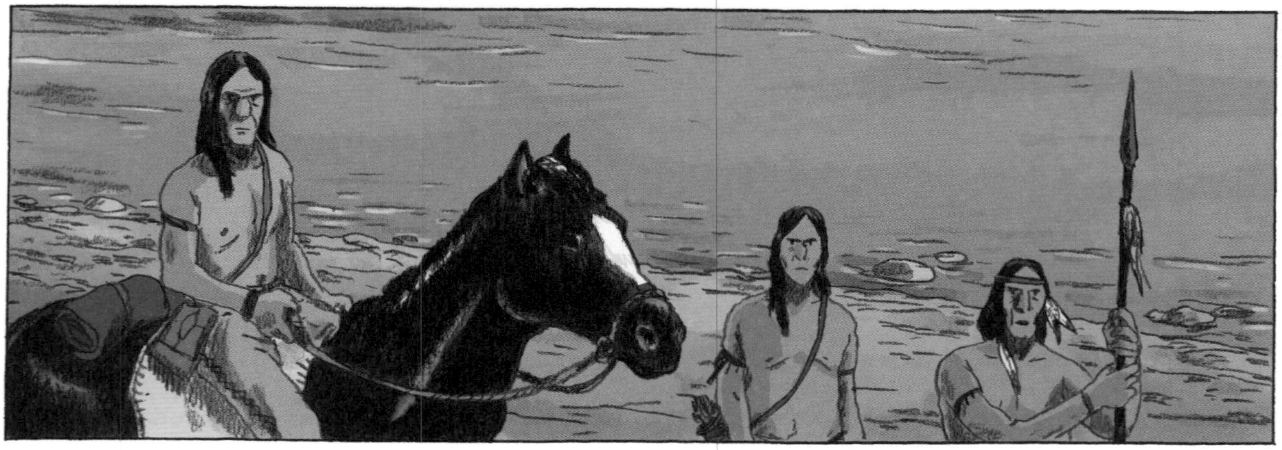

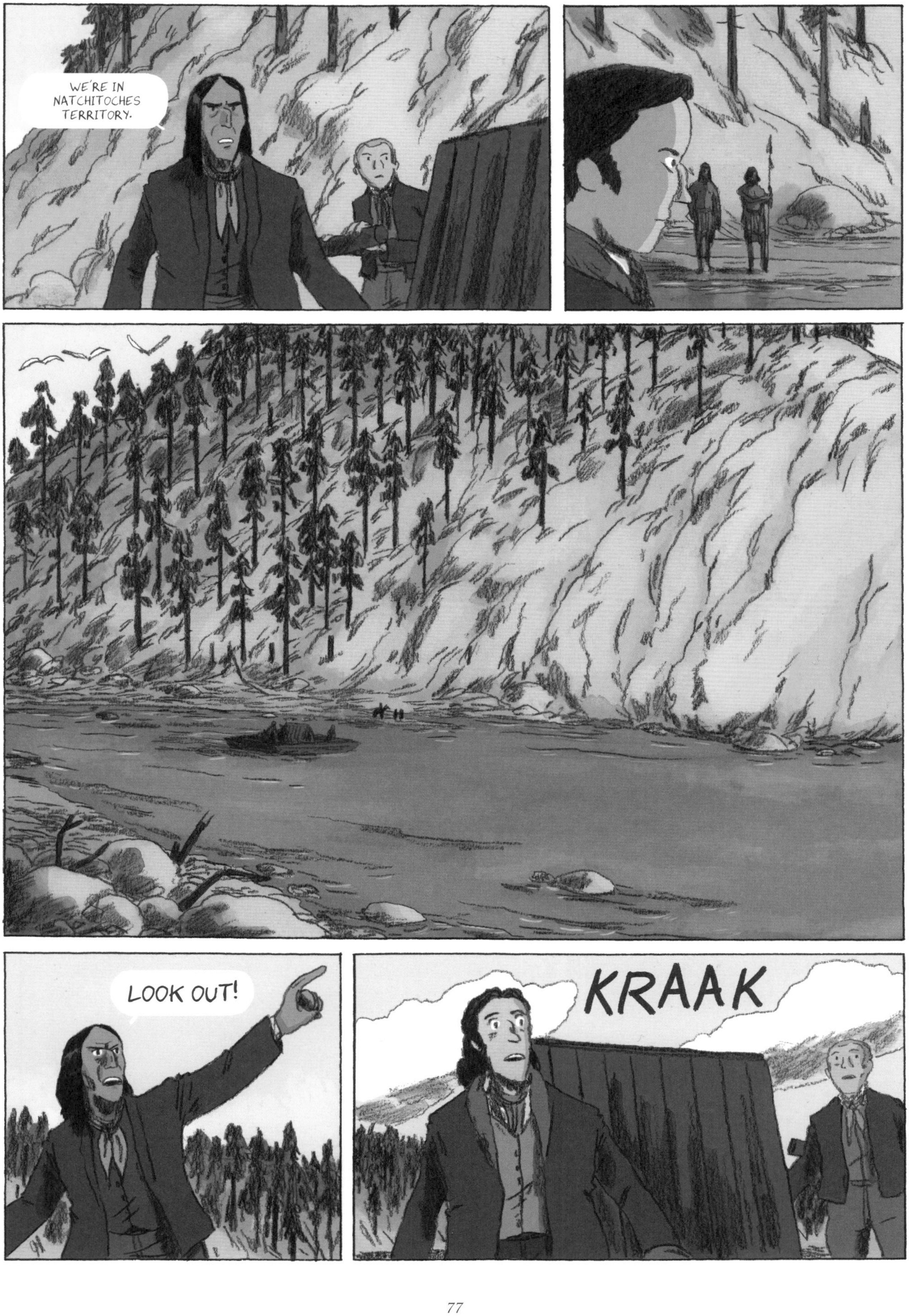
WE'RE IN NATCHITOCHES TERRITORY.
LOOK OUT!
KRAAK

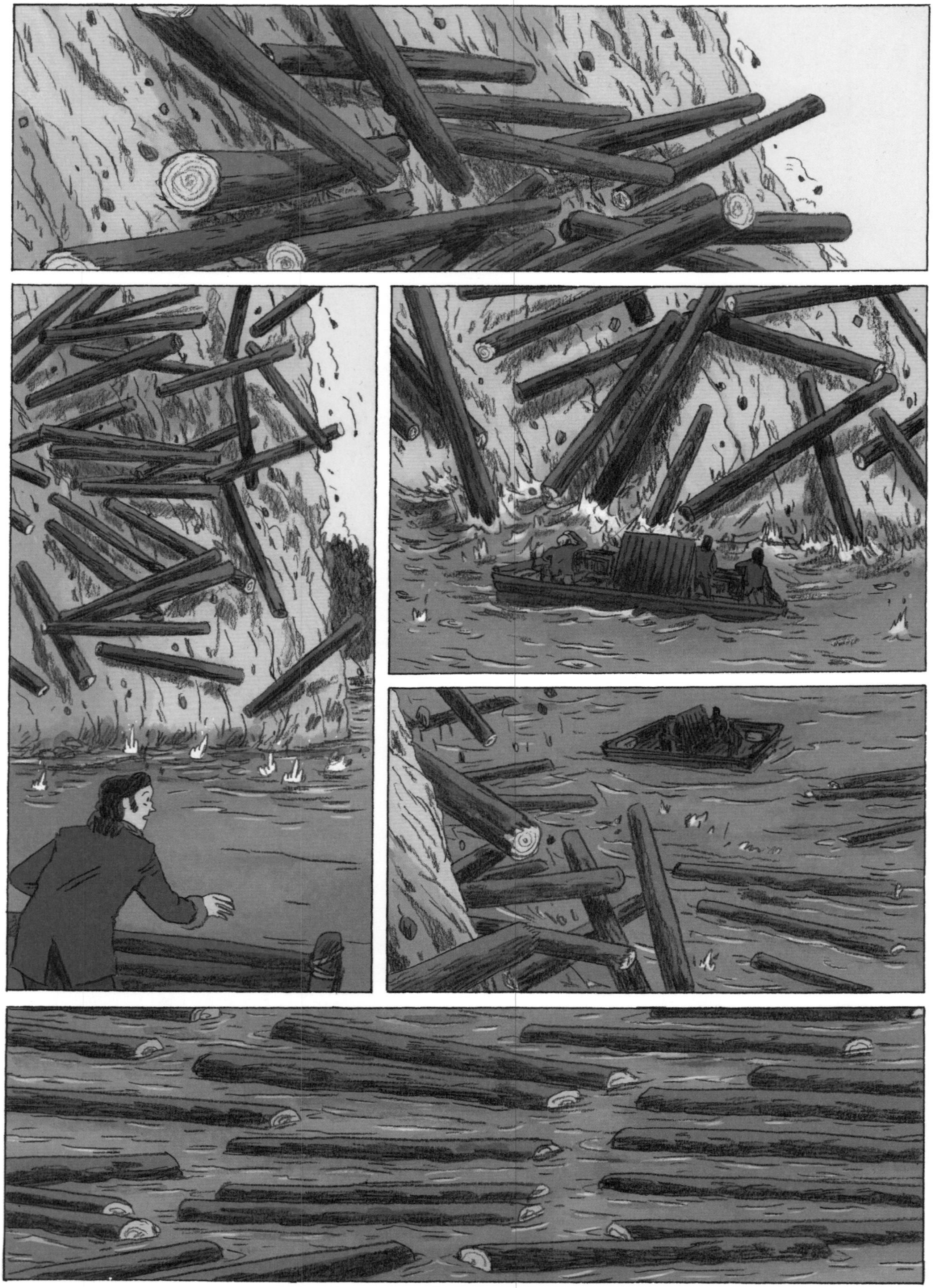

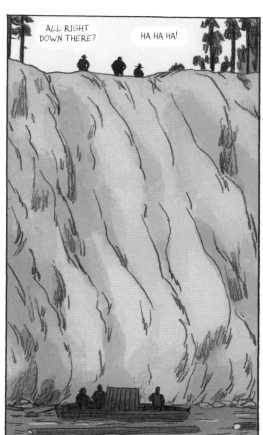

ALL RIGHT
DOWN THERE?

HA HA HA!

GOOD DAY, GENTLEMEN!
IT'S A BEAUTIFUL DAY,
DON'T YOU THINK?

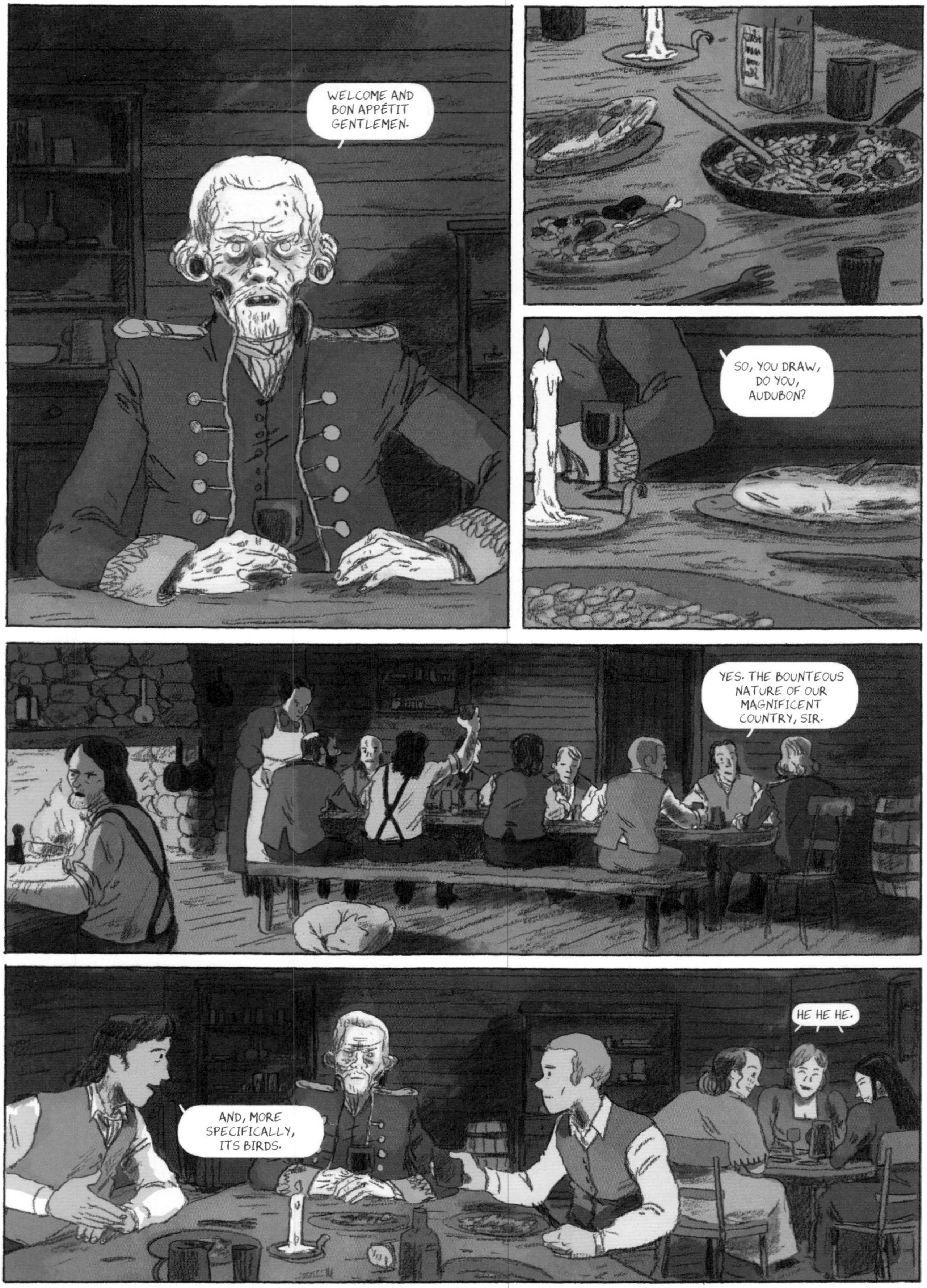
WELCOME AND BON APPÉTIT GENTLEMEN.
SO, YOU DRAW, DO YOU, AUDUBON?
YES. THE BOUNTEOUS NATURE OF OUR MAGNIFICENT COUNTRY, SIR.
AND, MORE SPECIFICALLY, ITS BIRDS.
HE HE HE.

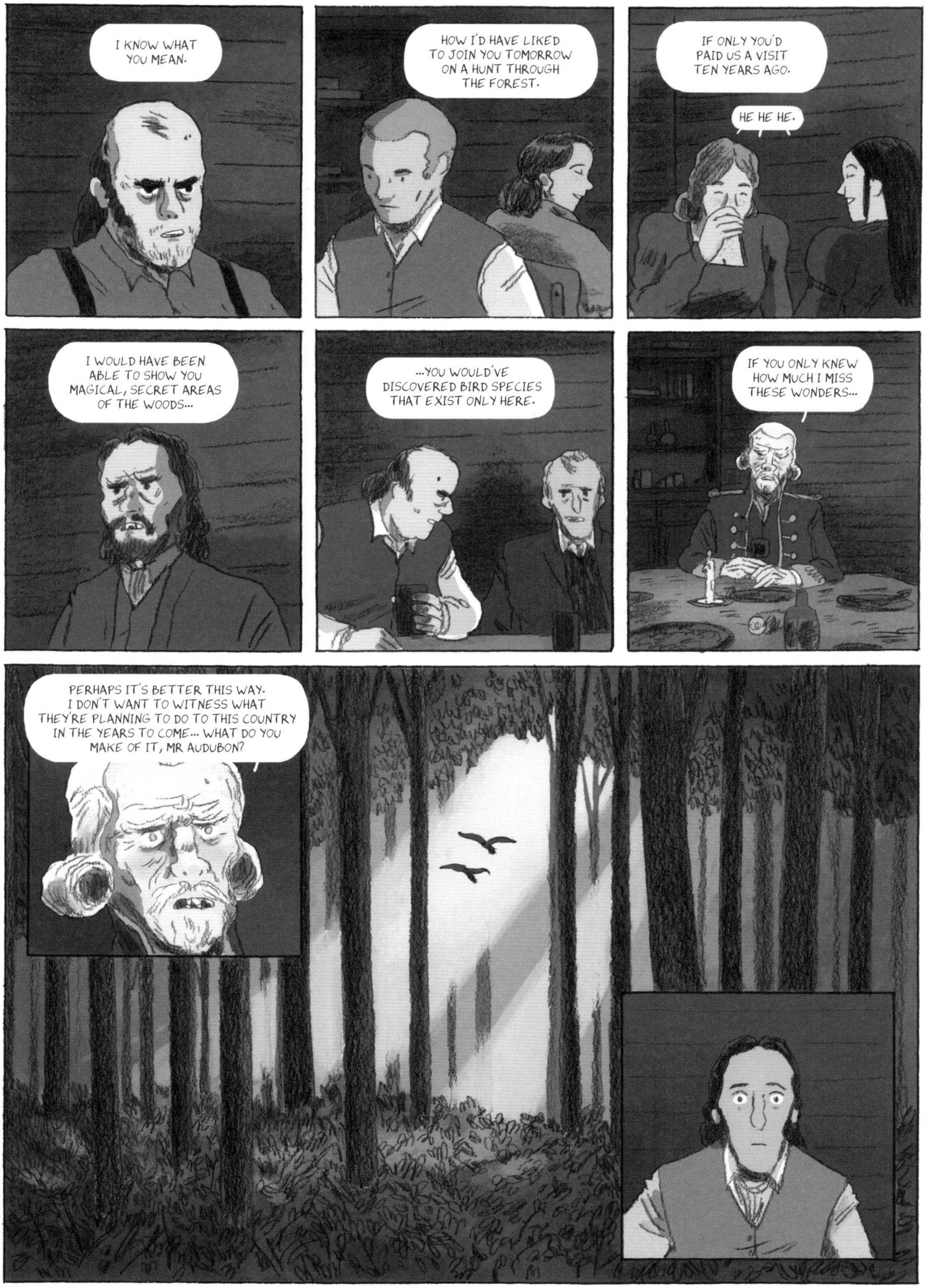
I KNOW WHAT YOU MEAN.
HOW I'D HAVE LIKED TO JOIN YOU TOMORROW ON A HUNT THROUGH THE FOREST.
IF ONLY YOU'D PAID US A VISIT TEN YEARS AGO.
HE HE HE.
I WOULD HAVE BEEN ABLE TO SHOW YOU MAGICAL, SECRET AREAS OF THE WOODS...
...YOU WOULD'VE DISCOVERED BIRD SPECIES THAT EXIST ONLY HERE.
IF YOU ONLY KNEW HOW MUCH I MISS THESE WONDERS...
PERHAPS IT'S BETTER THIS WAY. I DON'T WANT TO WITNESS WHAT THEY'RE PLANNING TO DO TO THIS COUNTRY IN THE YEARS TO COME... WHAT DO YOU MAKE OF IT, MR AUDUBON?

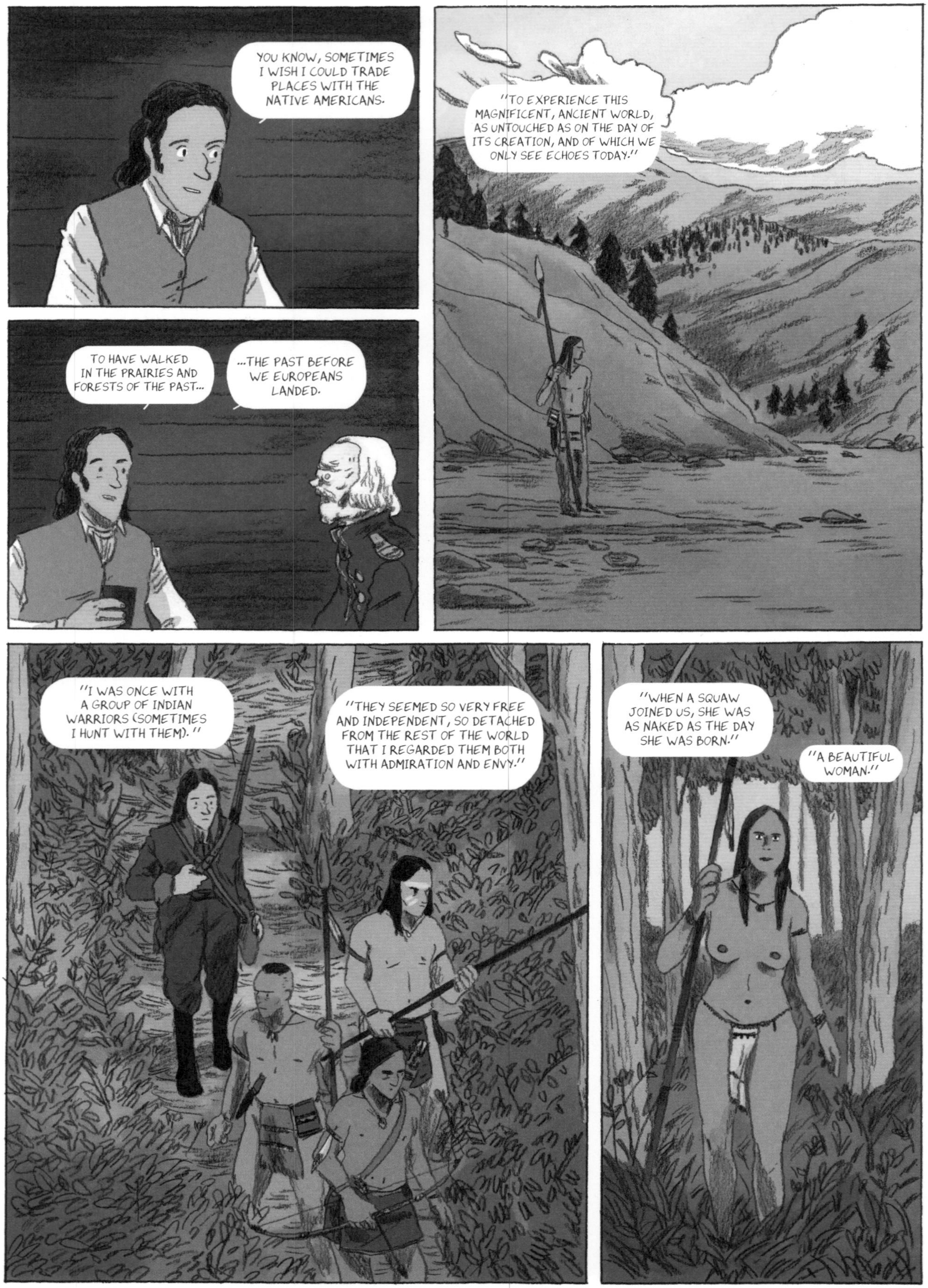
YOU KNOW, SOMETIMES I WISH I COULD TRADE PLACES WITH THE NATIVE AMERICANS.
TO HAVE WALKED IN THE PRAIRIES AND FORESTS OF THE PAST...
...THE PAST BEFORE WE EUROPEANS LANDED.
"TO EXPERIENCE THIS MAGNIFICENT, ANCIENT WORLD, AS UNTOUCHED AS ON THE DAY OF ITS CREATION, AND OF WHICH WE ONLY SEE ECHOES TODAY."
"I WAS ONCE WITH A GROUP OF INDIAN WARRIORS (SOMETIMES I HUNT WITH THEM)."
"THEY SEEMED SO VERY FREE AND INDEPENDENT, SO DETACHED FROM THE REST OF THE WORLD THAT I REGARDED THEM BOTH WITH ADMIRATION AND ENVY."
"WHEN A SQUAW JOINED US, SHE WAS AS NAKED AS THE DAY SHE WAS BORN."
"A BEAUTIFUL WOMAN."

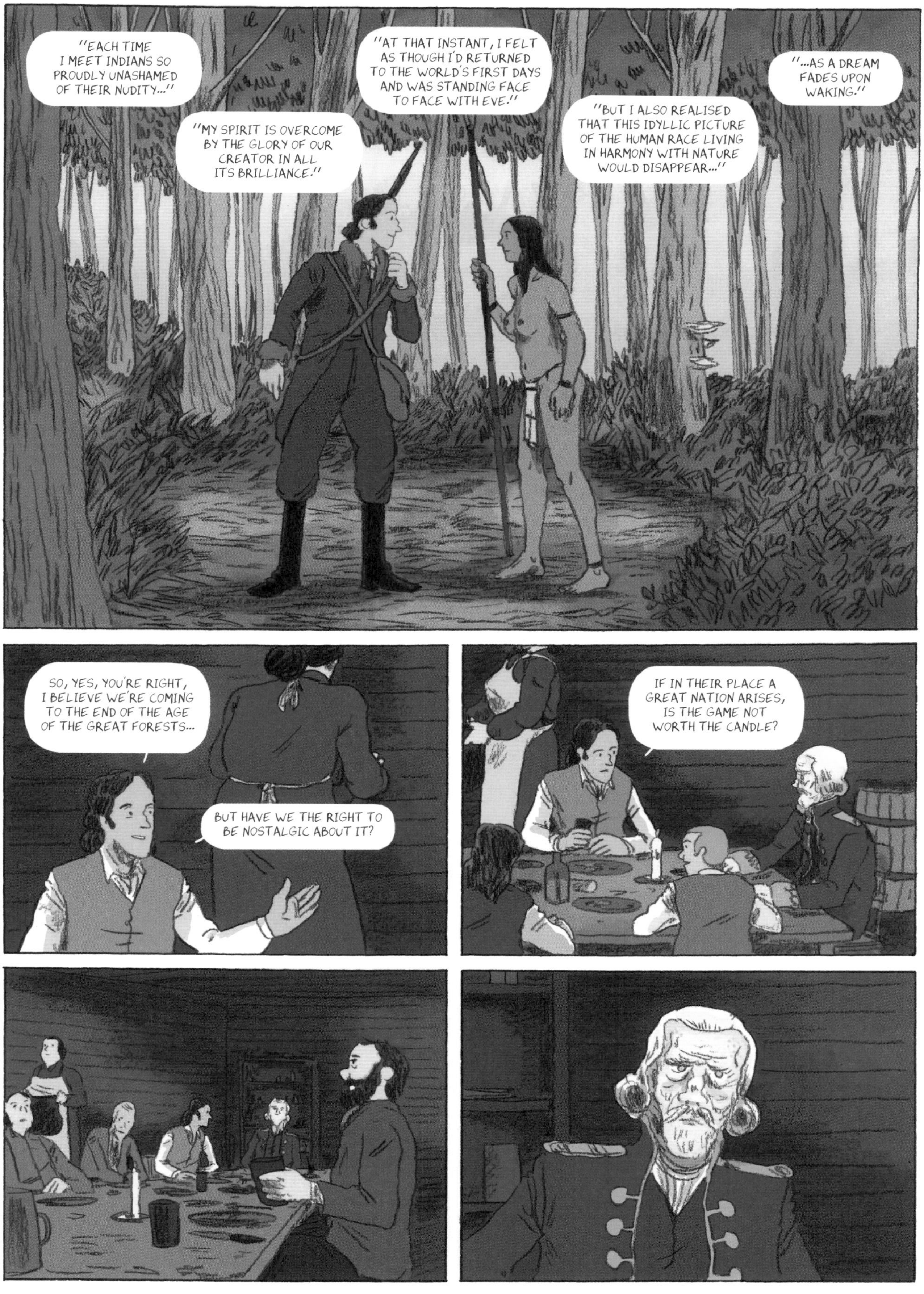
"EACH TIME I MEET INDIANS SO PROUDLY UNASHAMED OF THEIR NUDITY..."
"MY SPIRIT IS OVERCOME BY THE GLORY OF OUR CREATOR IN ALL ITS BRILLIANCE."
"AT THAT INSTANT, I FELT AS THOUGH I'D RETURNED TO THE WORLD'S FIRST DAYS AND WAS STANDING FACE TO FACE WITH EVE."
"BUT I ALSO REALISED THAT THIS IDYLLIC PICTURE OF THE HUMAN RACE LIVING IN HARMONY WITH NATURE WOULD DISAPPEAR..."
"...AS A DREAM FADES UPON WAKING."
SO, YES, YOU'RE RIGHT, I BELIEVE WE'RE COMING TO THE END OF THE AGE OF THE GREAT FORESTS...
BUT HAVE WE THE RIGHT TO BE NOSTALGIC ABOUT IT?
IF IN THEIR PLACE A GREAT NATION ARISES, IS THE GAME NOT WORTH THE CANDLE?

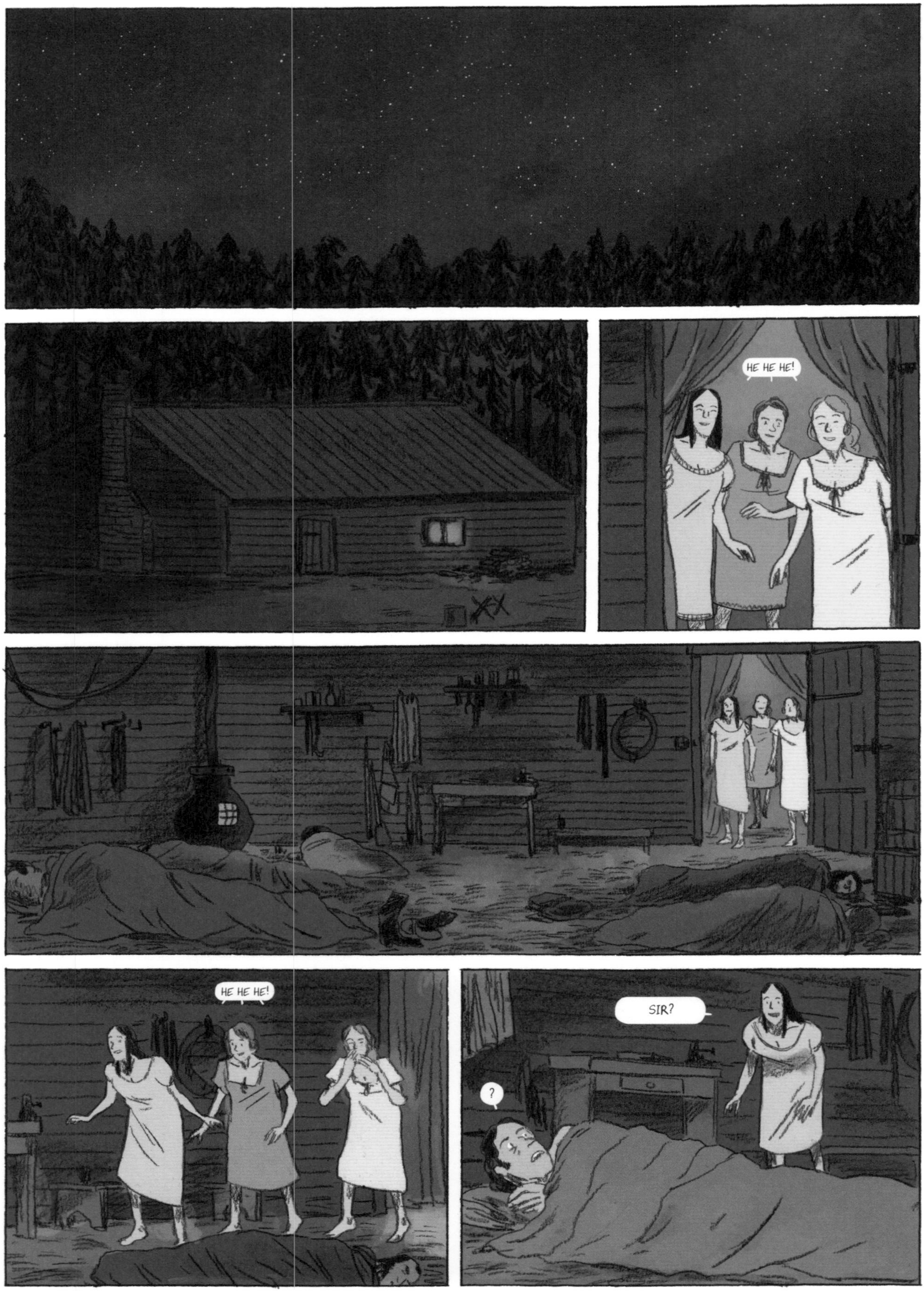
HE HE HE!
HE HE HE!
?
SIR?

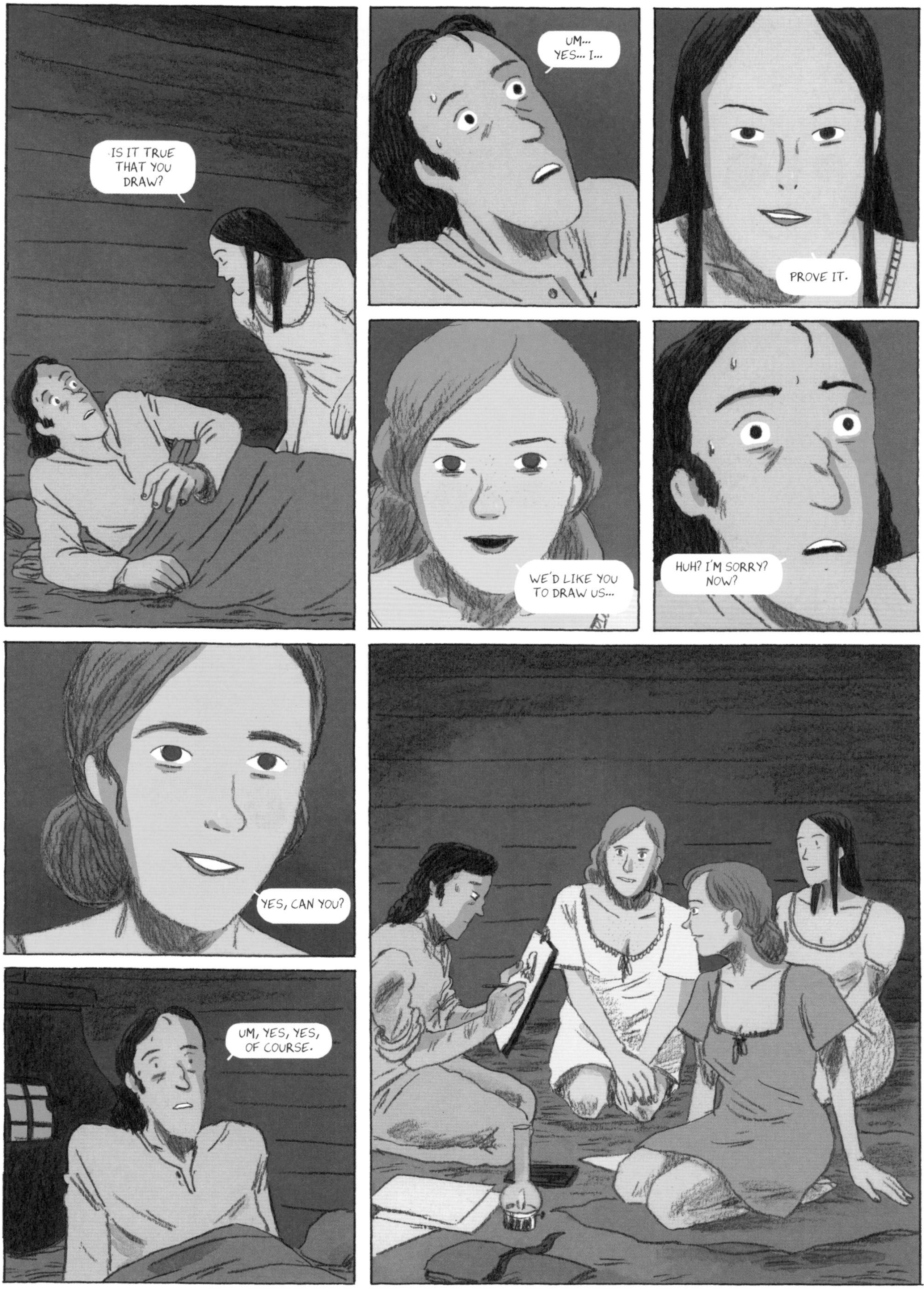
IS IT TRUE THAT YOU DRAW?
UM... YES... I...
PROVE IT.
WE'D LIKE YOU TO DRAW US...
HUH? I'M SORRY? NOW?
YES, CAN YOU?
UM, YES, YES, OF COURSE.

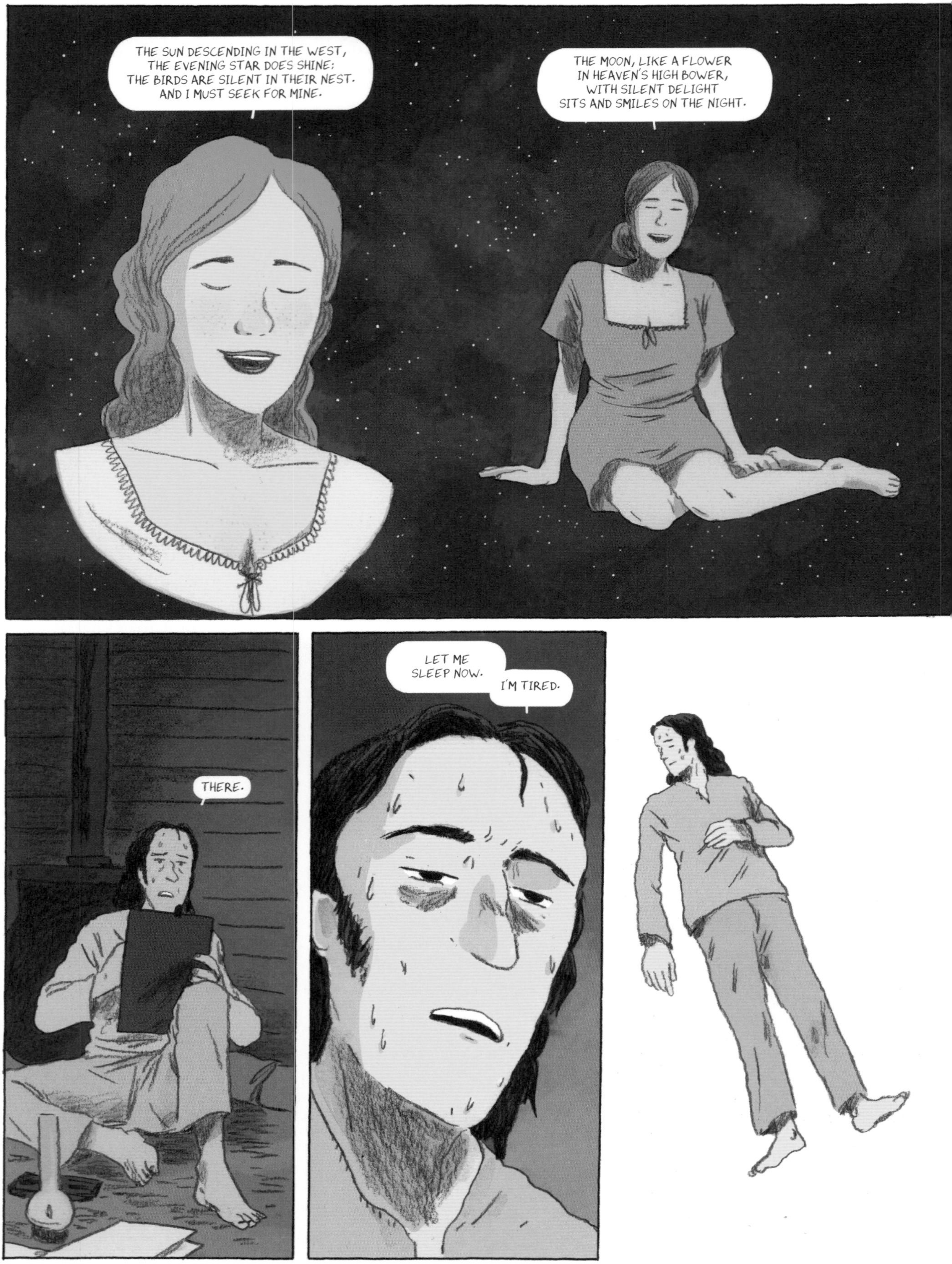
THE SUN DESCENDING IN THE WEST, THE EVENING STAR DOES SHINE; THE BIRDS ARE SILENT IN THEIR NEST. AND I MUST SEEK FOR MINE.
THE MOON, LIKE A FLOWER IN HEAVEN'S HIGH BOWER, WITH SILENT DELIGHT SITS AND SMILES ON THE NIGHT.
THERE.
LET ME SLEEP NOW.
I'M TIRED.

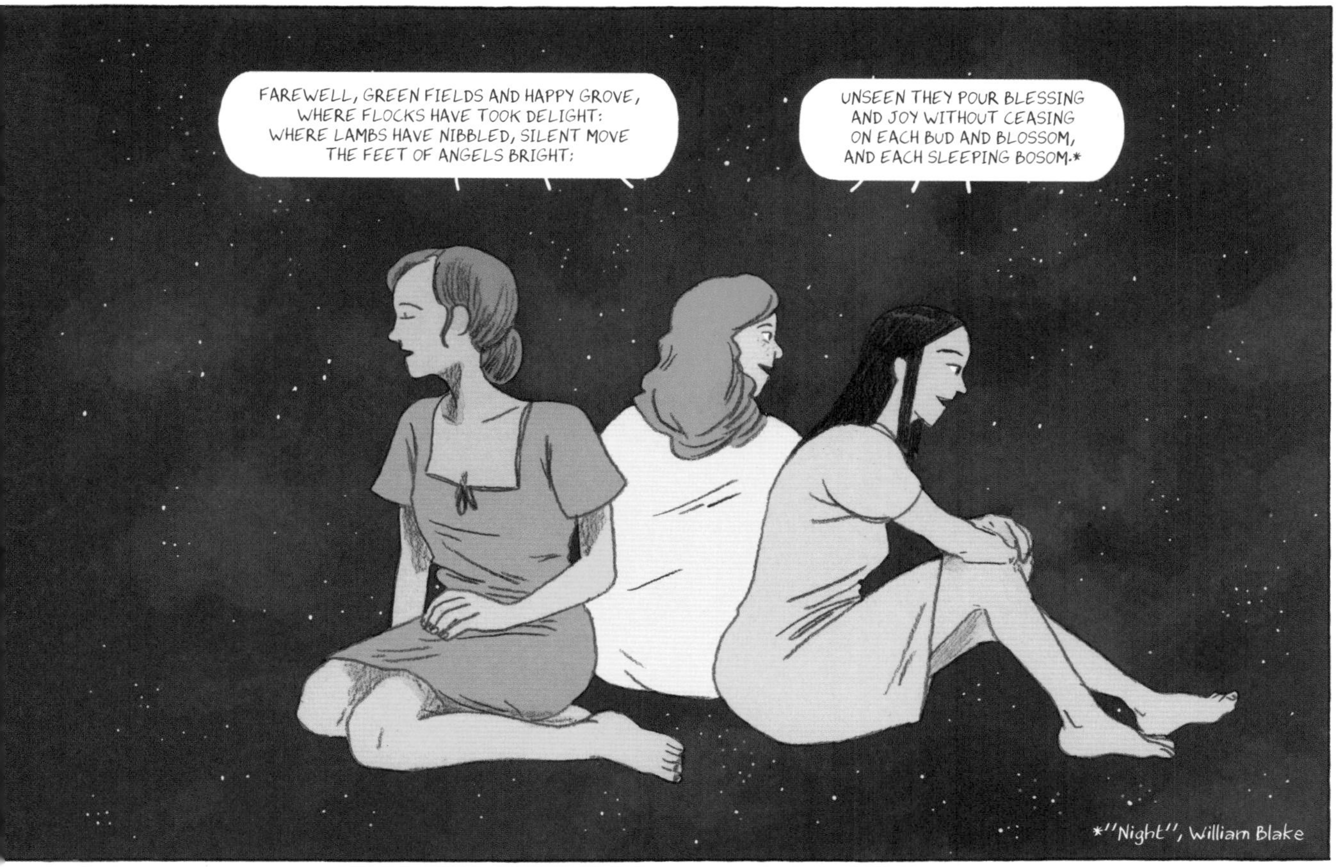
FAREWELL, GREEN FIELDS AND HAPPY GROVE, WHERE FLOCKS HAVE TOOK DELIGHT: WHERE LAMBS HAVE NIBBLED, SILENT MOVE THE FEET OF ANGELS BRIGHT:
UNSEEN THEY POUR BLESSING AND JOY WITHOUT CEASING ON EACH BUD AND BLOSSOM, AND EACH SLEEPING BOSOM.*
*"Night", William Blake

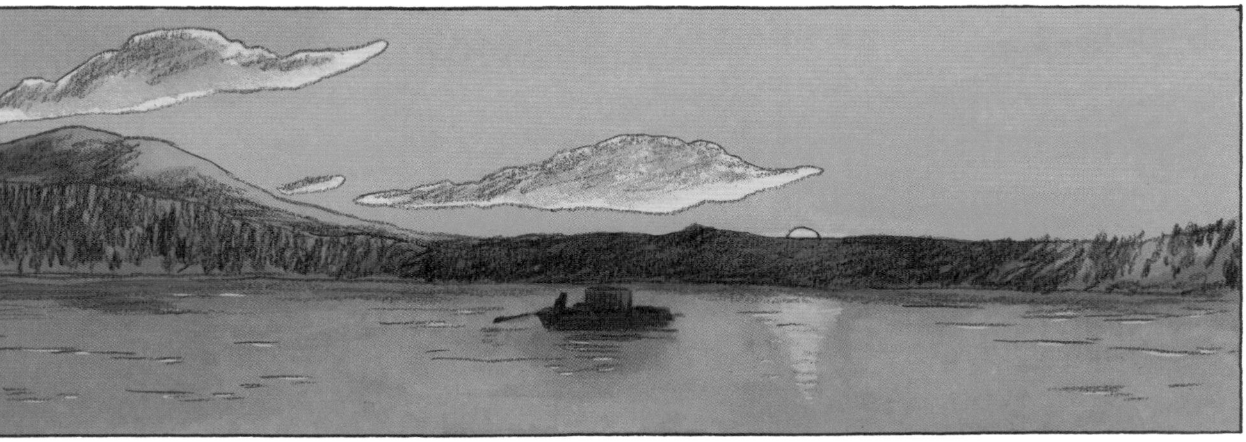

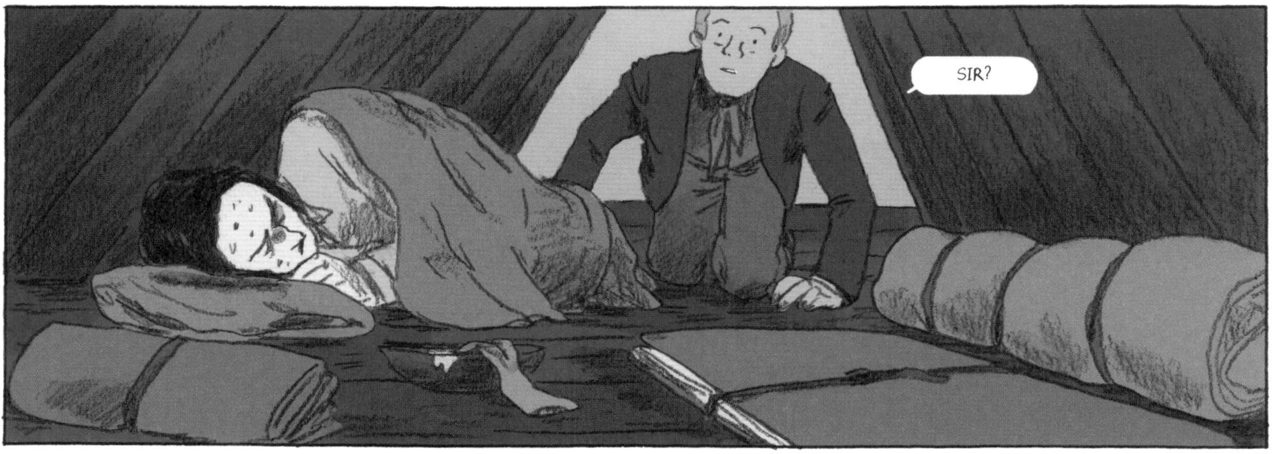
SIR?

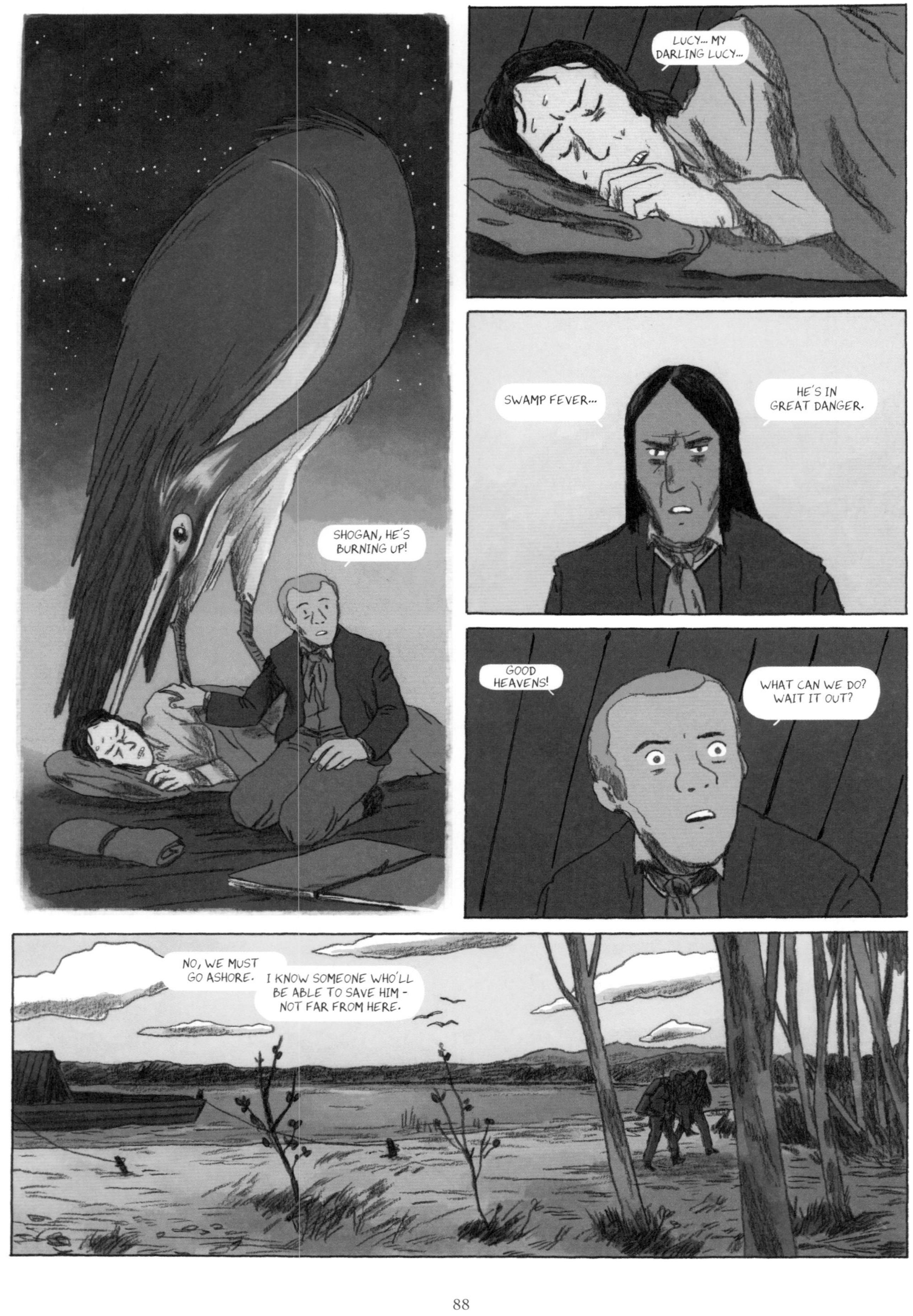
SHOGAN, HE'S BURNING UP!
LUCY... MY DARLING LUCY...
SWAMP FEVER...
HE'S IN GREAT DANGER.
GOOD HEAVENS!
WHAT CAN WE DO? WAIT IT OUT?
NO, WE MUST GO ASHORE.
I KNOW SOMEONE WHO'LL BE ABLE TO SAVE HIM - NOT FAR FROM HERE.

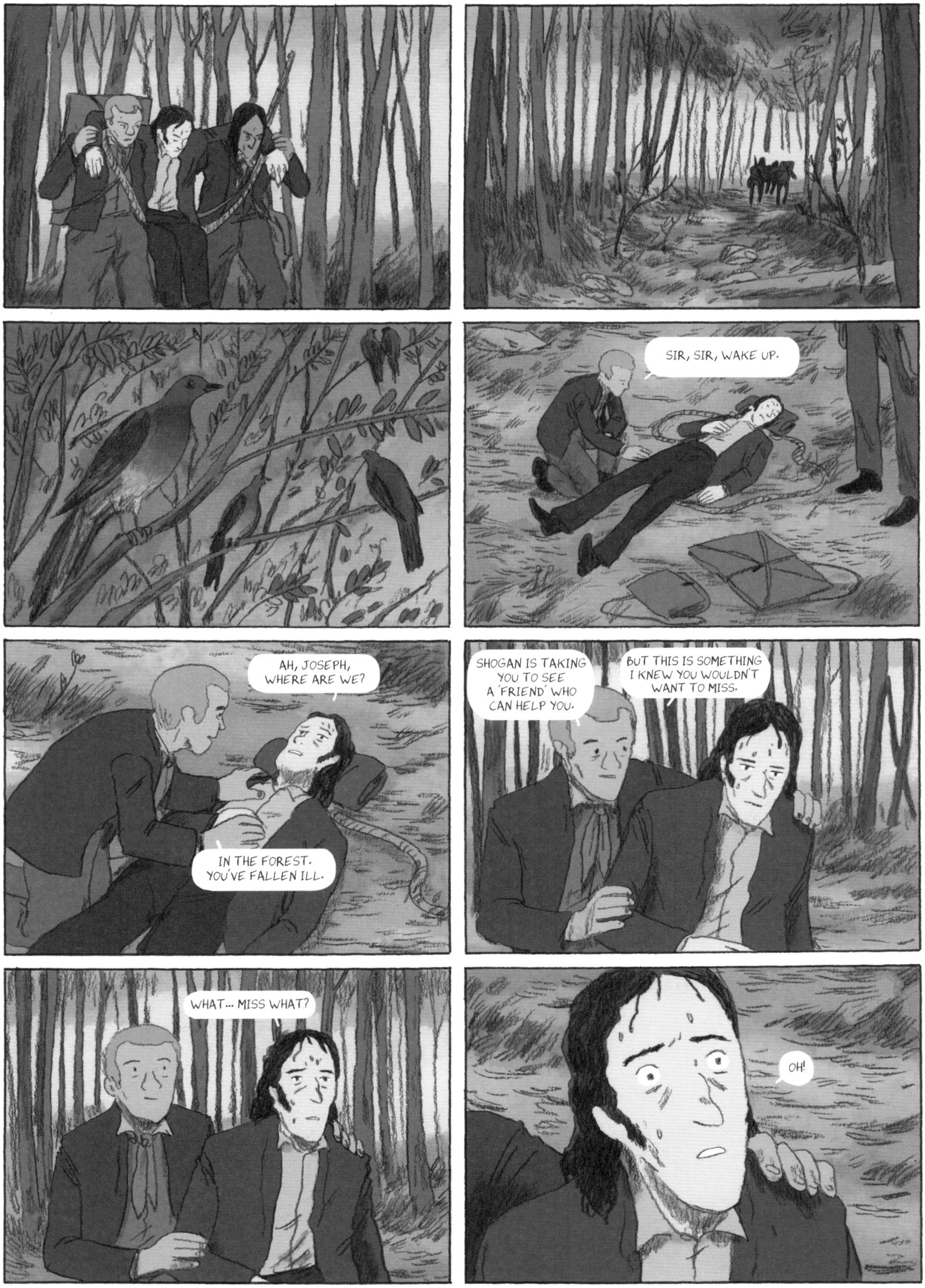
SIR, SIR, WAKE UP.
AH, JOSEPH, WHERE ARE WE?
IN THE FOREST. YOU'VE FALLEN ILL.
SHOGAN IS TAKING YOU TO SEE A 'FRIEND' WHO CAN HELP YOU.
BUT THIS IS SOMETHING I KNEW YOU WOULDN'T WANT TO MISS.
WHAT... MISS WHAT?
OH!

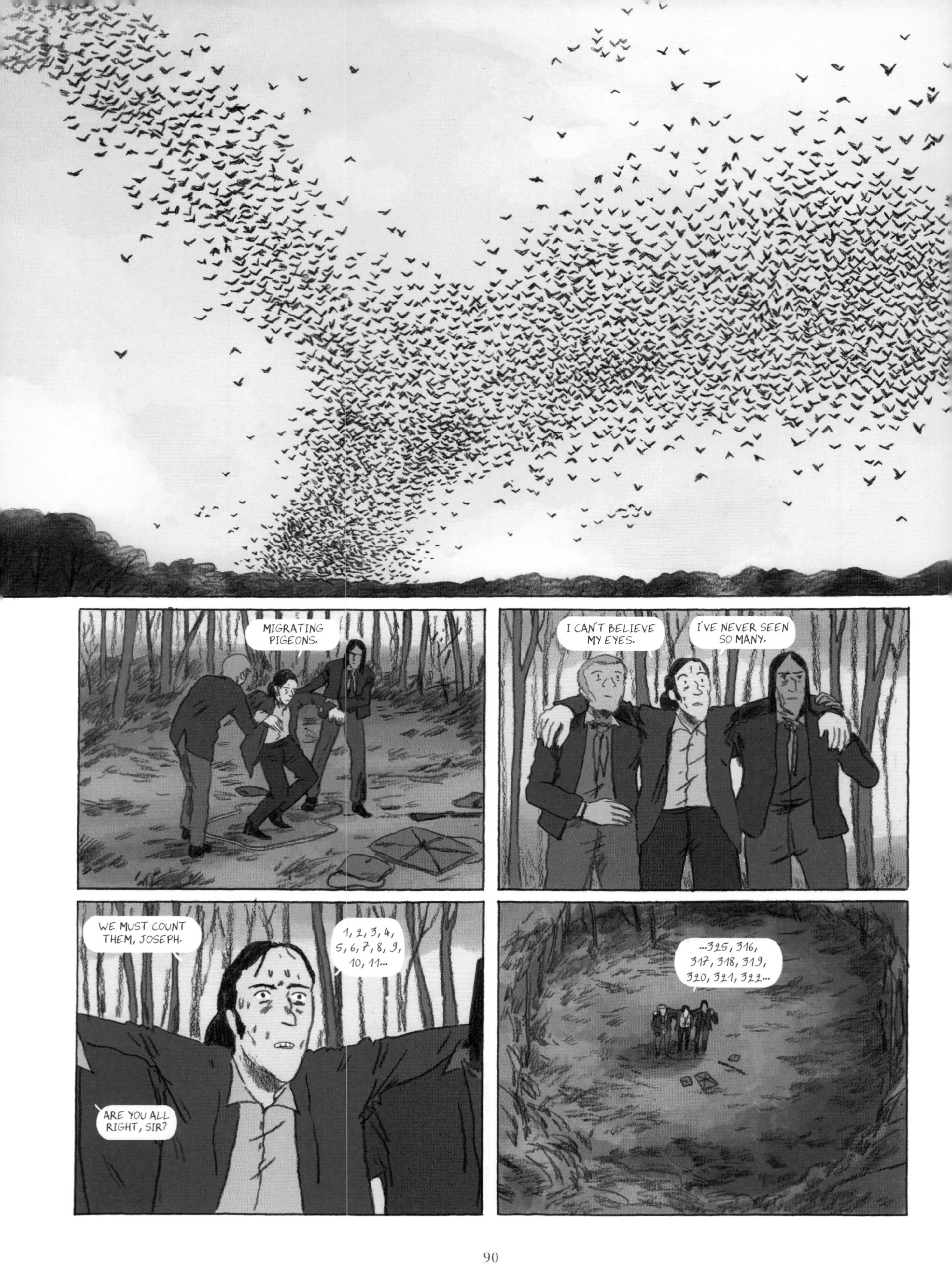
MIGRATING PIGEONS.
I CAN'T BELIEVE MY EYES.
I'VE NEVER SEEN SO MANY.
WE MUST COUNT THEM, JOSEPH.
1, 2, 3, 4, 5, 6, 7, 8, 9, 10, 11...
ARE YOU ALL RIGHT, SIR?
...315, 316, 317, 318, 319, 320, 321, 322...

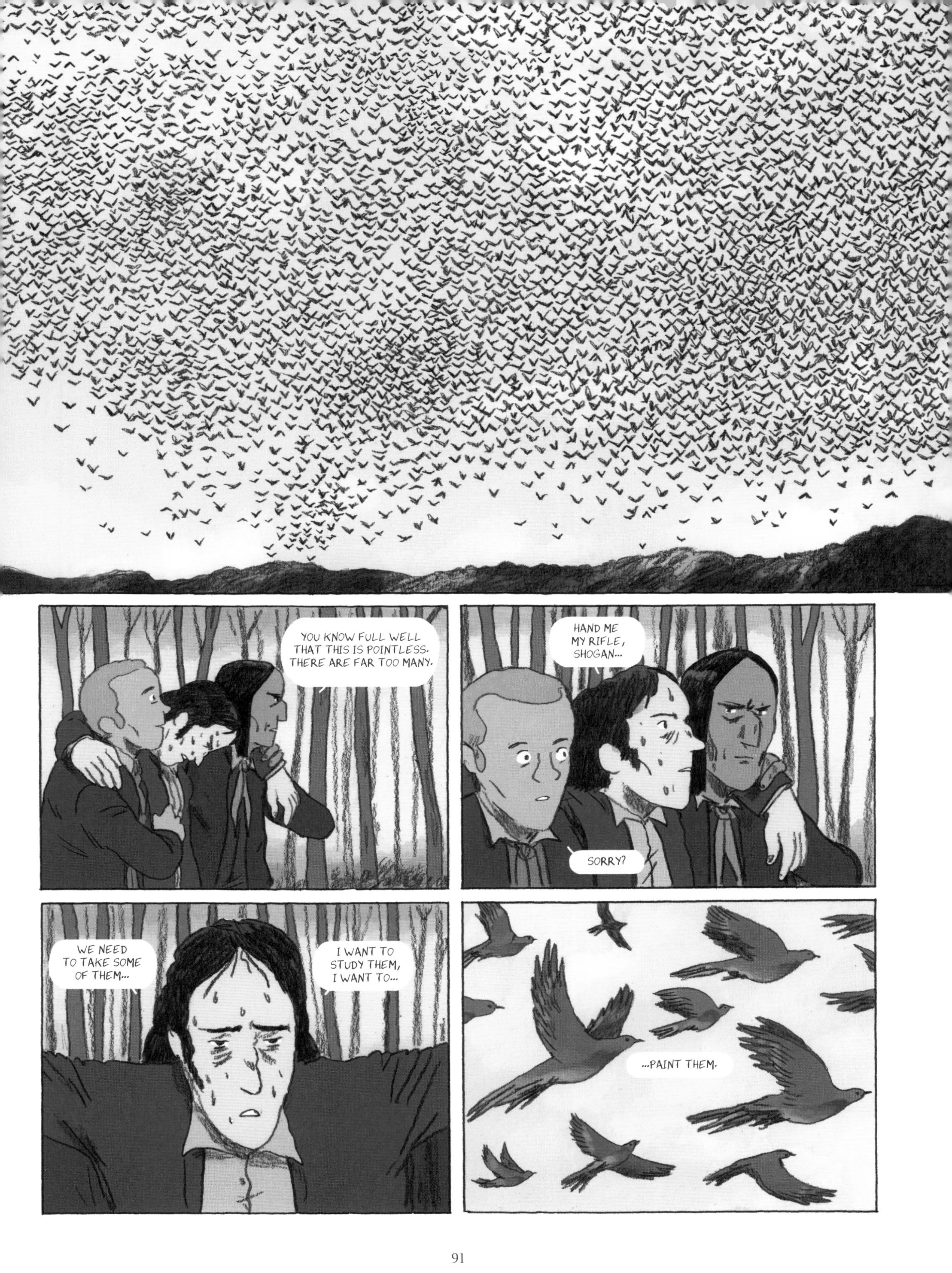

YOU KNOW FULL WELL THAT THIS IS POINTLESS. THERE ARE FAR TOO MANY.
HAND ME MY RIFLE, SHOGAN...
SORRY?
WE NEED TO TAKE SOME OF THEM...
I WANT TO STUDY THEM, I WANT TO...
...PAINT THEM.

BANG!

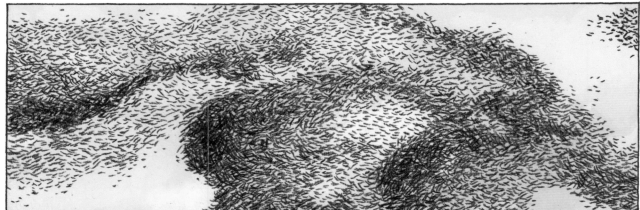

BANG!

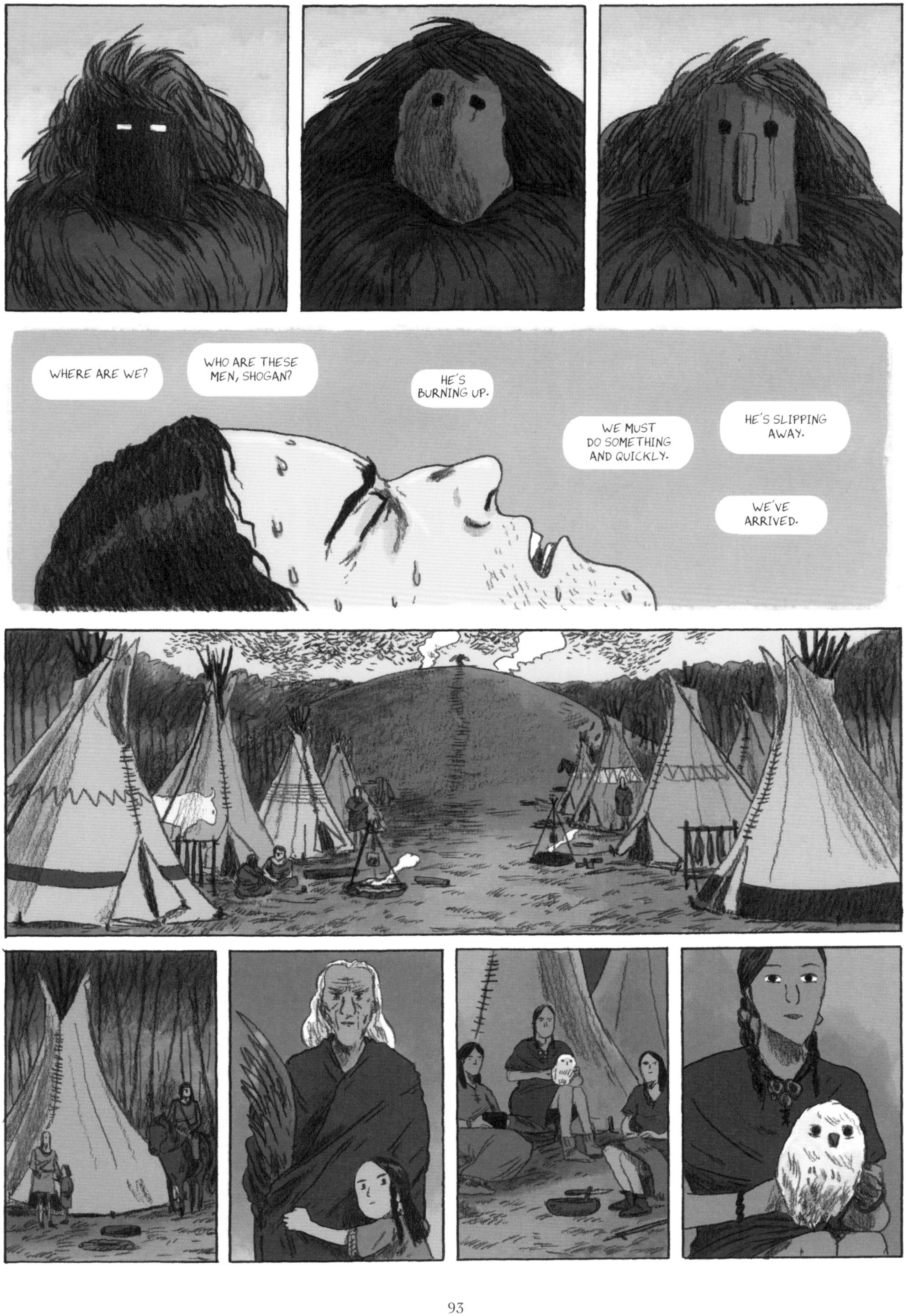
WHERE ARE WE?
WHO ARE THESE MEN, SHOGAN?
HE'S BURNING UP.
WE MUST DO SOMETHING AND QUICKLY.
HE'S SLIPPING AWAY.
WE'VE ARRIVED.

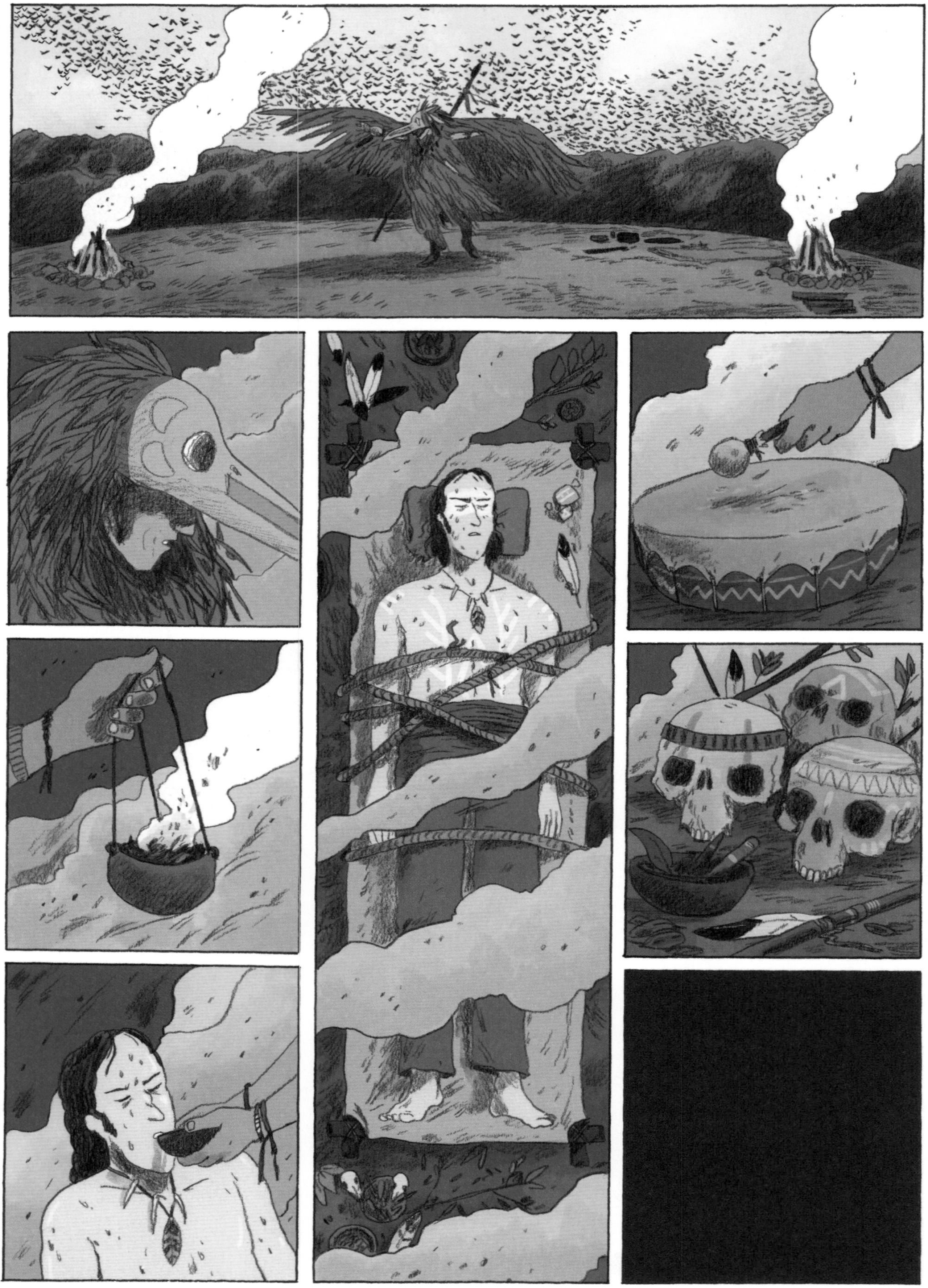

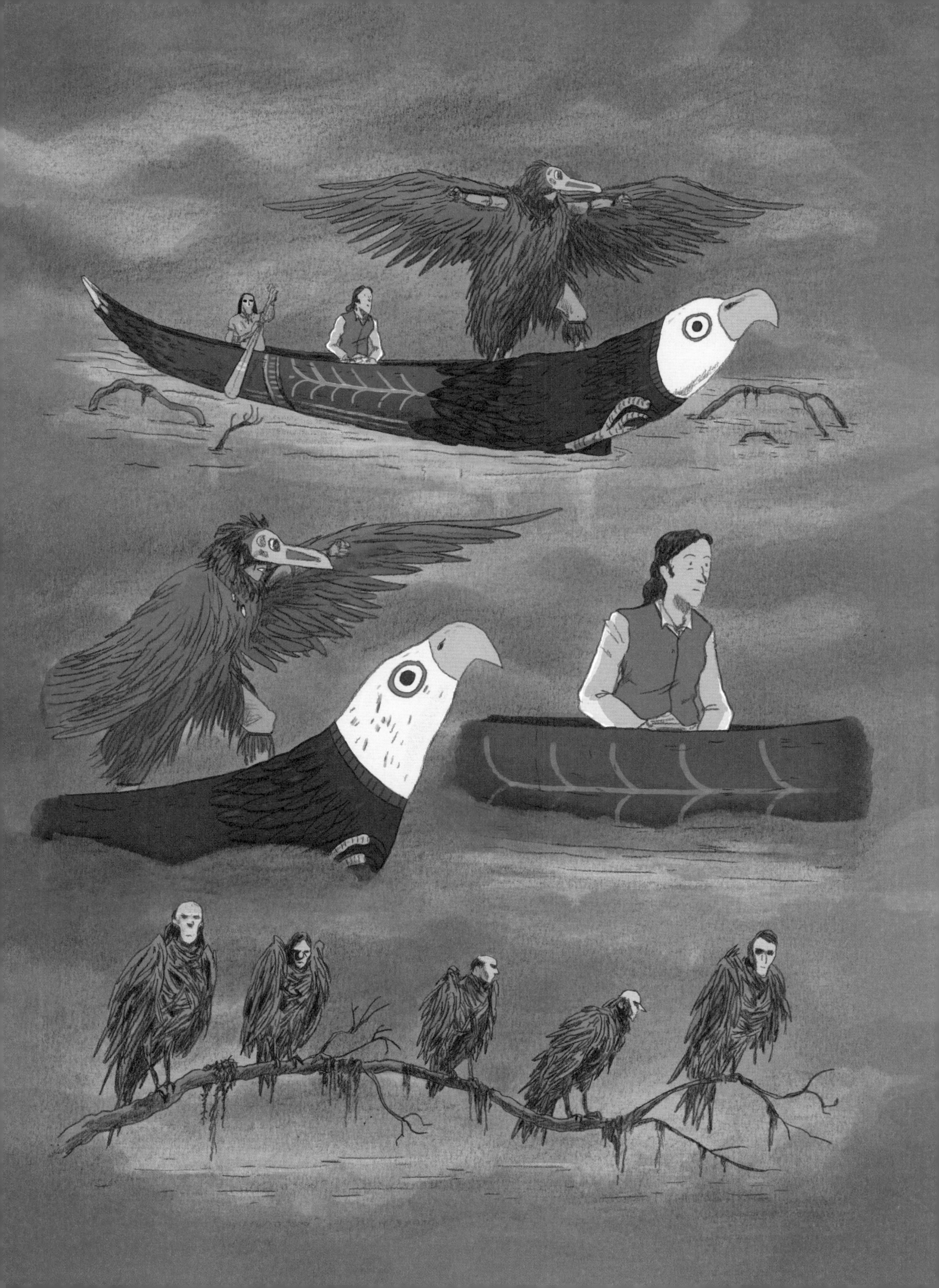

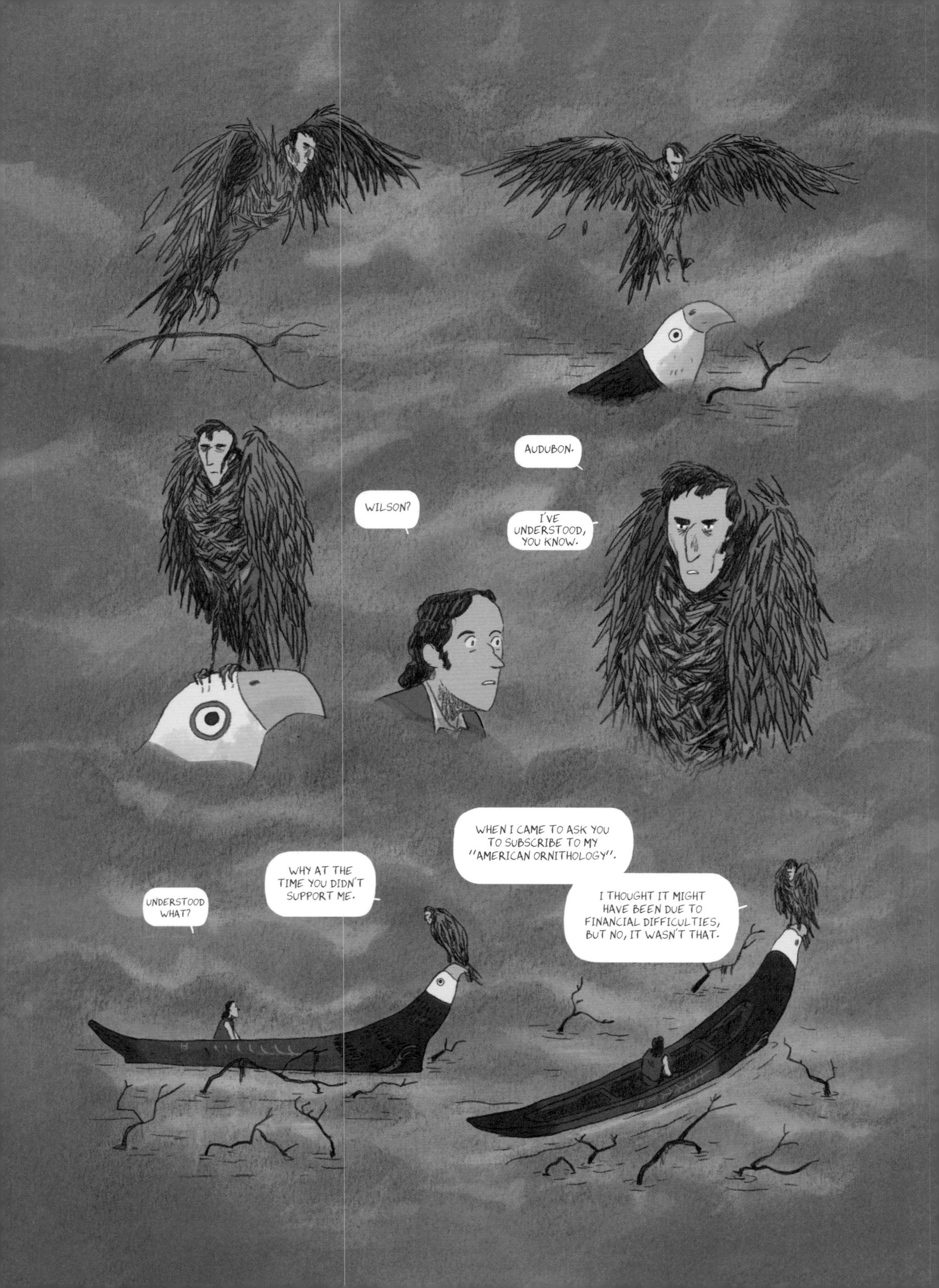
AUDUBON.
WILSON?
I'VE UNDERSTOOD, YOU KNOW.
UNDERSTOOD WHAT?
WHY AT THE TIME YOU DIDN'T SUPPORT ME.
WHEN I CAME TO ASK YOU TO SUBSCRIBE TO MY ''AMERICAN ORNITHOLOGY''.
I THOUGHT IT MIGHT HAVE BEEN DUE TO FINANCIAL DIFFICULTIES, BUT NO, IT WASN'T THAT.

THE TRUTH IS, YOU DIDN'T WANT THE BOOK TO SEE THE LIGHT OF DAY.
BECAUSE YOU WERE CONVINCED THAT YOUR DRAWINGS WERE BETTER, AM I MISTAKEN, AUDUBON?
NO, IT'S TRUE, YOU'RE RIGHT.
ONE DAY MY DRAWINGS WILL COME BACK TO HAUNT YOU. THEY'LL HAVE THE LAST LAUGH, AUDUBON.
"DRAWINGS"! AH, THIS DRAWING BUSINESS AGAIN, JEAN-JACQUES!
STILL DRAWING YOUR BLASTED BIRDS?
CONTENT YOURSELF WITH BIRDS ON A PLATE OR AT THE END OF YOUR RIFLE, SON.
YOU'RE TOO OLD TO BE RUNNING THROUGH FORESTS AS YOU ONCE DID AT LA GERBETIÈRE! GROW UP!
FATHER?
WHEN WILL YOU STOP WASTING YOUR LIFE ON THIS NONSENSE?
WAIT!
GET A MOVE ON! WE'RE WAITING FOR YOU.
WHO'S THERE? WHO'S AT THE HOUSE, FATHER?

WHO... WHO ARE YOU?
OH, MY GOD!
IT'S IMPOSSIBLE?! LUCY? IS IT YOU, MY DARLING LUCY?
AND YOU, YOU ARE MY SWEET... ROSE, NO?
HOW YOU'VE...
GROWN...
IF YOU ONLY KNEW HOW MUCH WE'VE MISSED YOU...
NOT A DAY GOES BY WITHOUT YOUR MOTHER THINKING ABOUT YOU... I...
HOW SHE WOULD HAVE LOVED TO HAVE KNOWN YOU...
ARE YOU COMING?
ADIEU, MY DARLINGS!
IT'S MADE ME SO HAPPY TO HAVE SEEN YOU SO...
...ALIVE.

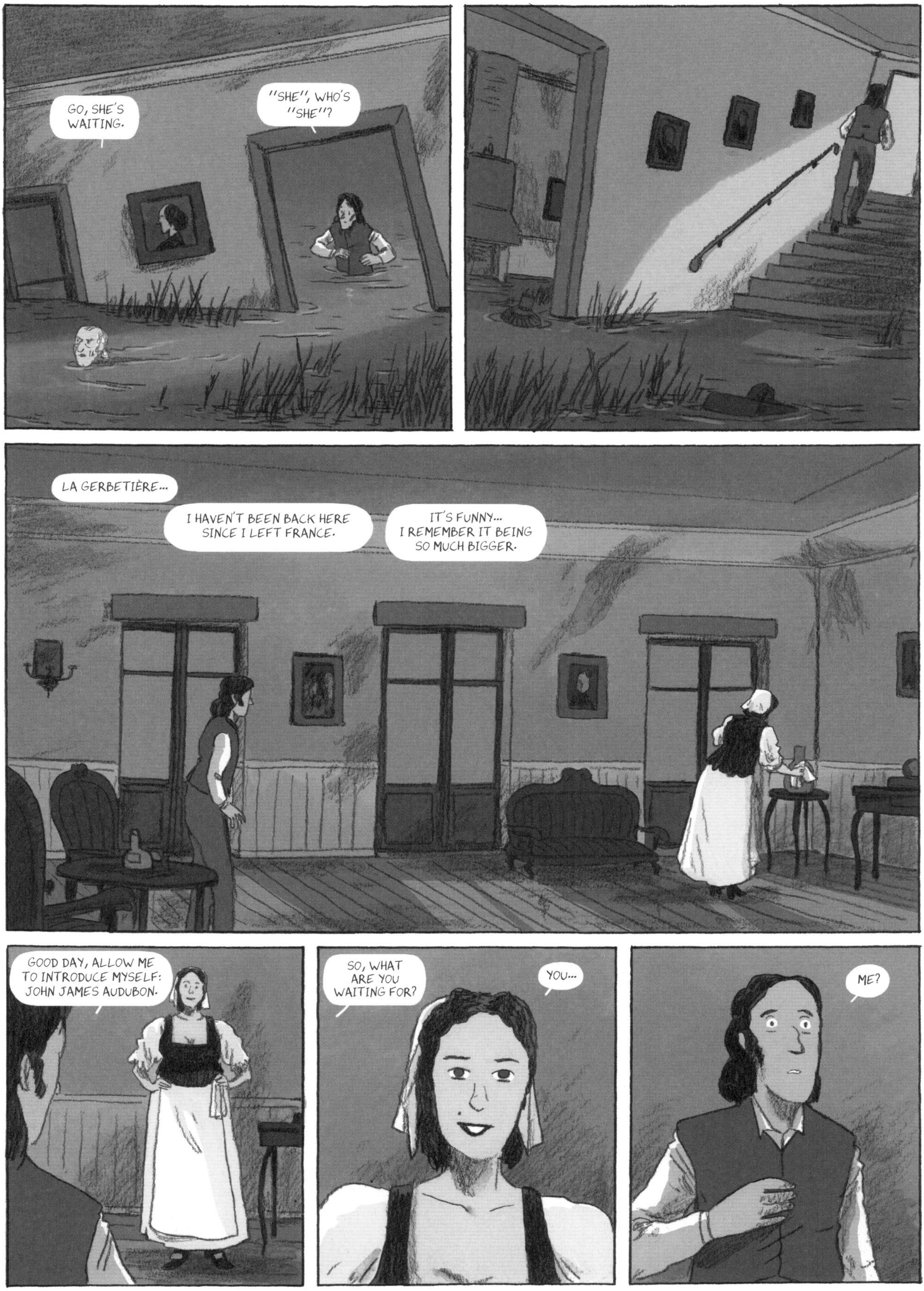
GO, SHE'S WAITING.
"SHE", WHO'S "SHE"?
LA GERBETIÈRE...
I HAVEN'T BEEN BACK HERE SINCE I LEFT FRANCE.
IT'S FUNNY... I REMEMBER IT BEING SO MUCH BIGGER.
GOOD DAY, ALLOW ME TO INTRODUCE MYSELF: JOHN JAMES AUDUBON.
SO, WHAT ARE YOU WAITING FOR?
YOU...
ME?

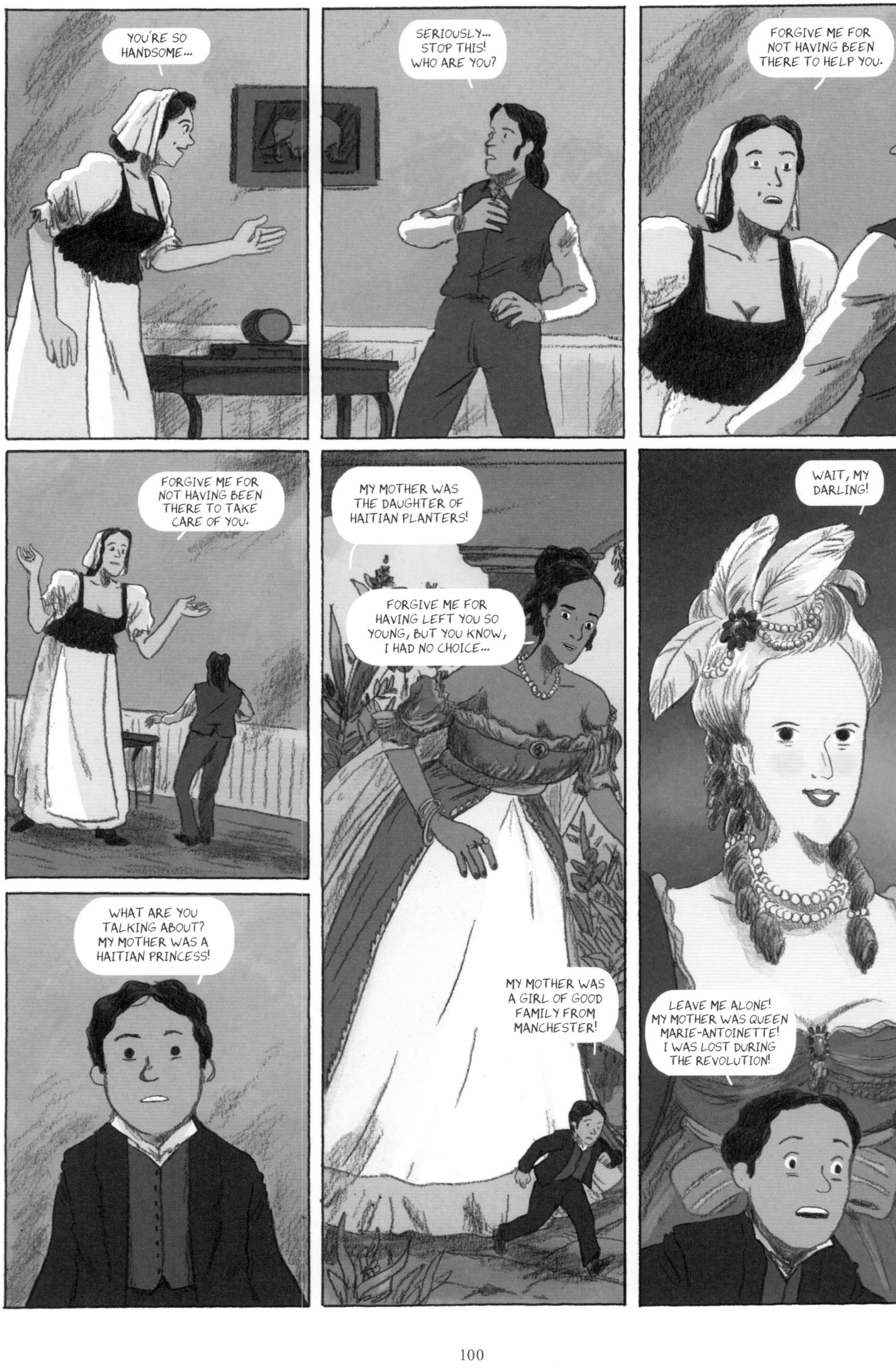
YOU'RE SO HANDSOME...
SERIOUSLY... STOP THIS! WHO ARE YOU?
FORGIVE ME FOR NOT HAVING BEEN THERE TO HELP YOU.
FORGIVE ME FOR NOT HAVING BEEN THERE TO TAKE CARE OF YOU.
WHAT ARE YOU TALKING ABOUT? MY MOTHER WAS A HAITIAN PRINCESS!
MY MOTHER WAS THE DAUGHTER OF HAITIAN PLANTERS!
FORGIVE ME FOR HAVING LEFT YOU SO YOUNG, BUT YOU KNOW, I HAD NO CHOICE...
MY MOTHER WAS A GIRL OF GOOD FAMILY FROM MANCHESTER!
WAIT, MY DARLING!
LEAVE ME ALONE! MY MOTHER WAS QUEEN MARIE-ANTOINETTE! I WAS LOST DURING THE REVOLUTION!

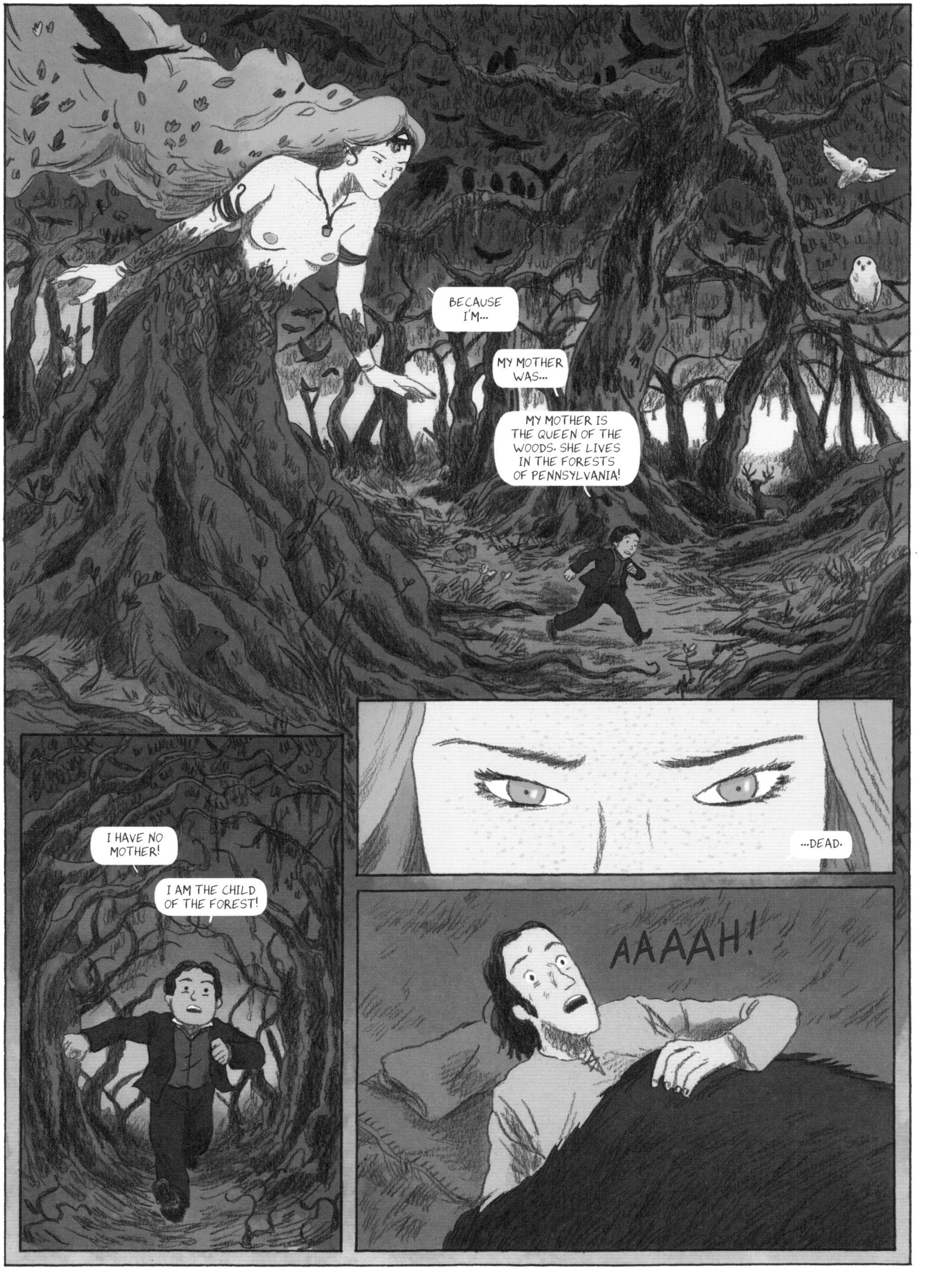

BECAUSE I'M...
MY MOTHER WAS...
MY MOTHER IS THE QUEEN OF THE WOODS. SHE LIVES IN THE FORESTS OF PENNSYLVANIA!
I HAVE NO MOTHER!
I AM THE CHILD OF THE FOREST!
...DEAD.
AAAAH!

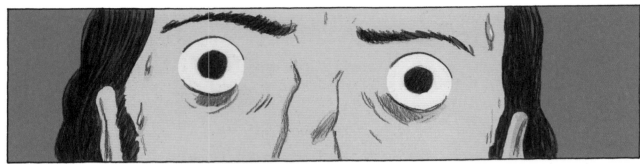

YOUR FEVER
HAS SUBSIDED,
SIR?

MY DRAWINGS!

EVERYTHING'S
FINE, SIR,
CALM DOWN!

JOSEPH, YOU MUSTN'T
LET THEM TAKE
MY DRAWINGS!

KOF KOF
KOF !

KOF KOF
KOF !

KOF KOF
KOF !

KOF
KOF !

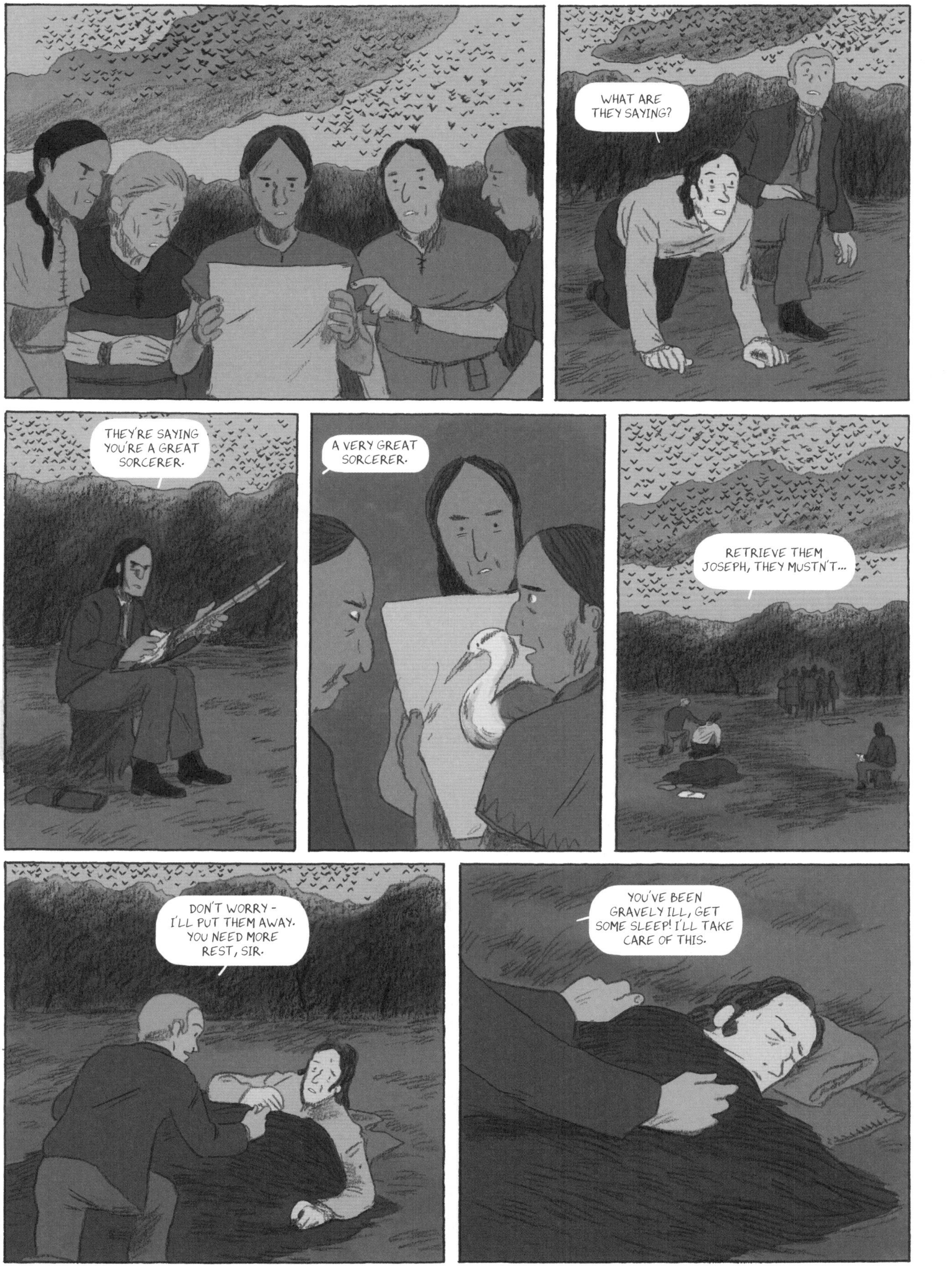
WHAT ARE THEY SAYING?
THEY'RE SAYING YOU'RE A GREAT SORCERER.
A VERY GREAT SORCERER.
RETRIEVE THEM JOSEPH, THEY MUSTN'T...
DON'T WORRY - I'LL PUT THEM AWAY. YOU NEED MORE REST, SIR.
YOU'VE BEEN GRAVELY ILL, GET SOME SLEEP! I'LL TAKE CARE OF THIS.

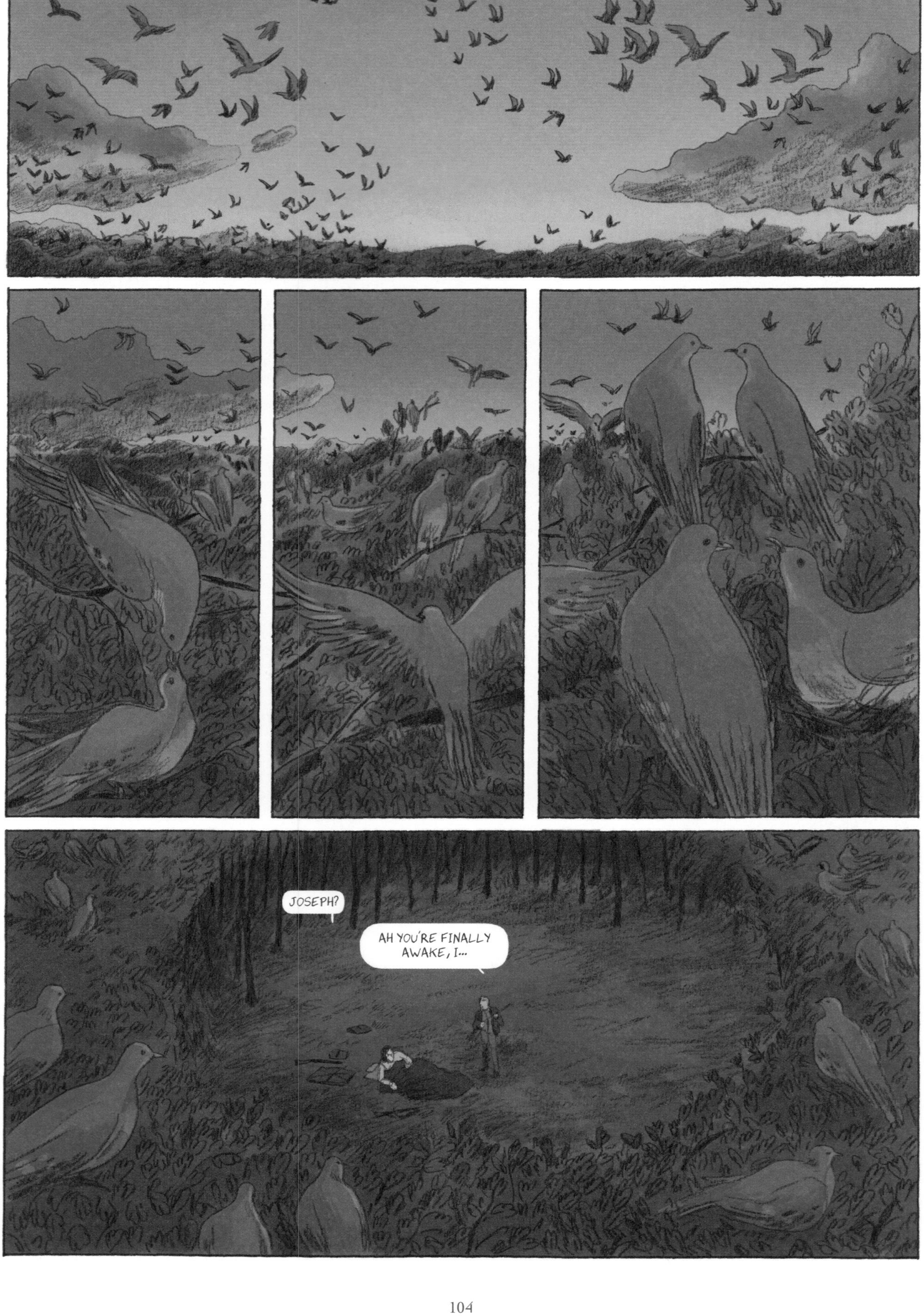
JOSEPH?
AH YOU'RE FINALLY AWAKE, I...

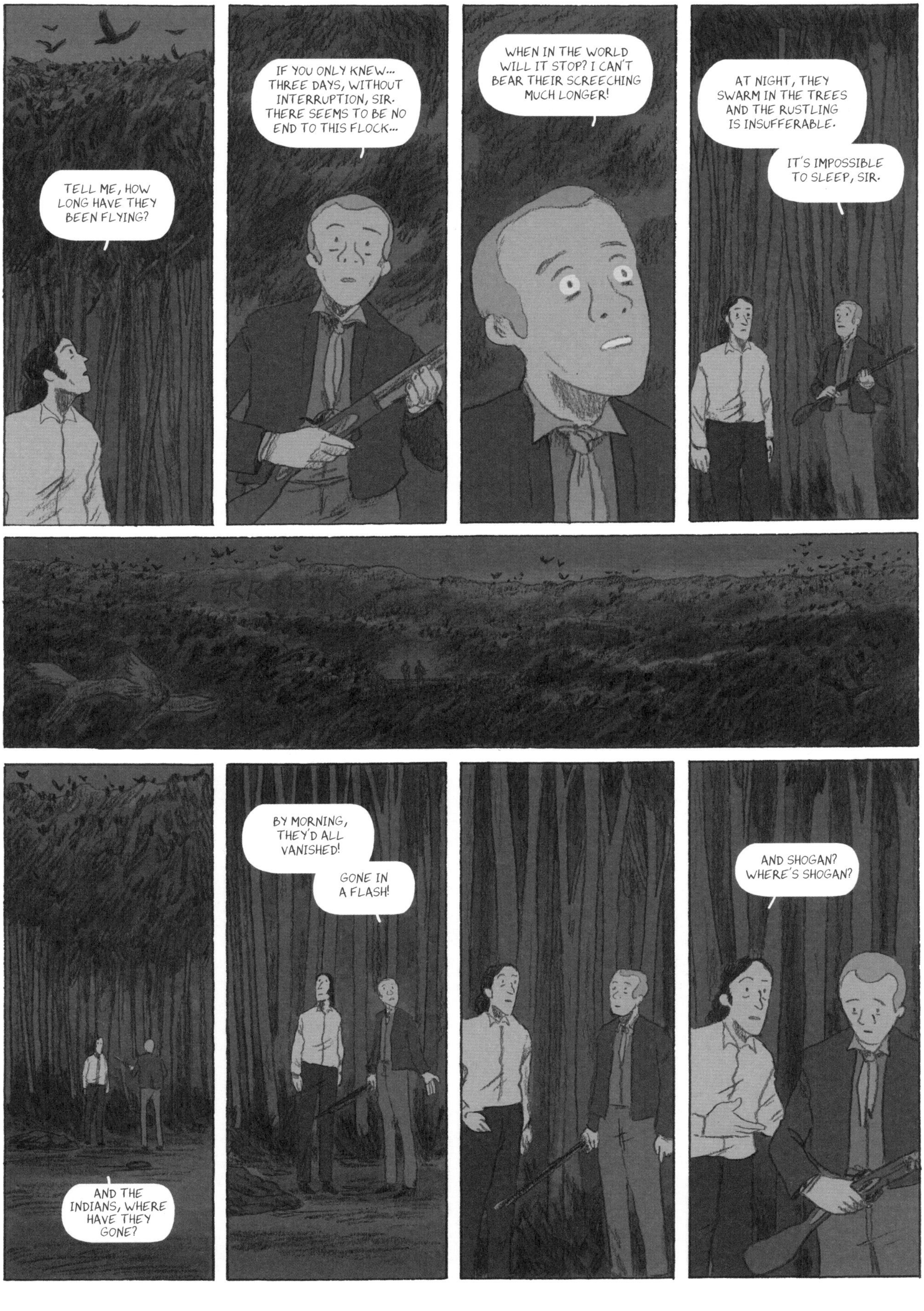
TELL ME, HOW LONG HAVE THEY BEEN FLYING?
IF YOU ONLY KNEW... THREE DAYS, WITHOUT INTERRUPTION, SIR. THERE SEEMS TO BE NO END TO THIS FLOCK...
WHEN IN THE WORLD WILL IT STOP? I CAN'T BEAR THEIR SCREECHING MUCH LONGER!
AT NIGHT, THEY SWARM IN THE TREES AND THE RUSTLING IS INSUFFERABLE.
IT'S IMPOSSIBLE TO SLEEP, SIR.
AND THE INDIANS, WHERE HAVE THEY GONE?
BY MORNING, THEY'D ALL VANISHED!
GONE IN A FLASH!
AND SHOGAN? WHERE'S SHOGAN?

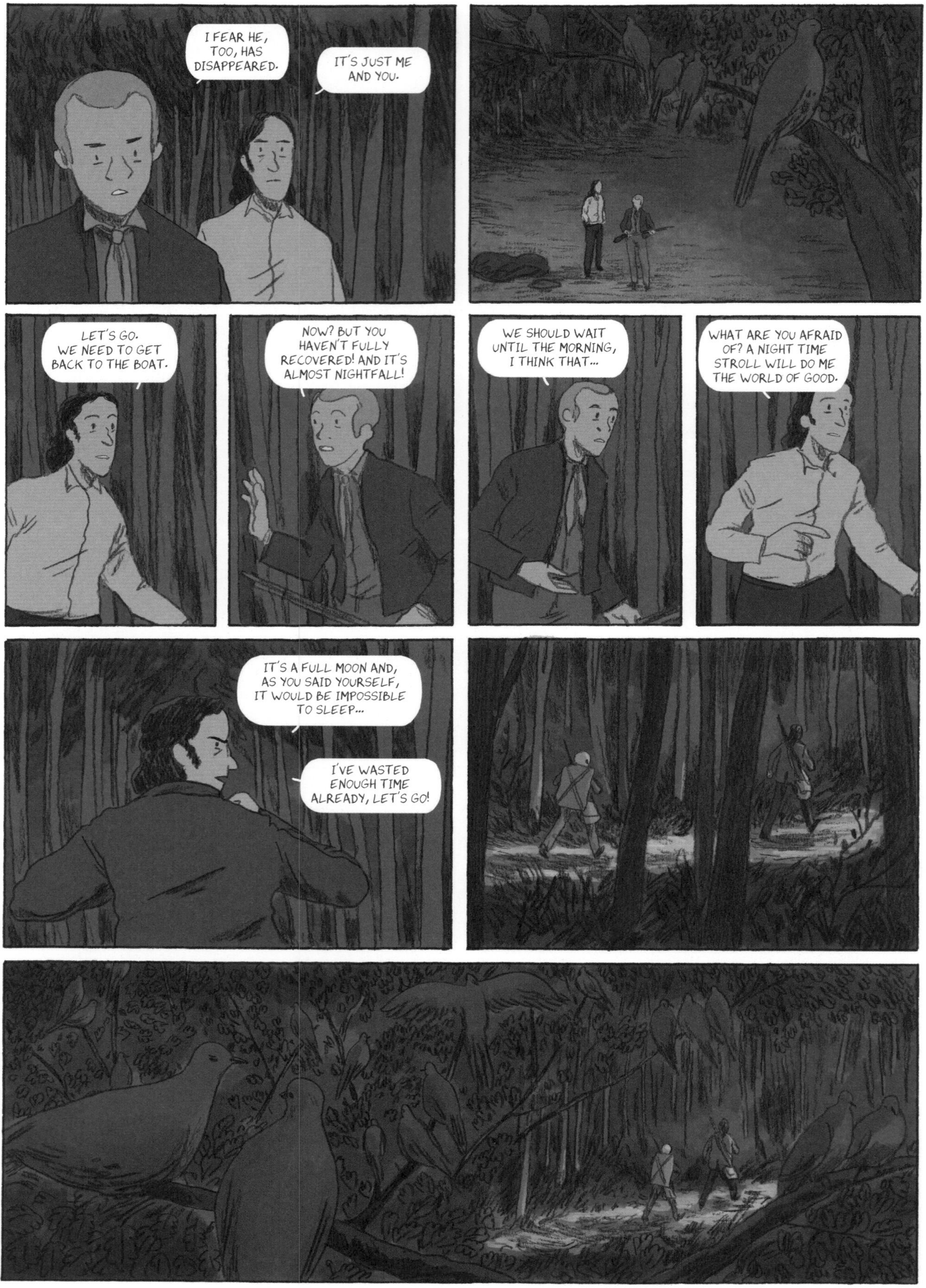
I FEAR HE, TOO, HAS DISAPPEARED.
IT'S JUST ME AND YOU.
LET'S GO. WE NEED TO GET BACK TO THE BOAT.
NOW? BUT YOU HAVEN'T FULLY RECOVERED! AND IT'S ALMOST NIGHTFALL!
WE SHOULD WAIT UNTIL THE MORNING, I THINK THAT...
WHAT ARE YOU AFRAID OF? A NIGHT TIME STROLL WILL DO ME THE WORLD OF GOOD.
IT'S A FULL MOON AND, AS YOU SAID YOURSELF, IT WOULD BE IMPOSSIBLE TO SLEEP...
I'VE WASTED ENOUGH TIME ALREADY, LET'S GO!

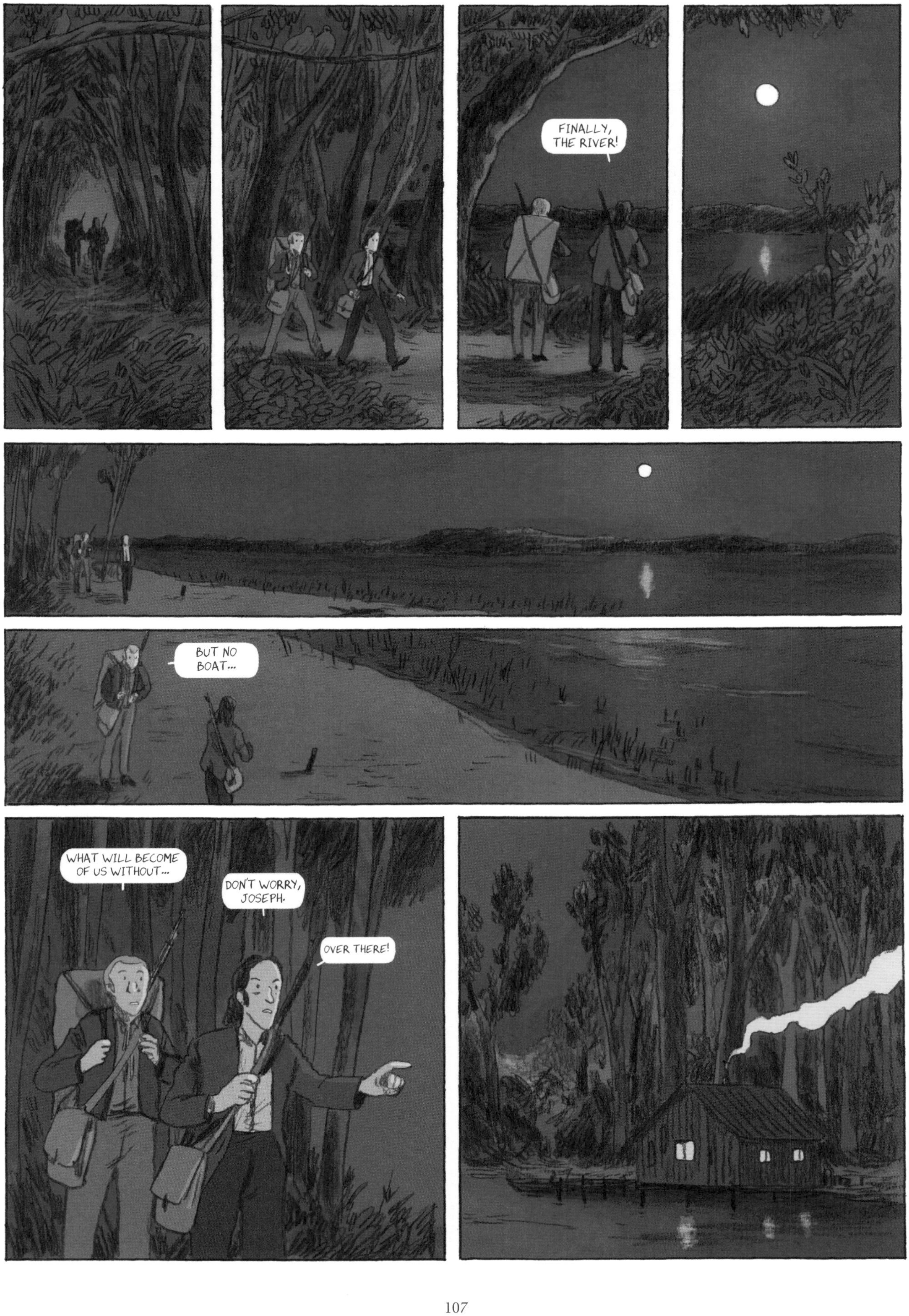

FINALLY, THE RIVER!
BUT NO BOAT...
WHAT WILL BECOME OF US WITHOUT...
DON'T WORRY, JOSEPH.
OVER THERE!

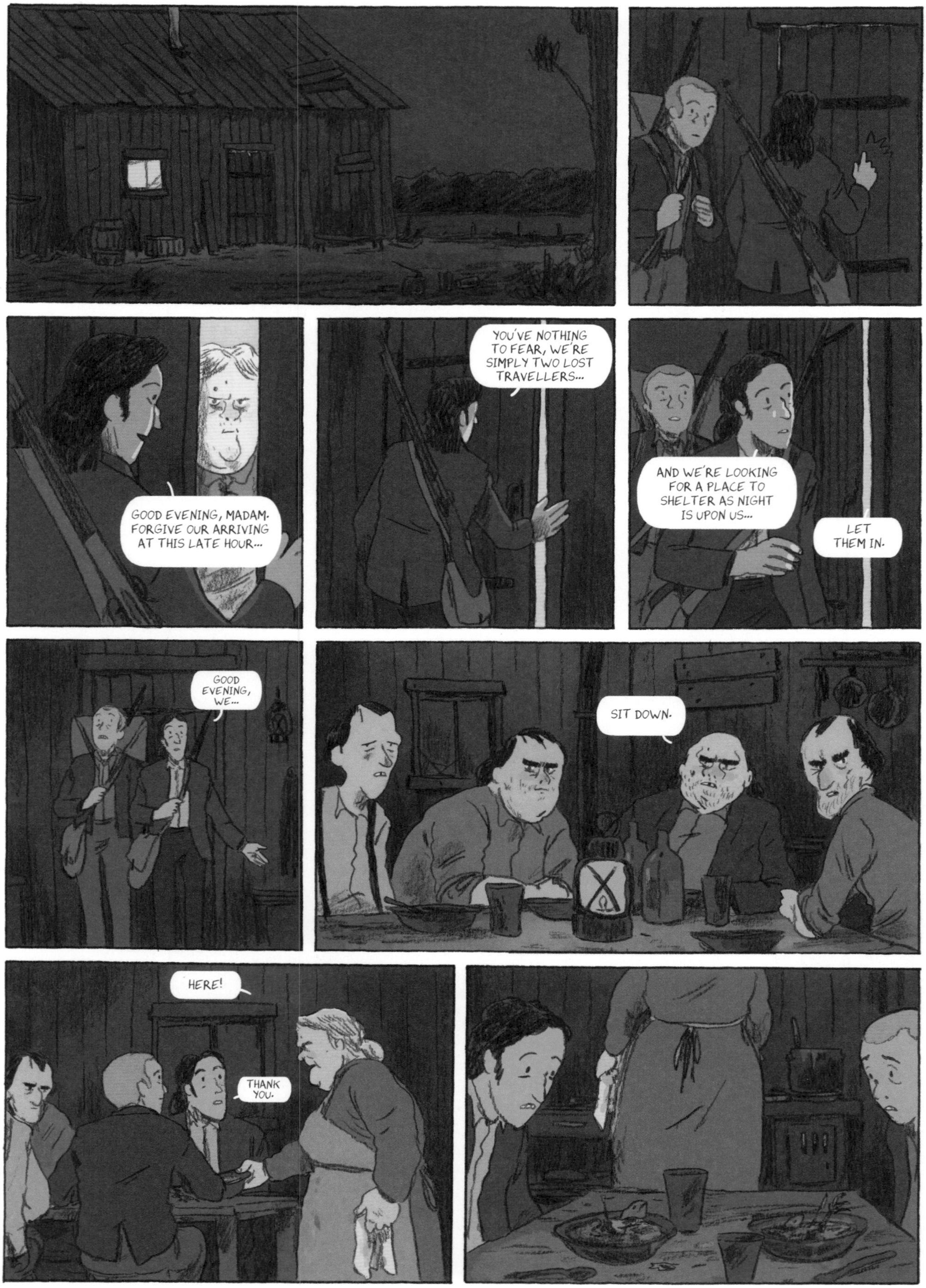
GOOD EVENING, MADAM. FORGIVE OUR ARRIVING AT THIS LATE HOUR...
YOU'VE NOTHING TO FEAR, WE'RE SIMPLY TWO LOST TRAVELLERS...
AND WE'RE LOOKING FOR A PLACE TO SHELTER AS NIGHT IS UPON US...
LET THEM IN.
GOOD EVENING, WE...
SIT DOWN.
HERE!
THANK YOU.

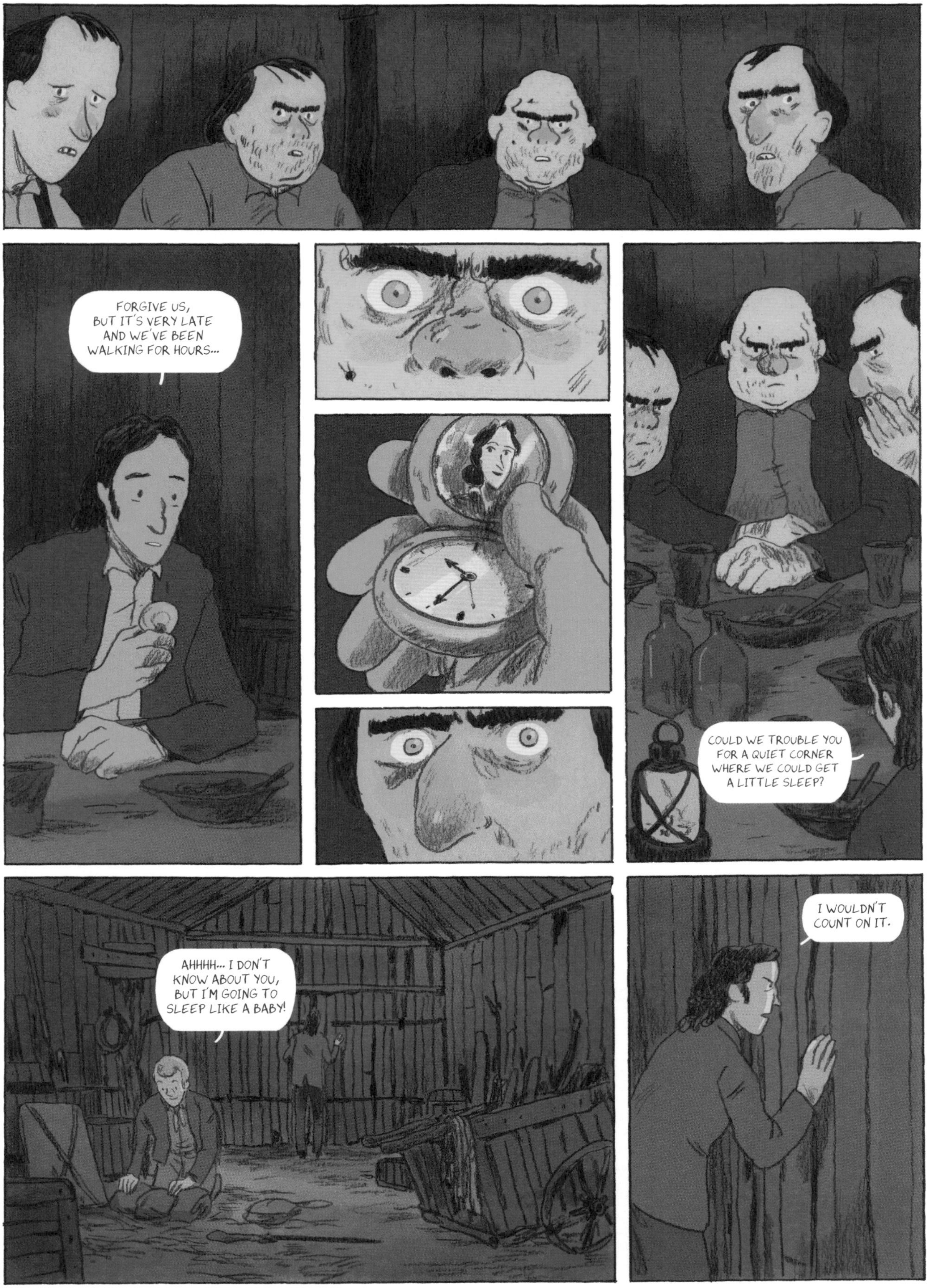
FORGIVE US, BUT IT'S VERY LATE AND WE'VE BEEN WALKING FOR HOURS...
COULD WE TROUBLE YOU FOR A QUIET CORNER WHERE WE COULD GET A LITTLE SLEEP?
AHHHH... I DON'T KNOW ABOUT YOU, BUT I'M GOING TO SLEEP LIKE A BABY!
I WOULDN'T COUNT ON IT.

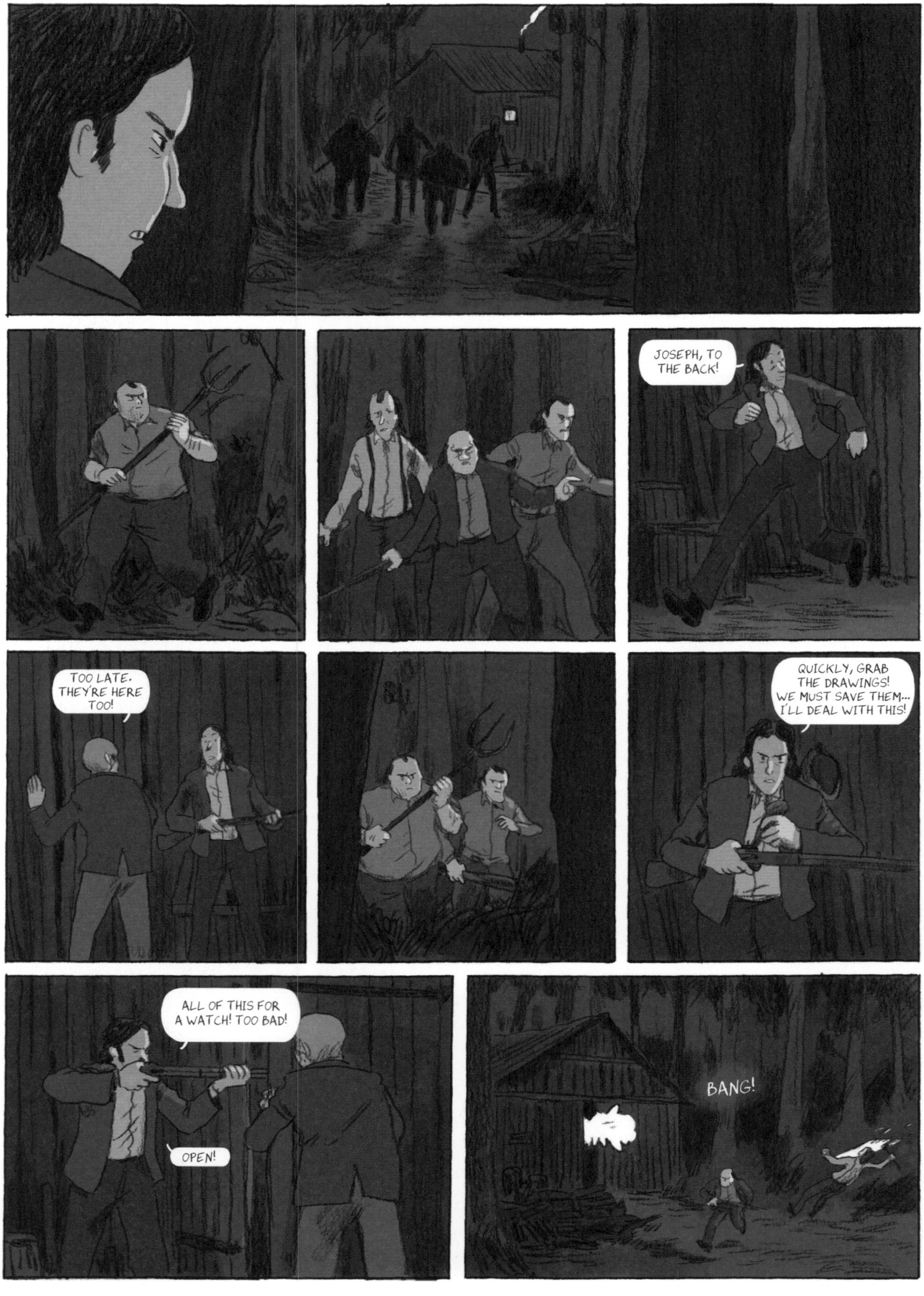
JOSEPH, TO THE BACK!
TOO LATE. THEY'RE HERE TOO!
QUICKLY, GRAB THE DRAWINGS! WE MUST SAVE THEM... I'LL DEAL WITH THIS!
ALL OF THIS FOR A WATCH! TOO BAD!
OPEN!
BANG!

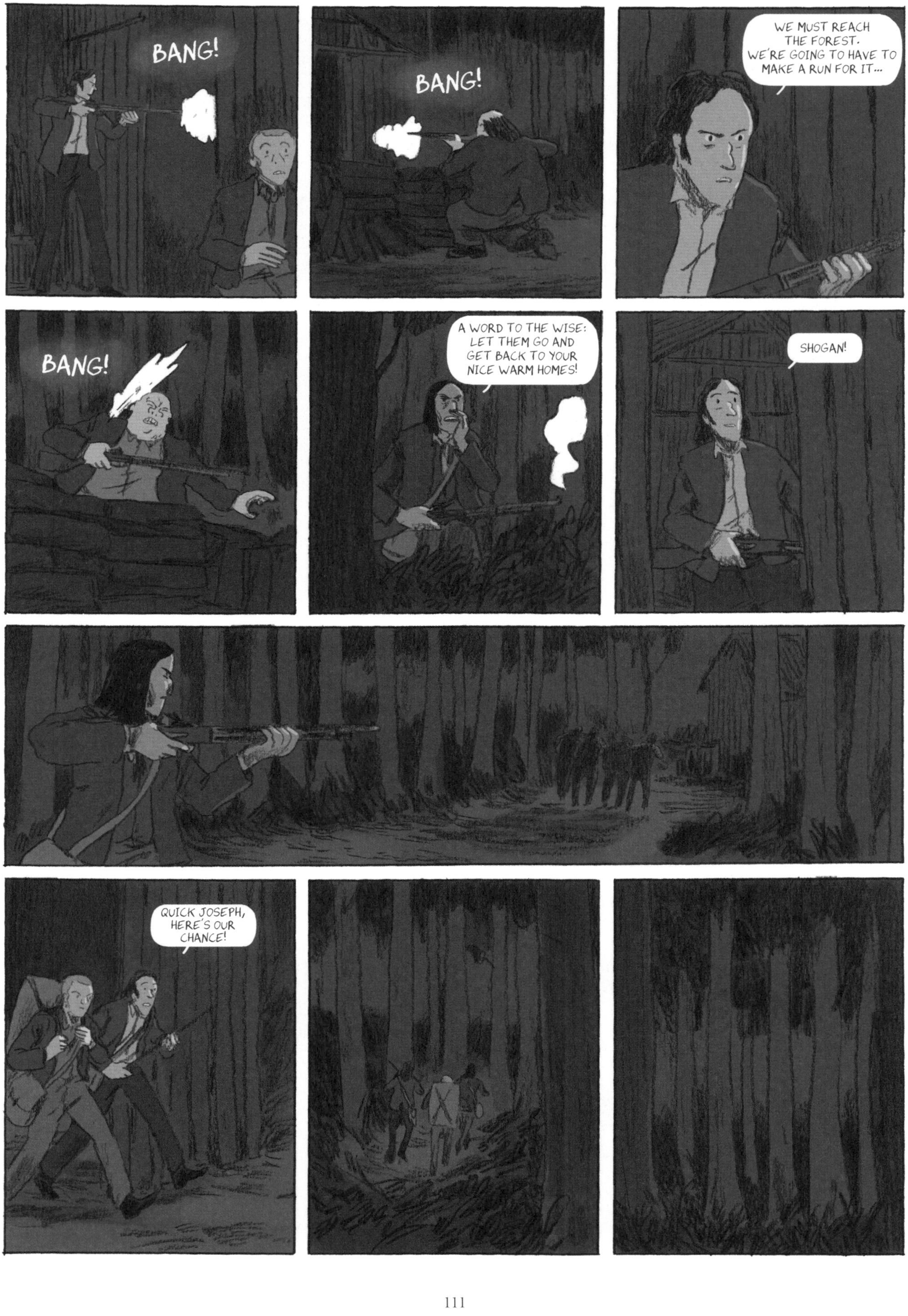
BANG!
BANG!
WE MUST REACH THE FOREST. WE'RE GOING TO HAVE TO MAKE A RUN FOR IT...
BANG!
A WORD TO THE WISE: LET THEM GO AND GET BACK TO YOUR NICE WARM HOMES!
SHOGAN!
QUICK JOSEPH, HERE'S OUR CHANCE!

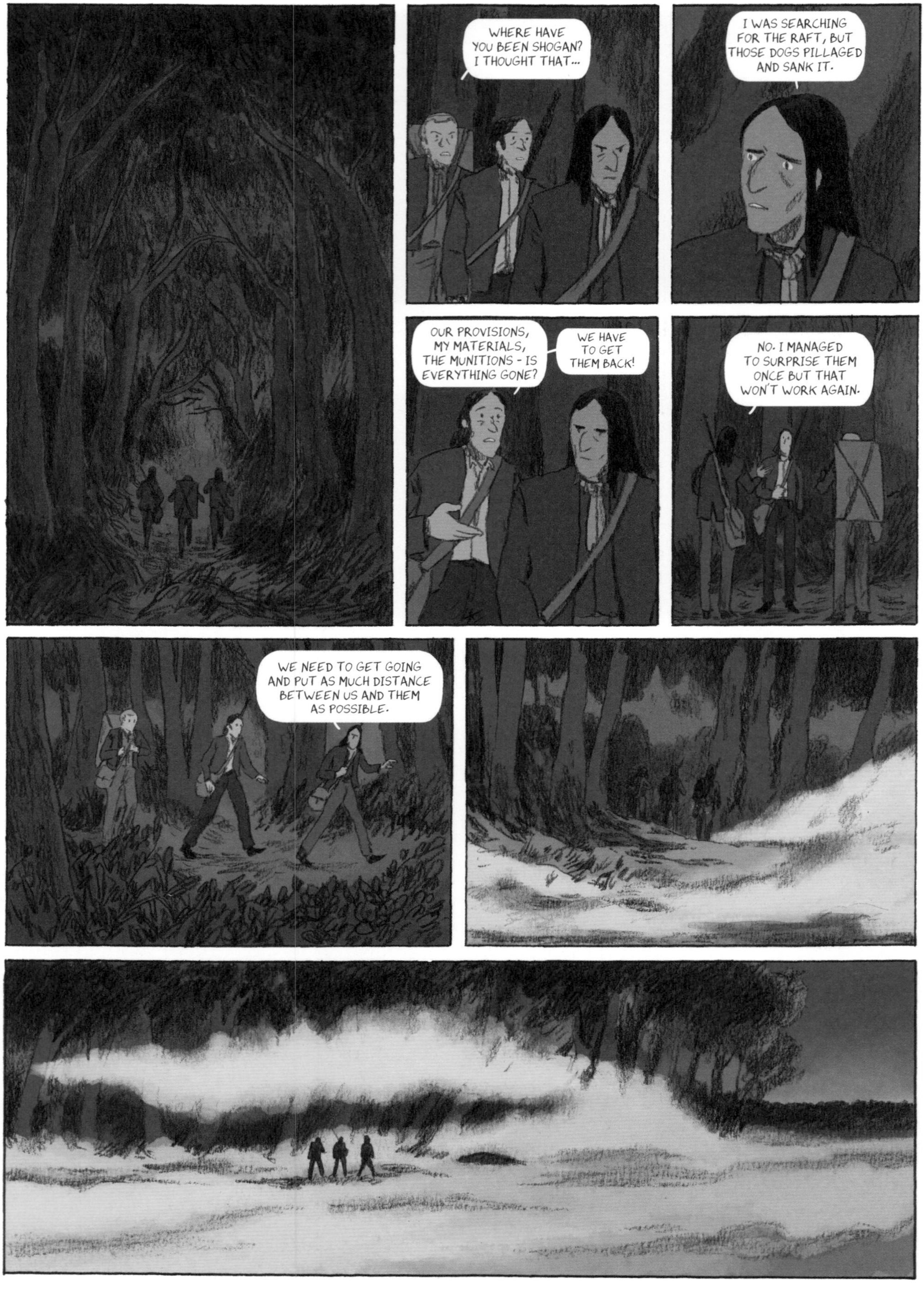
WHERE HAVE YOU BEEN SHOGAN? I THOUGHT THAT...
I WAS SEARCHING FOR THE RAFT, BUT THOSE DOGS PILLAGED AND SANK IT.
OUR PROVISIONS, MY MATERIALS, THE MUNITIONS - IS EVERYTHING GONE?
WE HAVE TO GET THEM BACK!
NO. I MANAGED TO SURPRISE THEM ONCE BUT THAT WON'T WORK AGAIN.
WE NEED TO GET GOING AND PUT AS MUCH DISTANCE BETWEEN US AND THEM AS POSSIBLE.

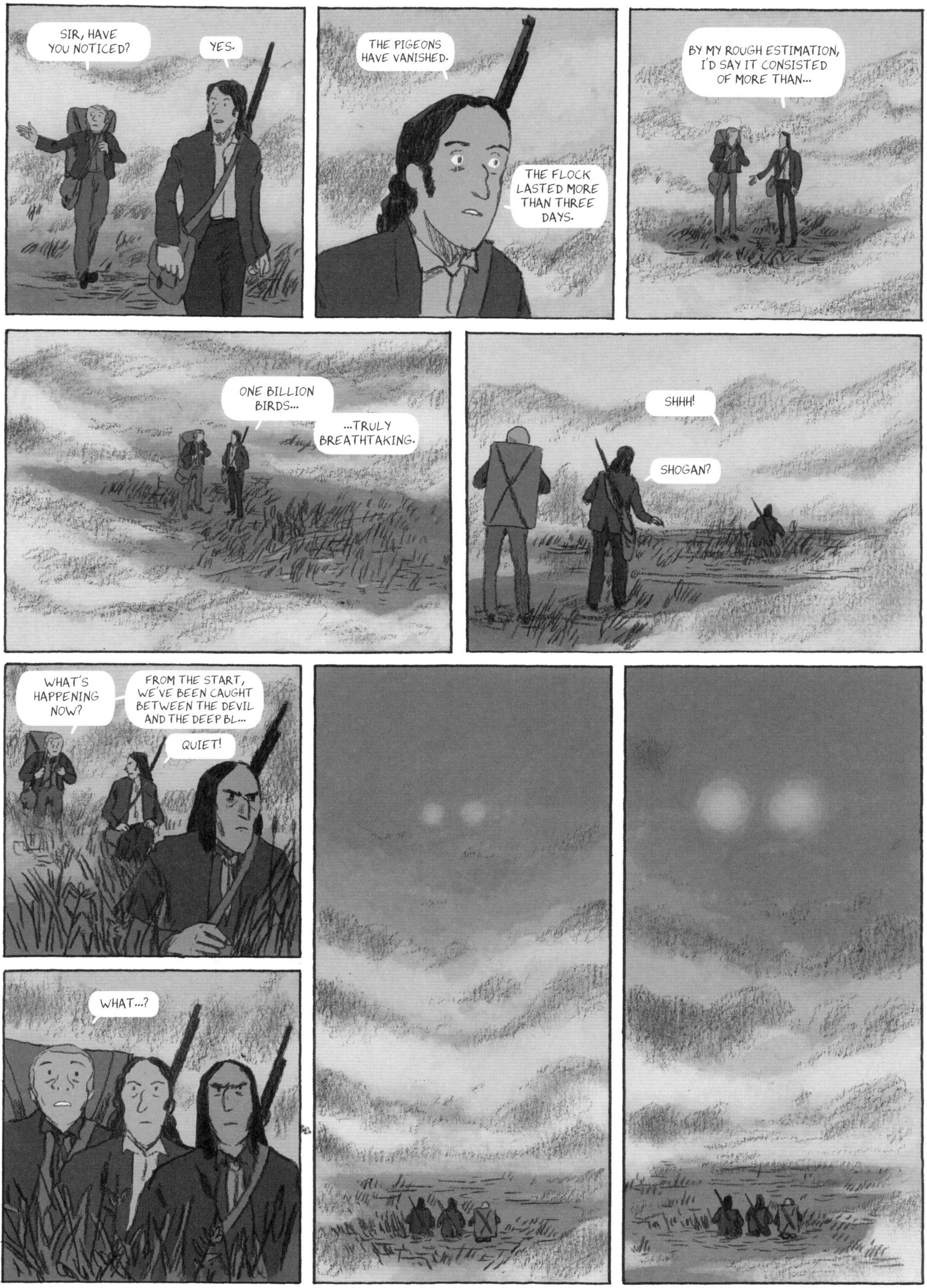
SIR, HAVE YOU NOTICED?
YES.
THE PIGEONS HAVE VANISHED.
THE FLOCK LASTED MORE THAN THREE DAYS.
BY MY ROUGH ESTIMATION, I'D SAY IT CONSISTED OF MORE THAN...
ONE BILLION BIRDS...
...TRULY BREATHTAKING.
SHHH!
SHOGAN?
WHAT'S HAPPENING NOW?
FROM THE START, WE'VE BEEN CAUGHT BETWEEN THE DEVIL AND THE DEEP BL...
QUIET!
WHAT...?

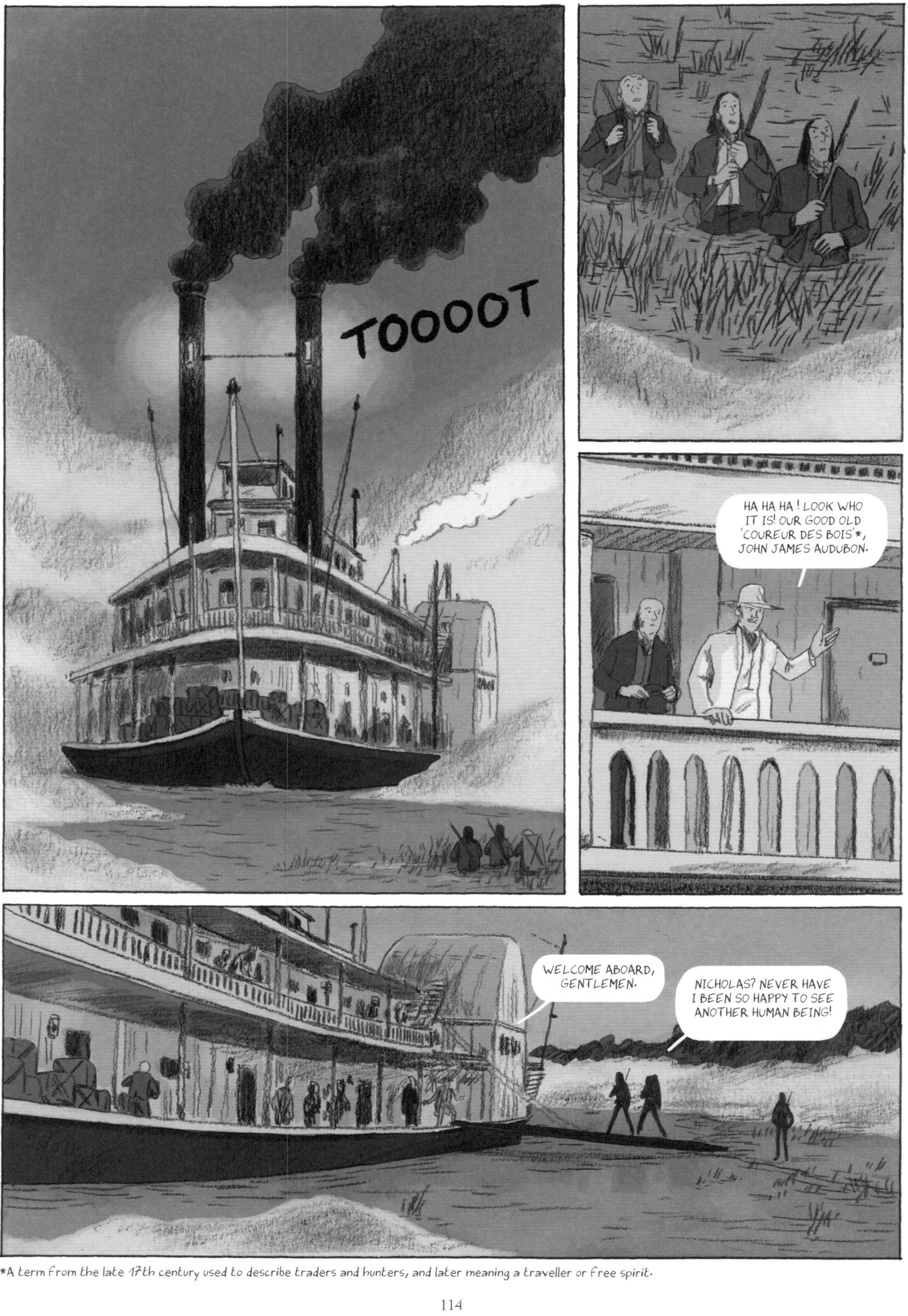
TOOOOT
HA HA HA ! LOOK WHO IT IS! OUR GOOD OLD 'COUREUR DES BOIS'*, JOHN JAMES AUDUBON.
WELCOME ABOARD, GENTLEMEN.
NICHOLAS? NEVER HAVE I BEEN SO HAPPY TO SEE ANOTHER HUMAN BEING!

*A term from the late 17th century used to describe traders and hunters, and later meaning a traveller or free spirit.

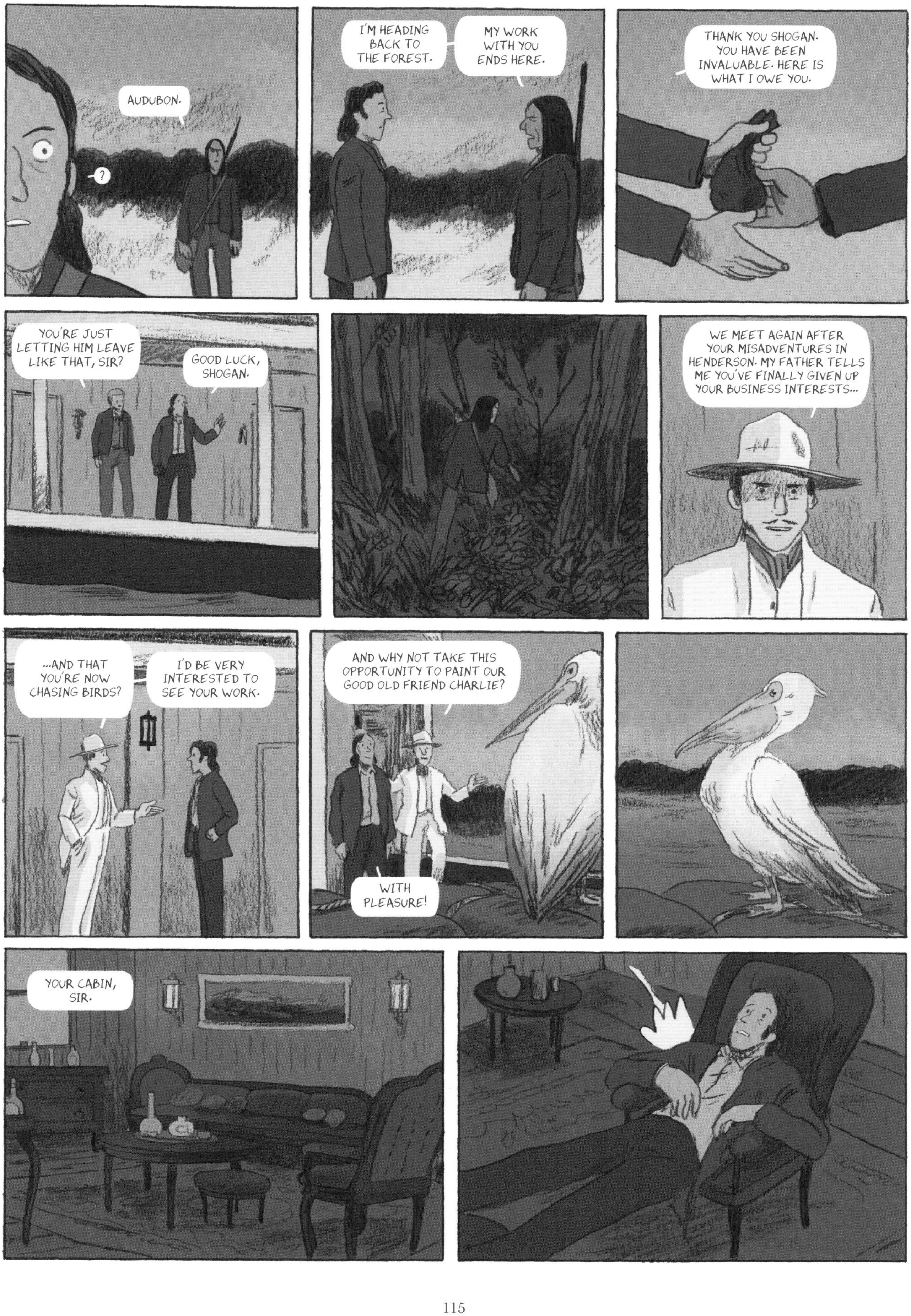

AUDUBON.
?
I'M HEADING BACK TO THE FOREST.
MY WORK WITH YOU ENDS HERE.
THANK YOU SHOGAN. YOU HAVE BEEN INVALUABLE. HERE IS WHAT I OWE YOU.
YOU'RE JUST LETTING HIM LEAVE LIKE THAT, SIR?
GOOD LUCK, SHOGAN.
WE MEET AGAIN AFTER YOUR MISADVENTURES IN HENDERSON. MY FATHER TELLS ME YOU'VE FINALLY GIVEN UP YOUR BUSINESS INTERESTS...
...AND THAT YOU'RE NOW CHASING BIRDS?
I'D BE VERY INTERESTED TO SEE YOUR WORK.
AND WHY NOT TAKE THIS OPPORTUNITY TO PAINT OUR GOOD OLD FRIEND CHARLIE?
WITH PLEASURE!
YOUR CABIN, SIR.

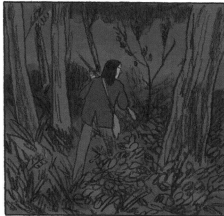

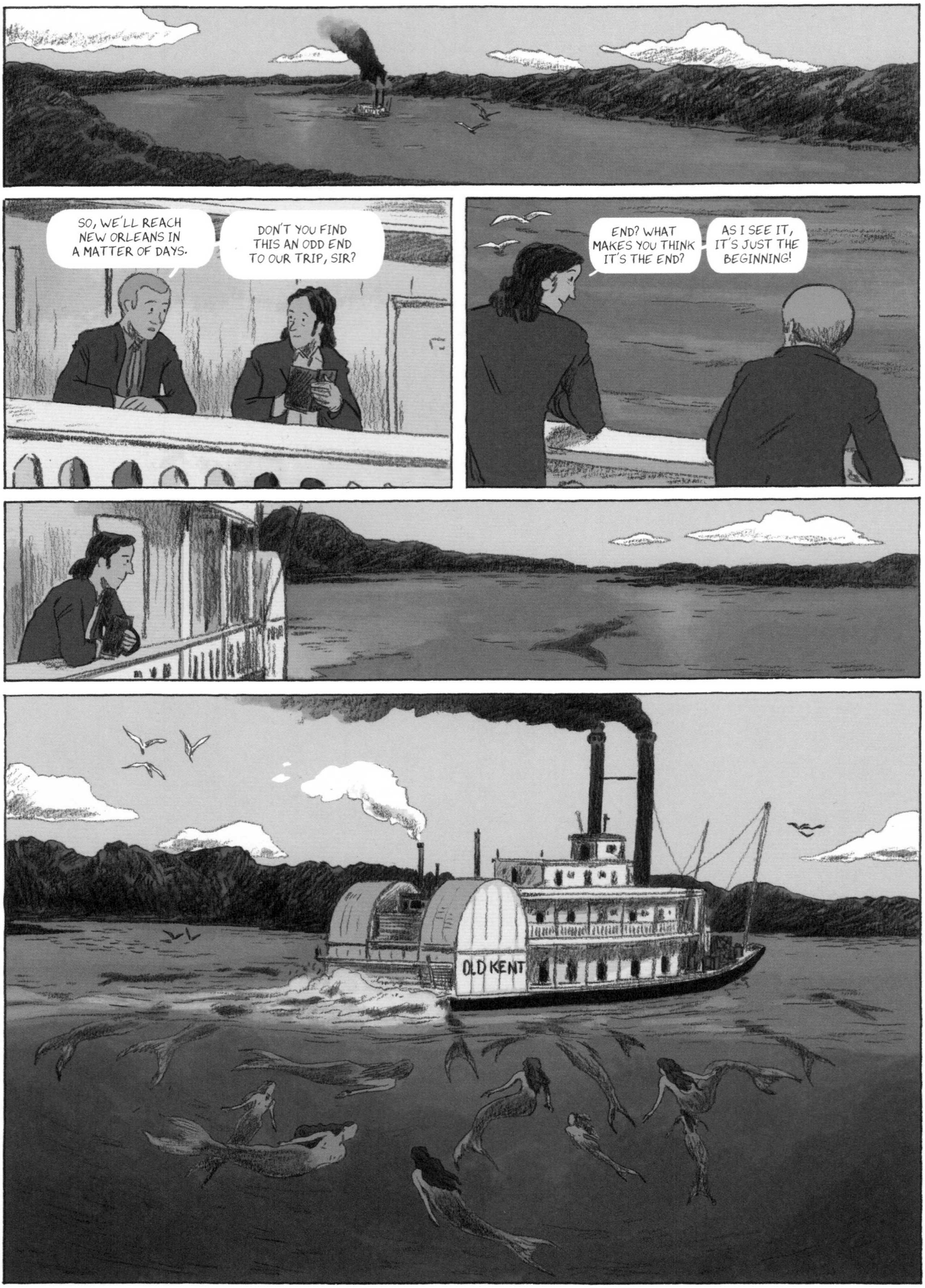
SO, WE'LL REACH NEW ORLEANS IN A MATTER OF DAYS.
DON'T YOU FIND THIS AN ODD END TO OUR TRIP, SIR?
END? WHAT MAKES YOU THINK IT'S THE END?
AS I SEE IT, IT'S JUST THE BEGINNING!
OLD KENT

·III· NEW ORLEANS

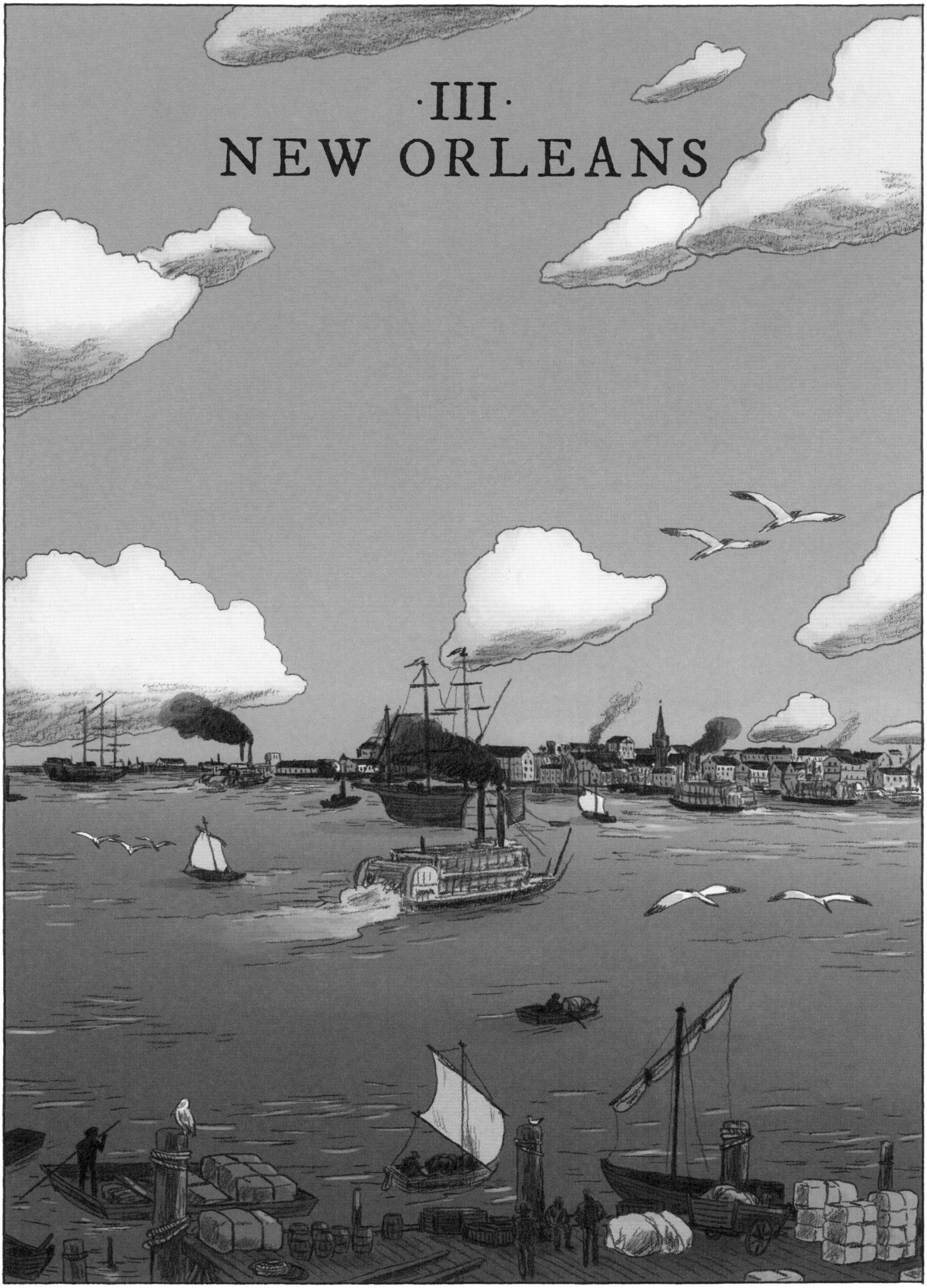

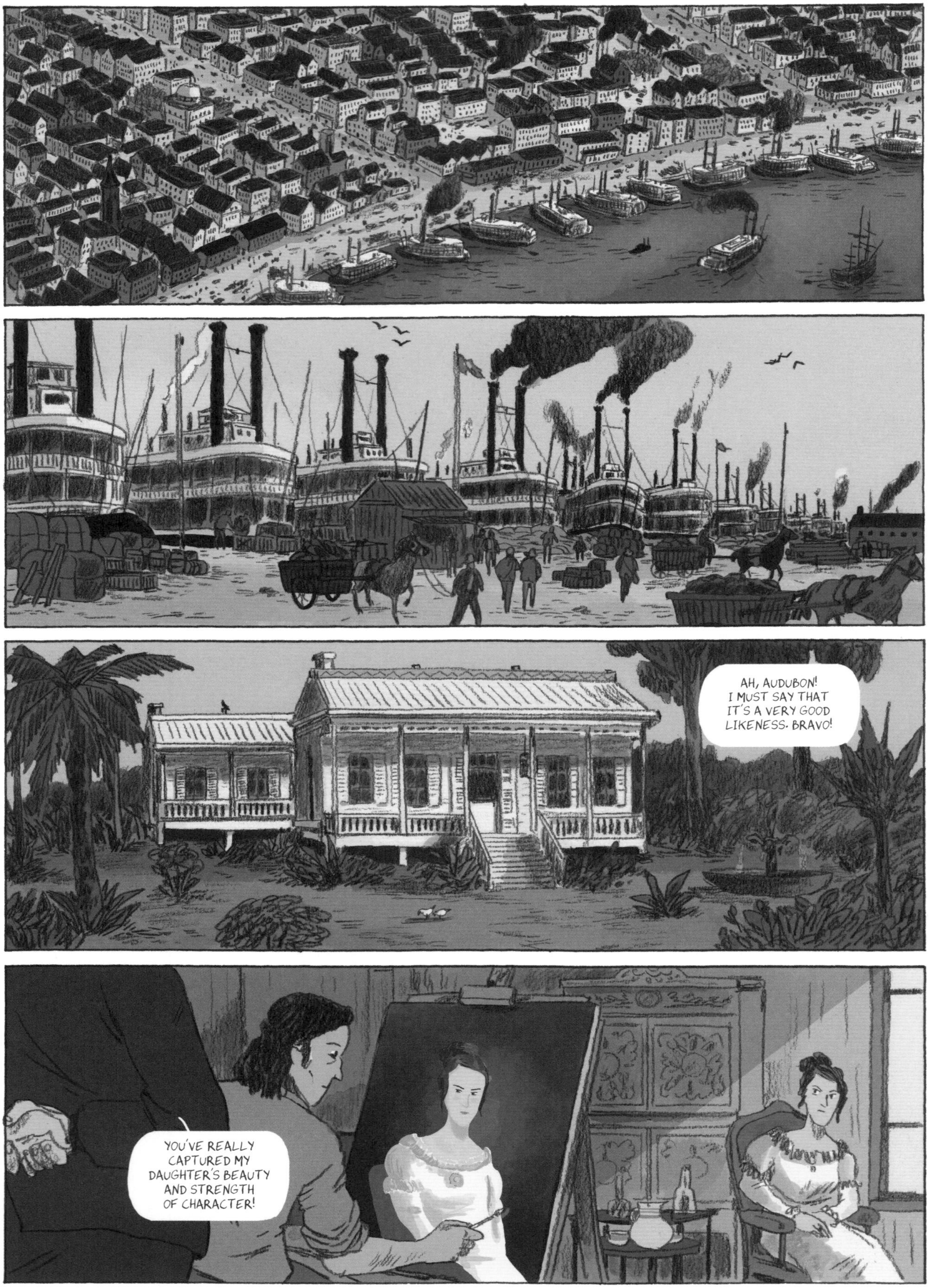
AH, AUDUBON! I MUST SAY THAT IT'S A VERY GOOD LIKENESS. BRAVO!
YOU'VE REALLY CAPTURED MY DAUGHTER'S BEAUTY AND STRENGTH OF CHARACTER!

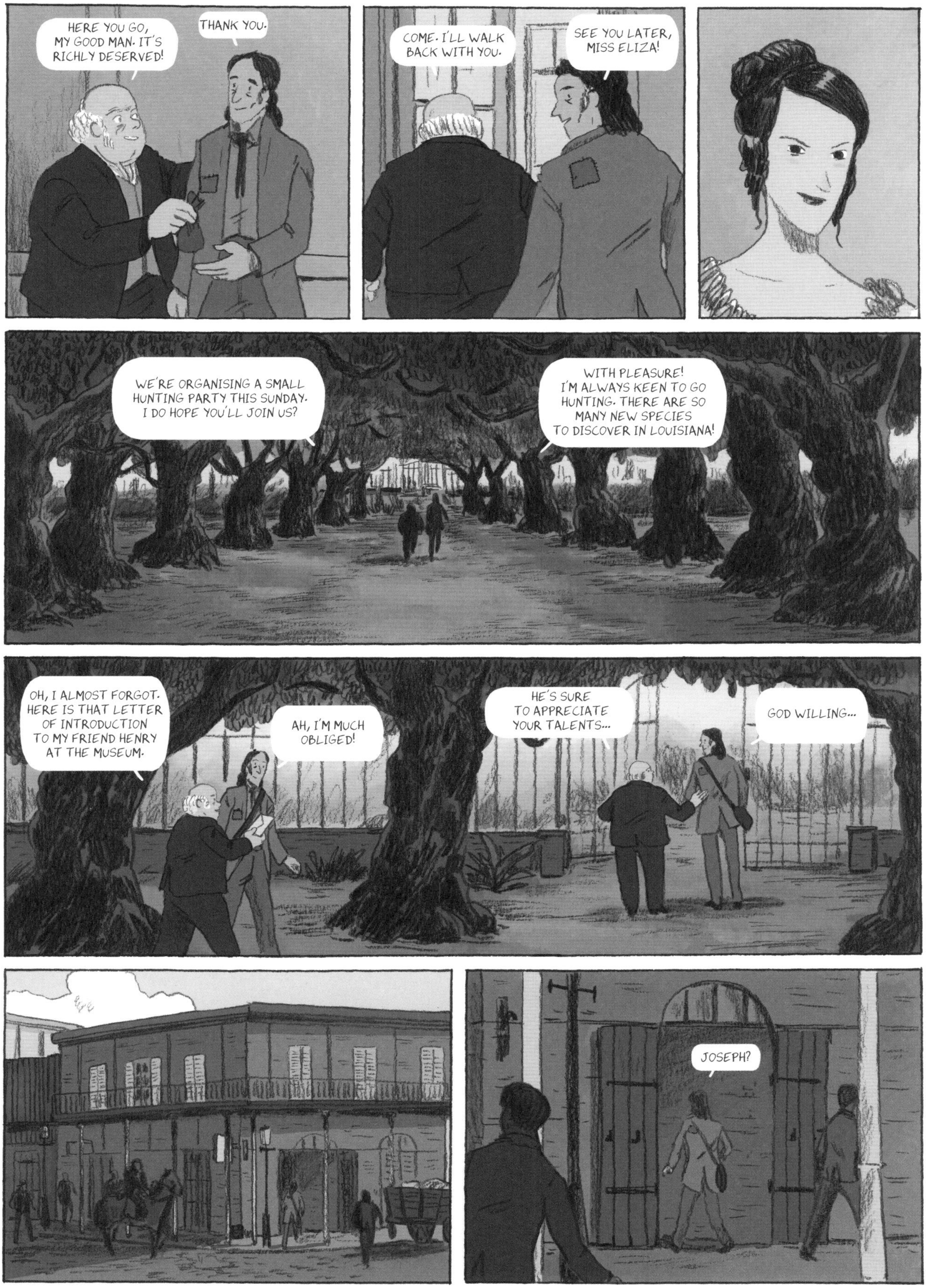
HERE YOU GO, MY GOOD MAN. IT'S RICHLY DESERVED!
THANK YOU.
COME. I'LL WALK BACK WITH YOU.
SEE YOU LATER, MISS ELIZA!
WE'RE ORGANISING A SMALL HUNTING PARTY THIS SUNDAY. I DO HOPE YOU'LL JOIN US?
WITH PLEASURE! I'M ALWAYS KEEN TO GO HUNTING. THERE ARE SO MANY NEW SPECIES TO DISCOVER IN LOUISIANA!
OH, I ALMOST FORGOT. HERE IS THAT LETTER OF INTRODUCTION TO MY FRIEND HENRY AT THE MUSEUM.
AH, I'M MUCH OBLIGED!
HE'S SURE TO APPRECIATE YOUR TALENTS...
GOD WILLING...
JOSEPH?

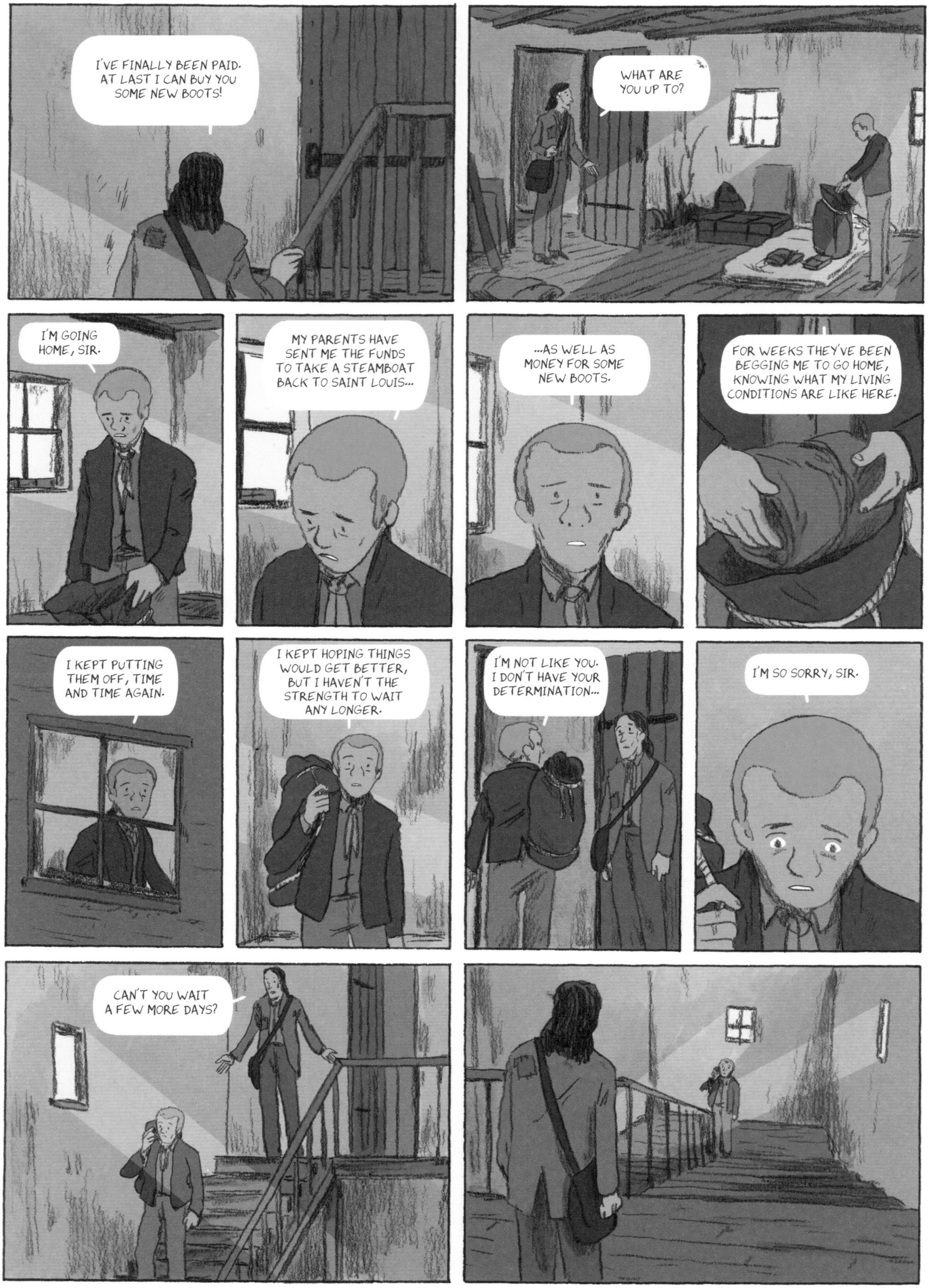
I'VE FINALLY BEEN PAID. AT LAST I CAN BUY YOU SOME NEW BOOTS!
WHAT ARE YOU UP TO?
I'M GOING HOME, SIR.
MY PARENTS HAVE SENT ME THE FUNDS TO TAKE A STEAMBOAT BACK TO SAINT LOUIS...
...AS WELL AS MONEY FOR SOME NEW BOOTS.
FOR WEEKS THEY'VE BEEN BEGGING ME TO GO HOME, KNOWING WHAT MY LIVING CONDITIONS ARE LIKE HERE.
I KEPT PUTTING THEM OFF, TIME AND TIME AGAIN.
I KEPT HOPING THINGS WOULD GET BETTER, BUT I HAVEN'T THE STRENGTH TO WAIT ANY LONGER.
I'M NOT LIKE YOU. I DON'T HAVE YOUR DETERMINATION...
I'M SO SORRY, SIR.
CAN'T YOU WAIT A FEW MORE DAYS?

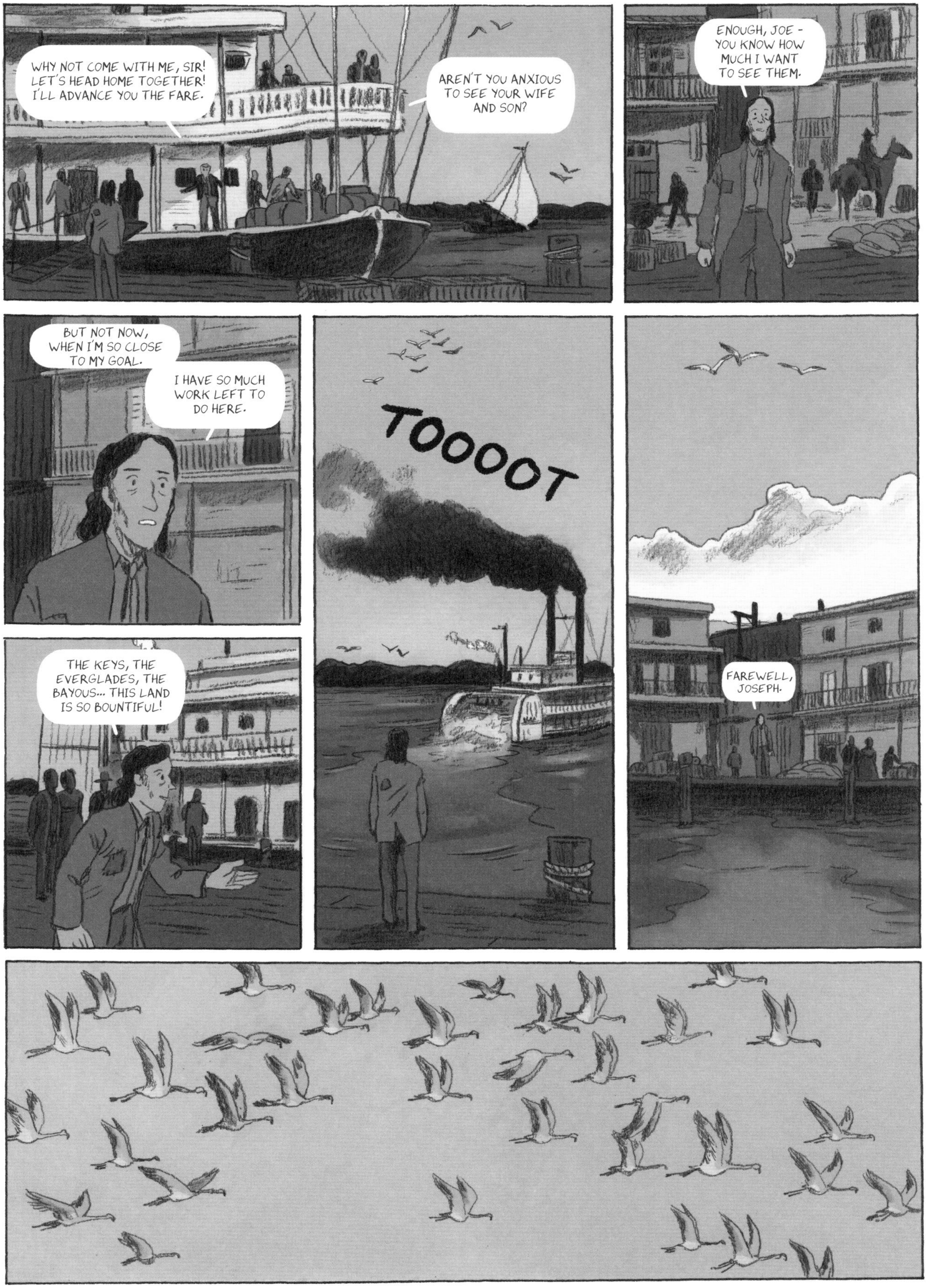
WHY NOT COME WITH ME, SIR! LET'S HEAD HOME TOGETHER! I'LL ADVANCE YOU THE FARE.
AREN'T YOU ANXIOUS TO SEE YOUR WIFE AND SON?
ENOUGH, JOE - YOU KNOW HOW MUCH I WANT TO SEE THEM.
BUT NOT NOW, WHEN I'M SO CLOSE TO MY GOAL.
I HAVE SO MUCH WORK LEFT TO DO HERE.
THE KEYS, THE EVERGLADES, THE BAYOUS... THIS LAND IS SO BOUNTIFUL!
TOOOOT
FAREWELL, JOSEPH.

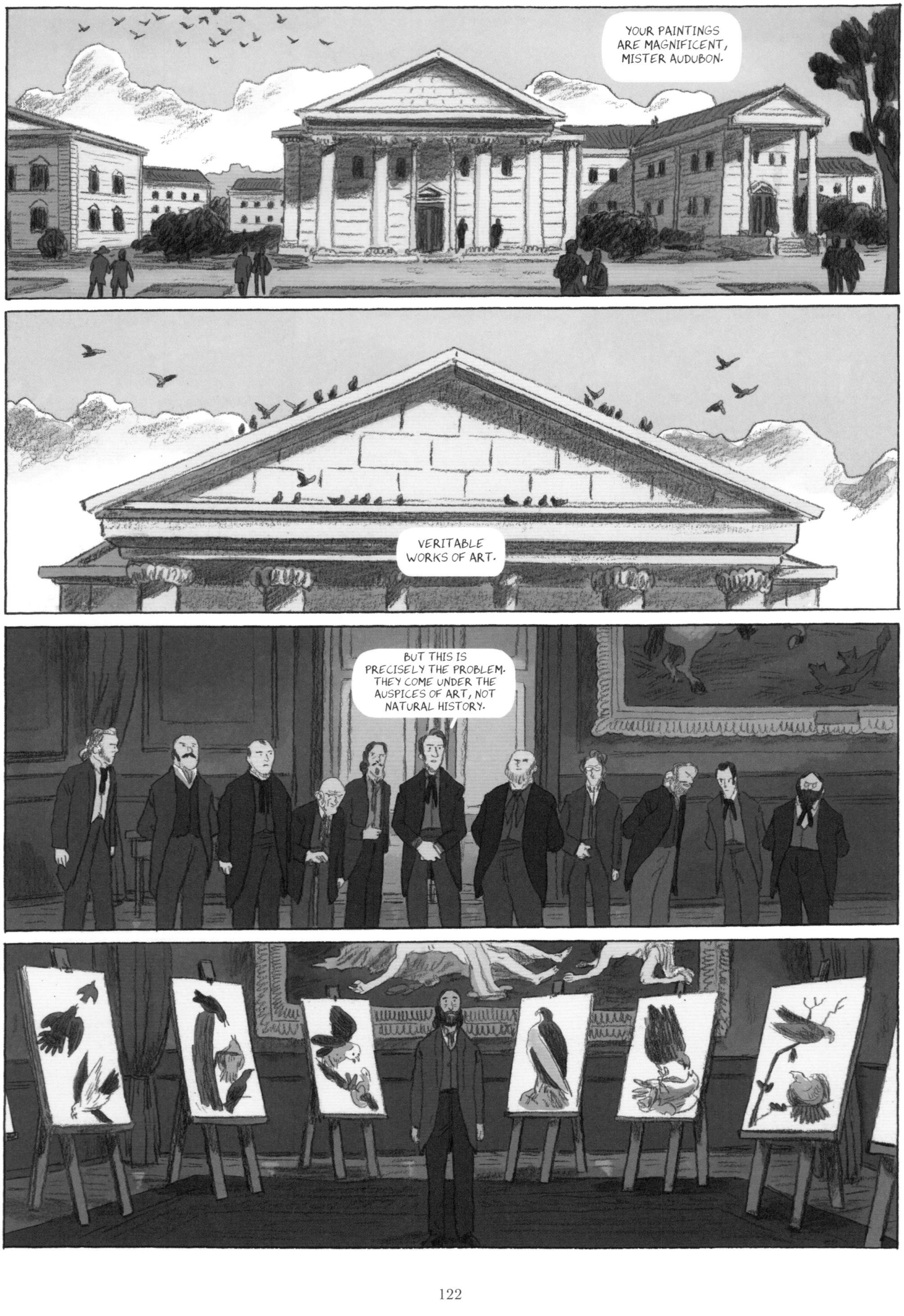
YOUR PAINTINGS ARE MAGNIFICENT, MISTER AUDUBON.
VERITABLE WORKS OF ART.
BUT THIS IS PRECISELY THE PROBLEM. THEY COME UNDER THE AUSPICES OF ART, NOT NATURAL HISTORY.

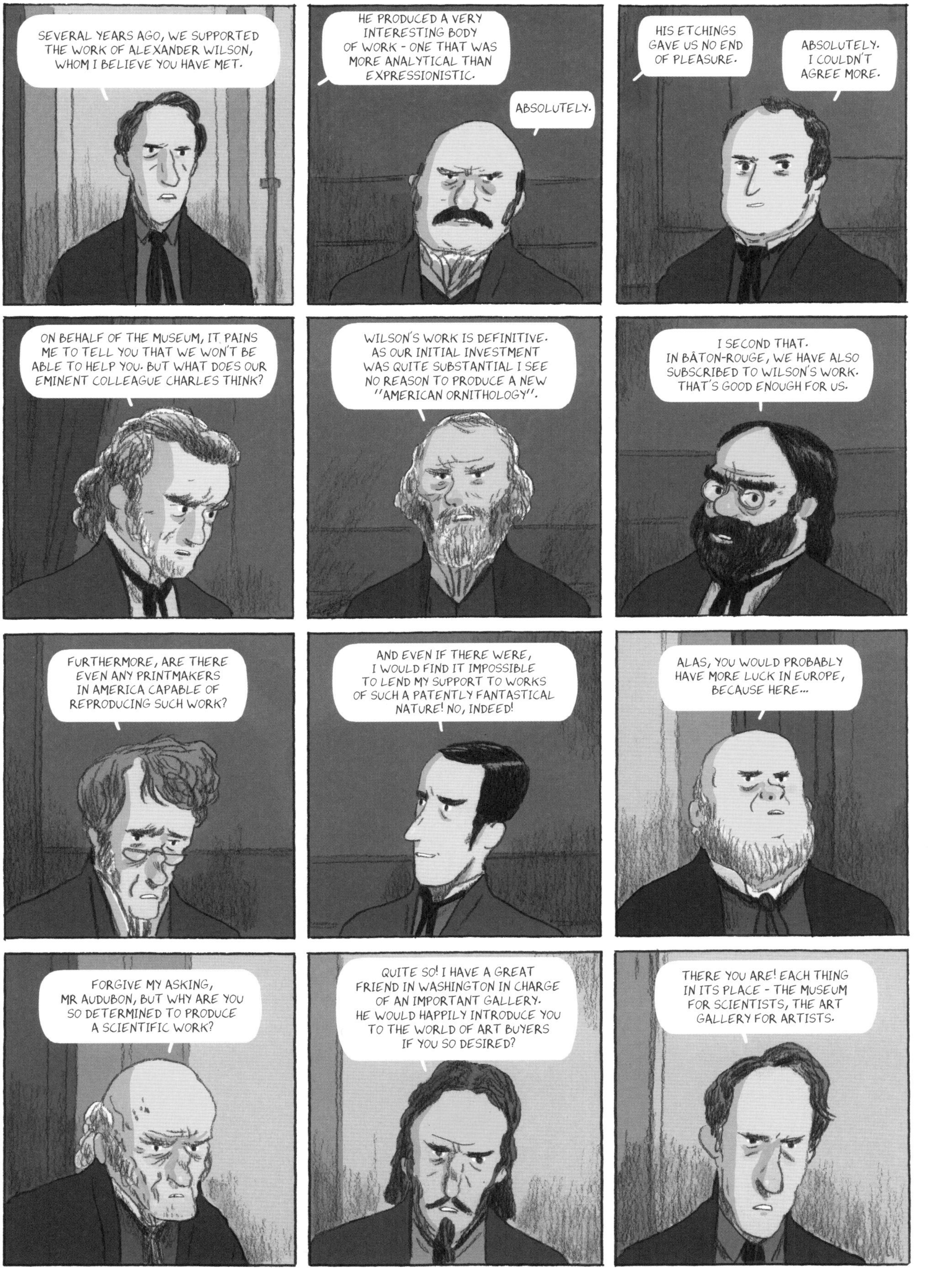
SEVERAL YEARS AGO, WE SUPPORTED THE WORK OF ALEXANDER WILSON, WHOM I BELIEVE YOU HAVE MET.
HE PRODUCED A VERY INTERESTING BODY OF WORK - ONE THAT WAS MORE ANALYTICAL THAN EXPRESSIONISTIC.
ABSOLUTELY.
HIS ETCHINGS GAVE US NO END OF PLEASURE.
ABSOLUTELY. I COULDN'T AGREE MORE.
ON BEHALF OF THE MUSEUM, IT PAINS ME TO TELL YOU THAT WE WON'T BE ABLE TO HELP YOU. BUT WHAT DOES OUR EMINENT COLLEAGUE CHARLES THINK?
WILSON'S WORK IS DEFINITIVE. AS OUR INITIAL INVESTMENT WAS QUITE SUBSTANTIAL I SEE NO REASON TO PRODUCE A NEW "AMERICAN ORNITHOLOGY".
I SECOND THAT. IN BÂTON-ROUGE, WE HAVE ALSO SUBSCRIBED TO WILSON'S WORK. THAT'S GOOD ENOUGH FOR US.
FURTHERMORE, ARE THERE EVEN ANY PRINTMAKERS IN AMERICA CAPABLE OF REPRODUCING SUCH WORK?
AND EVEN IF THERE WERE, I WOULD FIND IT IMPOSSIBLE TO LEND MY SUPPORT TO WORKS OF SUCH A PATENTLY FANTASTICAL NATURE! NO, INDEED!
ALAS, YOU WOULD PROBABLY HAVE MORE LUCK IN EUROPE, BECAUSE HERE...
FORGIVE MY ASKING, MR AUDUBON, BUT WHY ARE YOU SO DETERMINED TO PRODUCE A SCIENTIFIC WORK?
QUITE SO! I HAVE A GREAT FRIEND IN WASHINGTON IN CHARGE OF AN IMPORTANT GALLERY. HE WOULD HAPPILY INTRODUCE YOU TO THE WORLD OF ART BUYERS IF YOU SO DESIRED?
THERE YOU ARE! EACH THING IN ITS PLACE - THE MUSEUM FOR SCIENTISTS, THE ART GALLERY FOR ARTISTS.

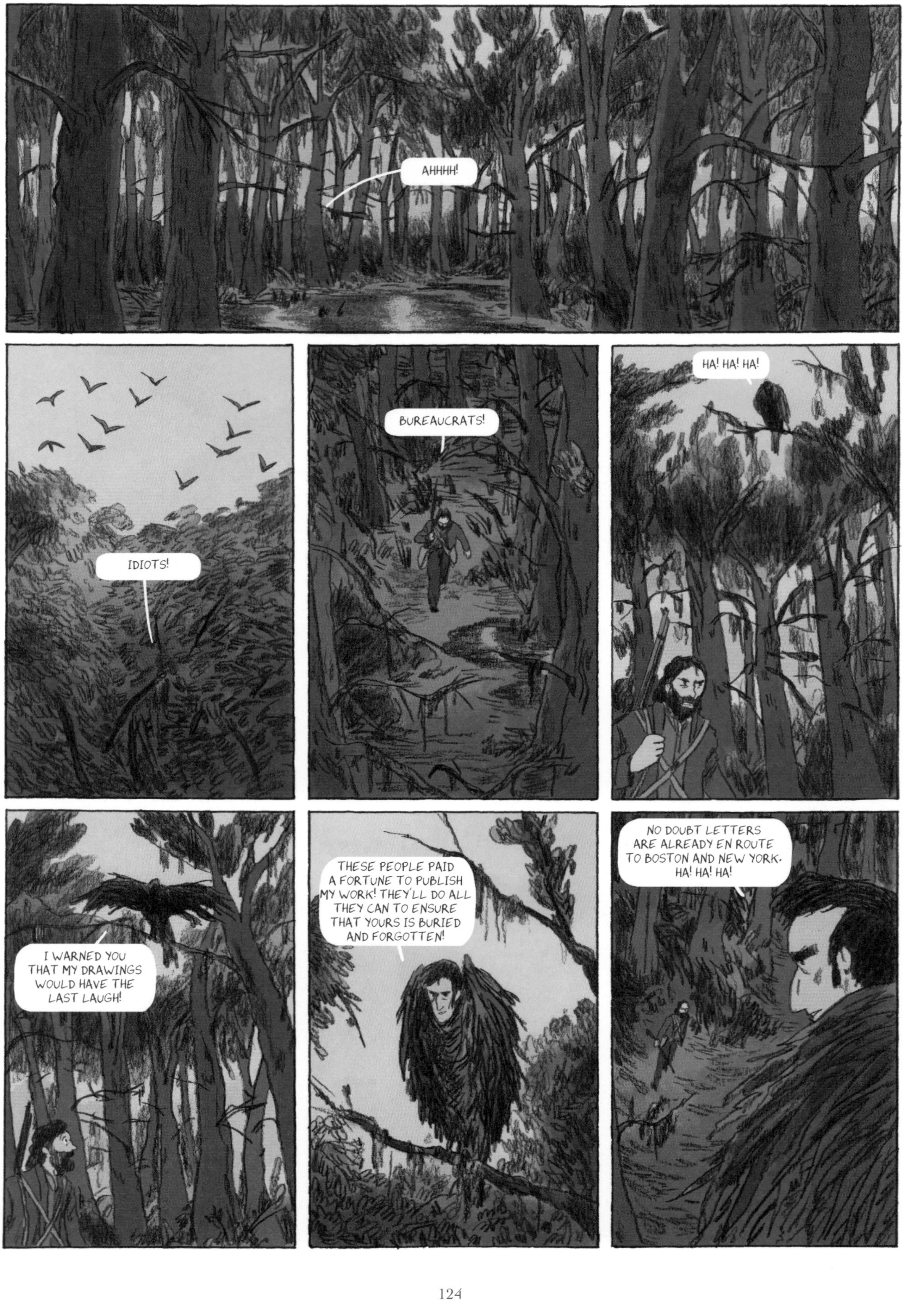
AHHHH!
IDIOTS!
BUREAUCRATS!
HA! HA! HA!
I WARNED YOU THAT MY DRAWINGS WOULD HAVE THE LAST LAUGH!
THESE PEOPLE PAID A FORTUNE TO PUBLISH MY WORK! THEY'LL DO ALL THEY CAN TO ENSURE THAT YOURS IS BURIED AND FORGOTTEN!
NO DOUBT LETTERS ARE ALREADY EN ROUTE TO BOSTON AND NEW YORK. HA! HA! HA!

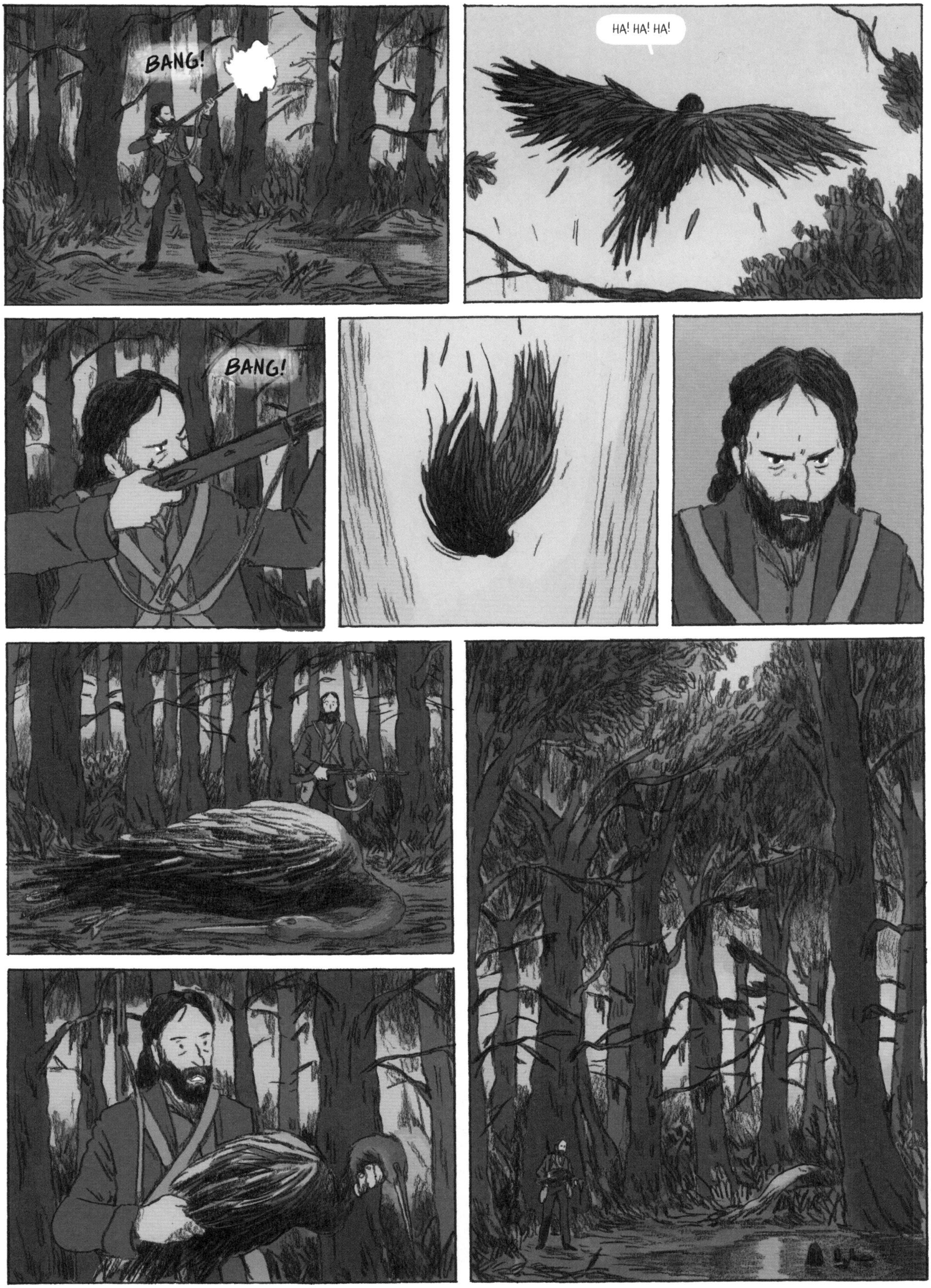
BANG!
HA! HA! HA!
BANG!

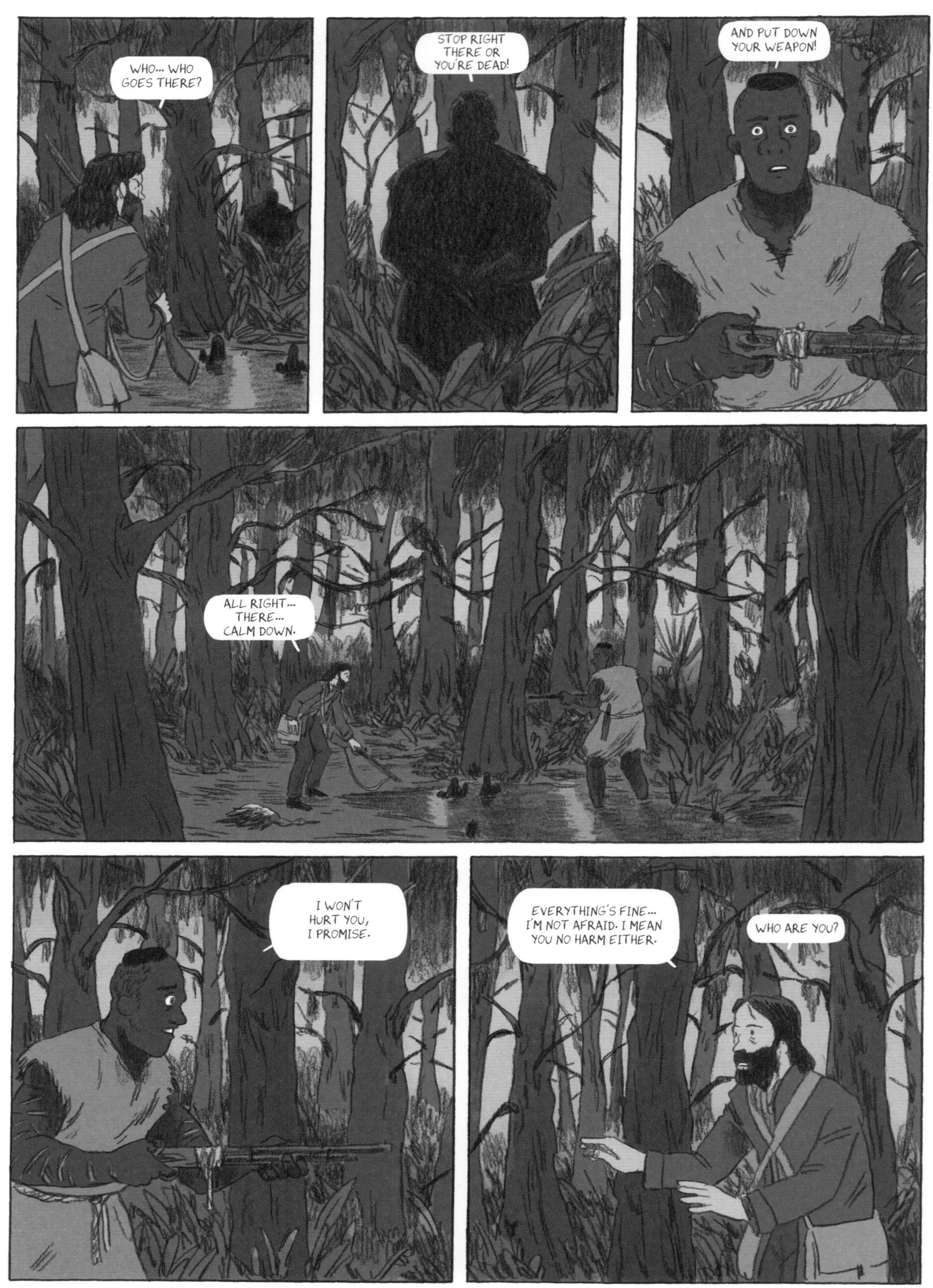
WHO... WHO GOES THERE?
STOP RIGHT THERE OR YOU'RE DEAD!
AND PUT DOWN YOUR WEAPON!
ALL RIGHT... THERE... CALM DOWN.
I WON'T HURT YOU, I PROMISE.
EVERYTHING'S FINE... I'M NOT AFRAID. I MEAN YOU NO HARM EITHER.
WHO ARE YOU?

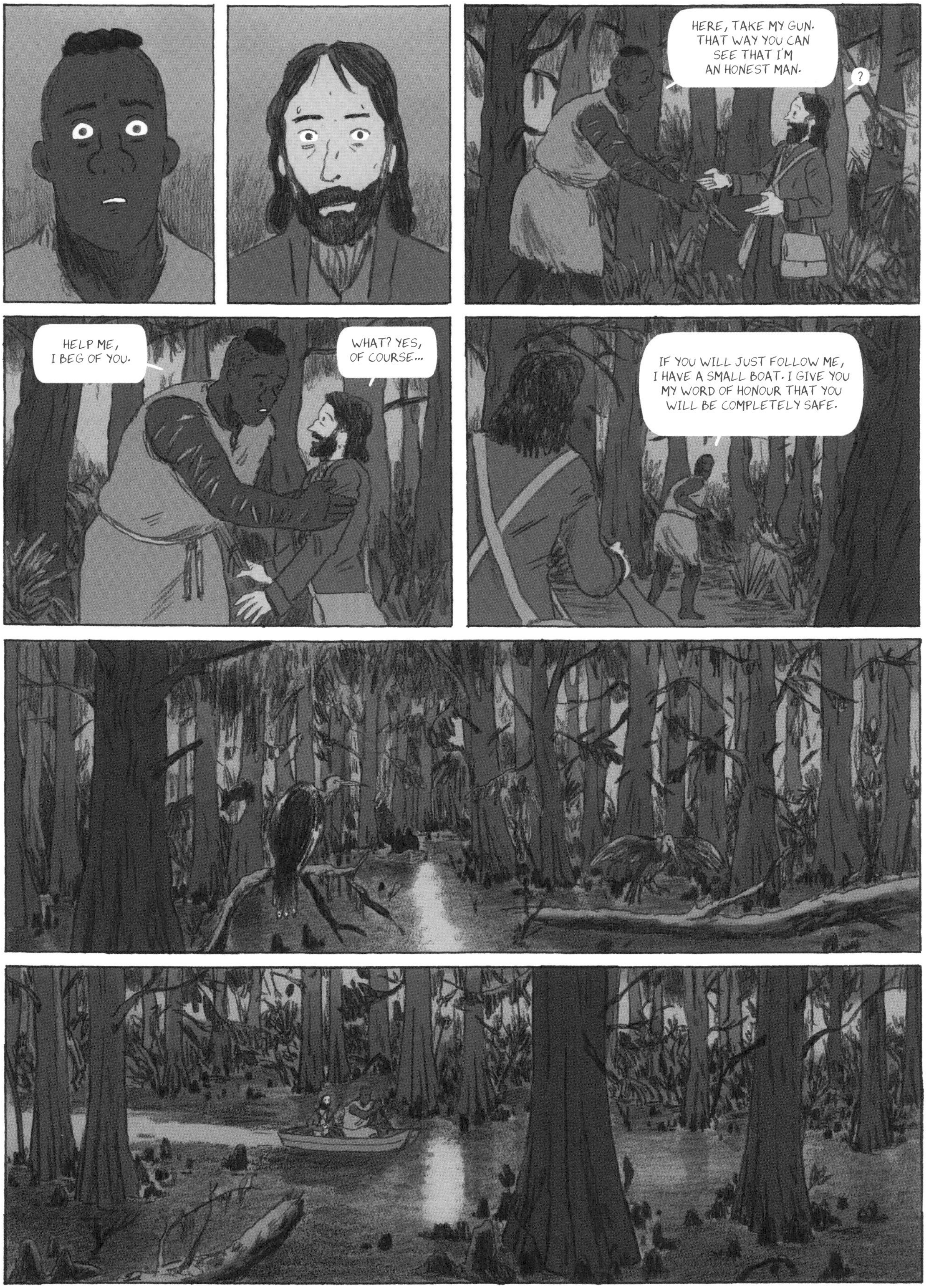
HERE, TAKE MY GUN. THAT WAY YOU CAN SEE THAT I'M AN HONEST MAN.
?
HELP ME, I BEG OF YOU.
WHAT? YES, OF COURSE...
IF YOU WILL JUST FOLLOW ME, I HAVE A SMALL BOAT. I GIVE YOU MY WORD OF HONOUR THAT YOU WILL BE COMPLETELY SAFE.

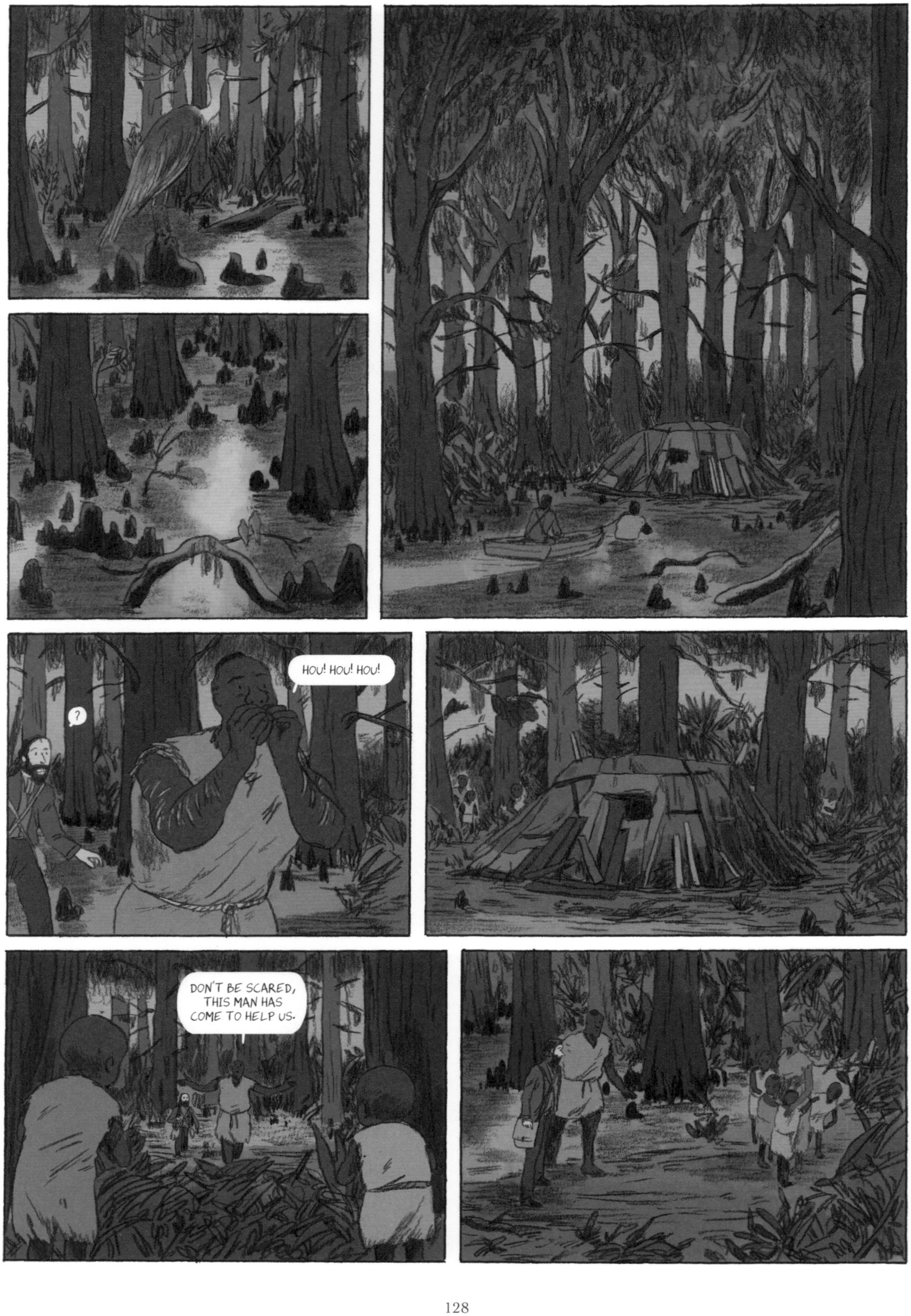
HOU! HOU! HOU!
?
DON'T BE SCARED, THIS MAN HAS COME TO HELP US.

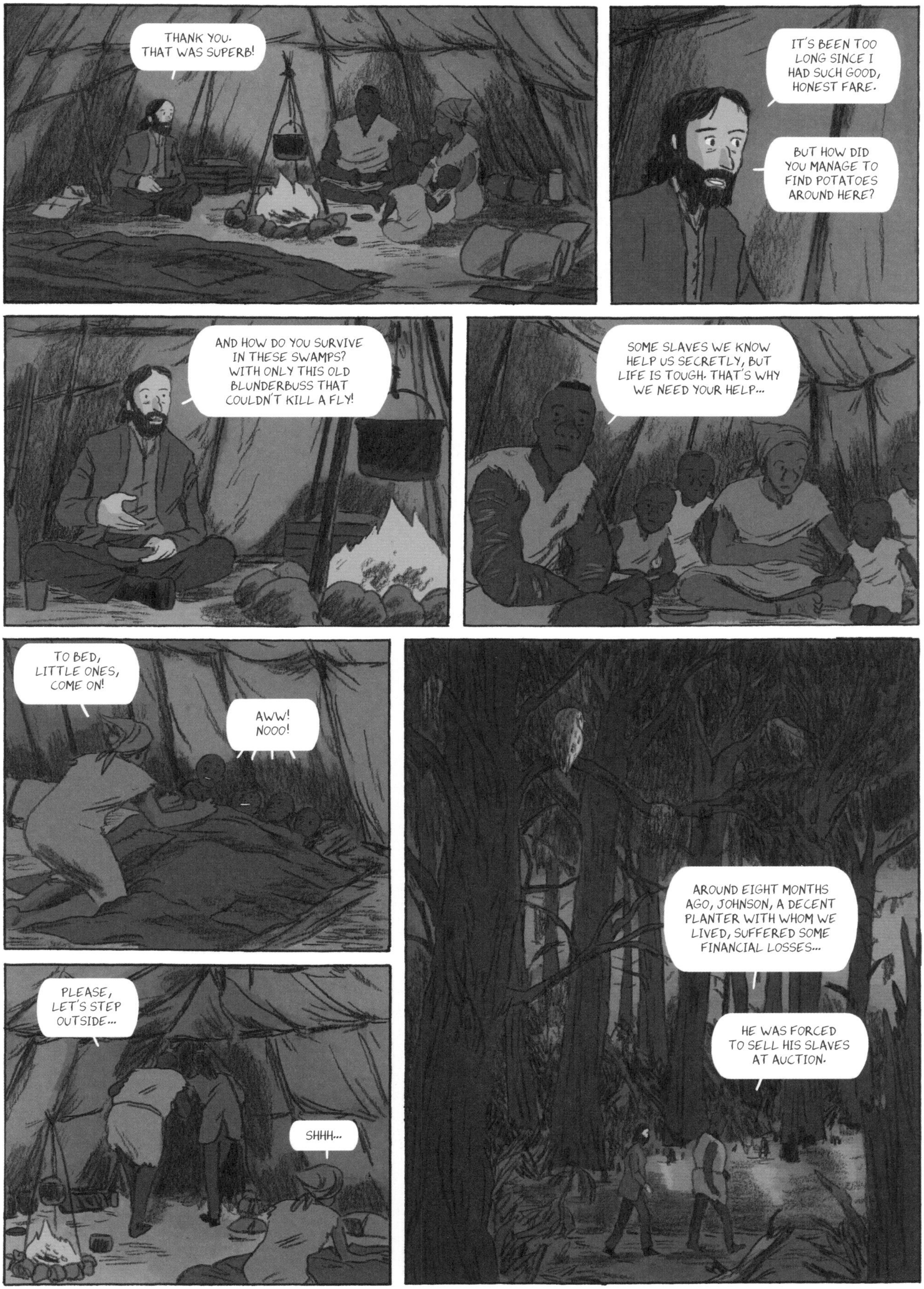
THANK YOU. THAT WAS SUPERB!
IT'S BEEN TOO LONG SINCE I HAD SUCH GOOD, HONEST FARE.
BUT HOW DID YOU MANAGE TO FIND POTATOES AROUND HERE?
AND HOW DO YOU SURVIVE IN THESE SWAMPS? WITH ONLY THIS OLD BLUNDERBUSS THAT COULDN'T KILL A FLY!
SOME SLAVES WE KNOW HELP US SECRETLY, BUT LIFE IS TOUGH. THAT'S WHY WE NEED YOUR HELP...
TO BED, LITTLE ONES, COME ON!
AWW! NOOO!
PLEASE, LET'S STEP OUTSIDE...
SHHH...
AROUND EIGHT MONTHS AGO, JOHNSON, A DECENT PLANTER WITH WHOM WE LIVED, SUFFERED SOME FINANCIAL LOSSES...
HE WAS FORCED TO SELL HIS SLAVES AT AUCTION.

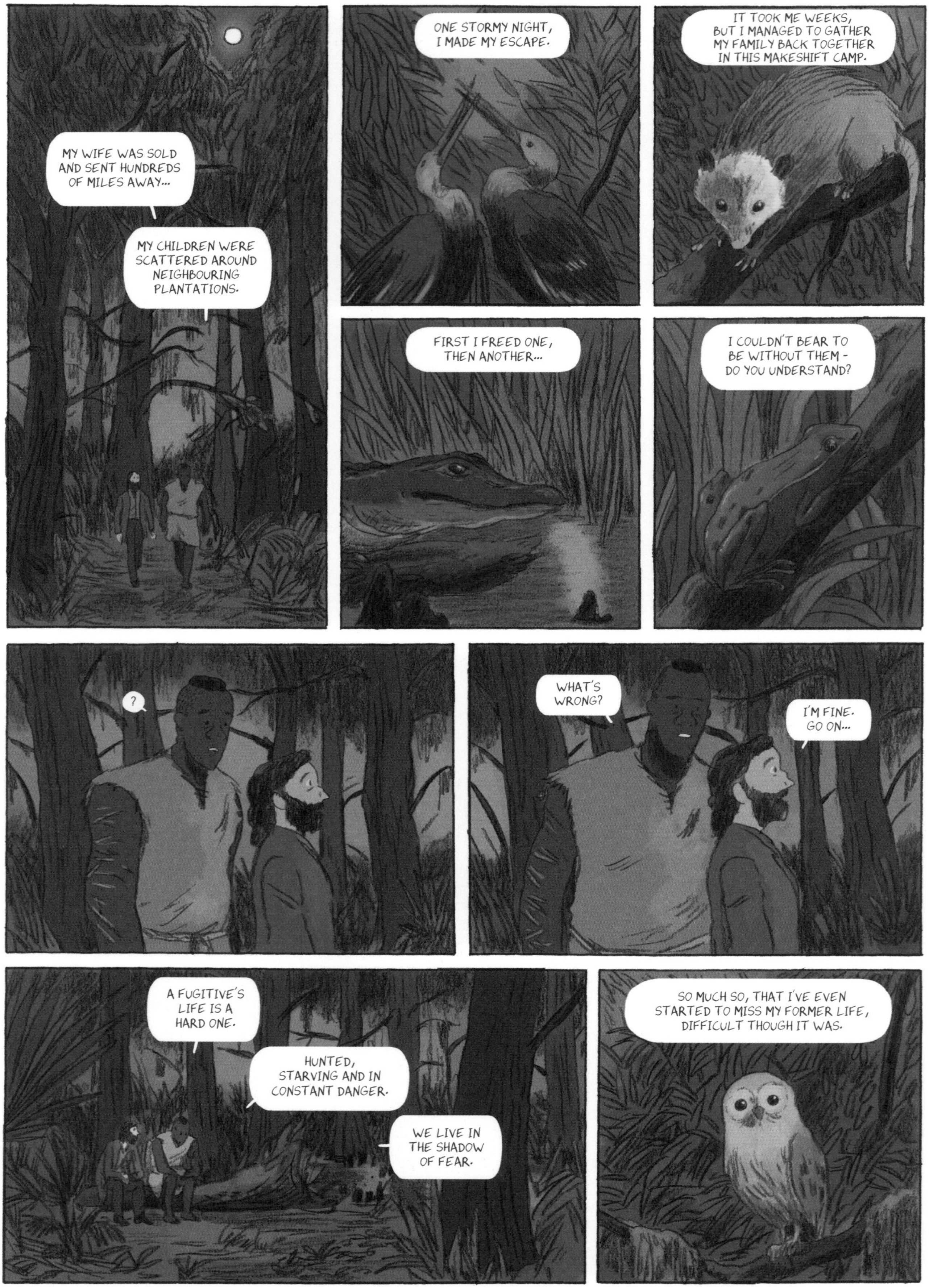
MY WIFE WAS SOLD AND SENT HUNDREDS OF MILES AWAY...
MY CHILDREN WERE SCATTERED AROUND NEIGHBOURING PLANTATIONS.
ONE STORMY NIGHT, I MADE MY ESCAPE.
IT TOOK ME WEEKS, BUT I MANAGED TO GATHER MY FAMILY BACK TOGETHER IN THIS MAKESHIFT CAMP.
FIRST I FREED ONE, THEN ANOTHER...
I COULDN'T BEAR TO BE WITHOUT THEM - DO YOU UNDERSTAND?
?
WHAT'S WRONG?
I'M FINE. GO ON...
A FUGITIVE'S LIFE IS A HARD ONE.
HUNTED, STARVING AND IN CONSTANT DANGER.
WE LIVE IN THE SHADOW OF FEAR.
SO MUCH SO, THAT I'VE EVEN STARTED TO MISS MY FORMER LIFE, DIFFICULT THOUGH IT WAS.

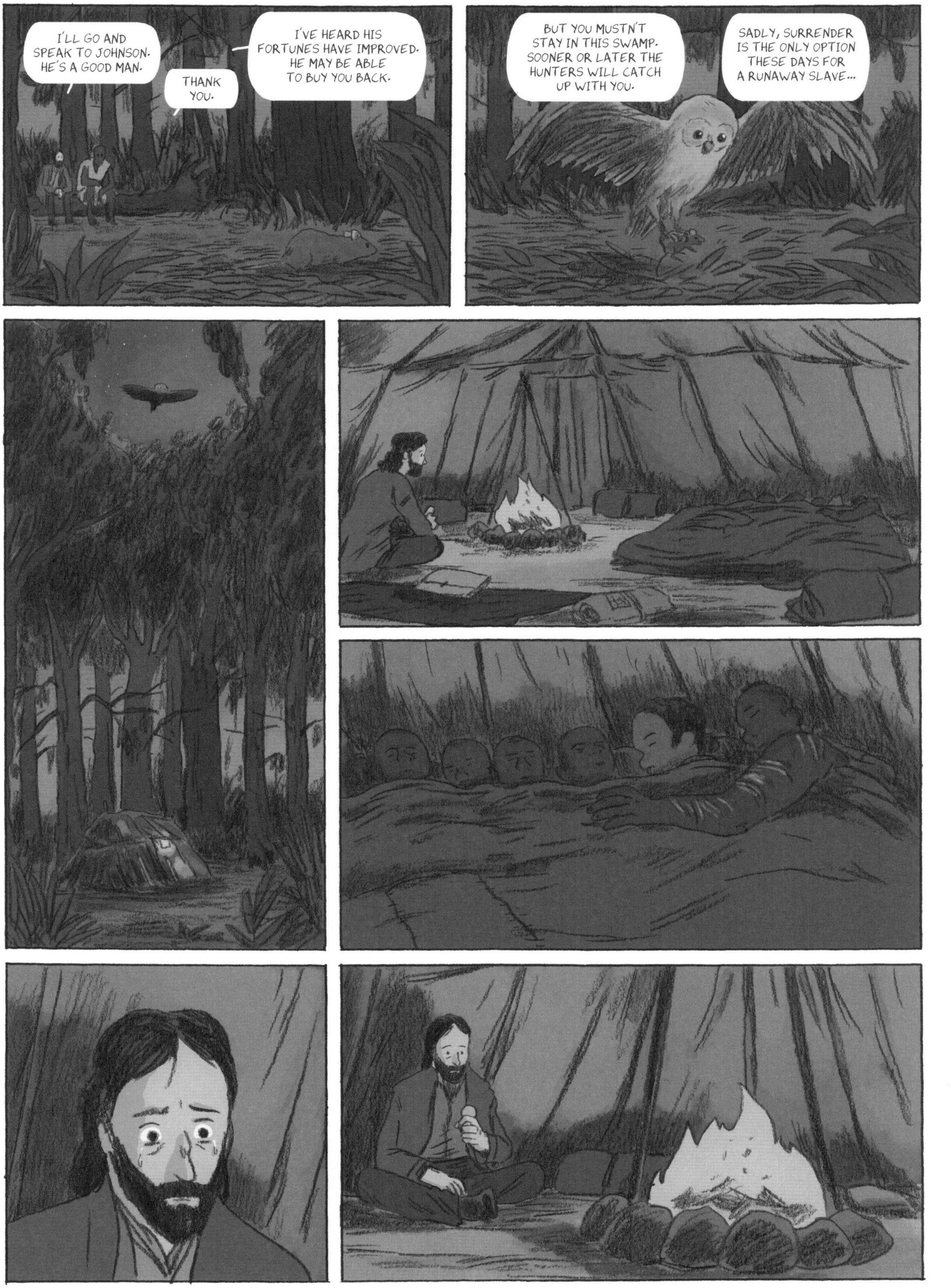
I'LL GO AND SPEAK TO JOHNSON. HE'S A GOOD MAN.
THANK YOU.
I'VE HEARD HIS FORTUNES HAVE IMPROVED. HE MAY BE ABLE TO BUY YOU BACK.
BUT YOU MUSTN'T STAY IN THIS SWAMP. SOONER OR LATER THE HUNTERS WILL CATCH UP WITH YOU.
SADLY, SURRENDER IS THE ONLY OPTION THESE DAYS FOR A RUNAWAY SLAVE...

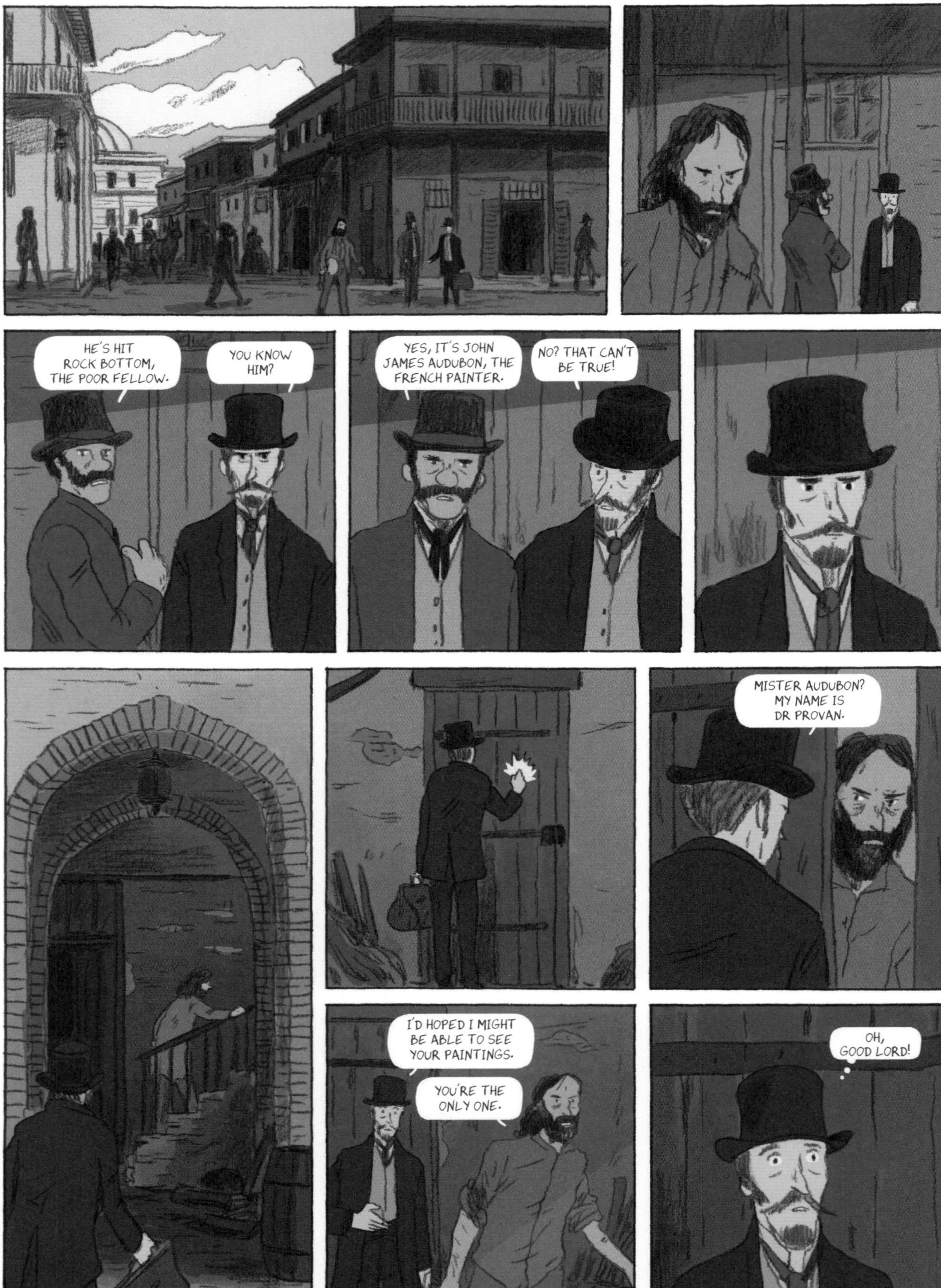
HE'S HIT ROCK BOTTOM, THE POOR FELLOW.
YOU KNOW HIM?
YES, IT'S JOHN JAMES AUDUBON, THE FRENCH PAINTER.
NO? THAT CAN'T BE TRUE!
MISTER AUDUBON? MY NAME IS DR PROVAN.
I'D HOPED I MIGHT BE ABLE TO SEE YOUR PAINTINGS.
YOU'RE THE ONLY ONE.
OH, GOOD LORD!

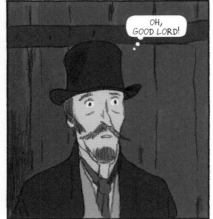

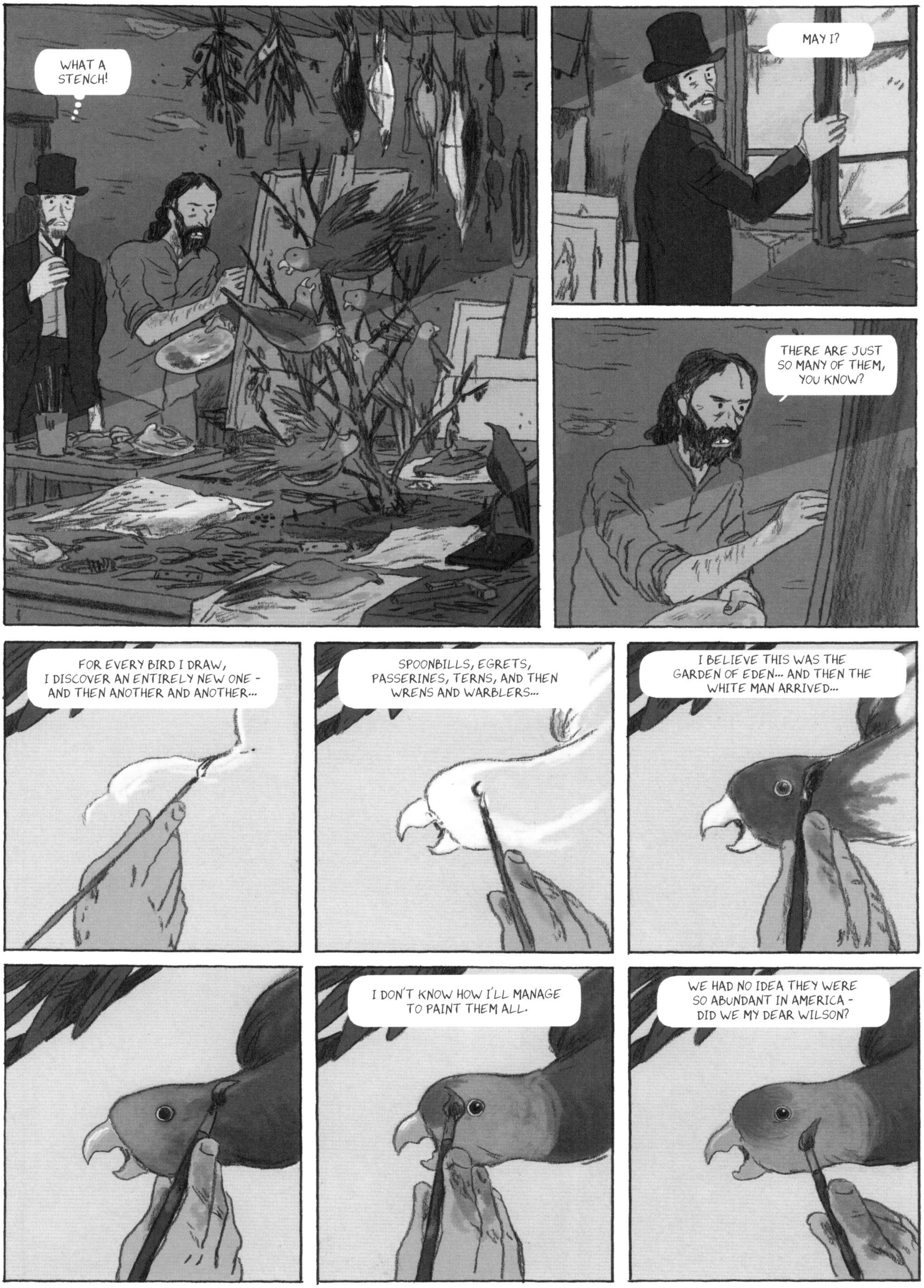
WHAT A STENCH!
MAY I?
THERE ARE JUST SO MANY OF THEM, YOU KNOW?
FOR EVERY BIRD I DRAW, I DISCOVER AN ENTIRELY NEW ONE - AND THEN ANOTHER AND ANOTHER...
SPOONBILLS, EGRETS, PASSERINES, TERNS, AND THEN WRENS AND WARBLERS...
I BELIEVE THIS WAS THE GARDEN OF EDEN... AND THEN THE WHITE MAN ARRIVED...
I DON'T KNOW HOW I'LL MANAGE TO PAINT THEM ALL.
WE HAD NO IDEA THEY WERE SO ABUNDANT IN AMERICA - DID WE MY DEAR WILSON?

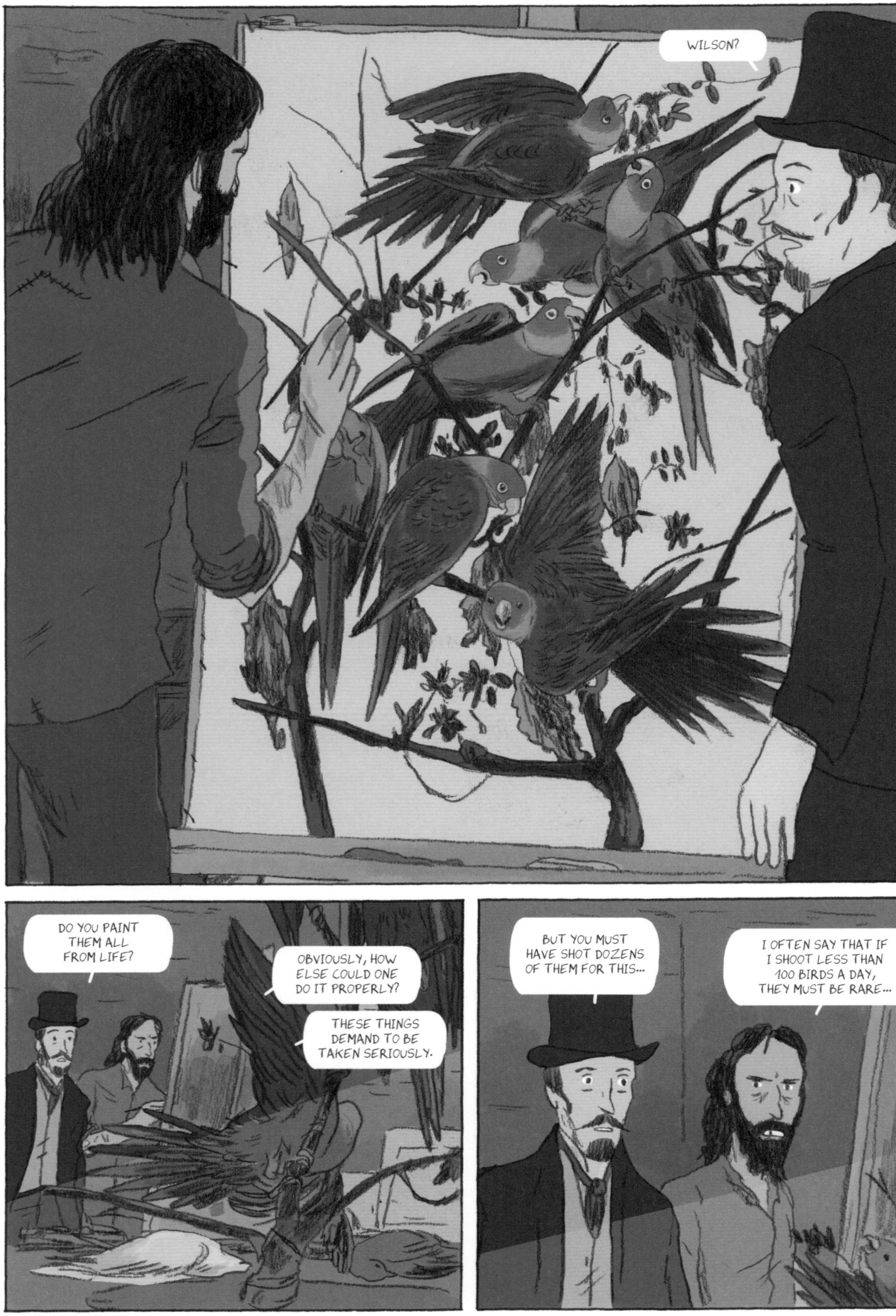

WILSON?
DO YOU PAINT THEM ALL FROM LIFE?
OBVIOUSLY, HOW ELSE COULD ONE DO IT PROPERLY?
THESE THINGS DEMAND TO BE TAKEN SERIOUSLY.
BUT YOU MUST HAVE SHOT DOZENS OF THEM FOR THIS...
I OFTEN SAY THAT IF I SHOOT LESS THAN 100 BIRDS A DAY, THEY MUST BE RARE...

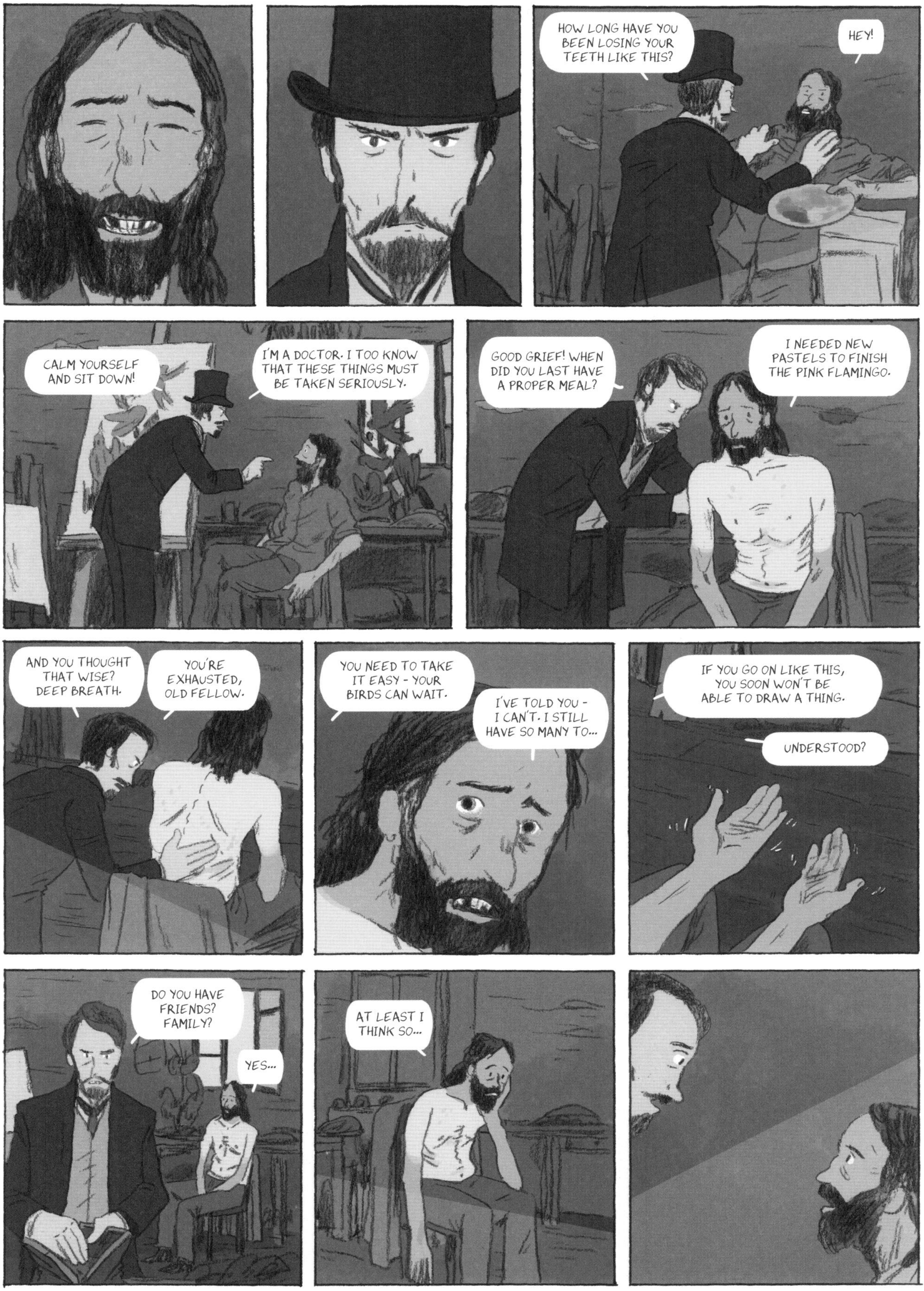
HOW LONG HAVE YOU BEEN LOSING YOUR TEETH LIKE THIS?
HEY!
CALM YOURSELF AND SIT DOWN!
I'M A DOCTOR. I TOO KNOW THAT THESE THINGS MUST BE TAKEN SERIOUSLY.
GOOD GRIEF! WHEN DID YOU LAST HAVE A PROPER MEAL?
I NEEDED NEW PASTELS TO FINISH THE PINK FLAMINGO.
AND YOU THOUGHT THAT WISE? DEEP BREATH.
YOU'RE EXHAUSTED, OLD FELLOW.
YOU NEED TO TAKE IT EASY - YOUR BIRDS CAN WAIT.
I'VE TOLD YOU - I CAN'T. I STILL HAVE SO MANY TO...
IF YOU GO ON LIKE THIS, YOU SOON WON'T BE ABLE TO DRAW A THING.
UNDERSTOOD?
DO YOU HAVE FRIENDS? FAMILY?
YES...
AT LEAST I THINK SO...

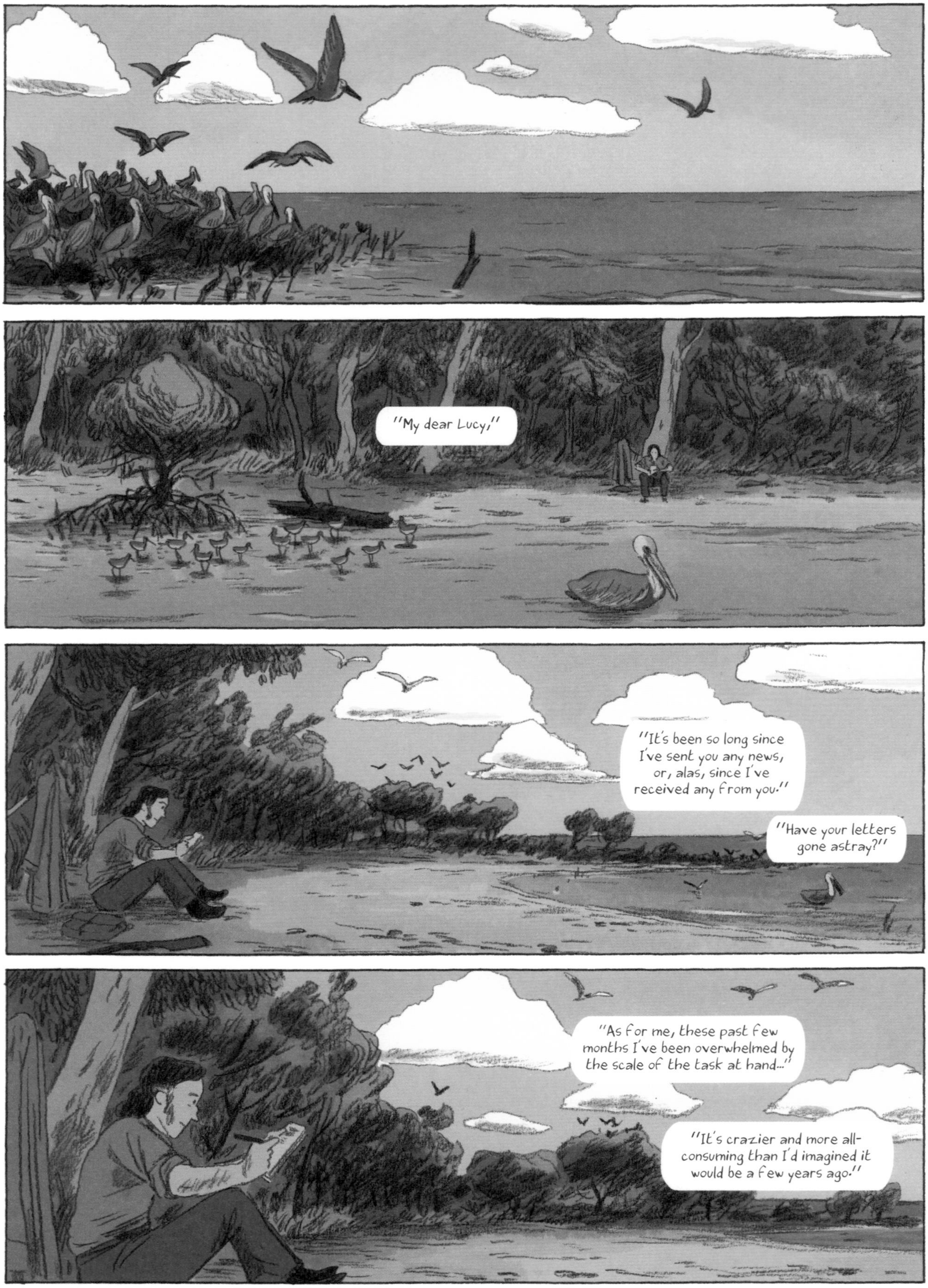
"My dear Lucy,"
"It's been so long since I've sent you any news, or, alas, since I've received any from you."
"Have your letters gone astray?"
"As for me, these past few months I've been overwhelmed by the scale of the task at hand..."
"It's crazier and more all-consuming than I'd imagined it would be a few years ago."

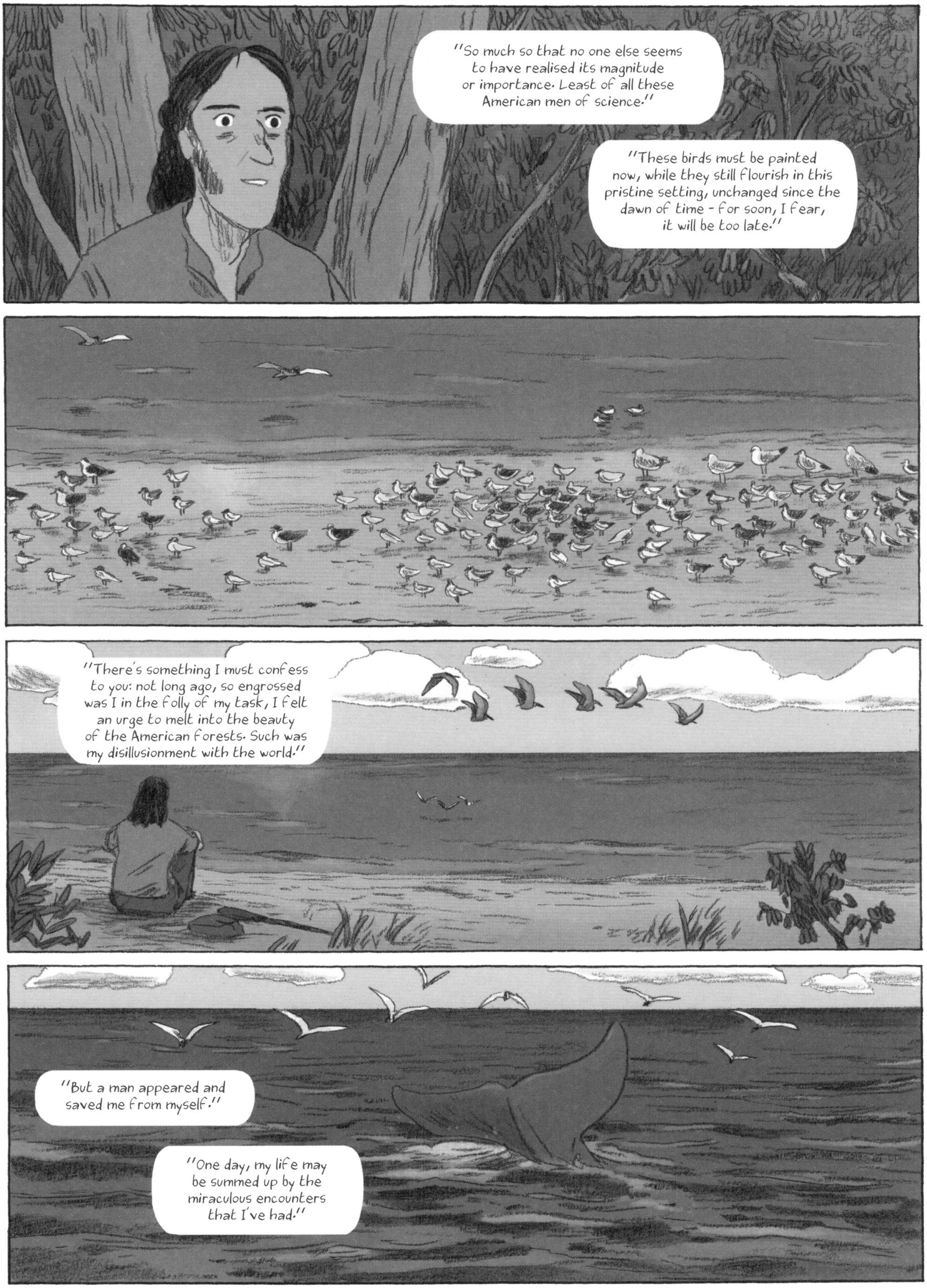
"So much so that no one else seems to have realised its magnitude or importance. Least of all these American men of science."
"These birds must be painted now, while they still flourish in this pristine setting, unchanged since the dawn of time - for soon, I fear, it will be too late."
"There's something I must confess to you: not long ago, so engrossed was I in the folly of my task, I felt an urge to melt into the beauty of the American forests. Such was my disillusionment with the world."
"But a man appeared and saved me from myself."
"One day, my life may be summed up by the miraculous encounters that I've had."

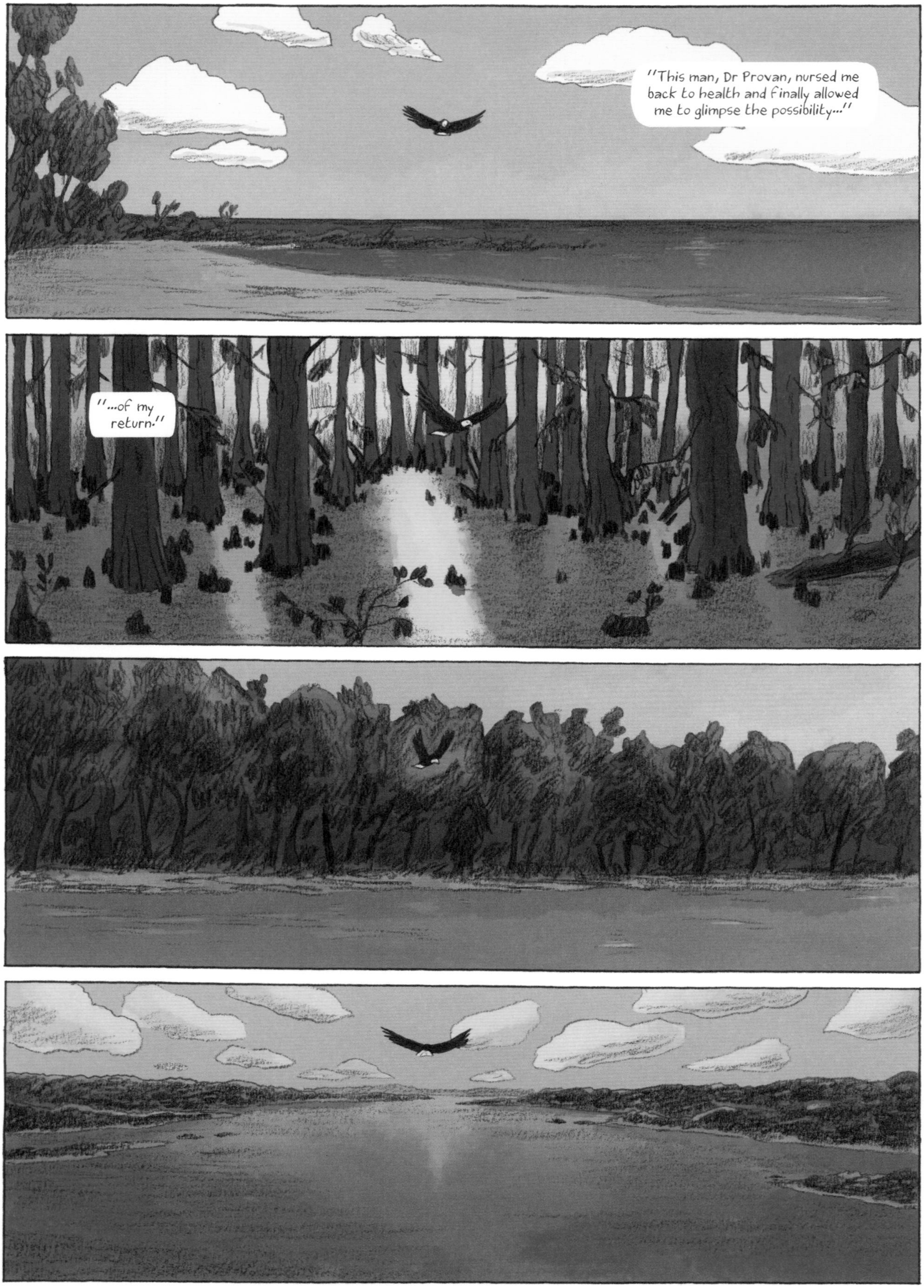
"This man, Dr Provan, nursed me back to health and finally allowed me to glimpse the possibility..."
"...of my return."

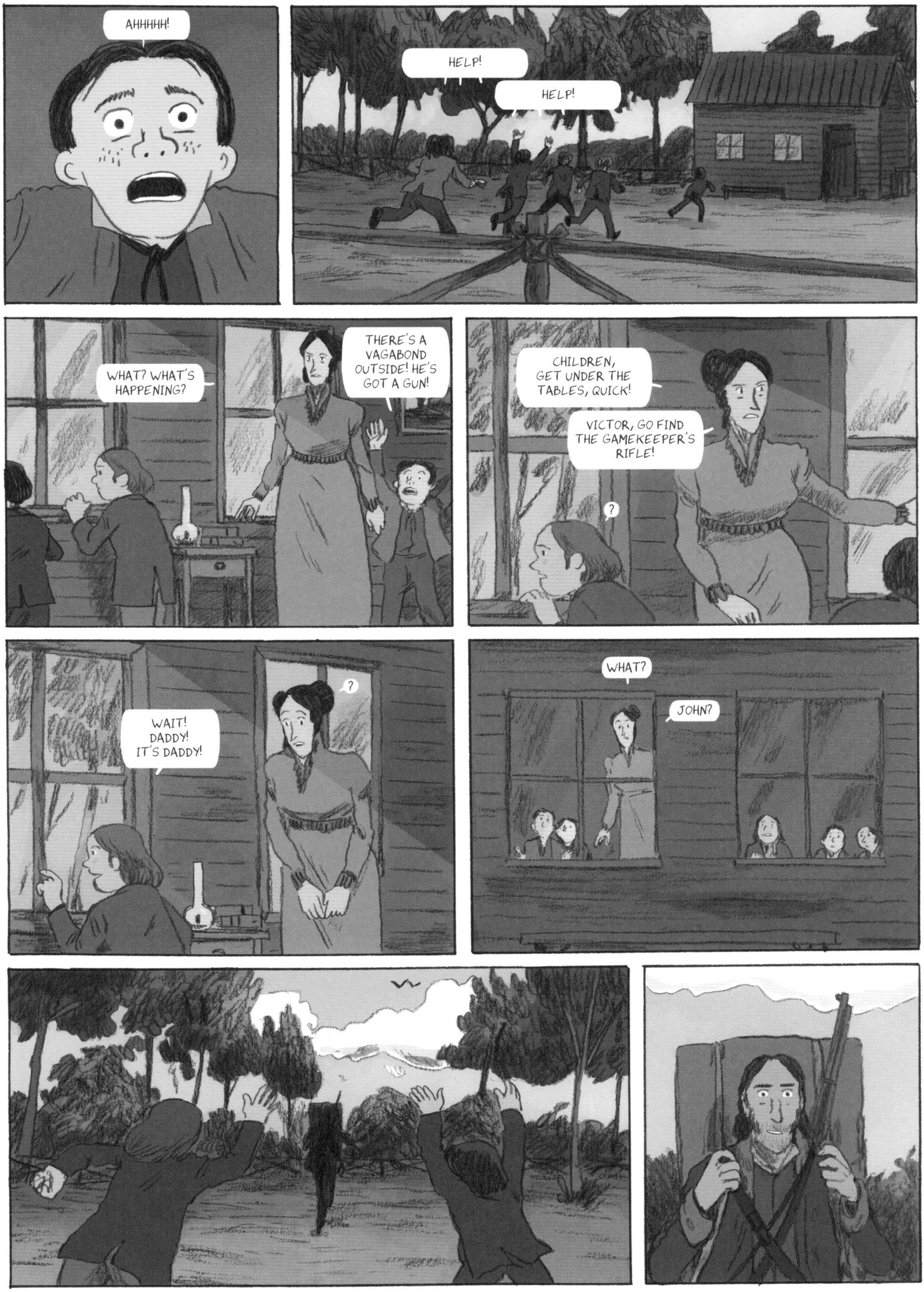
AHHHHH!
HELP!
HELP!
WHAT? WHAT'S HAPPENING?
THERE'S A VAGABOND OUTSIDE! HE'S GOT A GUN!
CHILDREN, GET UNDER THE TABLES, QUICK!
VICTOR, GO FIND THE GAMEKEEPER'S RIFLE!
?
?
WAIT! DADDY! IT'S DADDY!
WHAT?
JOHN?

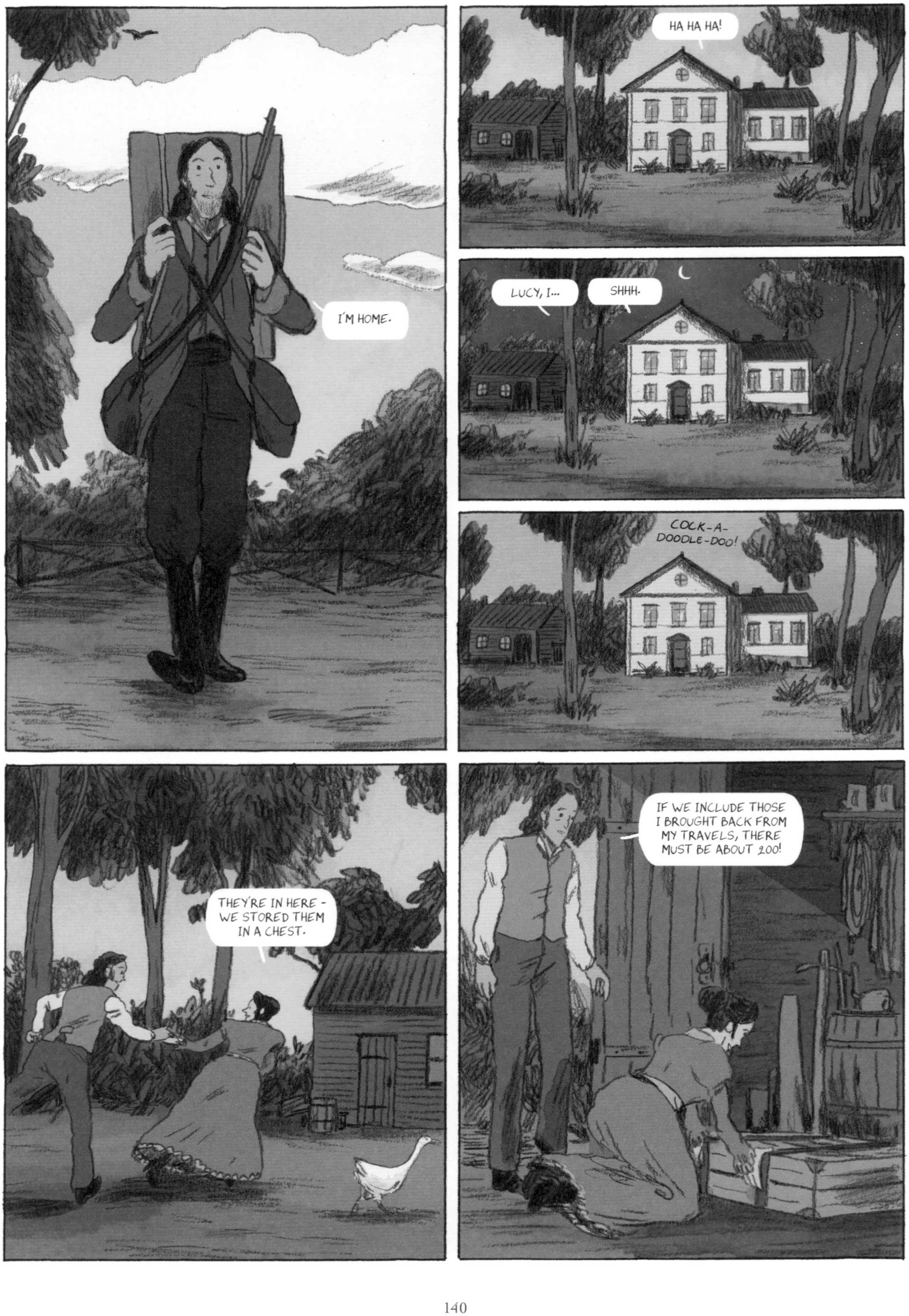
I'M HOME.
HA HA HA!
LUCY, I...
SHHH.
COCK-A-DOODLE-DOO!
THEY'RE IN HERE - WE STORED THEM IN A CHEST.
IF WE INCLUDE THOSE I BROUGHT BACK FROM MY TRAVELS, THERE MUST BE ABOUT 200!

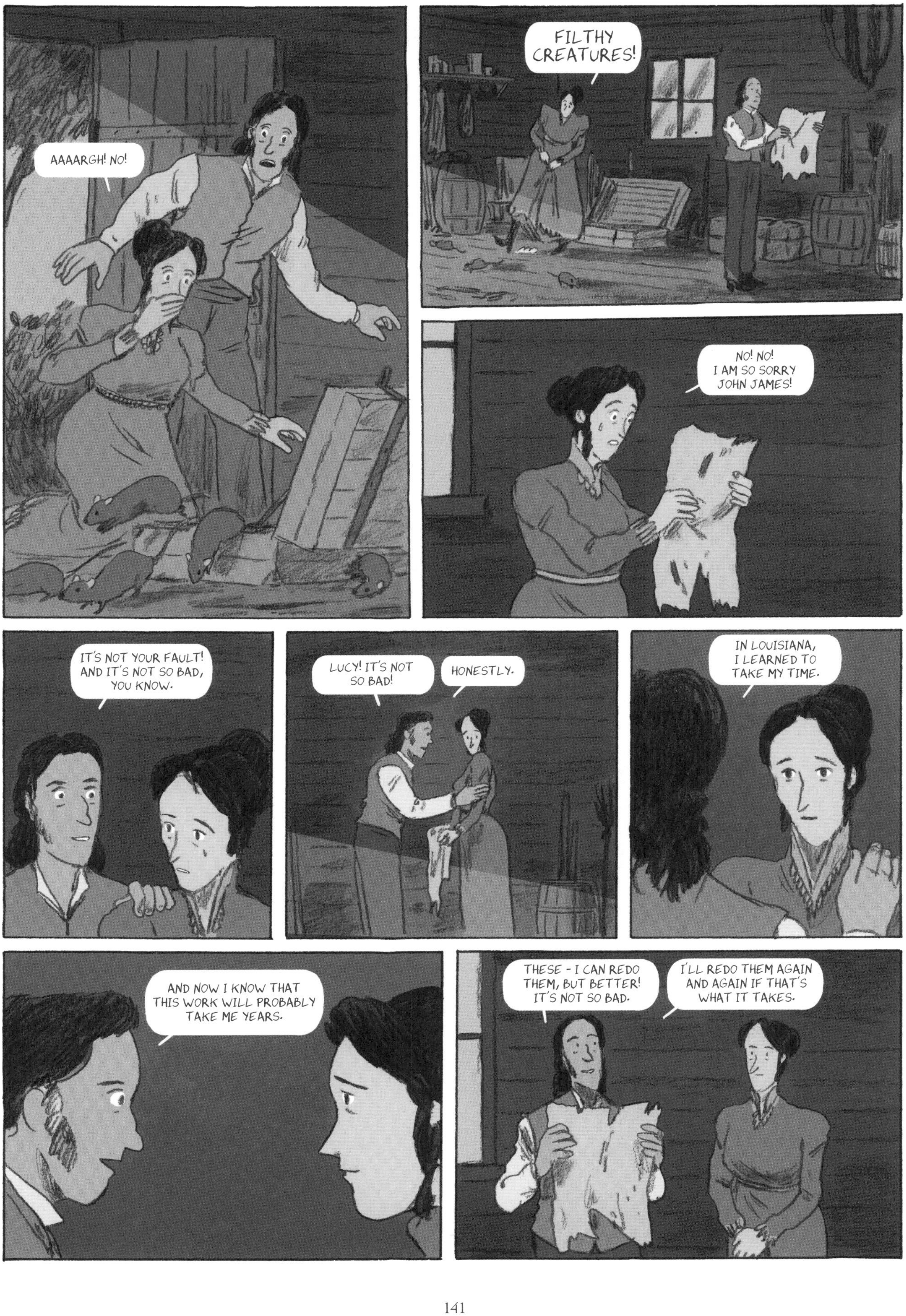
AAAARGH! NO!
FILTHY CREATURES!
NO! NO! I AM SO SORRY JOHN JAMES!
IT'S NOT YOUR FAULT! AND IT'S NOT SO BAD, YOU KNOW.
LUCY! IT'S NOT SO BAD!
HONESTLY.
IN LOUISIANA, I LEARNED TO TAKE MY TIME.
AND NOW I KNOW THAT THIS WORK WILL PROBABLY TAKE ME YEARS.
THESE - I CAN REDO THEM, BUT BETTER! IT'S NOT SO BAD.
I'LL REDO THEM AGAIN AND AGAIN IF THAT'S WHAT IT TAKES.

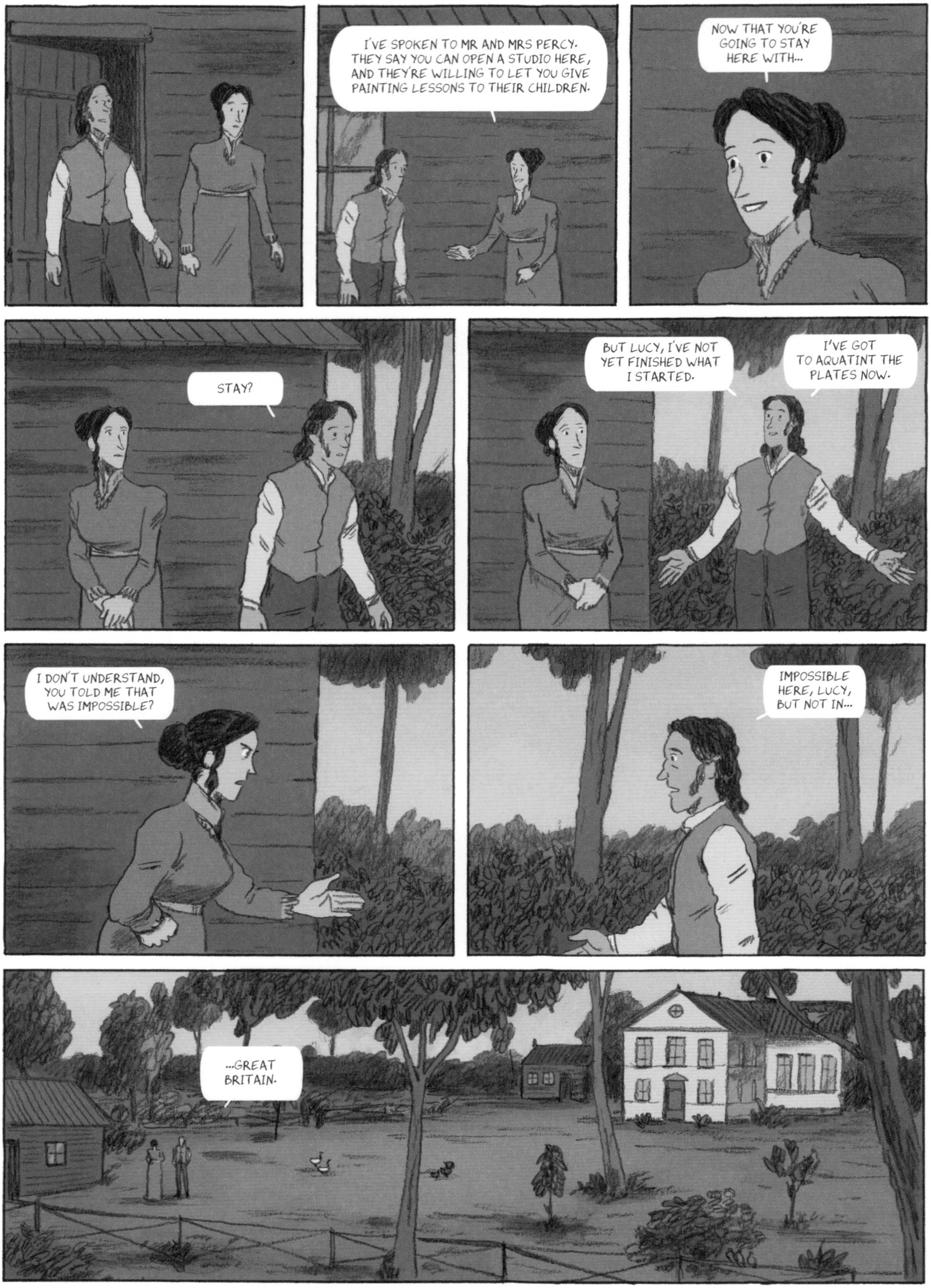
I'VE SPOKEN TO MR AND MRS PERCY. THEY SAY YOU CAN OPEN A STUDIO HERE, AND THEY'RE WILLING TO LET YOU GIVE PAINTING LESSONS TO THEIR CHILDREN.
NOW THAT YOU'RE GOING TO STAY HERE WITH...
STAY?
BUT LUCY, I'VE NOT YET FINISHED WHAT I STARTED.
I'VE GOT TO AQUATINT THE PLATES NOW.
I DON'T UNDERSTAND, YOU TOLD ME THAT WAS IMPOSSIBLE?
IMPOSSIBLE HERE, LUCY, BUT NOT IN...
...GREAT BRITAIN.

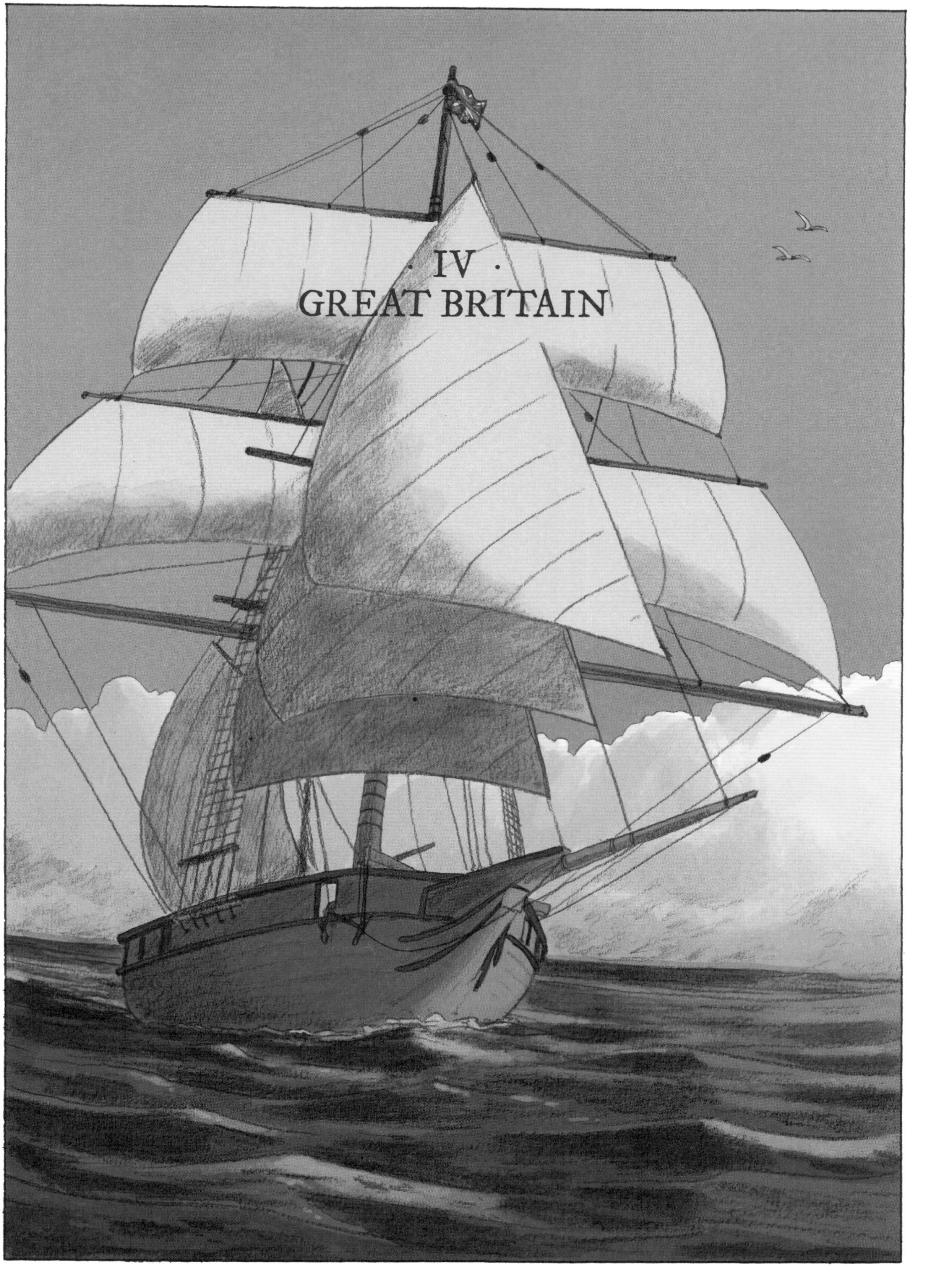
· IV ·
GREAT BRITAIN

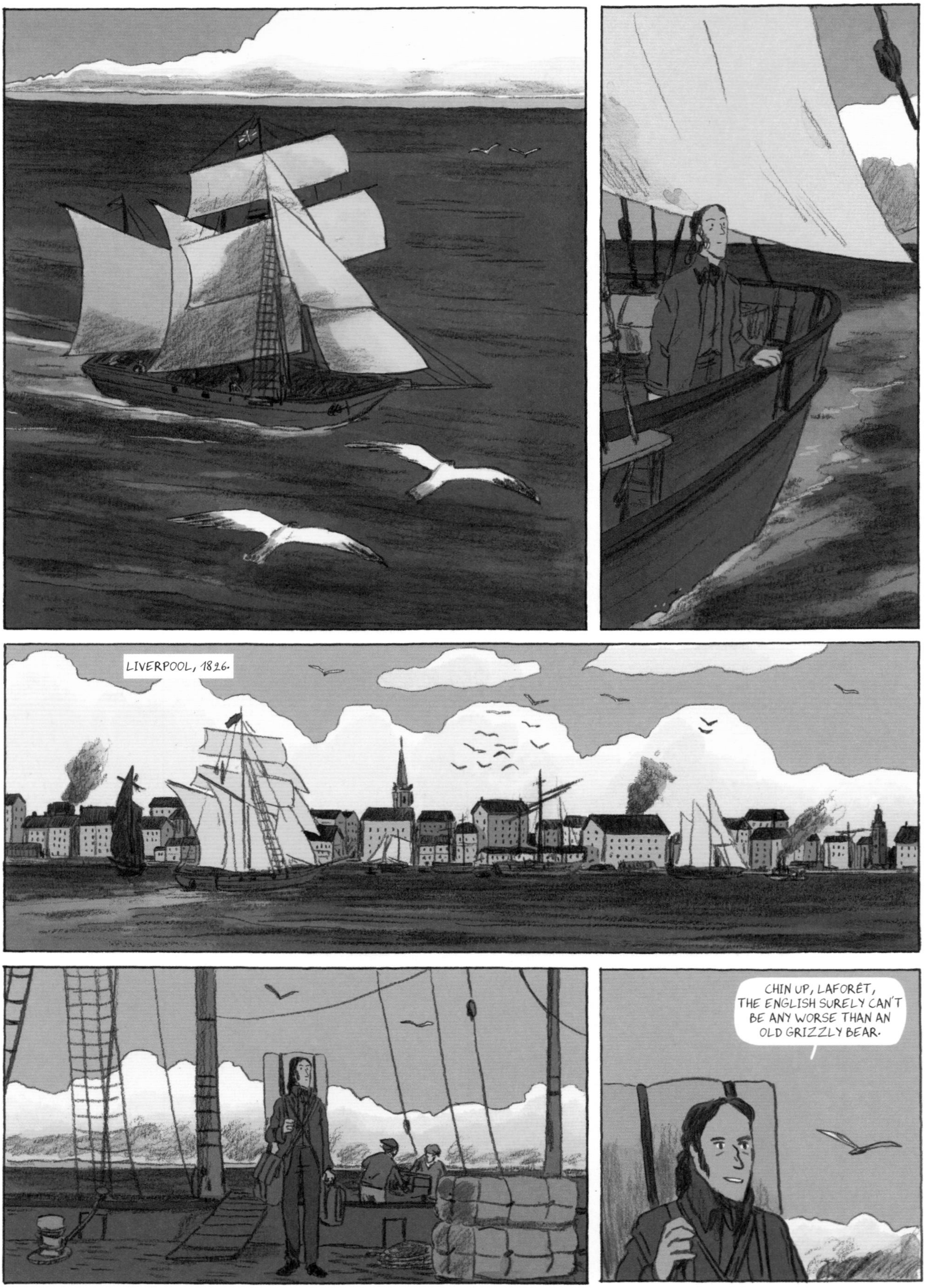
LIVERPOOL, 1826.
CHIN UP, LAFORÊT, THE ENGLISH SURELY CAN'T BE ANY WORSE THAN AN OLD GRIZZLY BEAR.

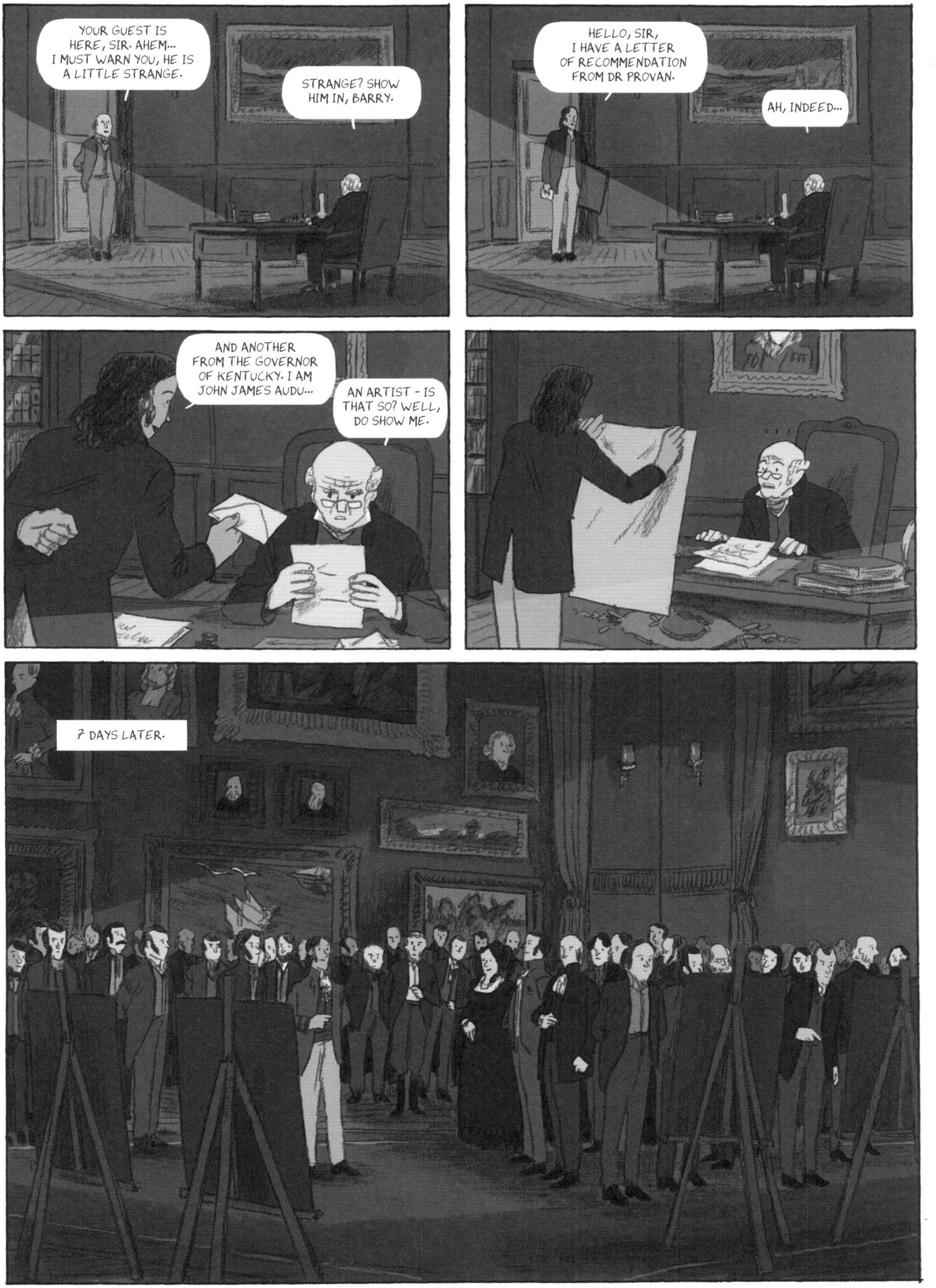
YOUR GUEST IS HERE, SIR. AHEM... I MUST WARN YOU, HE IS A LITTLE STRANGE.
STRANGE? SHOW HIM IN, BARRY.
HELLO, SIR, I HAVE A LETTER OF RECOMMENDATION FROM DR PROVAN.
AH, INDEED...
AND ANOTHER FROM THE GOVERNOR OF KENTUCKY. I AM JOHN JAMES AUDU...
AN ARTIST - IS THAT SO? WELL, DO SHOW ME.
7 DAYS LATER.

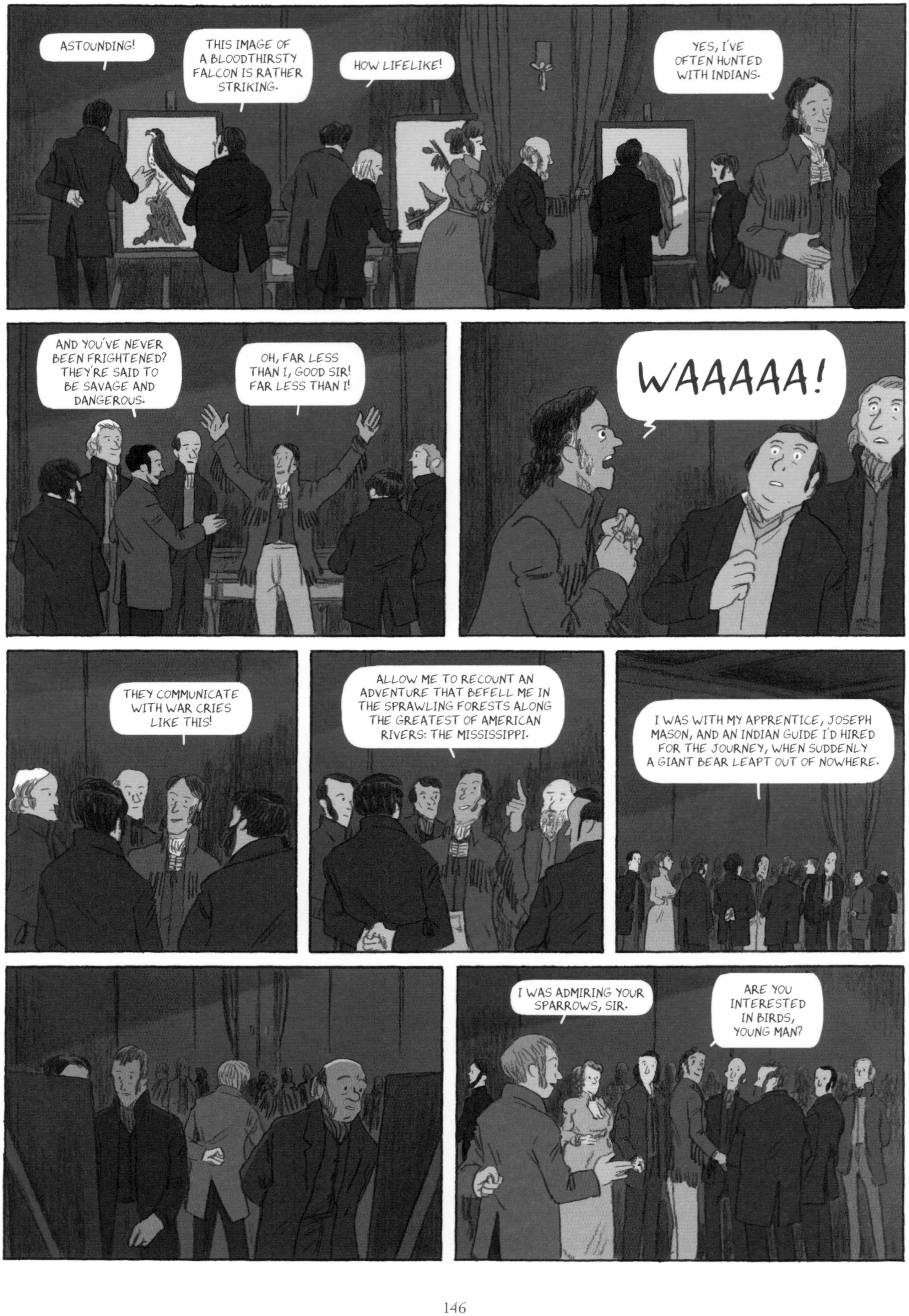
ASTOUNDING!
THIS IMAGE OF A BLOODTHIRSTY FALCON IS RATHER STRIKING.
HOW LIFELIKE!
YES, I'VE OFTEN HUNTED WITH INDIANS.
AND YOU'VE NEVER BEEN FRIGHTENED? THEY'RE SAID TO BE SAVAGE AND DANGEROUS.
OH, FAR LESS THAN I, GOOD SIR! FAR LESS THAN I!
WAAAAA!
THEY COMMUNICATE WITH WAR CRIES LIKE THIS!
ALLOW ME TO RECOUNT AN ADVENTURE THAT BEFELL ME IN THE SPRAWLING FORESTS ALONG THE GREATEST OF AMERICAN RIVERS: THE MISSISSIPPI.
I WAS WITH MY APPRENTICE, JOSEPH MASON, AND AN INDIAN GUIDE I'D HIRED FOR THE JOURNEY, WHEN SUDDENLY A GIANT BEAR LEAPT OUT OF NOWHERE.
I WAS ADMIRING YOUR SPARROWS, SIR.
ARE YOU INTERESTED IN BIRDS, YOUNG MAN?

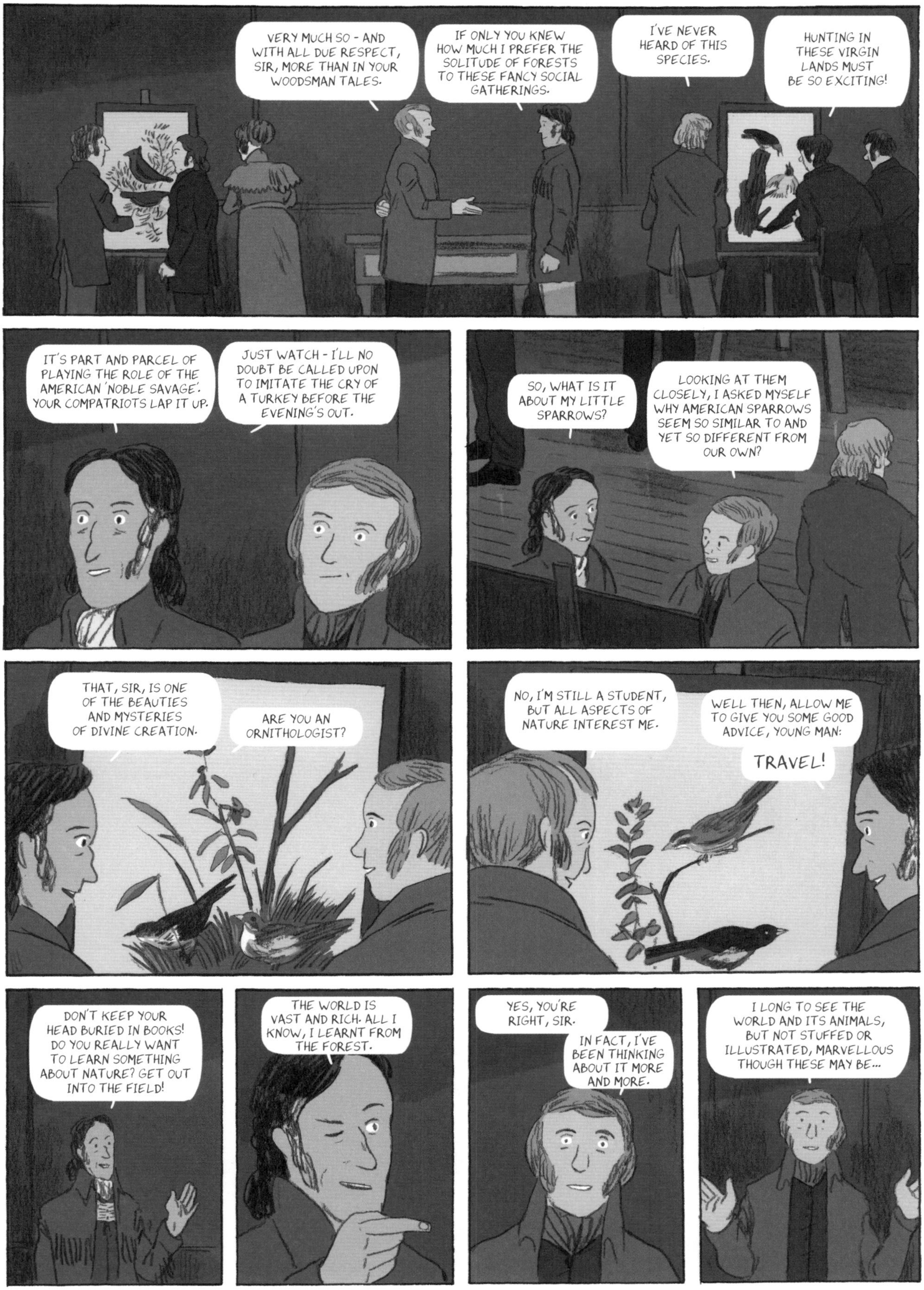
VERY MUCH SO - AND WITH ALL DUE RESPECT, SIR, MORE THAN IN YOUR WOODSMAN TALES.
IF ONLY YOU KNEW HOW MUCH I PREFER THE SOLITUDE OF FORESTS TO THESE FANCY SOCIAL GATHERINGS.
I'VE NEVER HEARD OF THIS SPECIES.
HUNTING IN THESE VIRGIN LANDS MUST BE SO EXCITING!
IT'S PART AND PARCEL OF PLAYING THE ROLE OF THE AMERICAN 'NOBLE SAVAGE'. YOUR COMPATRIOTS LAP IT UP.
JUST WATCH - I'LL NO DOUBT BE CALLED UPON TO IMITATE THE CRY OF A TURKEY BEFORE THE EVENING'S OUT.
SO, WHAT IS IT ABOUT MY LITTLE SPARROWS?
LOOKING AT THEM CLOSELY, I ASKED MYSELF WHY AMERICAN SPARROWS SEEM SO SIMILAR TO AND YET SO DIFFERENT FROM OUR OWN?
THAT, SIR, IS ONE OF THE BEAUTIES AND MYSTERIES OF DIVINE CREATION.
ARE YOU AN ORNITHOLOGIST?
NO, I'M STILL A STUDENT, BUT ALL ASPECTS OF NATURE INTEREST ME.
WELL THEN, ALLOW ME TO GIVE YOU SOME GOOD ADVICE, YOUNG MAN:
TRAVEL!
DON'T KEEP YOUR HEAD BURIED IN BOOKS! DO YOU REALLY WANT TO LEARN SOMETHING ABOUT NATURE? GET OUT INTO THE FIELD!
THE WORLD IS VAST AND RICH. ALL I KNOW, I LEARNT FROM THE FOREST.
YES, YOU'RE RIGHT, SIR.
IN FACT, I'VE BEEN THINKING ABOUT IT MORE AND MORE.
I LONG TO SEE THE WORLD AND ITS ANIMALS, BUT NOT STUFFED OR ILLUSTRATED, MARVELLOUS THOUGH THESE MAY BE...

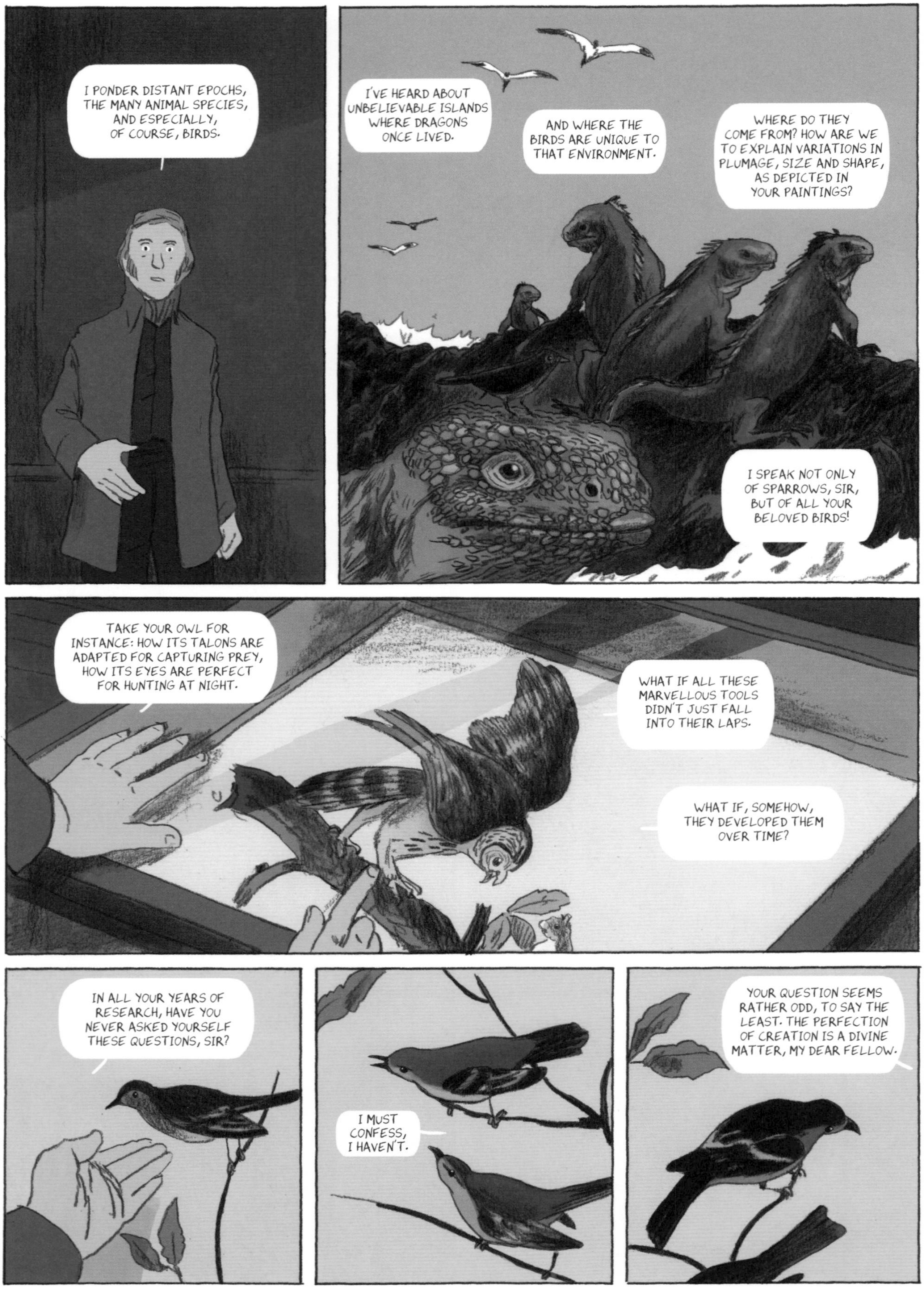
I PONDER DISTANT EPOCHS, THE MANY ANIMAL SPECIES, AND ESPECIALLY, OF COURSE, BIRDS.
I'VE HEARD ABOUT UNBELIEVABLE ISLANDS WHERE DRAGONS ONCE LIVED.
AND WHERE THE BIRDS ARE UNIQUE TO THAT ENVIRONMENT.
WHERE DO THEY COME FROM? HOW ARE WE TO EXPLAIN VARIATIONS IN PLUMAGE, SIZE AND SHAPE, AS DEPICTED IN YOUR PAINTINGS?
I SPEAK NOT ONLY OF SPARROWS, SIR, BUT OF ALL YOUR BELOVED BIRDS!
TAKE YOUR OWL FOR INSTANCE: HOW ITS TALONS ARE ADAPTED FOR CAPTURING PREY, HOW ITS EYES ARE PERFECT FOR HUNTING AT NIGHT.
WHAT IF ALL THESE MARVELLOUS TOOLS DIDN'T JUST FALL INTO THEIR LAPS.
WHAT IF, SOMEHOW, THEY DEVELOPED THEM OVER TIME?
IN ALL YOUR YEARS OF RESEARCH, HAVE YOU NEVER ASKED YOURSELF THESE QUESTIONS, SIR?
I MUST CONFESS, I HAVEN'T.
YOUR QUESTION SEEMS RATHER ODD, TO SAY THE LEAST. THE PERFECTION OF CREATION IS A DIVINE MATTER, MY DEAR FELLOW.

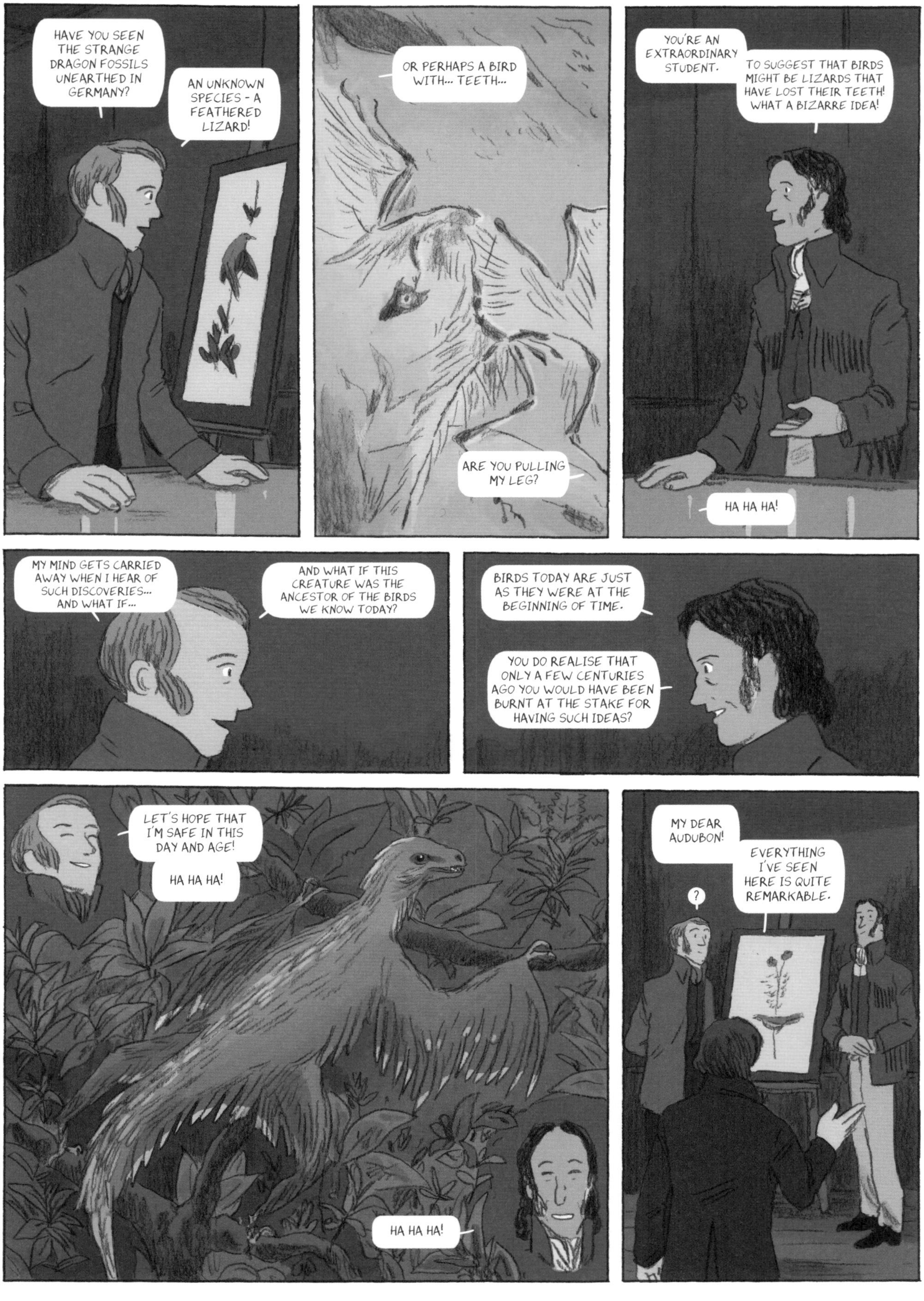
HAVE YOU SEEN THE STRANGE DRAGON FOSSILS UNEARTHED IN GERMANY?
AN UNKNOWN SPECIES - A FEATHERED LIZARD!
OR PERHAPS A BIRD WITH... TEETH...
ARE YOU PULLING MY LEG?
YOU'RE AN EXTRAORDINARY STUDENT.
TO SUGGEST THAT BIRDS MIGHT BE LIZARDS THAT HAVE LOST THEIR TEETH! WHAT A BIZARRE IDEA!
HA HA HA!
MY MIND GETS CARRIED AWAY WHEN I HEAR OF SUCH DISCOVERIES... AND WHAT IF...
AND WHAT IF THIS CREATURE WAS THE ANCESTOR OF THE BIRDS WE KNOW TODAY?
BIRDS TODAY ARE JUST AS THEY WERE AT THE BEGINNING OF TIME.
YOU DO REALISE THAT ONLY A FEW CENTURIES AGO YOU WOULD HAVE BEEN BURNT AT THE STAKE FOR HAVING SUCH IDEAS?
LET'S HOPE THAT I'M SAFE IN THIS DAY AND AGE!
HA HA HA!
HA HA HA!
MY DEAR AUDUBON!
EVERYTHING I'VE SEEN HERE IS QUITE REMARKABLE.
?

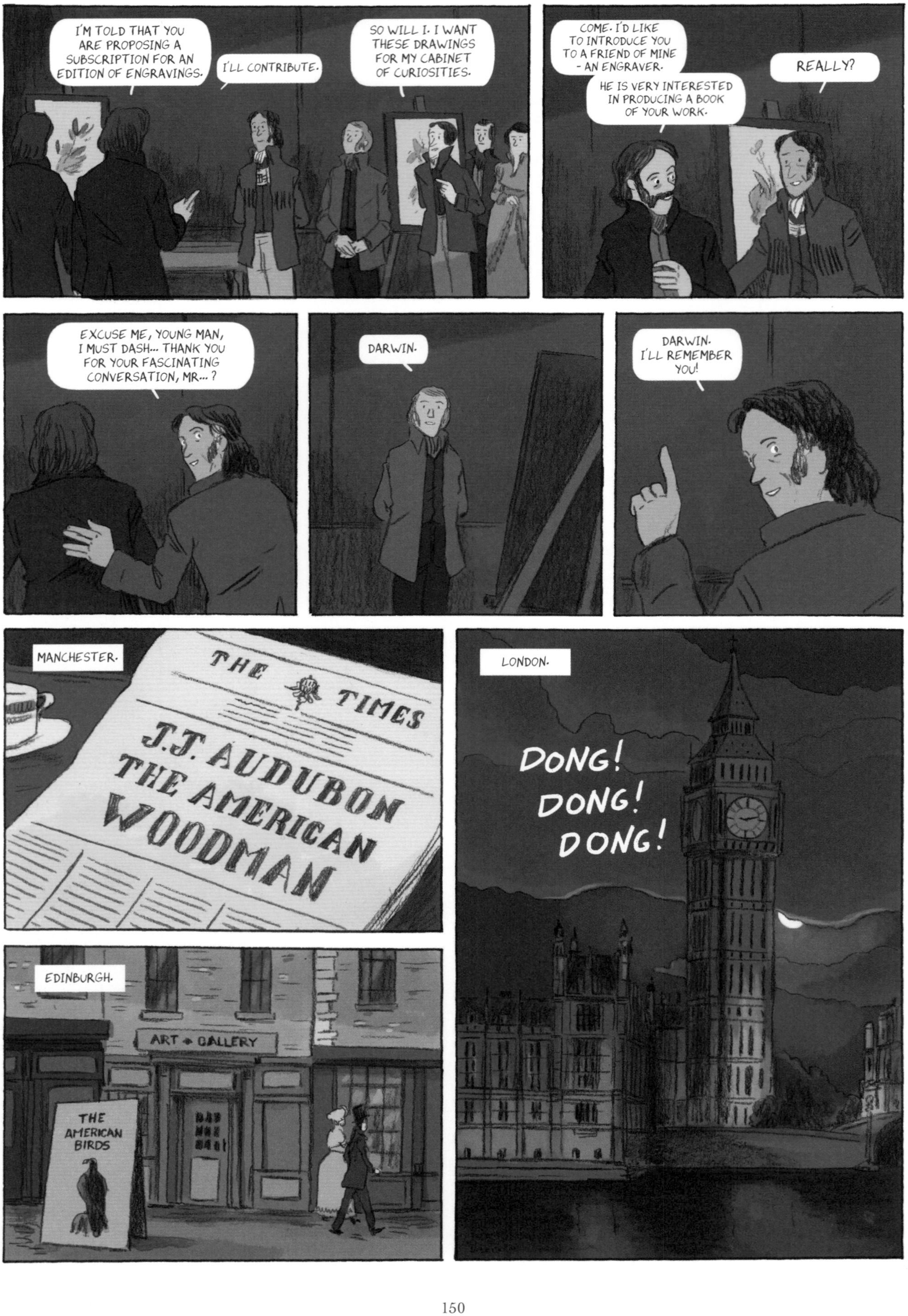
I'M TOLD THAT YOU ARE PROPOSING A SUBSCRIPTION FOR AN EDITION OF ENGRAVINGS.
I'LL CONTRIBUTE.
SO WILL I. I WANT THESE DRAWINGS FOR MY CABINET OF CURIOSITIES.
COME. I'D LIKE TO INTRODUCE YOU TO A FRIEND OF MINE - AN ENGRAVER.
HE IS VERY INTERESTED IN PRODUCING A BOOK OF YOUR WORK.
REALLY?
EXCUSE ME, YOUNG MAN, I MUST DASH... THANK YOU FOR YOUR FASCINATING CONVERSATION, MR...?
DARWIN.
DARWIN. I'LL REMEMBER YOU!
MANCHESTER.
THE TIMES
J.J. AUDUBON THE AMERICAN WOODMAN
LONDON.
DONG! DONG! DONG!
EDINBURGH.
ART GALLERY
THE AMERICAN BIRDS

· V ·
MISSOURI

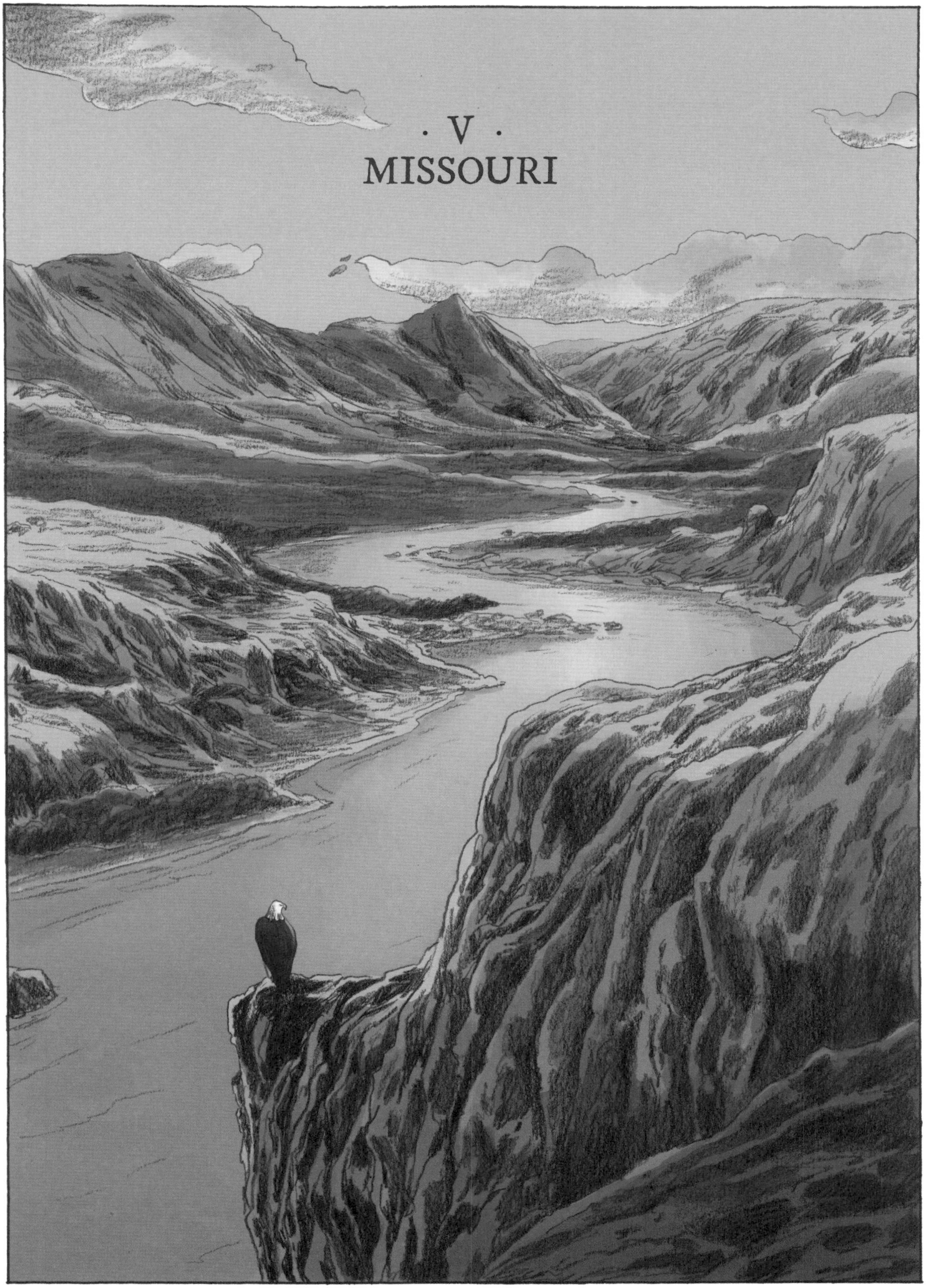

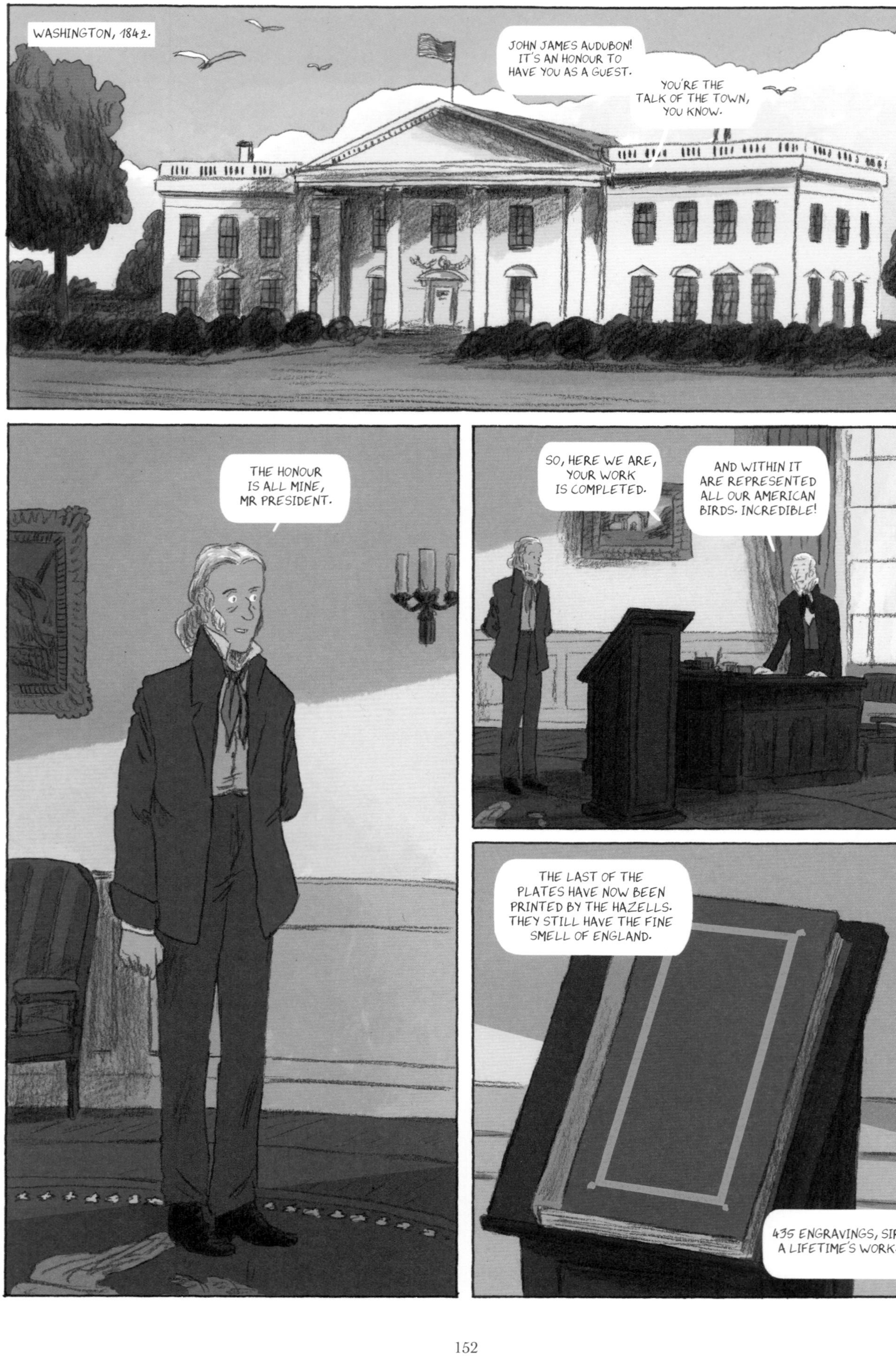
WASHINGTON, 1842.
JOHN JAMES AUDUBON! IT'S AN HONOUR TO HAVE YOU AS A GUEST.
YOU'RE THE TALK OF THE TOWN, YOU KNOW.
THE HONOUR IS ALL MINE, MR PRESIDENT.
SO, HERE WE ARE, YOUR WORK IS COMPLETED.
AND WITHIN IT ARE REPRESENTED ALL OUR AMERICAN BIRDS. INCREDIBLE!
THE LAST OF THE PLATES HAVE NOW BEEN PRINTED BY THE HAZELLS. THEY STILL HAVE THE FINE SMELL OF ENGLAND.
435 ENGRAVINGS, SIR: A LIFETIME'S WORK.

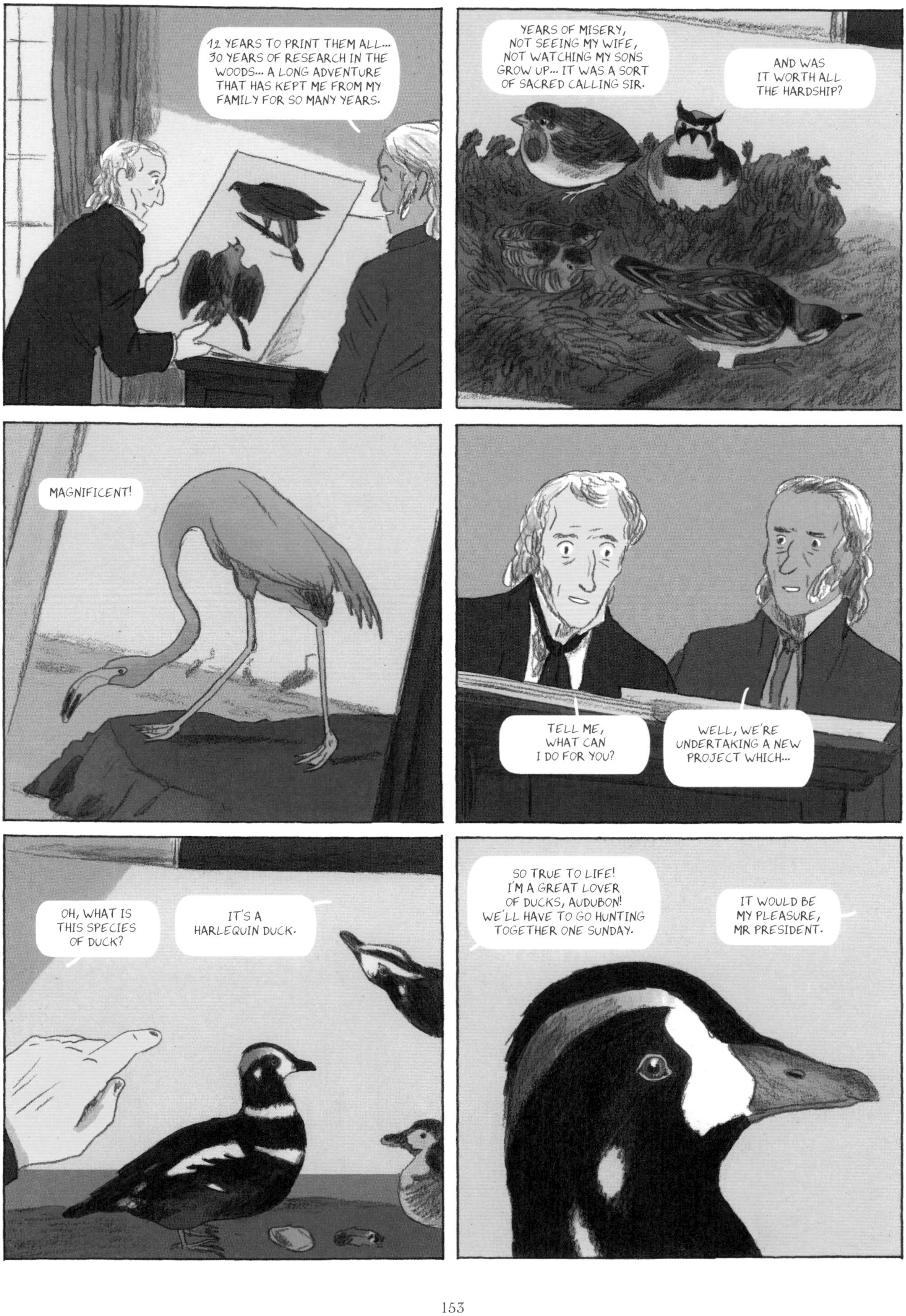
12 YEARS TO PRINT THEM ALL... 30 YEARS OF RESEARCH IN THE WOODS... A LONG ADVENTURE THAT HAS KEPT ME FROM MY FAMILY FOR SO MANY YEARS.
YEARS OF MISERY, NOT SEEING MY WIFE, NOT WATCHING MY SONS GROW UP... IT WAS A SORT OF SACRED CALLING SIR.
AND WAS IT WORTH ALL THE HARDSHIP?
MAGNIFICENT!
TELL ME, WHAT CAN I DO FOR YOU?
WELL, WE'RE UNDERTAKING A NEW PROJECT WHICH...
OH, WHAT IS THIS SPECIES OF DUCK?
IT'S A HARLEQUIN DUCK.
SO TRUE TO LIFE! I'M A GREAT LOVER OF DUCKS, AUDUBON! WE'LL HAVE TO GO HUNTING TOGETHER ONE SUNDAY.
IT WOULD BE MY PLEASURE, MR PRESIDENT.

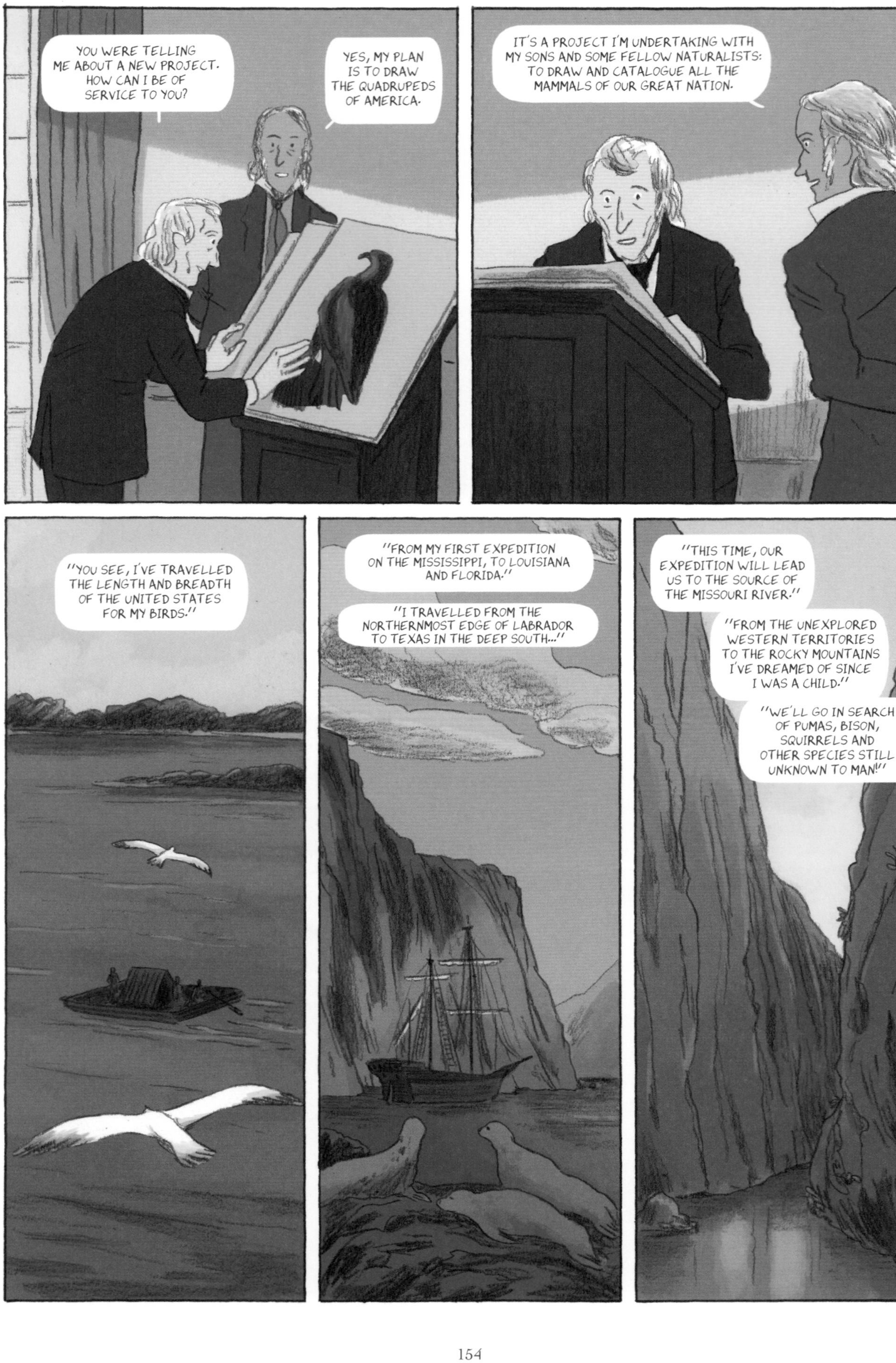

YOU WERE TELLING ME ABOUT A NEW PROJECT. HOW CAN I BE OF SERVICE TO YOU?
YES, MY PLAN IS TO DRAW THE QUADRUPEDS OF AMERICA.
IT'S A PROJECT I'M UNDERTAKING WITH MY SONS AND SOME FELLOW NATURALISTS: TO DRAW AND CATALOGUE ALL THE MAMMALS OF OUR GREAT NATION.
"YOU SEE, I'VE TRAVELLED THE LENGTH AND BREADTH OF THE UNITED STATES FOR MY BIRDS."
"FROM MY FIRST EXPEDITION ON THE MISSISSIPPI, TO LOUISIANA AND FLORIDA."
"I TRAVELLED FROM THE NORTHERNMOST EDGE OF LABRADOR TO TEXAS IN THE DEEP SOUTH..."
"THIS TIME, OUR EXPEDITION WILL LEAD US TO THE SOURCE OF THE MISSOURI RIVER."
"FROM THE UNEXPLORED WESTERN TERRITORIES TO THE ROCKY MOUNTAINS I'VE DREAMED OF SINCE I WAS A CHILD."
"WE'LL GO IN SEARCH OF PUMAS, BISON, SQUIRRELS AND OTHER SPECIES STILL UNKNOWN TO MAN!"

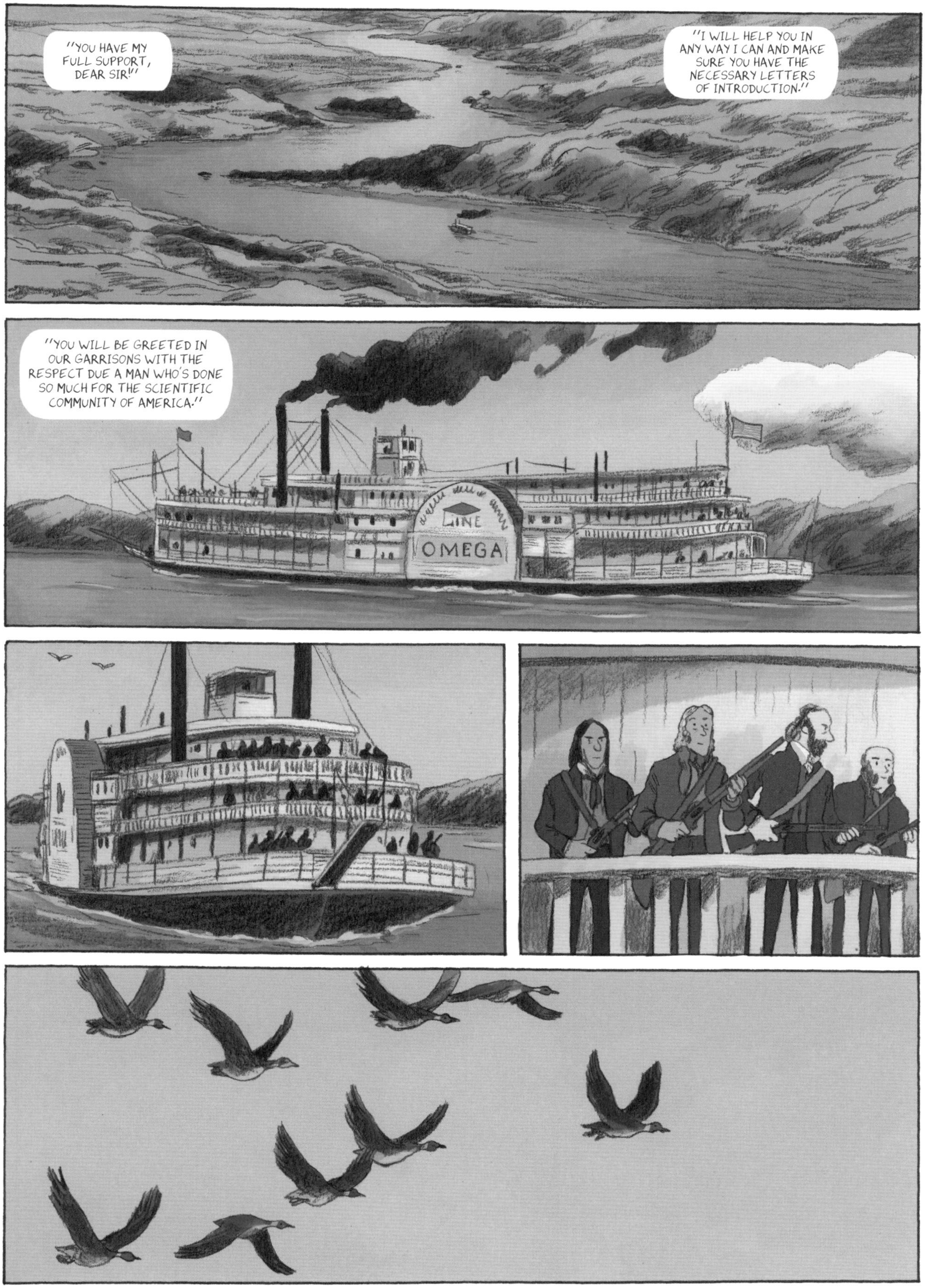
"YOU HAVE MY FULL SUPPORT, DEAR SIR!"
"I WILL HELP YOU IN ANY WAY I CAN AND MAKE SURE YOU HAVE THE NECESSARY LETTERS OF INTRODUCTION."
"YOU WILL BE GREETED IN OUR GARRISONS WITH THE RESPECT DUE A MAN WHO'S DONE SO MUCH FOR THE SCIENTIFIC COMMUNITY OF AMERICA."
LINE
OMEGA

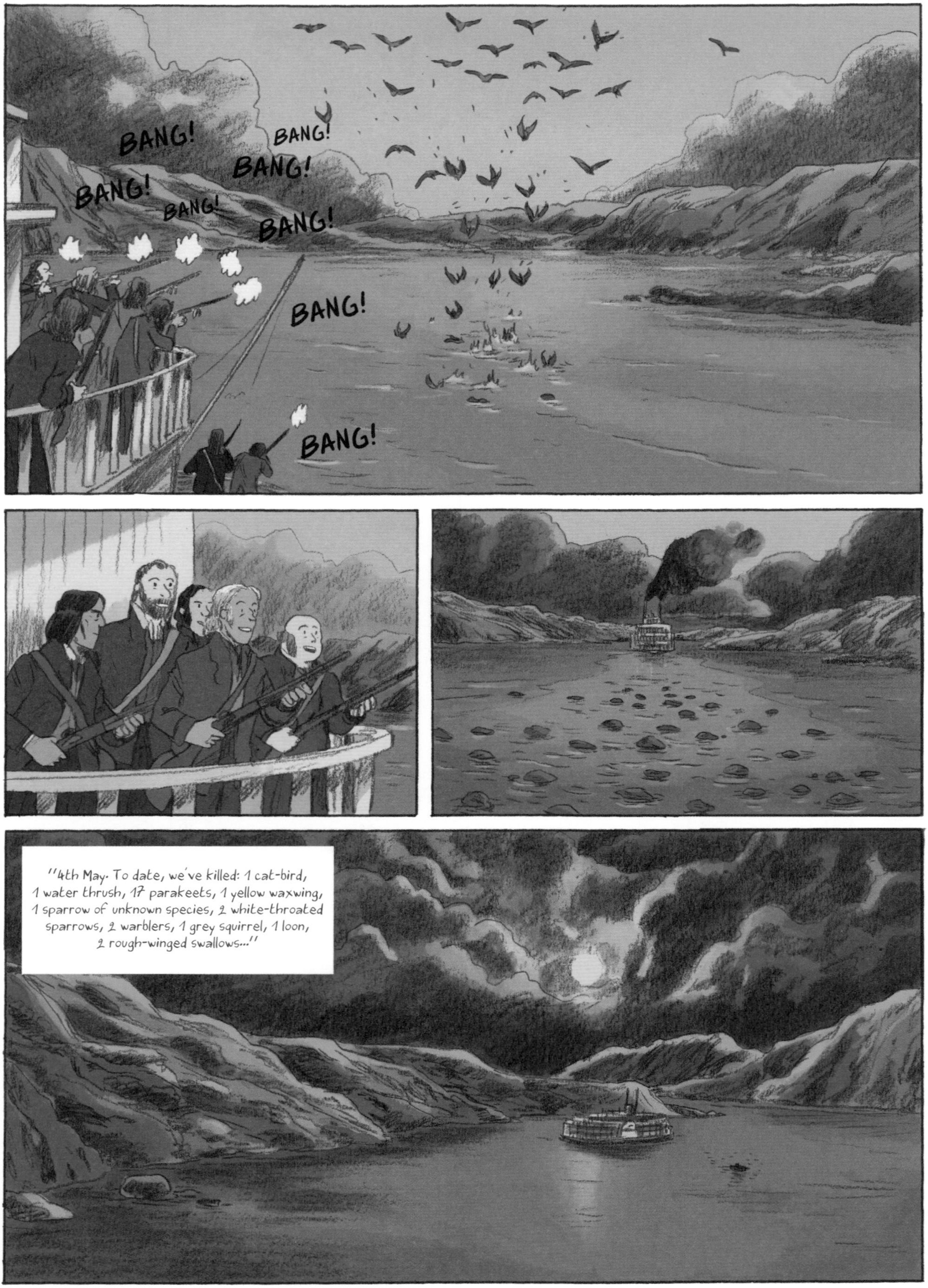
BANG!
BANG!
BANG!
BANG!
BANG!
BANG!
BANG!
BANG!
"4th May. To date, we've killed: 1 cat-bird, 1 water thrush, 17 parakeets, 1 yellow waxwing, 1 sparrow of unknown species, 2 white-throated sparrows, 2 warblers, 1 grey squirrel, 1 loon, 2 rough-winged swallows..."

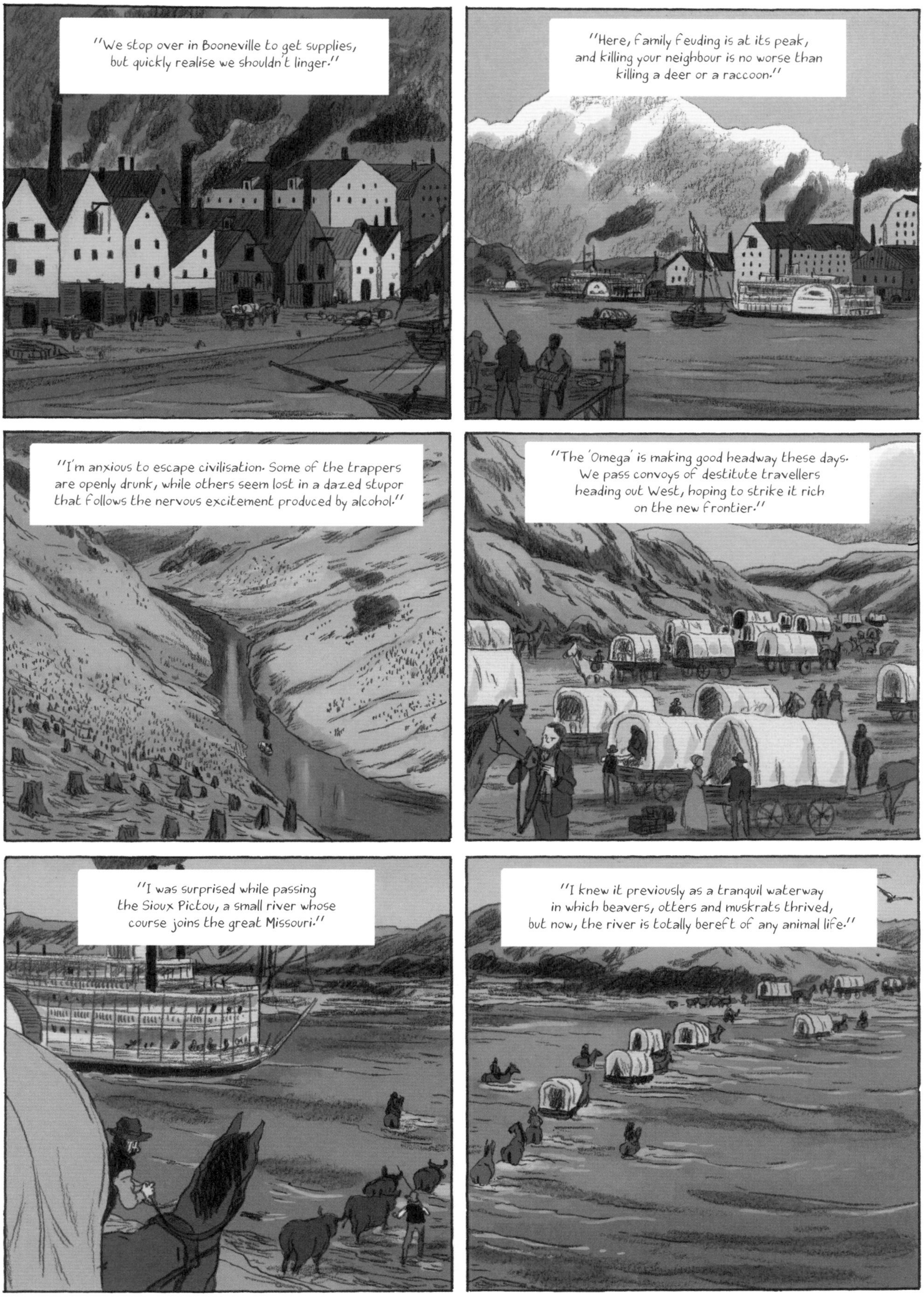
"We stop over in Booneville to get supplies, but quickly realise we shouldn't linger."
"Here, family feuding is at its peak, and killing your neighbour is no worse than killing a deer or a raccoon."
"I'm anxious to escape civilisation. Some of the trappers are openly drunk, while others seem lost in a dazed stupor that follows the nervous excitement produced by alcohol."
"The 'Omega' is making good headway these days. We pass convoys of destitute travellers heading out West, hoping to strike it rich on the new frontier."
"I was surprised while passing the Sioux Pictou, a small river whose course joins the great Missouri."
"I knew it previously as a tranquil waterway in which beavers, otters and muskrats thrived, but now, the river is totally bereft of any animal life."

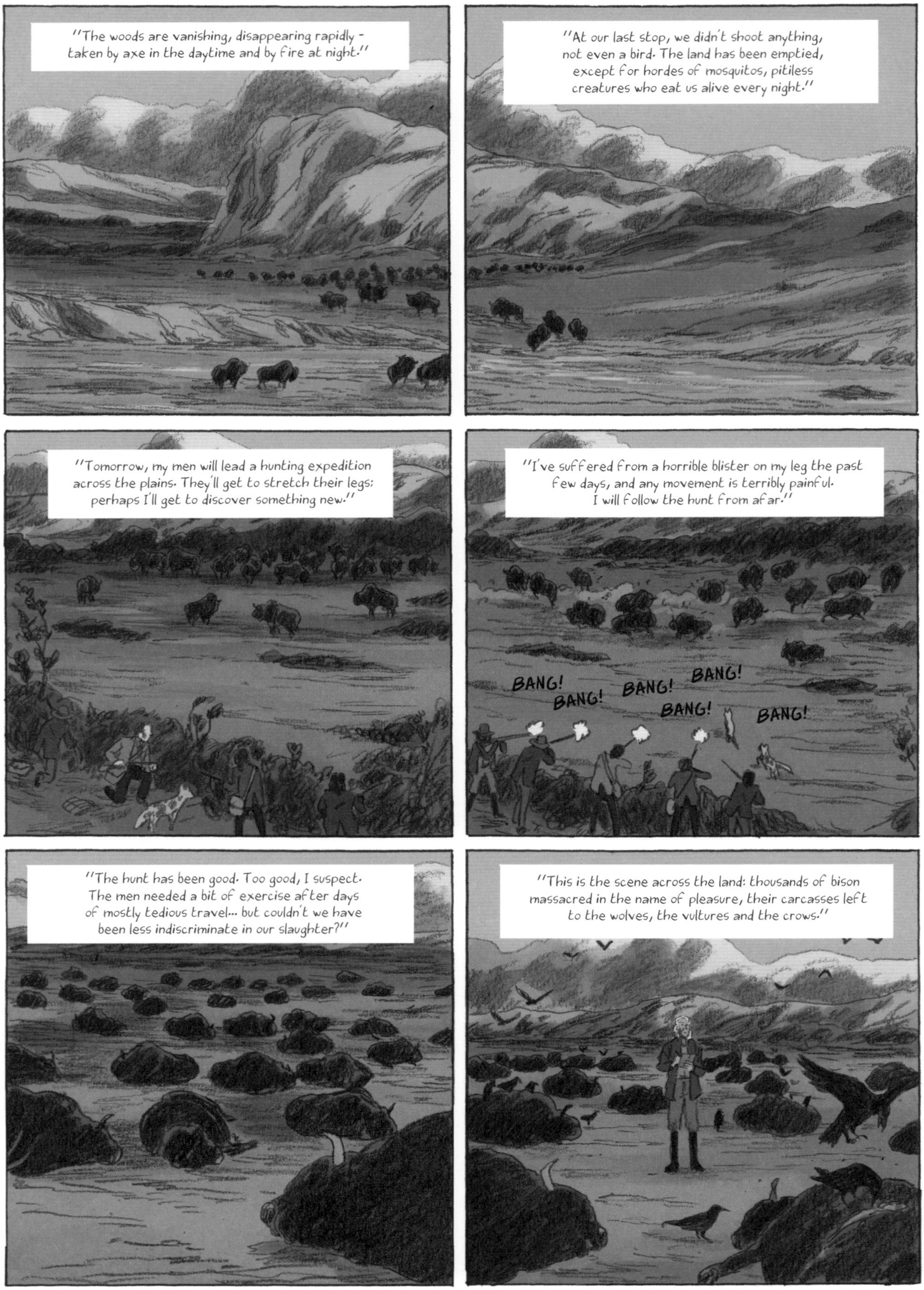
"The woods are vanishing, disappearing rapidly - taken by axe in the daytime and by fire at night."
"At our last stop, we didn't shoot anything, not even a bird. The land has been emptied, except for hordes of mosquitos, pitiless creatures who eat us alive every night."
"Tomorrow, my men will lead a hunting expedition across the plains. They'll get to stretch their legs; perhaps I'll get to discover something new."
"I've suffered from a horrible blister on my leg the past few days, and any movement is terribly painful. I will follow the hunt from afar."
BANG!
BANG!
BANG!
BANG!
BANG!
BANG!
"The hunt has been good. Too good, I suspect. The men needed a bit of exercise after days of mostly tedious travel... but couldn't we have been less indiscriminate in our slaughter?"
"This is the scene across the land: thousands of bison massacred in the name of pleasure, their carcasses left to the wolves, the vultures and the crows."

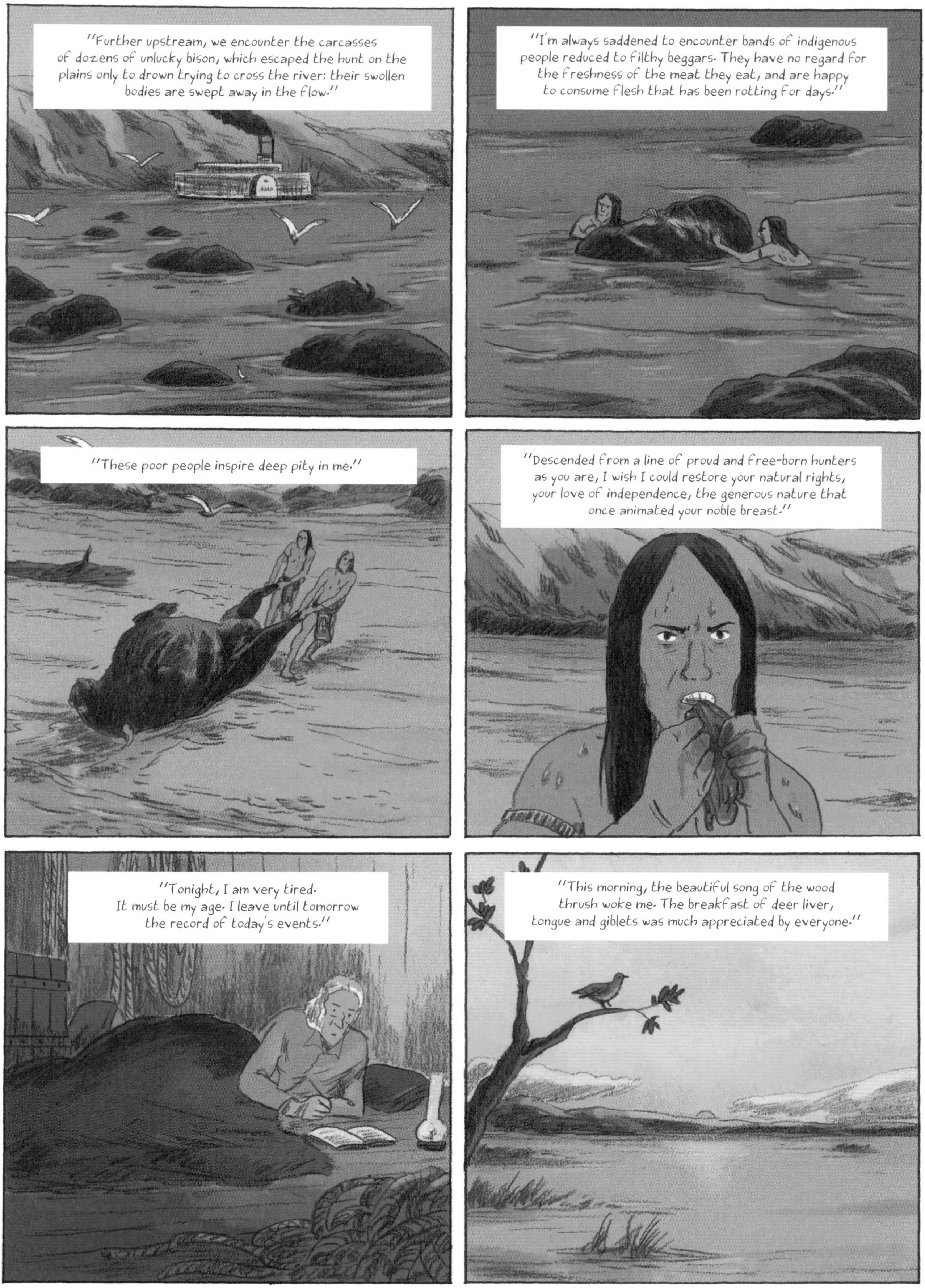
"Further upstream, we encounter the carcasses of dozens of unlucky bison, which escaped the hunt on the plains only to drown trying to cross the river: their swollen bodies are swept away in the flow."
"I'm always saddened to encounter bands of indigenous people reduced to filthy beggars. They have no regard for the freshness of the meat they eat, and are happy to consume flesh that has been rotting for days."
"These poor people inspire deep pity in me."
"Descended from a line of proud and free-born hunters as you are, I wish I could restore your natural rights, your love of independence, the generous nature that once animated your noble breast."
"Tonight, I am very tired. It must be my age. I leave until tomorrow the record of today's events."
"This morning, the beautiful song of the wood thrush woke me. The breakfast of deer liver, tongue and giblets was much appreciated by everyone."

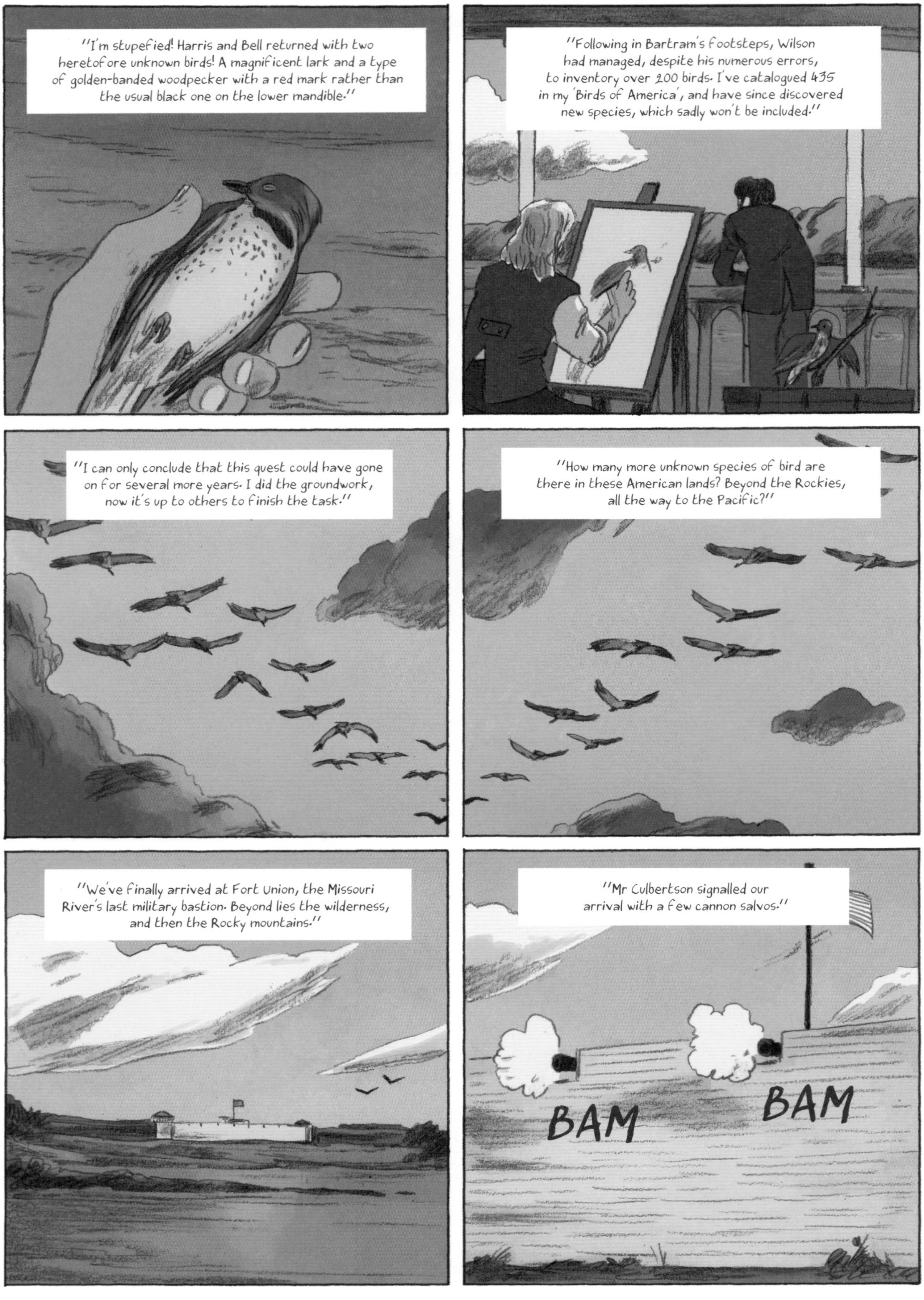
"I'm stupefied! Harris and Bell returned with two heretofore unknown birds! A magnificent lark and a type of golden-banded woodpecker with a red mark rather than the usual black one on the lower mandible."
"Following in Bartram's footsteps, Wilson had managed, despite his numerous errors, to inventory over 200 birds. I've catalogued 435 in my 'Birds of America', and have since discovered new species, which sadly won't be included."
"I can only conclude that this quest could have gone on for several more years. I did the groundwork, now it's up to others to finish the task."
"How many more unknown species of bird are there in these American lands? Beyond the Rockies, all the way to the Pacific?"
"We've finally arrived at Fort Union, the Missouri River's last military bastion. Beyond lies the wilderness, and then the Rocky mountains."
"Mr Culbertson signalled our arrival with a few cannon salvos."
BAM
BAM

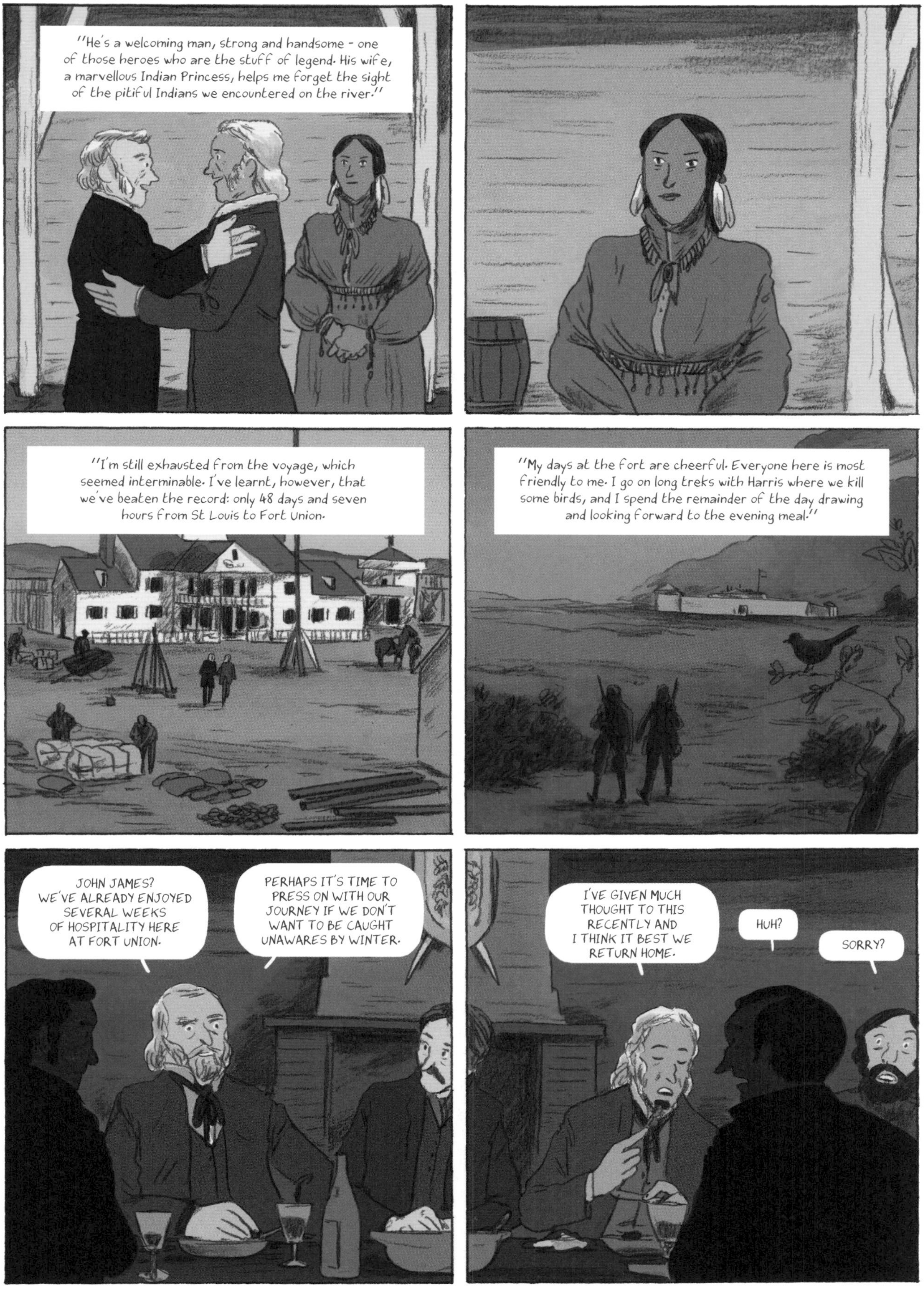
"He's a welcoming man, strong and handsome - one of those heroes who are the stuff of legend. His wife, a marvellous Indian Princess, helps me forget the sight of the pitiful Indians we encountered on the river."
"I'm still exhausted from the voyage, which seemed interminable. I've learnt, however, that we've beaten the record: only 48 days and seven hours from St Louis to Fort Union.
"My days at the fort are cheerful. Everyone here is most friendly to me. I go on long treks with Harris where we kill some birds, and I spend the remainder of the day drawing and looking forward to the evening meal."
JOHN JAMES? WE'VE ALREADY ENJOYED SEVERAL WEEKS OF HOSPITALITY HERE AT FORT UNION.
PERHAPS IT'S TIME TO PRESS ON WITH OUR JOURNEY IF WE DON'T WANT TO BE CAUGHT UNAWARES BY WINTER.
I'VE GIVEN MUCH THOUGHT TO THIS RECENTLY AND I THINK IT BEST WE RETURN HOME.
HUH?
SORRY?

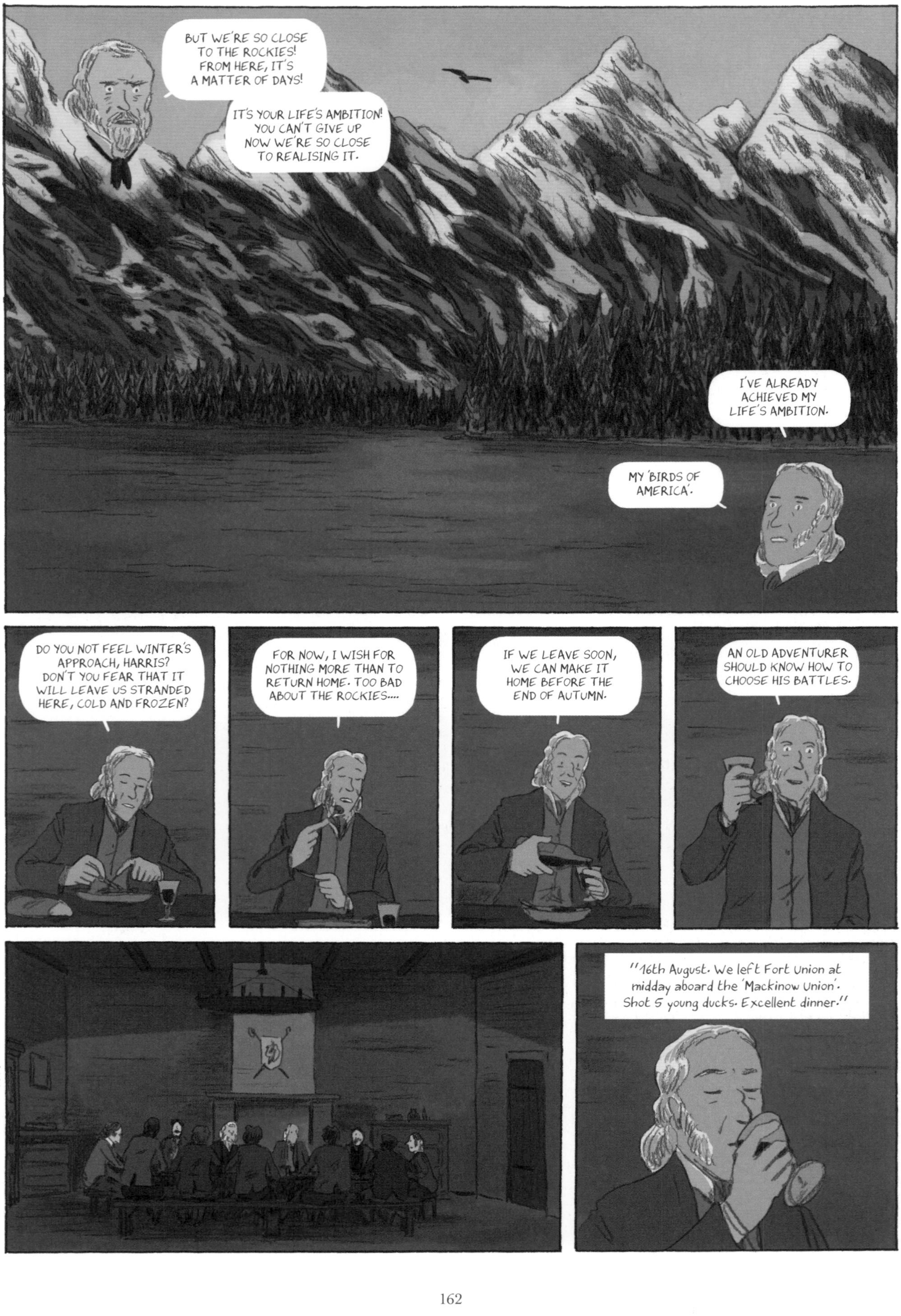

BUT WE'RE SO CLOSE TO THE ROCKIES! FROM HERE, IT'S A MATTER OF DAYS!
IT'S YOUR LIFE'S AMBITION! YOU CAN'T GIVE UP NOW WE'RE SO CLOSE TO REALISING IT.
I'VE ALREADY ACHIEVED MY LIFE'S AMBITION.
MY 'BIRDS OF AMERICA'.
DO YOU NOT FEEL WINTER'S APPROACH, HARRIS? DON'T YOU FEAR THAT IT WILL LEAVE US STRANDED HERE, COLD AND FROZEN?
FOR NOW, I WISH FOR NOTHING MORE THAN TO RETURN HOME. TOO BAD ABOUT THE ROCKIES....
IF WE LEAVE SOON, WE CAN MAKE IT HOME BEFORE THE END OF AUTUMN.
AN OLD ADVENTURER SHOULD KNOW HOW TO CHOOSE HIS BATTLES.
"16th August. We left Fort Union at midday aboard the 'Mackinow Union'. Shot 5 young ducks. Excellent dinner."

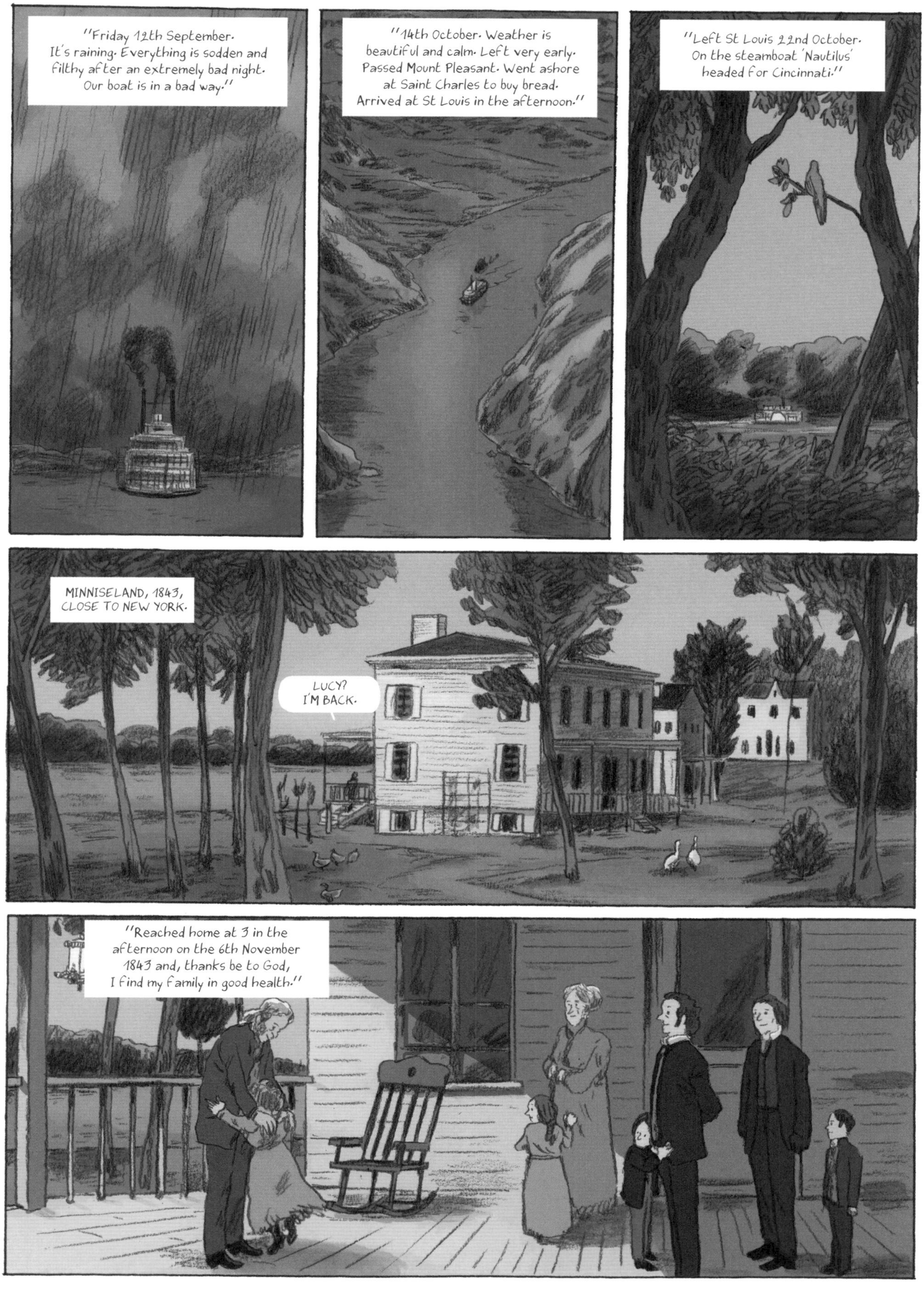
"Friday 12th September. It's raining. Everything is sodden and filthy after an extremely bad night. Our boat is in a bad way."
"14th October. Weather is beautiful and calm. Left very early. Passed Mount Pleasant. Went ashore at Saint Charles to buy bread. Arrived at St Louis in the afternoon."
"Left St Louis 22nd October. On the steamboat 'Nautilus' headed for Cincinnati."
MINNISELAND, 1843, CLOSE TO NEW YORK.
LUCY? I'M BACK.
"Reached home at 3 in the afternoon on the 6th November 1843 and, thanks be to God, I find my family in good health."

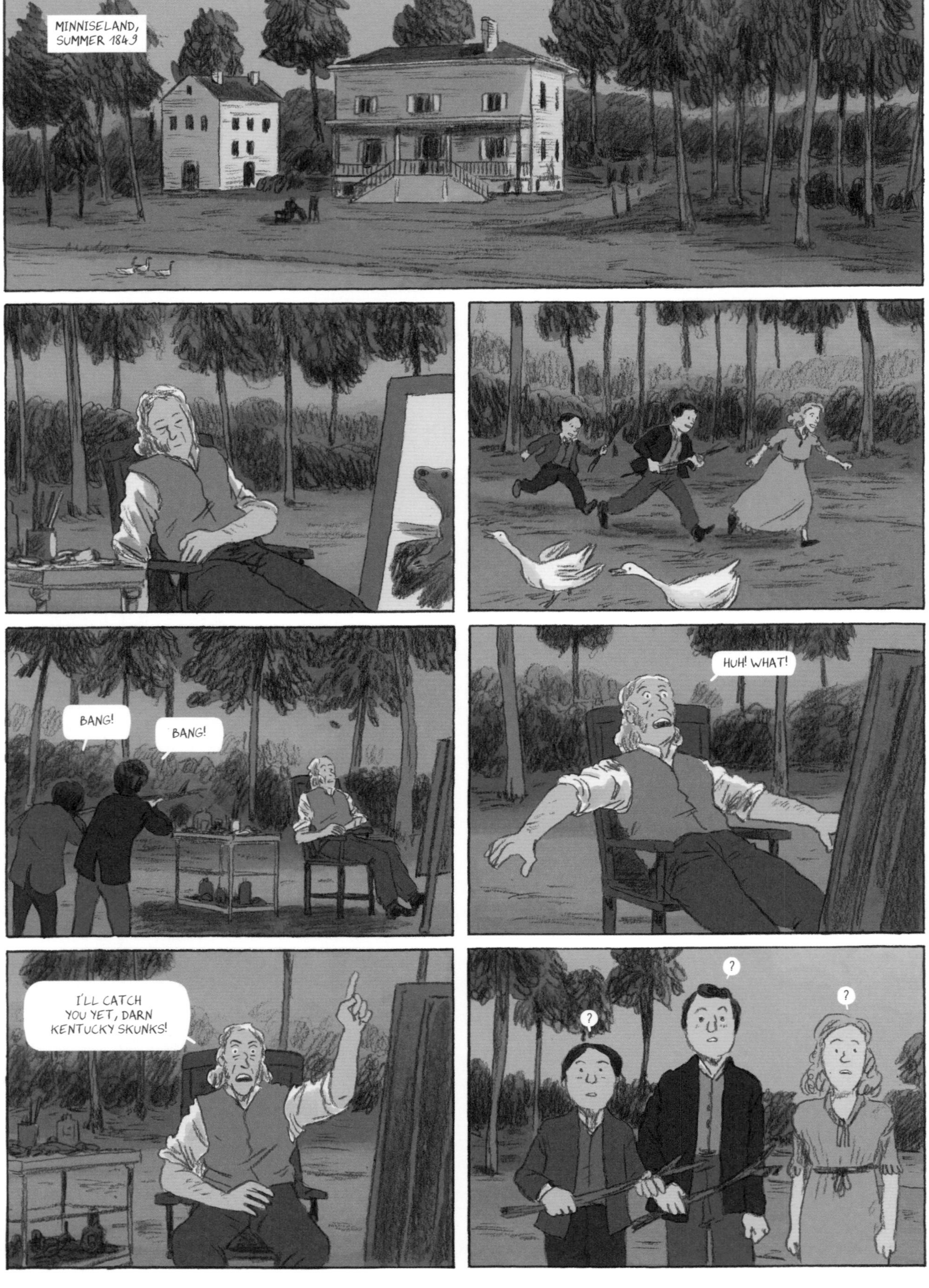
MINNISELAND, SUMMER 1849
BANG!
BANG!
HUH! WHAT!
I'LL CATCH YOU YET, DARN KENTUCKY SKUNKS!
?
?
?

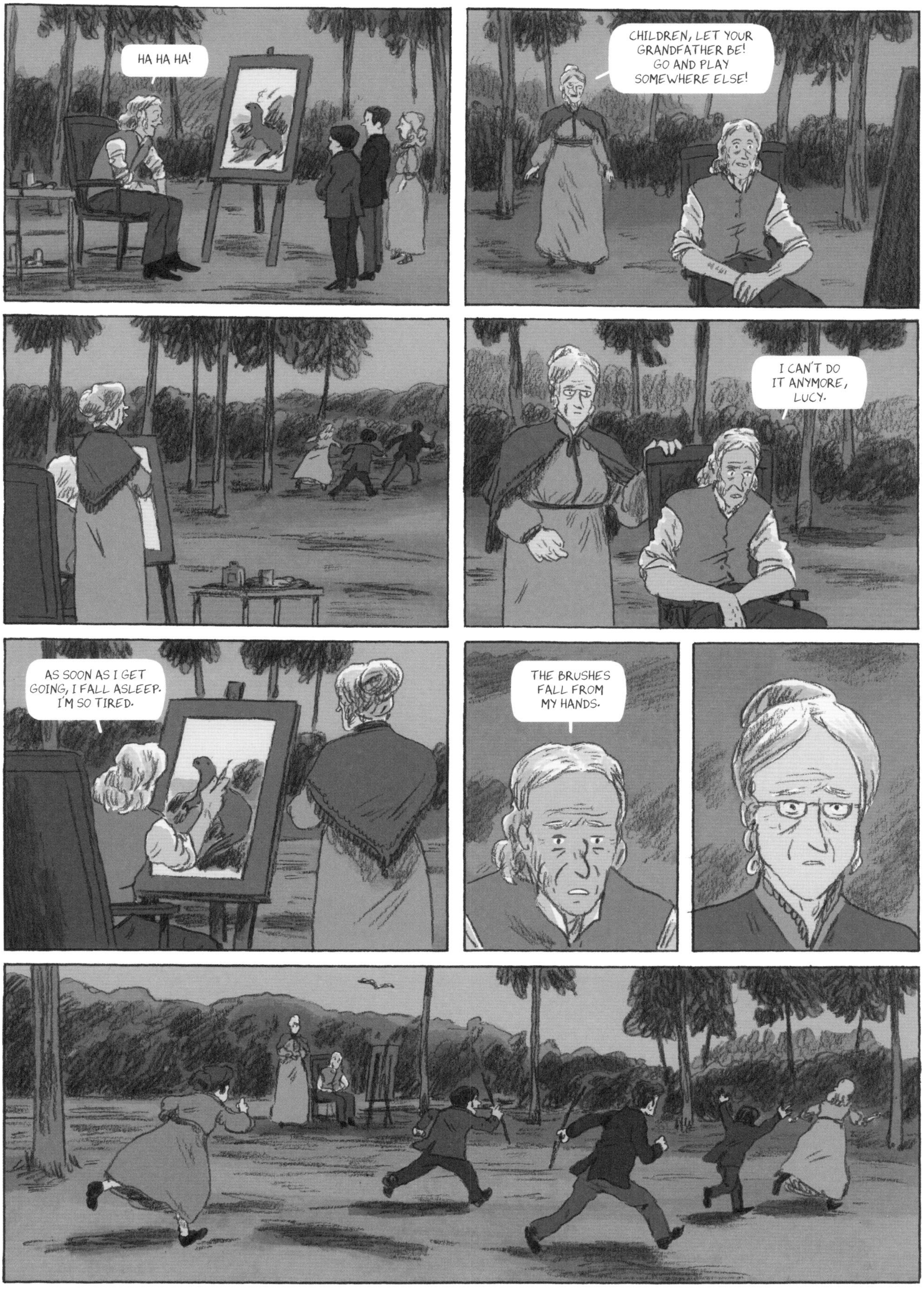

HA HA HA!
CHILDREN, LET YOUR GRANDFATHER BE! GO AND PLAY SOMEWHERE ELSE!
I CAN'T DO IT ANYMORE, LUCY.
AS SOON AS I GET GOING, I FALL ASLEEP. I'M SO TIRED.
THE BRUSHES FALL FROM MY HANDS.

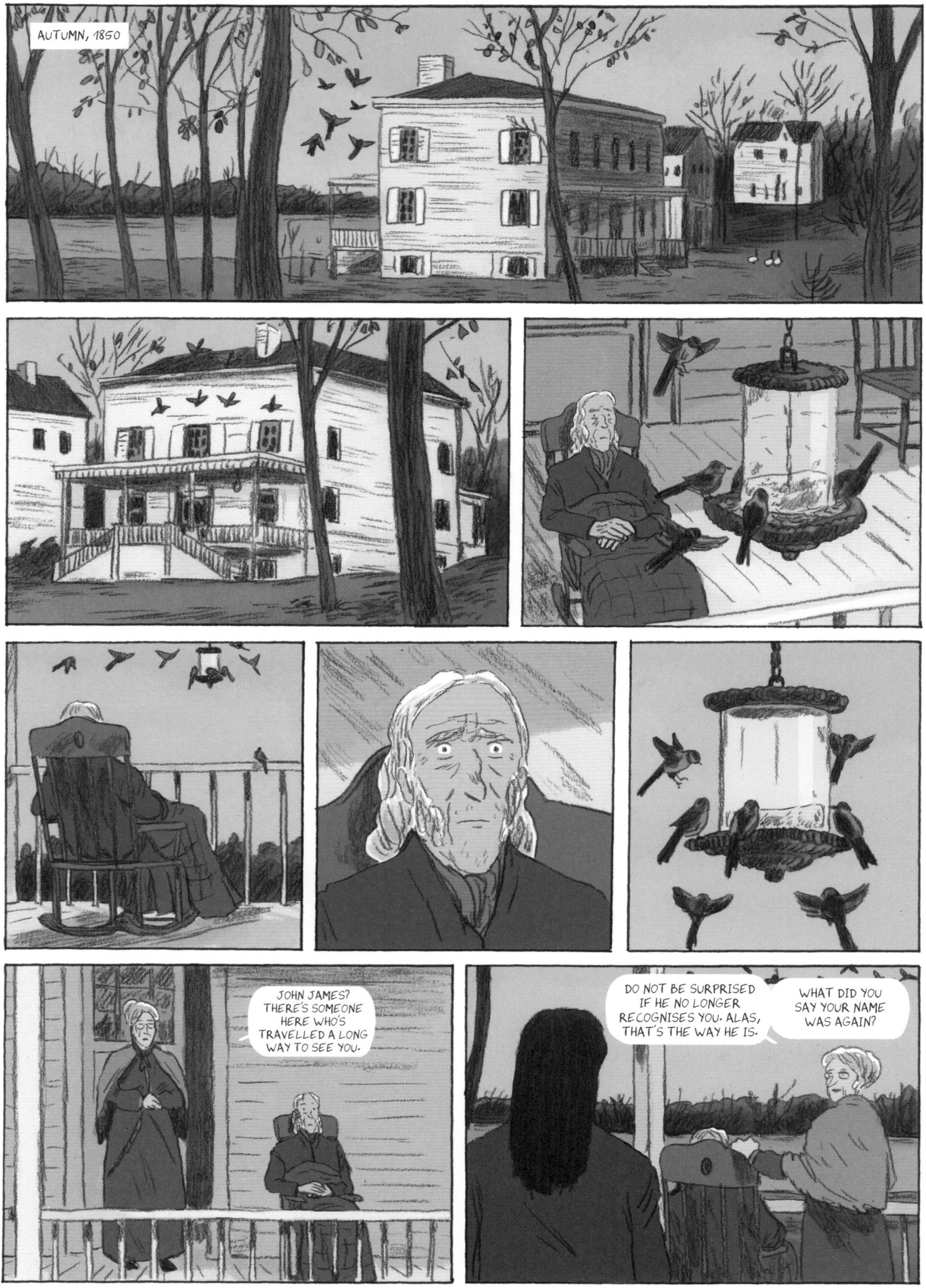
AUTUMN, 1850
JOHN JAMES? THERE'S SOMEONE HERE WHO'S TRAVELLED A LONG WAY TO SEE YOU.
DO NOT BE SURPRISED IF HE NO LONGER RECOGNISES YOU. ALAS, THAT'S THE WAY HE IS.
WHAT DID YOU SAY YOUR NAME WAS AGAIN?

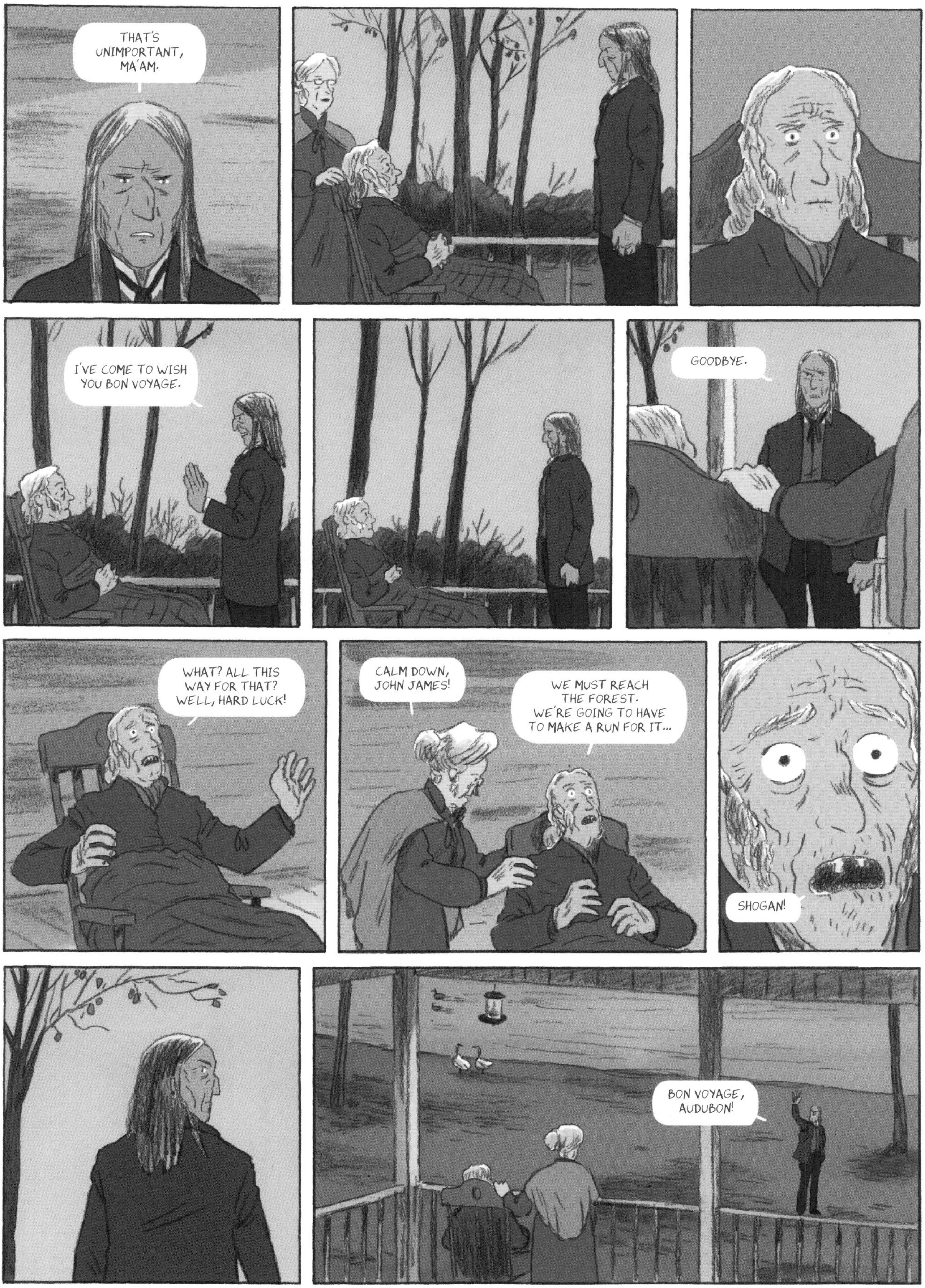
THAT'S UNIMPORTANT, MA'AM.
I'VE COME TO WISH YOU BON VOYAGE.
GOODBYE.
WHAT? ALL THIS WAY FOR THAT? WELL, HARD LUCK!
CALM DOWN, JOHN JAMES!
WE MUST REACH THE FOREST. WE'RE GOING TO HAVE TO MAKE A RUN FOR IT...
SHOGAN!
BON VOYAGE, AUDUBON!

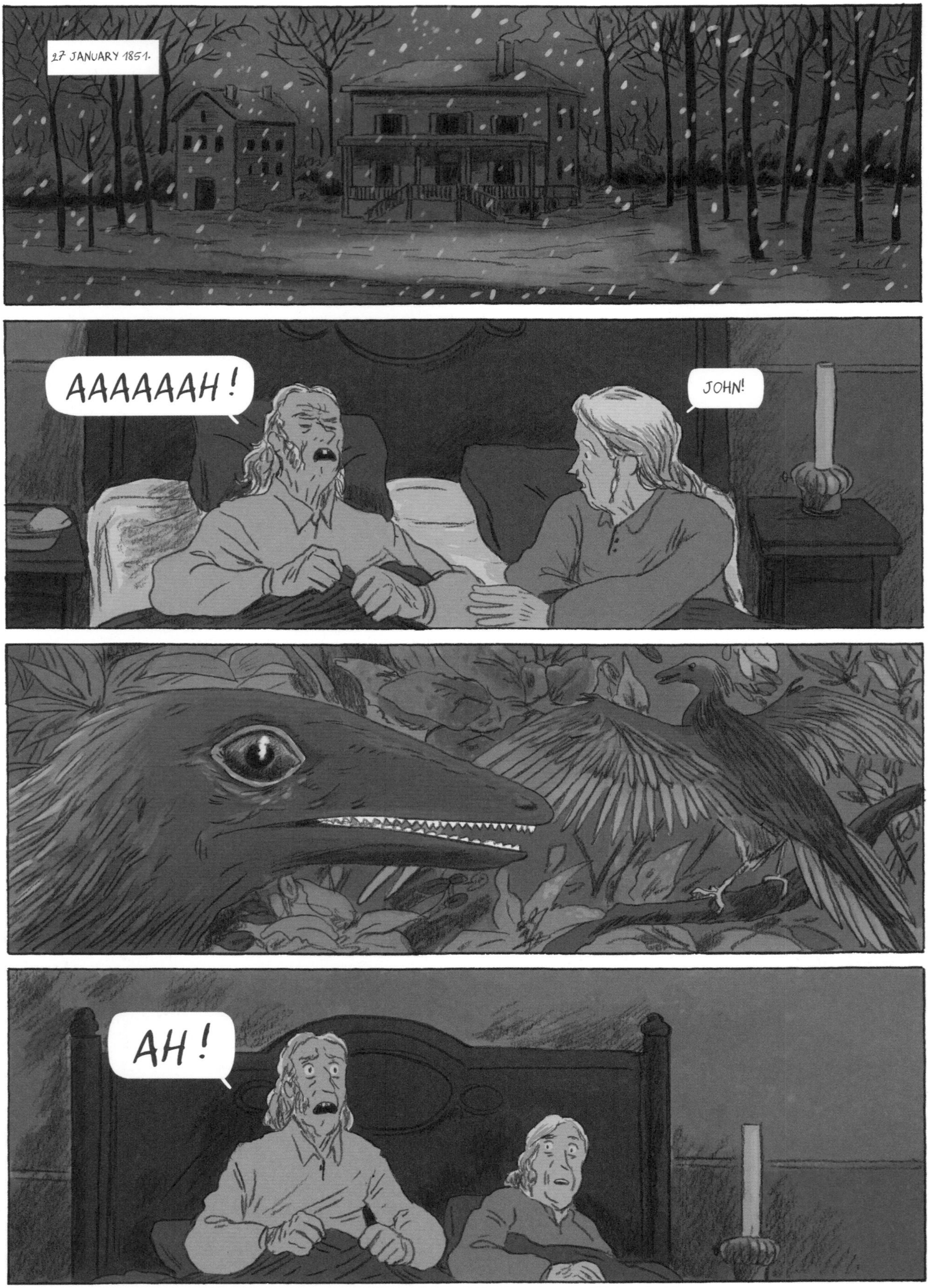
27 JANUARY 1851.
AAAAAAH!
JOHN!
AH!

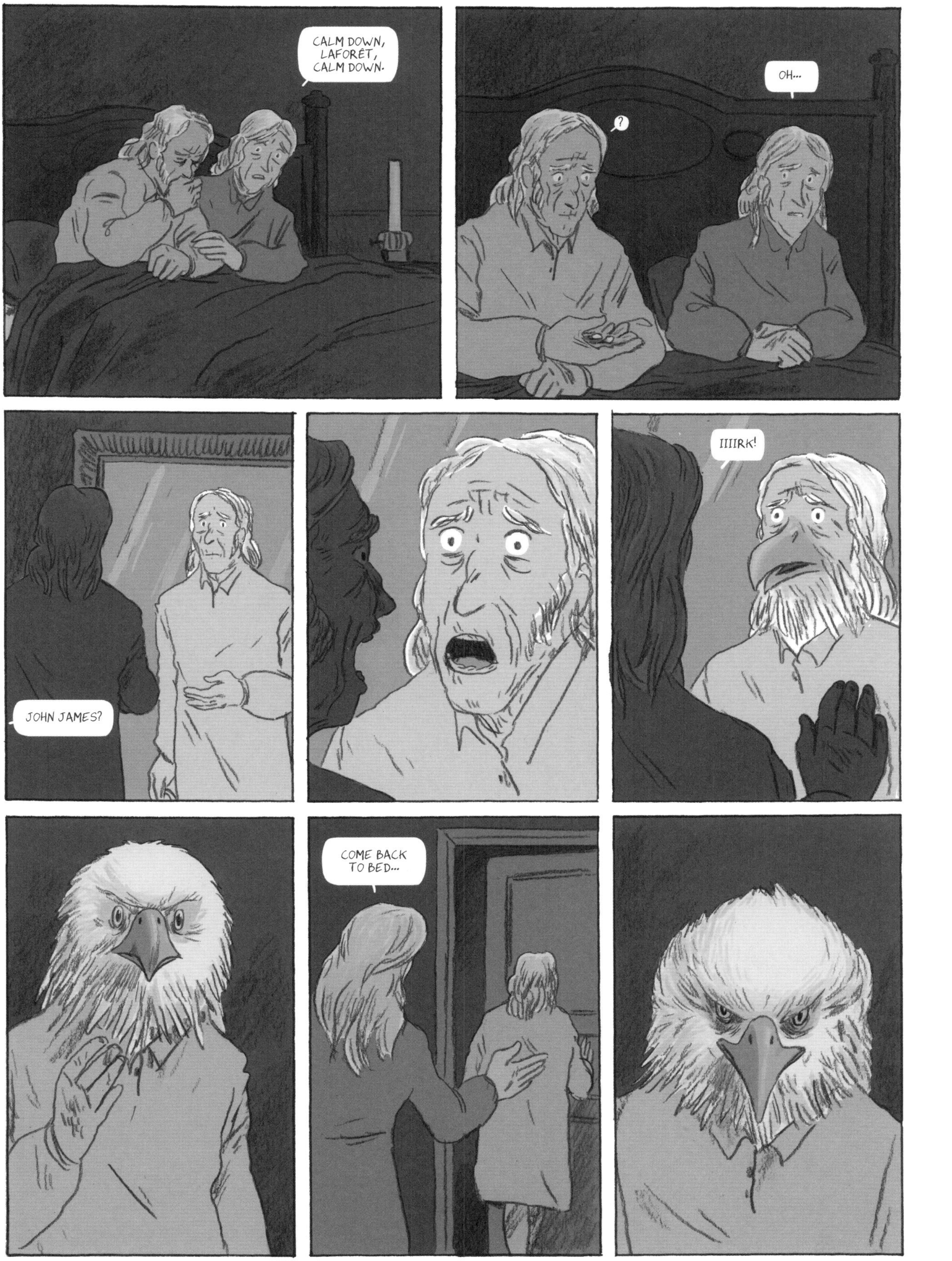
CALM DOWN, LAFORÊT, CALM DOWN.
OH...
?
JOHN JAMES?
IIIIRK!
COME BACK TO BED...

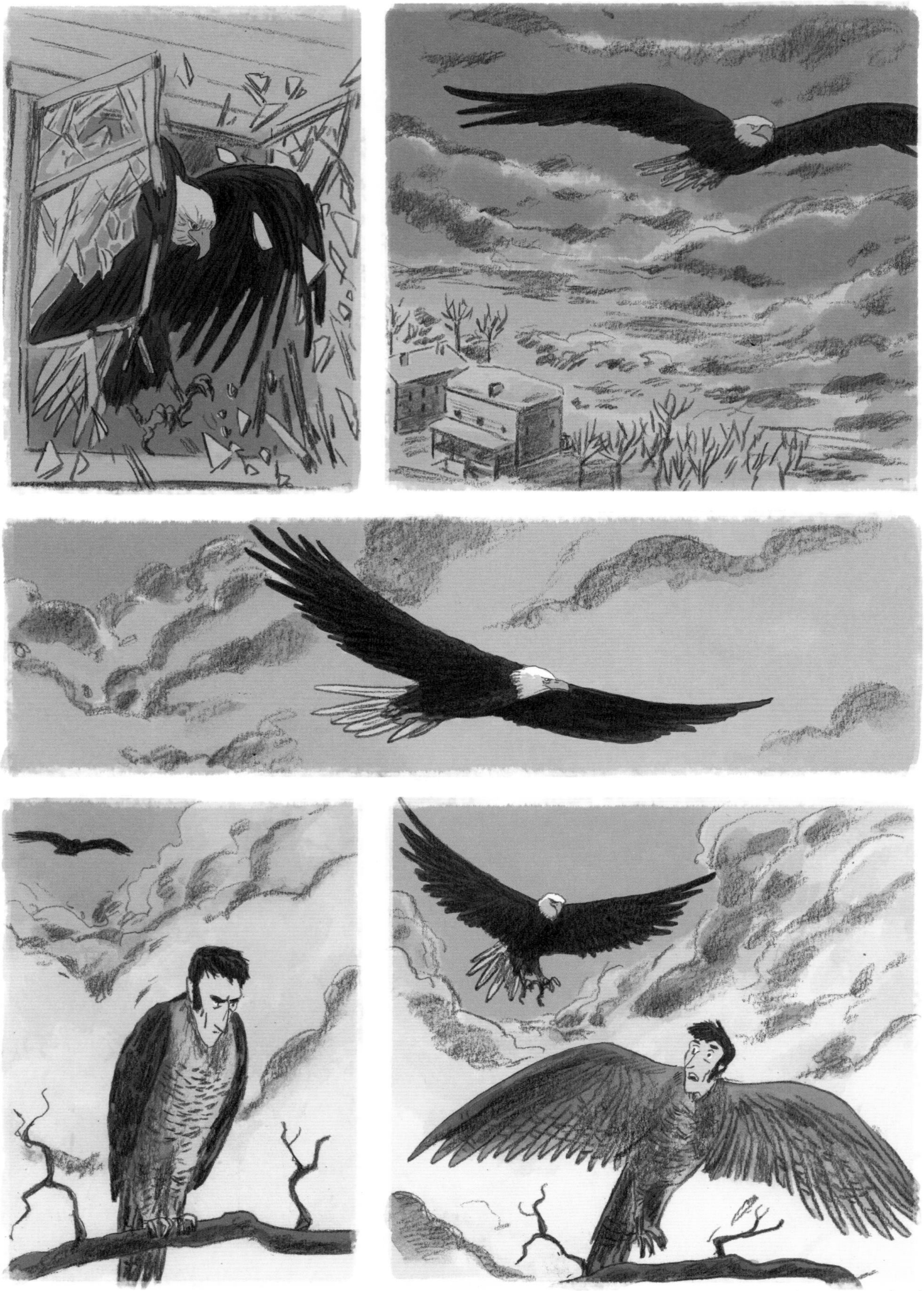

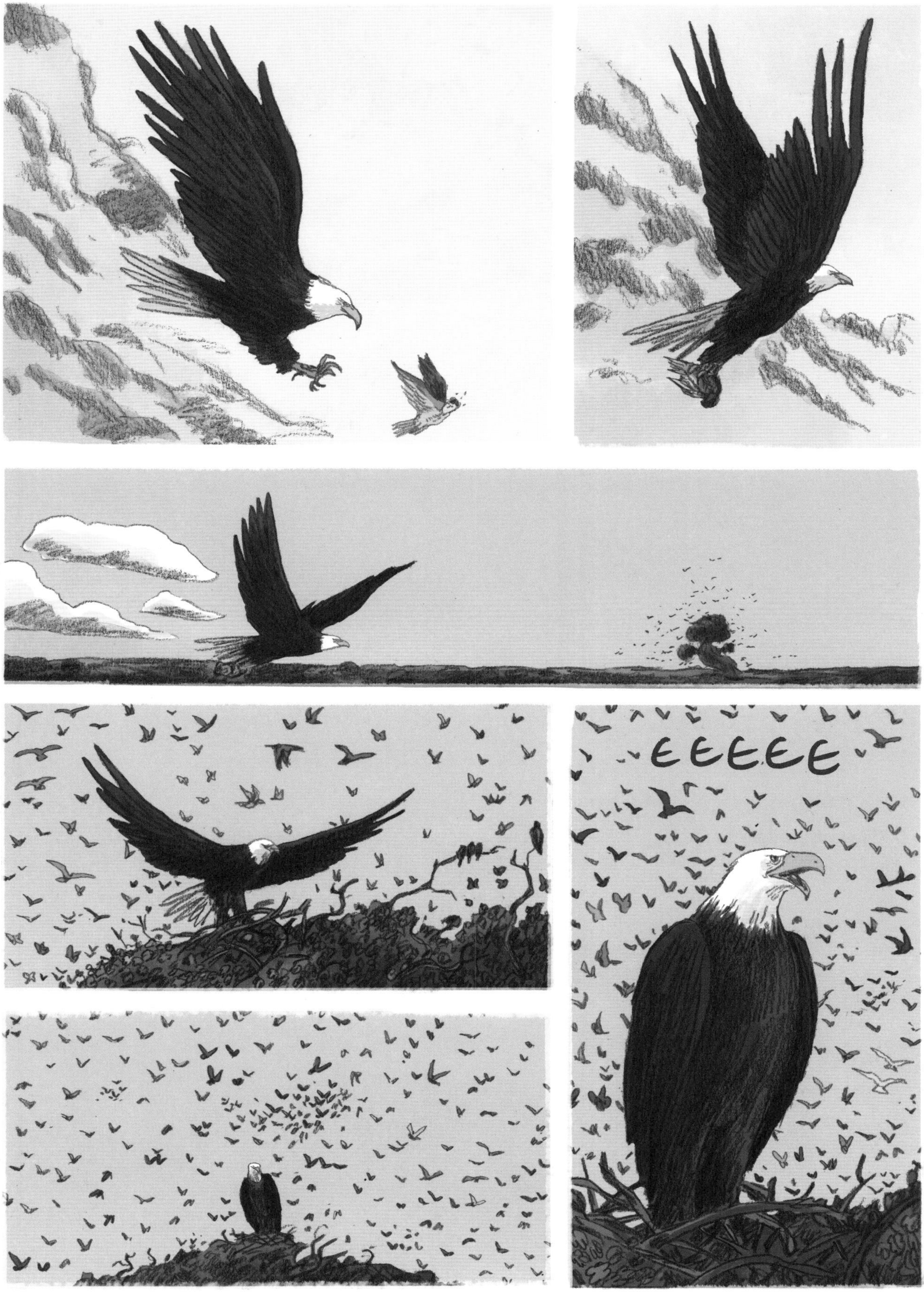
EEEEE

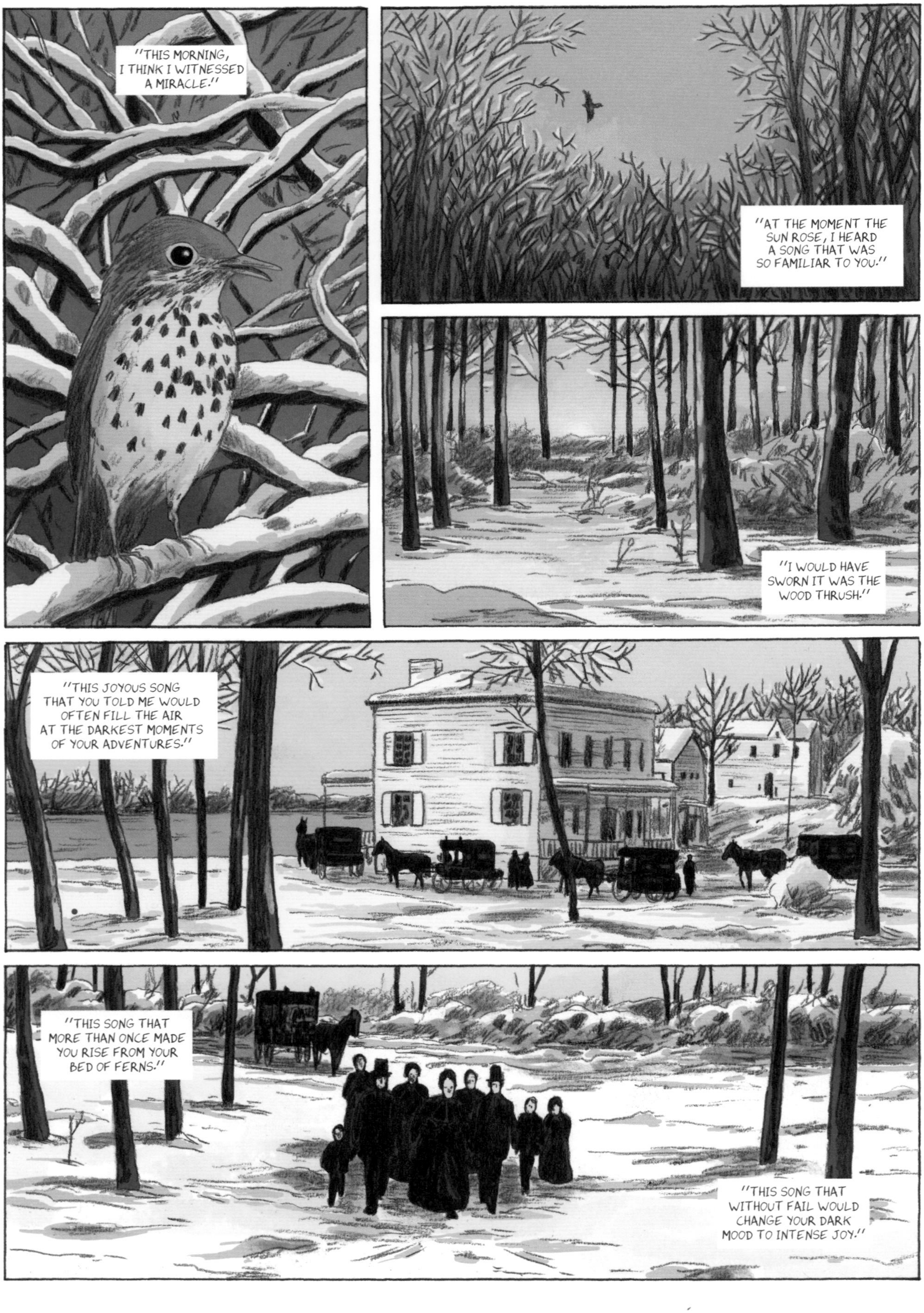
"THIS MORNING, I THINK I WITNESSED A MIRACLE."
"AT THE MOMENT THE SUN ROSE, I HEARD A SONG THAT WAS SO FAMILIAR TO YOU."
"I WOULD HAVE SWORN IT WAS THE WOOD THRUSH."
"THIS JOYOUS SONG THAT YOU TOLD ME WOULD OFTEN FILL THE AIR AT THE DARKEST MOMENTS OF YOUR ADVENTURES."
"THIS SONG THAT MORE THAN ONCE MADE YOU RISE FROM YOUR BED OF FERNS."
"THIS SONG THAT WITHOUT FAIL WOULD CHANGE YOUR DARK MOOD TO INTENSE JOY."

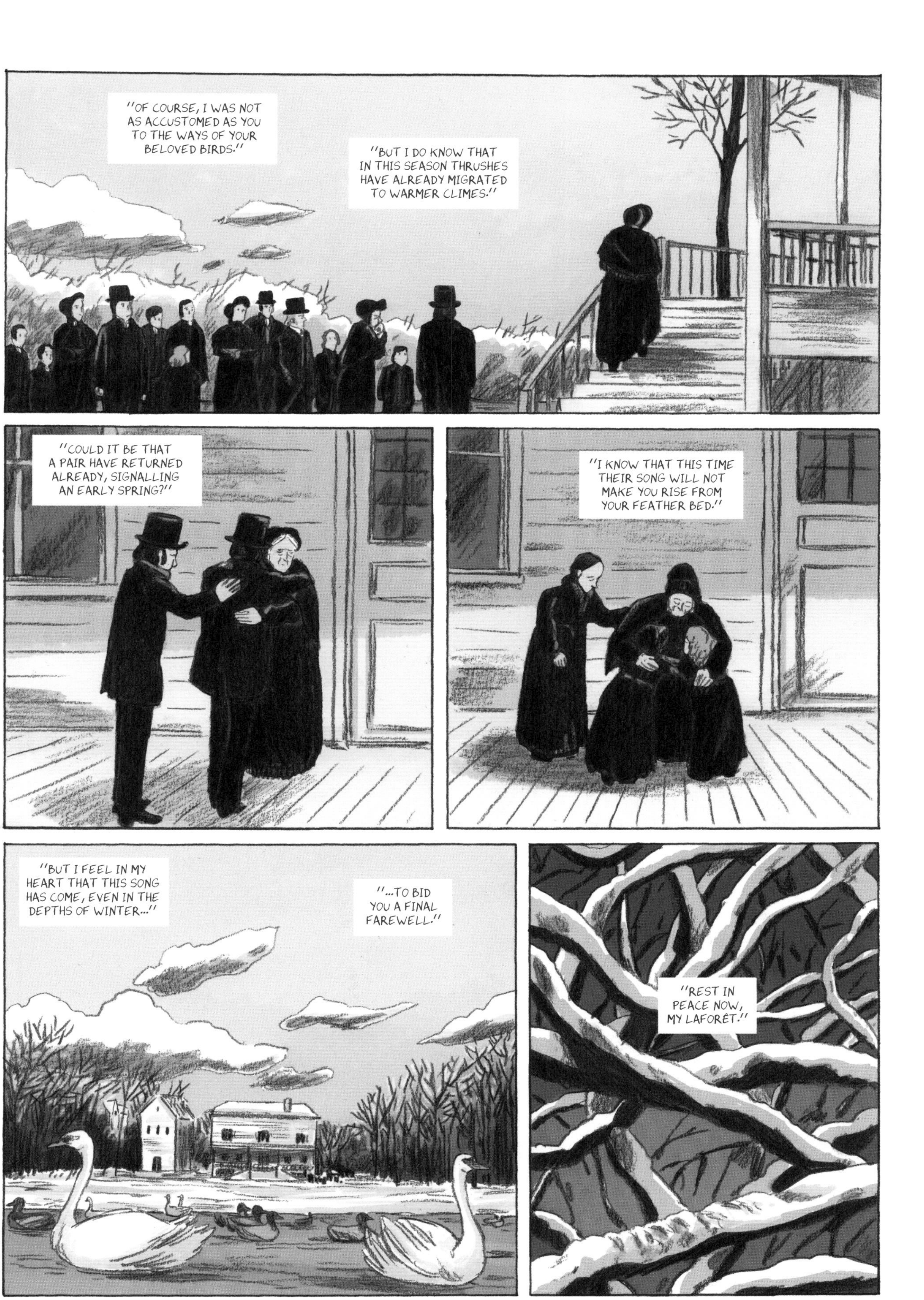
"OF COURSE, I WAS NOT AS ACCUSTOMED AS YOU TO THE WAYS OF YOUR BELOVED BIRDS."
"BUT I DO KNOW THAT IN THIS SEASON THRUSHES HAVE ALREADY MIGRATED TO WARMER CLIMES."
"COULD IT BE THAT A PAIR HAVE RETURNED ALREADY, SIGNALLING AN EARLY SPRING?"
"I KNOW THAT THIS TIME THEIR SONG WILL NOT MAKE YOU RISE FROM YOUR FEATHER BED."
"BUT I FEEL IN MY HEART THAT THIS SONG HAS COME, EVEN IN THE DEPTHS OF WINTER..."
"...TO BID YOU A FINAL FAREWELL."
"REST IN PEACE NOW, MY LAFORÊT."

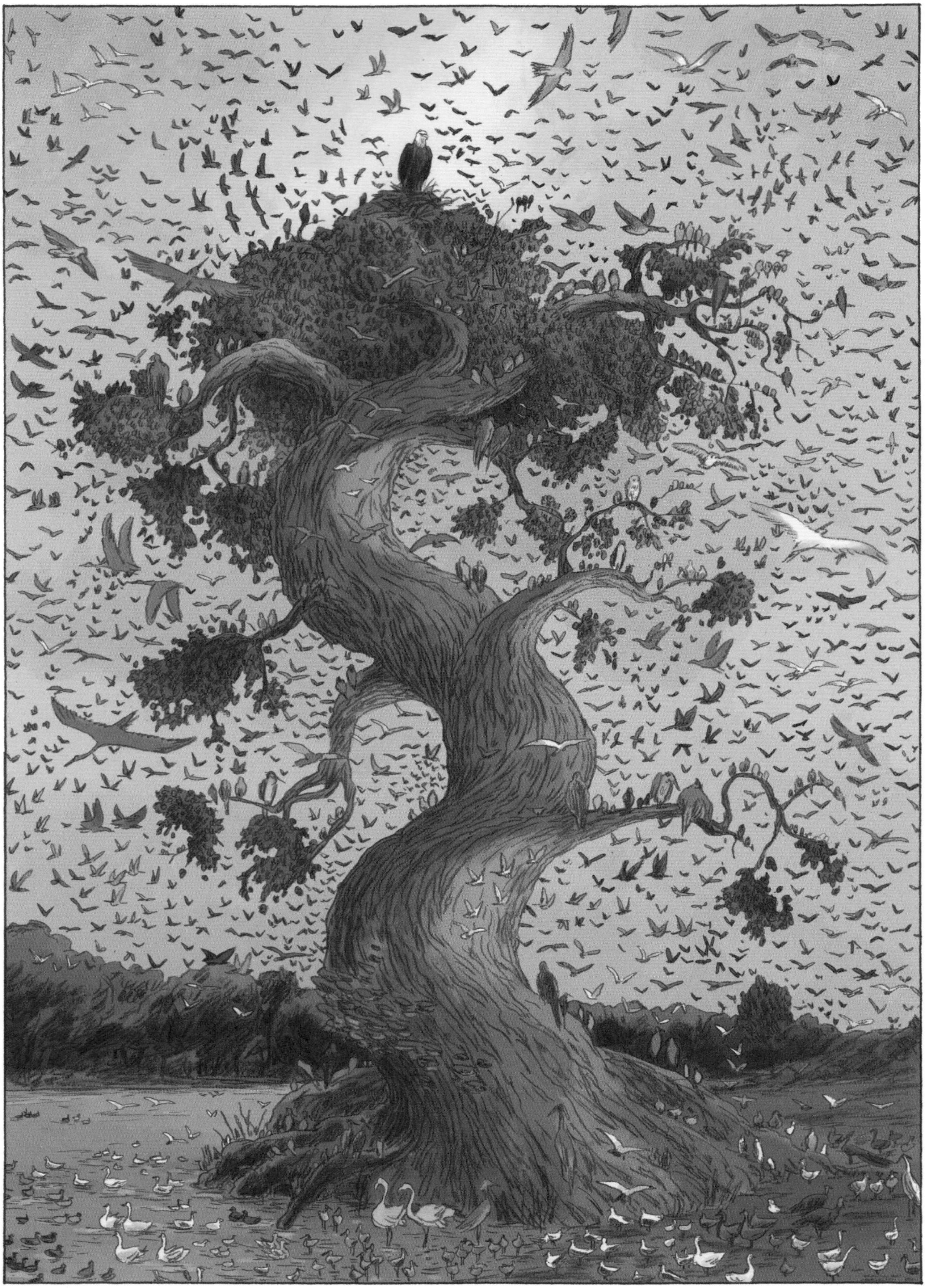

NOTES:

Numerous episodes in this book were inspired by Audubon's writings, most notably
*Ornithological Biography or, An Account of the Habits of the Birds of the United States of America;
Accompanied by Descriptions of the Objects Represented in the Work Entitled The Birds of America,
and Interspersed with Delineations of American Scenery and Manners.*

Page 18: Adapted from "Chimney Swallow or American Swift"
Pages 36-37: Text extracted from "Wild Turkey"
Pages 36-37: Adapted from "Ferruginous Thrush"
Page 60: Text extracted from "Summer, or Wood Duck"
Page 79: Adapted from "The Live-Oakers" and "Meadville"
Page 90: Adapted from "Passenger Pigeon"

Audubon's anecdote about the flight of passenger pigeons lasting several days is a credible one:
the species numbered a few billion in the 19th century. These gigantic migrations caused enormous
damage. An intensive cull, but especially the disappearance of vast tracts of American forests,
brought about the extinction of the species; the last surviving specimen died in captivity in 1914.

Page 108: Adapted from "The Prairie"

Page 126: Adapted from "The Runaway"

This book does not show that Audubon kept slaves. The subject deserves a book of its own;
we've chosen to evoke it only in this episode, inspired by his writings.

Page 146: Darwin was a student at the University of Edinburgh when Audubon went there to
give a lecture and present 'Birds of America'. Their imaginary encounter is therefore possible,
but the nineteen year old Darwin would not have known about adaptation yet.

Page 149: The archaeopteryx was, in reality, discovered in 1860, 10 years after Audubon's death,
but here the writer and illustrator have invoked a little artistic licence.

Page 156: Adapted from the Missouri Journal by John James Audubon.
The text includes various citations of Audubon.

The character of Shogan is an amalgam of various people whom Audubon encountered on his
travels; guides he met along the way, and Native Americans with whom he hunted. The final
scene is based on fact – an old friend did visit Audubon before his death, witnessing his declining
mental and physical health.

SELECTIVE BIBLIOGRAPHY

Audubon: peintre, naturaliste, aventurier
By Yvon Chatelin – France-Empire

*Ornithological Biography or, An Account of the Habits of the Birds
of the United States of America; Accompanied by Descriptions
of the Objects Represented in the Work Entitled The Birds of America,
and Interspersed with Delineations of American Scenery and Manners*
By Jean-Jacques Audubon – FB Éditions

The Missouri River Journals
By John James Audubon – Petite Bibliothèque Payot

Jean-Jacques Audubon, 1785-1851
By Henri Gourdin – Actes Sud

The Birds of America
By John James Audubon – Citadelles et Mazenol

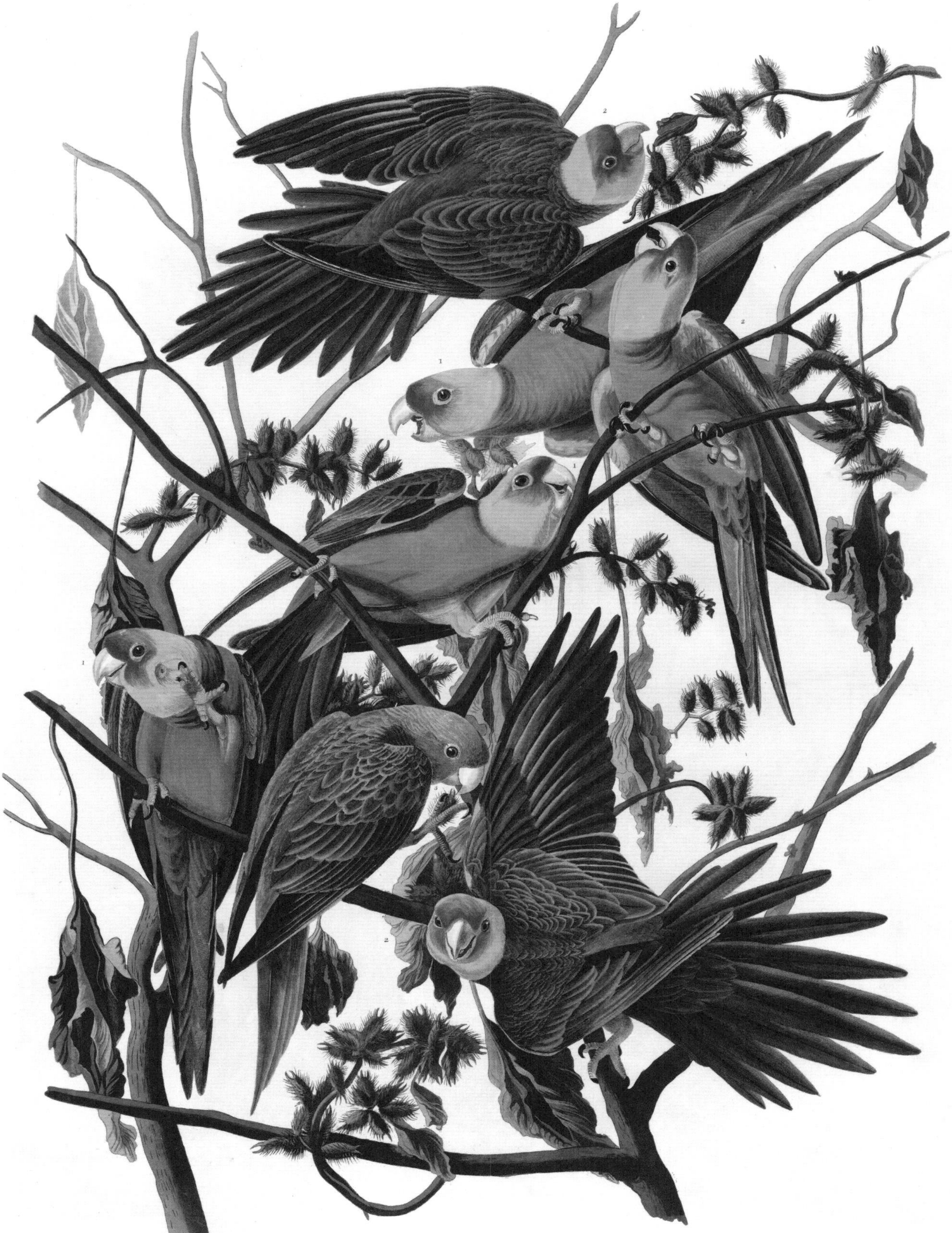

CAROLINA PARROT
JOHN JAMES AUDUBON

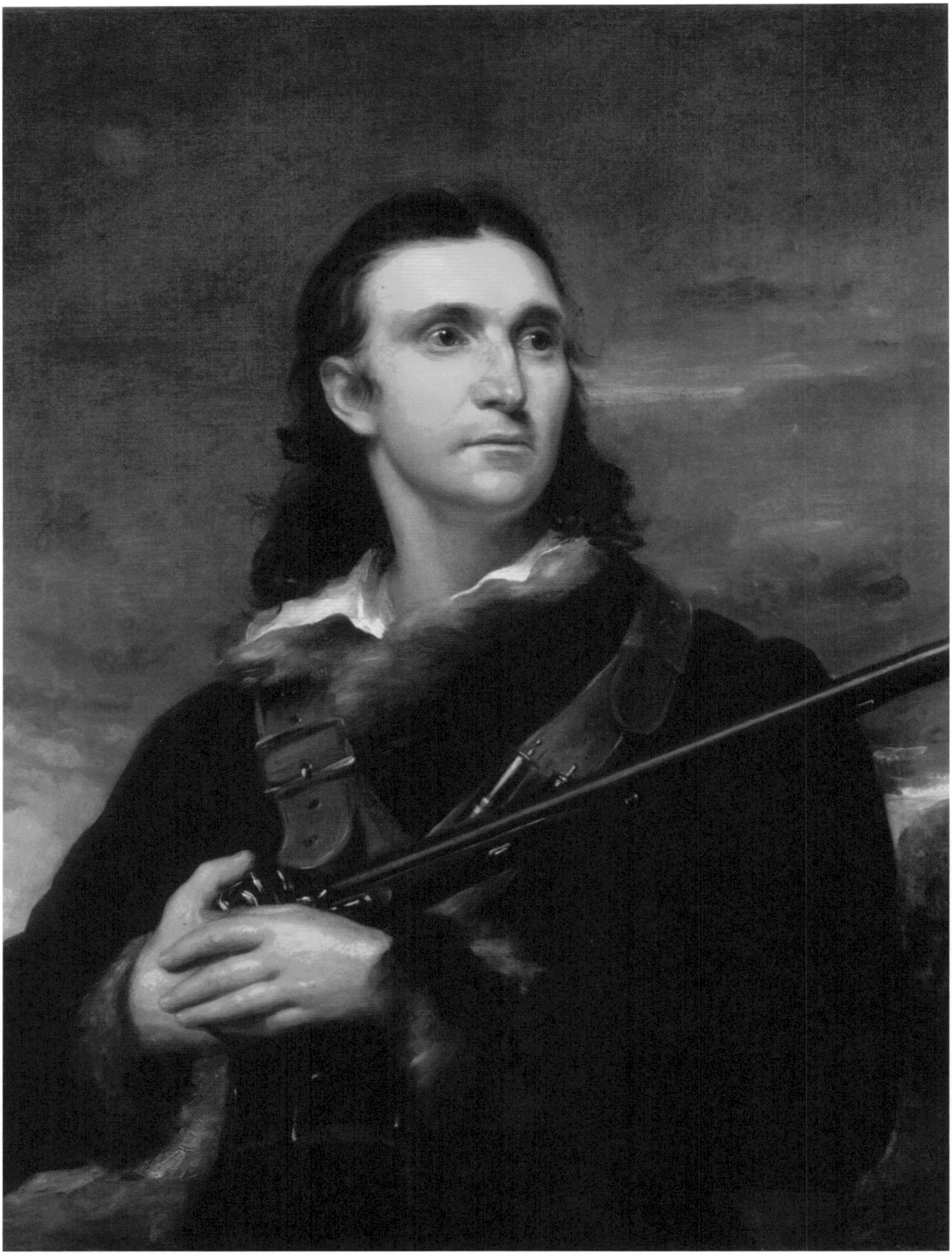

AUDUBON
BY JOHN SYME, 1826

BIOGRAPHY

Jean-Jacques Audubon was born in Haiti in 1785, an illegitimate child. (His father Jean Audubon, a businessman and adventurer, had seduced a servant, Jeanne Rabine, who died a few months after childbirth.) His childhood was spent in Nantes; his holidays at the family villa La Gerbetière, at Couëron, not far from the city.

In the marshes that today bear his name, he studied nature whilst skipping school. Now formally adopted by his father, he was given the name 'Fougère' (fern), perhaps hinting at his future as a woodsman. In 1803, to escape conscription into Napoleon's army, he was sent by his father to Mill Grove, a family property on the east coast of the United States. He became an American citizen and took the name John James Audubon. Here, he met Lucy Bakewell, a neighbour, who would later become his wife. Together they would have four children: Victor Gifford and John Woodhouse, who worked with their father and survived him, and Rose and Lucy who both died in childhood.

Initially encouraged to follow in his father's footsteps, Audubon threw himself into various businesses and ventures, at first with some success. Investing his fortune into a steam-powered sawmill, though, proved to be a financial catastrophe. Indebted and imprisoned, he was forced to declare bankruptcy and later renounced business to pursue his great passion: birds. For years he traversed America's great forests, hunting, drawing, and exploring the country far and wide, often a long way from his home and family.

As his work progressed and his reputation grew, he floated a subscription to the scientists of Cincinnati and New Orleans; this failed, however, when they remained faithful to Alexander Wilson, who had written and illustrated the then-definitive 'American Ornithology' some years earlier. In 1826, Audubon, hoping to find both sponsors and talented engravers – in short supply in the US – travelled to Britain. Here he met with great success, bringing, as he did, a taste of American exoticism to the upper class salons and scientific establishments of England. He also visited France where he succeeded in convincing Cuvier and other rich Frenchmen to support him. In London, he found the talented engravers of Havell, who would print 'Birds of America' over an eleven-year period.

The final plates engraved by Havell were released in 1838, realising the work of a lifetime: 'Birds of America' comprised 435 aquatint plates. A smaller octavo edition was published between 1840-44, which enjoyed wild success. Now rich and famous, Audubon continued his travels:

his final expedition was to Missouri in pursuit of his new project, 'Viviparous Quadrupeds of North America', which would be finished by his son. Now suffering from dementia, Audubon passed away in 1851 in New York, aged sixty-one.

AUDUBON'S LEGACY:

Audubon would be forgotten for some time before his art and legacy were rediscovered. In 1896, the Massachusetts Audubon Society was founded, the first such society bearing his name. In 1905, the Audubon Society was born, today one of the biggest organisations promoting conservation in the United States. The Audubon Society boasts thousands of branches and hundreds of thousands of members spread across the whole of North America.

John James Audubon, the great lover of nature, is considered one of the founders of American ecology (even if his activities as a hunter would horrify the majority of nature lovers today). There are countless roads, parks, zoos, museums and schools named in his honour.

In the United States, John James is the only Frenchman as well known as Lafayette. In France, he remains practically unknown.

The initial print of 'Birds of America' was for two hundred copies. Many of these are now incomplete having been broken up. Of the fourteen French copies, only four have survived intact. On the 7th December 2010, a complete edition was sold at auction for £7.3 million by Sotheby's of London. 'Birds of America' is currently one of the most expensive and sought after printed works in the world.

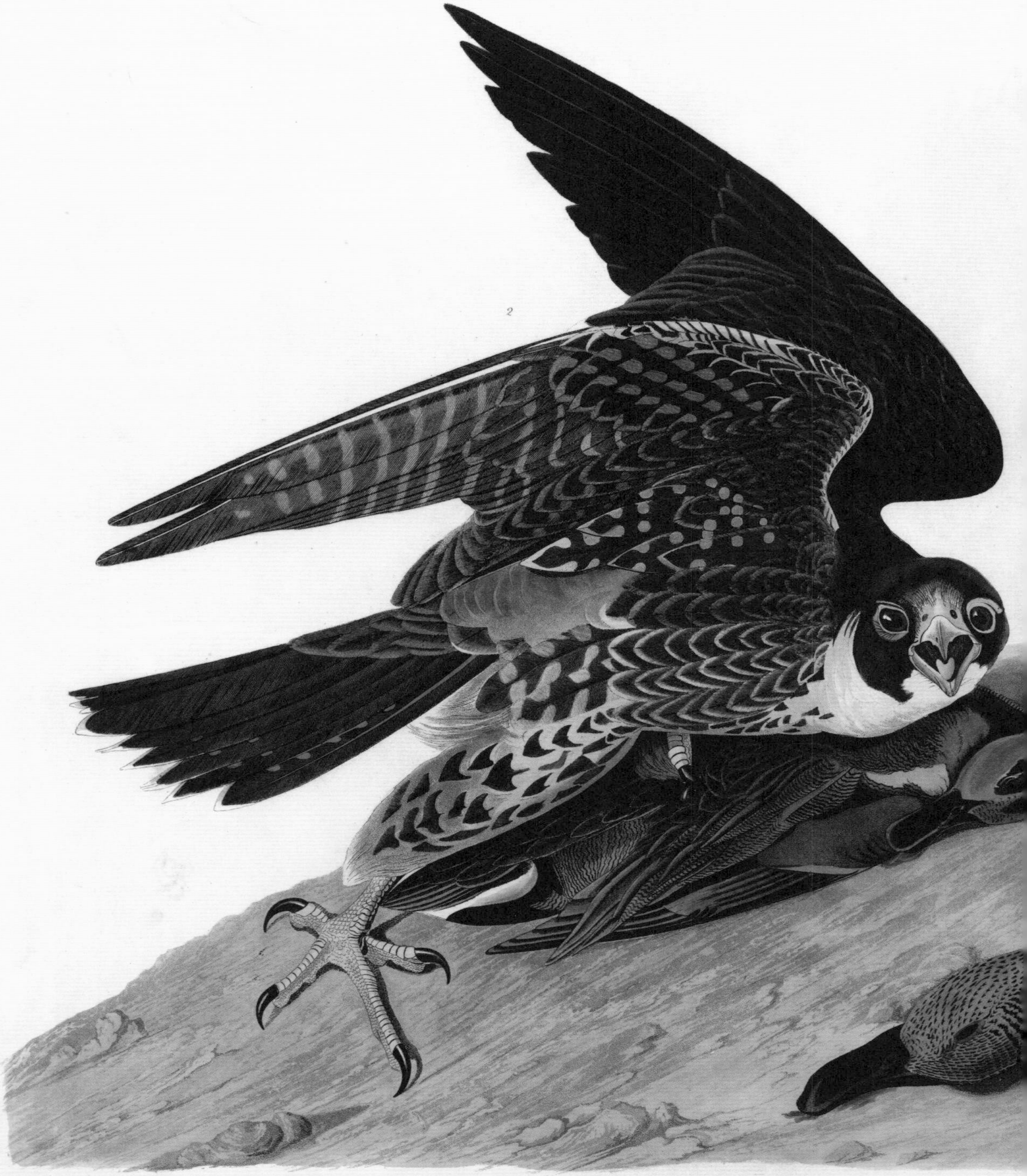
2

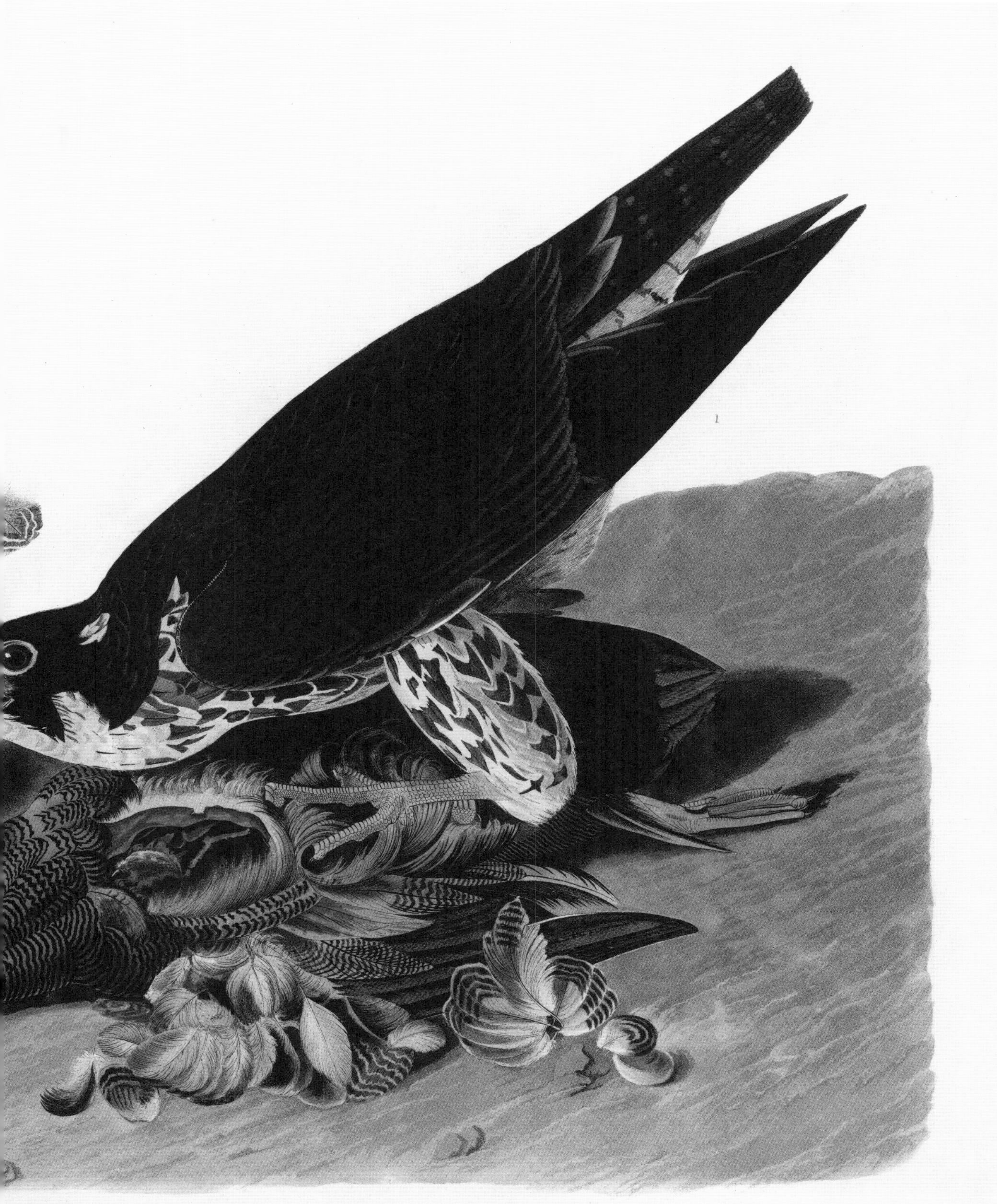

GREAT-FOOTED HAWK

JOHN JAMES AUDUBON

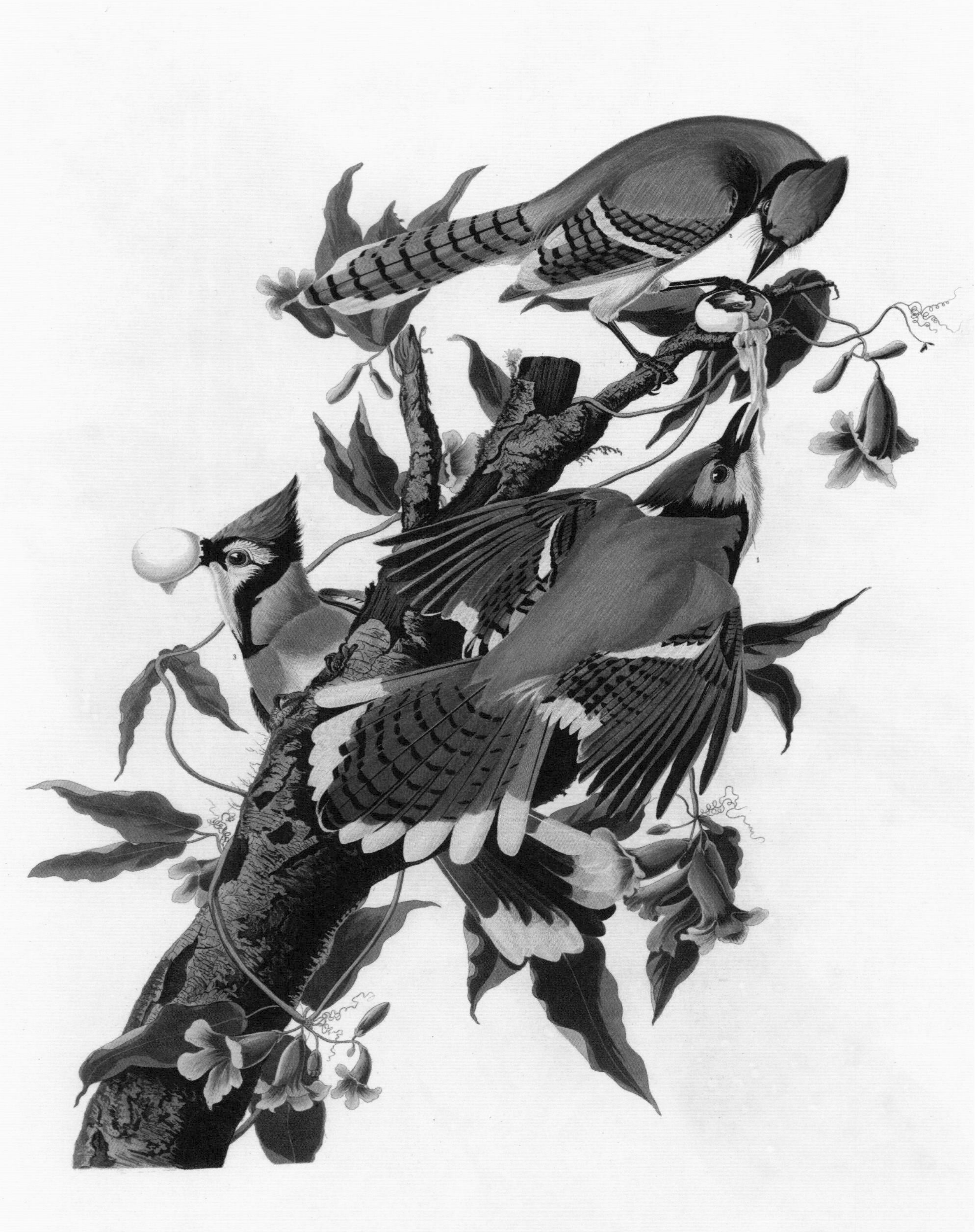

BLUE JAY
JOHN JAMES AUDUBON

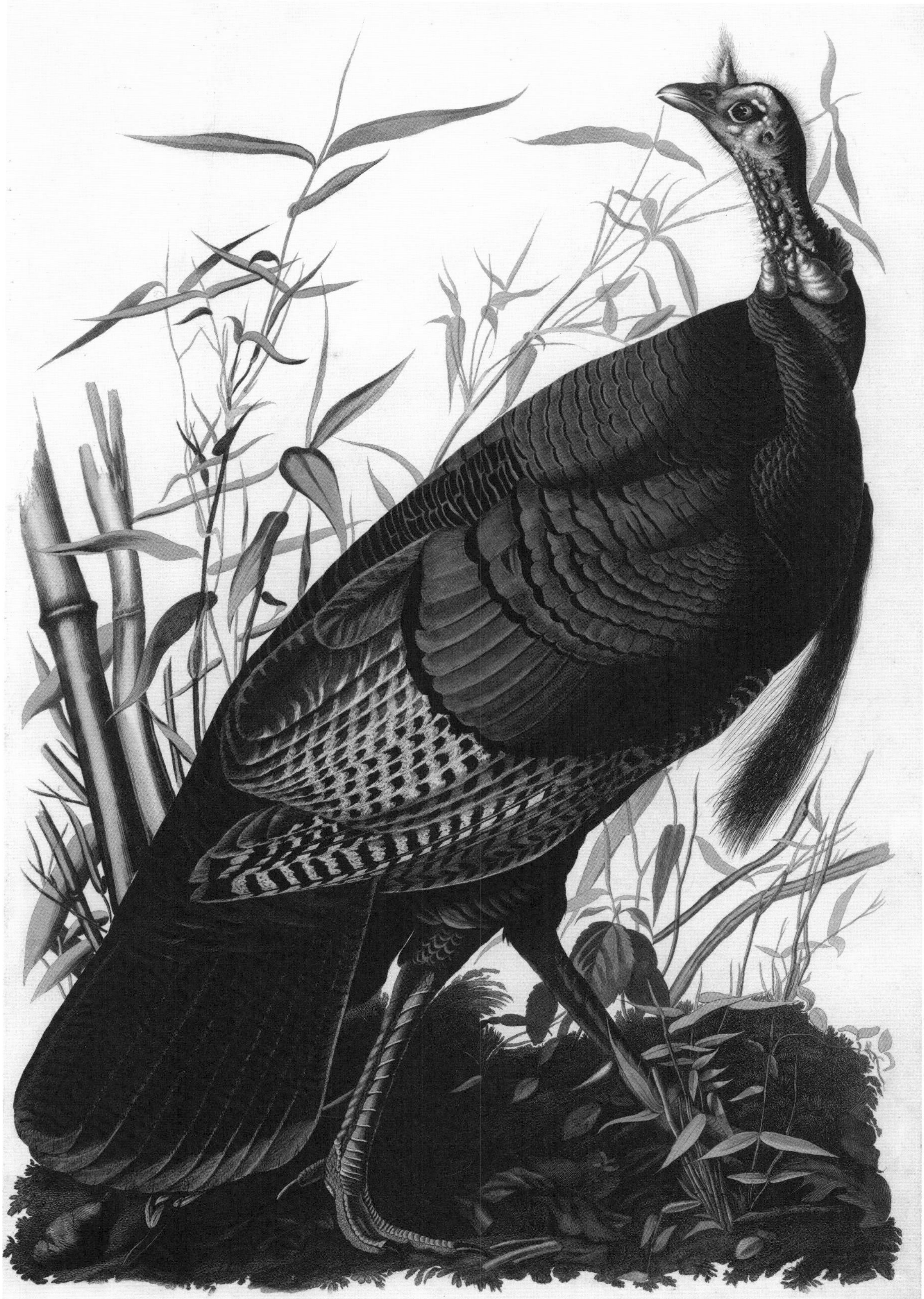

WILD TURKEY
JOHN JAMES AUDUBON

Thanks to the Natural History Museum at La Rochelle.
Thanks to Jean-Yves Noblet of the Couëron Audubon Atlantic Association.
Thanks to the Couëron town hall. Thanks to Yvon Chatelin.

To my parents.

F.G.

The author received a grant from the
Wallonia-Brussels Federation for this work.

FÉDÉRATION
WALLONIE-BRUXELLES

A special thanks to Christoph Irmscher and the Audubon Society.

Sur les Ailes du monde, Audubon © DARGAUD 2016, by Grolleau, Royer
www.dargaud.com

This is a first English edition published in 2016
by Nobrow Ltd. 27 Westgate Street, London E8 3RL.

Translated by Etienne Gilfillan.

Published in the US by Nobrow (US) Inc.
Printed in Poland on FSC assured paper.

ISBN: 978-1-910620-15-1

Order from www.nobrow.net